BRONZEVILLE
BURNHAM PARK
Shore Drive
STICKNEY
LYONS
FOREST VIEW
McCOOK
SUMMIT
GAGE PARK
CHICAGO LAWN
ENGLEWOOD
WASHINGTON PARK
HYDE PARK
JACKSON PARK
University of Chicago
page 234
DuSable Museum of African American History
Chicago Portage National Historic Site
Chicago Midway Airport
Sanitary and Ship Canal
Michigan Canal
Adlai E. Stevenson Expressway
Dan Ryan Expressway
Calumet Expway
Tri-State Tollway
South Archer Avenue
Columbus Avenue
West Pershing Road
West 47th Street
West 51st Street
West 55th Street
West 59th Street
West 63rd Street
West 67th Street
West 71st Street
West 75th Street
West 79th Street
West 83rd Street
West 87th Street
West 95th Street
West 103rd Street
West 111th Street
West 115th Street
W. 71st St
East 47th Street
East 51st Street
East 63rd Street
East 67th Street
East 71st Street
East 87th Street
East 103rd
E. 111th St
Garfield Boulevard
Drexel Blvd
MARQUETTE PARK
BEDFORD PARK
BRIDGE-VIEW
ASHBURN
BURBANK
HOMETOWN
EVERGREEN PARK
CHATHAM
BEVERLY
OAK LAWN
HICKORY HILLS
PALOS HILLS
CHICAGO RIDGE
WORTH
Pullman Historic District
South Harlem Avenue
South Central Avenue
South Cicero Avenue
South Pulaski Road
South Kedzie Avenue
South Western Avenue
South Damen Avenue
South Ashland Avenue
South Halsted Street
South State Street
South Dr Martin Luther King Drive
South Cottage Grove Avenue
South Stony Island Avenue
South Ridgeland Avenue
South Roberts Road
State Road
Joliet Road

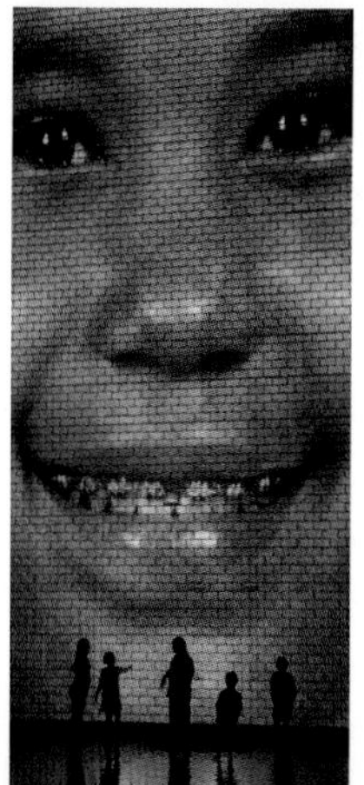

INSIGHT GUIDES

# CHICAGO

Part of the Langenscheidt Publishing Group

INSIGHT GUIDES
CHICAGO

*Project Editor*
**John Gattuso**
*Principal Photographer*
**Dávid Dunai**
*Managing Editor*
**Brian Bell**
*Art Director*
**Ian Spick**
*Cartography Editor*
**Zoë Goodwin**
*Production*
**Kenneth Chan**

**Distribution**

*United States*
**Langenscheidt Publishers, Inc.**
36–36 33rd Street 4th Floor
Long Island City, NY 11106
Fax: (1) 718 784-0640

*UK & Ireland*
**GeoCenter International Ltd**
Meridian House, Churchill Way West,
Basingstoke, Hampshire, RG21 6YR
Fax: (44) 1256-817988

*Australia*
**Universal Publishers**
1 Waterloo Road
Macquarie Park, NSW 2113
Fax: (61) 2 9888 9074

*New Zealand*
**Hema Maps New Zealand Ltd (HNZ)**
Unit D, 24 Ra ORA Drive
East Tamaki, Auckland
Fax: (64) 9 273 6479

*Worldwide*
**Apa Publications GmbH & Co. Verlag KG (Singapore branch)**
38 Joo Koon Road, Singapore 628990
Tel: (65) 6865-1600.
Fax: (65) 6861-6438

**Printing**

**Insight Print Services (Pte) Ltd**
38 Joo Koon Road, Singapore 628990
Tel: (65) 6865-1600.
Fax: (65) 6861-6438



*First Edition 1992*
*Fifth Edition 2008*



**www.insightguides.com**

# About This Book

What makes an Insight Guide different? Since our first book pioneered the use of creative full-color photography in travel guides in 1970, we have aimed to provide not only reliable information but also the key to a real understanding of a destination and its people.

Now, when the internet can supply inexhaustible (but not always reliable) facts, our books marry text and pictures to provide that most elusive quality: knowledge. To achieve this, they rely on the authority of locally based writers and photographers.

This book turns the spotlight on what may be the most American of cities – a robust metropolis that grew from a frontier outpost in an industrial powerhouse. At the start of a new millennium Chicago is bringing a characteristically bold vision to yet another reinvention of itself for the postindustrial age. *Insight Guide: Chicago* reflects the transformation with nearly all new text and pictures, providing everything you need to know about this broad-shouldered city.

## CONTACTING THE EDITORS

*We would appreciate it if readers would alert us to errors or outdated information by writing to:*

**Insight Guides, P.O. Box 7910, London se1 1WE, England.**
**Fax: (44) 20 7403-0290.**
**insight@apaguide.co.uk**

## The Contributors To This Book

This new edition was produced by **John Gattuso**, who has managed dozens of Insight Guides. He assembled a team of Chicago experts to provide comprehensive updates to the previous edition and to assess the city's latest hotspots.

**Martha Bayne** is a writer and critic whose work has appeared in the *Washington Post*, the *Baffler*, and – most frequently – the *Chicago Reader*, where she was an editor and staff writer for nine years. She handled all restaurant reviews and chapters on Wicker Park, cuisine, literature, and several other topics.

A relative newcomer to Chicago, **Caroline Lascom** compiled Travel Tips and covered the Loop. Her credits include guides to Lisbon, Havana, Mexico, and Costa Rica. **Anna H. Blessing**, writer and photographer of the *eat.shop* city guides, covered the South Side and Hyde Park.

**Anne Ford** wrote about several neighborhoods, including Lakeview, the South Loop, and Grant Park; **Eiren Caffall** drew upon her experience as an arts educator for her piece on the city's cultural scene. Chicago native **Heather Kenny** scoured the streets of the Near North, Lincoln Park, and the West Side; she writes often for *Chicago* and *North Shore* magazines.

**Ted Cox** and **Lynn Becker** write for the *Chicago Reader* – Cox on sports and Becker on architecture, which they also cover here. Veteran Insight Guide contributor **Edward A. Jardim** revamped sections on history and politics.

The spectacular photography in this edition is the work of Hungarian-born **Dávid Dunai**, a photojournalist who divides his time mainly between San Francisco and Budapest. The book was indexed by **Elizabeth Coo**

CHICAGO
CHICAGO
MONDAY SEPT 18
DANCING WITH THE
GIORDANO STARS
NOW PLAYING DOWNSTAIRS

# THE GUIDE AT A GLANCE

The book is carefully structured both to convey an understanding of the city and its culture and to guide readers through its attractions and activities:

◆ The Best Of section at the front of the book helps you to prioritize. The first spread contains all the Top Sights, while Editor's Choice details unique experiences, the best buys, or other recommendations.

◆ To understand Chicago, you need to know something of its past. The city's history and culture are described in authoritative essays written by specialists in their fields who have lived in and documented Chicago for many years.

◆ The Places section details all the attractions worth seeing. The main places of interest are coordinated by number with the maps.

◆ A list of recommended restaurants, bars, and cafés is printed at the end of each chapter.

◆ Photographs throughout the book are chosen not only to illustrate geography and buildings, but also to convey the moods of the city and the life of its people.

◆ The Travel Tips section includes all the practical information you will need, divided into five key sections: transportation, accommodations, activities (including nightlife, events, tours, and sports), shopping, and an A–Z of practic tips. Information may be locate quickly by using the index on t back cover flap of the book.

◆ Two detailed street atlases are included at the back of the book, complete with a full inde On the second one, you will fir restaurants and hotels plotted for your convenience.

## PLACES & SIGHTS

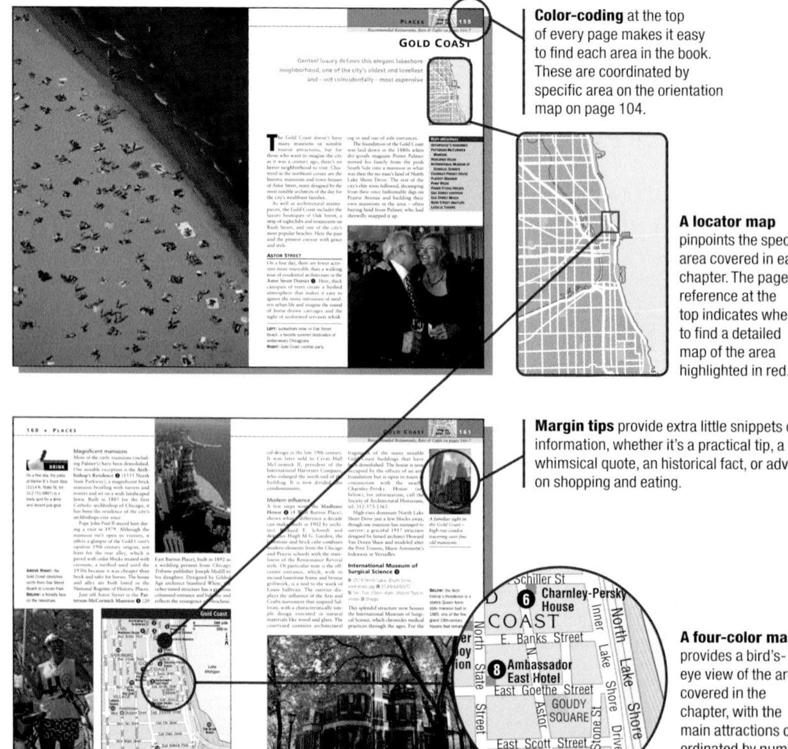

Color-coding at the top of every page makes it easy to find each area in the book. These are coordinated by specific area on the orientation map on page 104.
A locator map pinpoints the speci area covered in ea chapter. The page reference at the top indicates wher to find a detailed map of the area highlighted in red.
Margin tips provide extra little snippets o information, whether it's a practical tip, a whimsical quote, an historical fact, or advic on shopping and eating.
A four-color map provides a bird's-eye view of the are covered in the chapter, with the main attractions co ordinated by numb with the main text.
GOLD COAST
Schiller St
6 Charnley-Persky House
COAST
E. Banks Street
8 Ambassador East Hotel
East Goethe Street
GOUDY SQUARE
East Scott Street
9 Fisher Studio Houses
North State Street
Astor
N. Stone St.
Inner Lake Shore Drive
North Lake Shore

## PHOTO FEATURES

**Photo Features** offer visual coverage of the major sights. The map shows the sight's location, while "The essentials" panel conveys practical information: address, contact details, website, opening times, and if there's a charge.

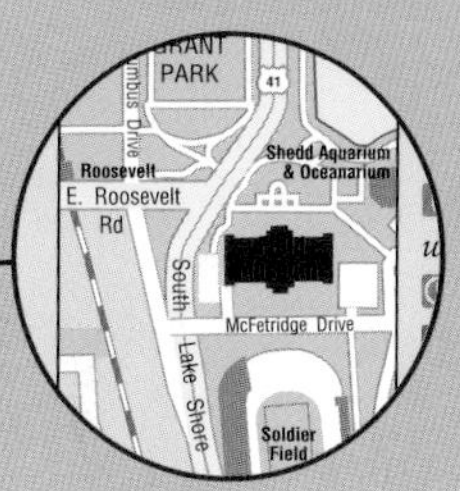


## RESTAURANT LISTINGS

**Restaurant listings** feature the best establishments within each area, giving the address, phone number, opening times, and price category followed by a useful review. The grid reference refers to the atlas at the back of the book.

**Shikago**
✉ 190 S. LaSalle St ☎ 312-781-7300 🕒 L Mon–Fri, D Mon–Sat **$$$** [p306, C2]
This new contemporary pan-Asian fusion comes from chef Kevin Shikami (he also runs River North's Kevin), who is being hailed lately as

## TRAVEL TIPS

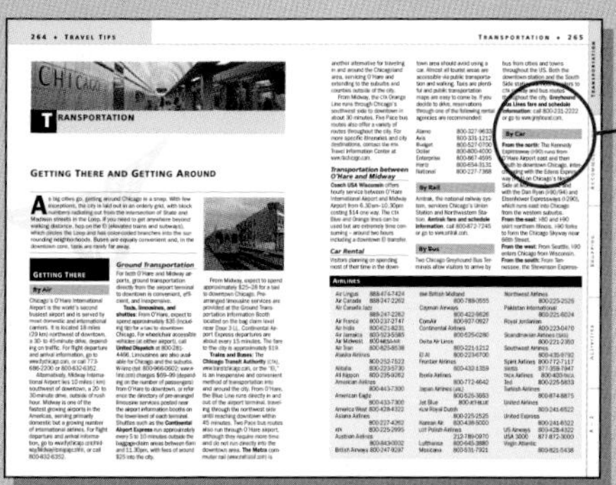


**Advice-packed Travel Tips** provide all the practical knowledge you'll need before and during your trip: how to get there, getting around, where to stay, and what to do. The A–Z section is a handy summary of practical information, arranged alphabetically.

# Contents

## Best of Chicago

**Top Sights** 8

Art Institute of Chicago ..... 130
Chicago Blues Festival ..... 135
John Hancock Center ...... 147
Macy's (formerly Marshall Field's) ............... 116
Magnificent Mile ......... 143
Millennium Park .......... 136
Navy Pier ............... 151
Sears Tower ............. 114
Wicker Park ............. 203
Wrigley Field ............ 180

**Editor's Choice** 10

## Introduction

Guide at a Glance ...................... 4
Master of Reinvention .............. 19

## History

The Making of Chicago ............ 21
Law and Disorder .................... 39
The Winds of Politics .............. 45
Decisive Dates ........................ 50

## Features

Literary Chicago ...................... 5
Chicago Blues ........................ 6
Art and Culture ...................... 7
Chicago Eats .......................... 7
Good Sports .......................... 8
Chicago Architecture ............. 9

## Photo Features

***Mini Features:***

Murder Castle ......................... 4
Built on Beer .......................... 8
'Say It Ain't So, Joe' ................ 8
Egos in the White City .............. 9
The Chicago River.................. 12
The Gallery Scene ................ 15
Oprah: Tough and Tender........ 19
Nelson Algren ....................... 21
The Real Blues Brothers ........ 22
Frank Lloyd Wright ................. 25

***Picture Stories:***

Chicago in the Movies.............. 6
Shopping................................ 9
Art Institute of Chicago .......... 13
Public Art ........................... 14
Feasts and Festivals.............. 18
Field Museum......................... 22
Museum of Science & Industry.. 24

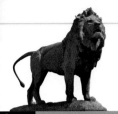

## Places


rientation .......................... **105**
The Loop........................ **111**
Grant and Millennium Parks .......................... **135**
Near North .................... **143**
Gold Coast .................... **159**
Lincoln Park and Old Town .......................**169**
Lakeview to Andersonville ..............**179**
West Side ...................... **191**
Wicker Park, Bucktown, and Ukrainian Village ....**203**
South Loop .................... **217**
South Side and Hyde Park .................... **231**
Oak Park ........................ **245**
Day Trips........................ **253**


## Restaurants & Bars


he Loop ............................. **128**
rant and Millennium Parks ............................... **139**
lear North ......................... **156**
old Coast ......................... **166**
incoln Park and Old Town........................... **176**
akeview to Andersonville ......................**186**
Vest Side .......................... **200**
Vicker Park, Bucktown, and Ukrainian Village ..........**214**
outh Loop...........................**224**
outh Side and Hyde Park ......................... **240**
ak Park ............................. **250**
ay Trips ............................. **260**


## Travel Tips


**TRANSPORTATION**

Getting There **264**
Getting Around **266**

**ACCOMMODATIONS**

Choosing a Hotel **267**
The Loop **268**
Near North **268**
Gold Coast **271**
Lincoln Park **272**
Lakeview **272**
Wicker Park and Bucktown **272**

**SHOPPING**

Where to Shop **273**
Malls and Marketplaces **273**
Antiques **274**
Art Galleries **274**
Bookstores **275**
Department Stores **276**
Food and Drink **276**
Women's Clothing **276**
Men's Clothing **277**
Music **277**

**ACTIVITIES**

The Arts **278**
Nightlife **282**
Events **283**
Tours **286**
Sports **286**

**A–Z of PRACTICAL INFORMATION**

**288**

**FURTHER READING**

**293**


## Maps

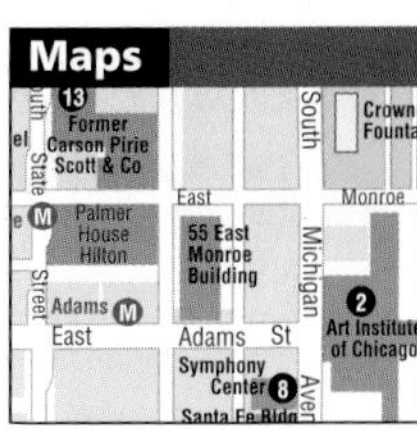



Chicago **front flap** and **106–7**

Orientation map **104**

Map Legend **295**

Street Atlas **296**

Restaurants and Accommodations **304**

The Loop **108–9**
Grant and Millennium Parks **136**
Near North **144**
Gold Coast **160**
Lincoln Park and Old Town **170**
Lakeview to Andersonville **180**
West Side **192**
Wicker Park, Bucktown, and Ukrainian Village **204**
South Loop **218**
South Side **232**
Hyde Park and the University of Chicago **234**
Oak Park **246**
Day Trips **254**
Chicago Transit Authority **321**

Around Chicago **back flap**

# THE BEST OF CHICAGO: TOP SIGHTS

At a glance, everything you can't afford to miss when you visit the Windy City, from the historic architecture of the Loop and world-class museums to legendary blues clubs and an old-time ballpark

△ **Millennium Park** has breathed new life into the once-neglected northern section of Grant Park. Part playground, part sculpture garden, part concert venue, the spectacular new park attracts millions of visitors a year. *See pages 136–37.*

▽ **Navy Pier** is the Midwest's most visited tourist destination. Jutting some 3,300 ft (1,010 meters) into Lake Michigan, the complex includes an amusement park, a children's museum, and live entertainment as well as frequent summer fireworks, an ice skating rink in winter, and a variety of cruises. *See page 151.*

▷ **Sears Tower** was the world's tallest building when it was erected in 1973. It is only one of the landmark skyscrapers in the Loop. *See pages 114–15.*

◁ When it comes to the blues, Chicago's got its mojo workin'. Check out classic **blues clubs** like Buddy Guy's Legends and Kingston Mines or the three-day Chicago Blues Festival in Grant Park. *See pages 65–9.*

▷ Marshall Field built his retail empire on a simple proposition: "Give the lady what she wants." It's worth visiting this icon of old Chicago – now **Macy's** – even if you're not shopping. *See pages 116–17.*

. 100-story, modernist obelisk, the **.n Hancock Center** has an open-air .ervatory on the 94th floor, where .tors can thrill to breathtaking .vs of the city and lakeshore. *. pages 147–48.*

▽ Tradition lives on at **Wrigley Field**, home to the Chicago Cubs and one of the oldest and most beloved stadiums in Major League Baseball, with its ivy-covered outfield wall, hand-operated scoreboard, and loyal but often disappointed fans. *See pages 86 and 180.*

▽ The **Magnificent Mile** on North Michigan Avenue is a grand boulevard with the city's most stylish shops. *See pages 143–48.*

▽ With numerous galleries, boutiques, cafés, and nightclubs, **Wicker Park** remains a center of bohemian culture despite a recent wave of gentrification. *See pages 203–10.*

.n extensive collec- of Impressionist and .-Impressionist .tings anchor the .ings of the **Art Insti- . of Chicago**, which .mpasses works both .ent and contempo- A new Modern Wing .pected to open in 9. *See pages –113 and 130-133.*

# THE BEST OF CHICAGO

**Unique attractions, festivals and events, food favorites, the best of the blues, family outings ... here are our recommendations, plus some money-saving tips and tricks**

**RIGHT:** an ancient Greek vase on display at the Art Institute of Chicago.

## BEST SKYSCRAPERS

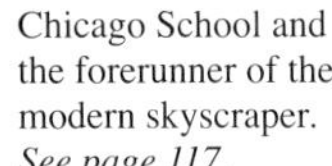

- **Sears Tower** Experience dizzying panoramas from the 110th-floor Skydeck. An engineering marvel, the Sears Tower was the world's tallest building at the time of its construction in 1973. *See page 114.*
- **Federal Center** Mies van der Rohe's seminal structure marked the transition from the Chicago School to Modernism. Beautiful in its simplicity, the building's geometric precision and purity embody the architect's maxim: "less is more." *See page 122.*

- **Reliance Building** Now site of the Burnham Hotel, the Reliance Building is a paradigm of the Chicago School and the forerunner of the modern skyscraper. *See page 117.*
- **Marquette Building** This pioneering Chicago School structure was built in 1895. The classical lobby features sublime Tiffany mosaics and bronze reliefs illustrating Chicago's founding. *See page 121.*
- **Marina City** Bertrand Goldberg's 1959 "corncobs" are a reply to the stark angularity of the glass box skyscraper. *See page 152.*
- **John Hancock Center** Tall, dark, and handsome, Chicago's signature skyscraper manages to convey both power and grace. *See pages 147–48.*
- **Wrigley Building** This triangular structure modeled after Seville's Giralda Tower is spectacular at night. *See page 145.*
- **Monadnock Building** Built in two stages starting in 1891, the 16-story tower marks a shift from masonry to steel-frame construction. *See page 124.*

## BEST PUBLIC SCULPTURES

- **The Picasso** This enigmatic, untitled piece, donated to the city by the Spanish maestro, has been embraced by Chicagoans as a symbol of the city. *See pages 119 and 141.*
- **Cloud Gate** Known as "The Bean," Anish Kapoor's reflective, elliptical sculpture has become a sym of the city's ambitions for the new millennium. *See page 136.*
- **Four Seasons** Ma Chagall's glass and tile mosaic humani the concrete expans of Chase Plaza. *See pages 118–19.*

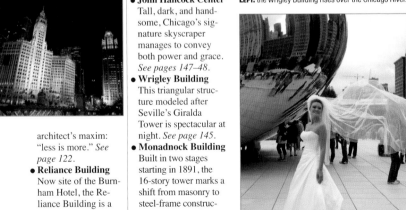

**BELOW:** a bride pays a visit to "The Bean" in Millennium P
**LEFT:** the Wrigley Building rises over the Chicago River.

## 3est Blues and Jazz Clubs

3uddy Guy's .egends Owned by olues giant Buddy Guy, this dark honky-onk is a fixture on the Chicago blues circuit; he Cajun food is oretty good, too. *See page 224.*
3.L.U.E.S. A knowl-edgeable crowd pays homage to rising local alent and famed na-ional artists in a raw, ıpbeat setting. *See page 172.*
Kingston Mines One of the oldest and largest clubs in town with acclaimed artists playing two stages, communal tables, and a welcoming ambi-ence. *See page 172.*
- **Green Mill** One of Al Capone's "friends" ran this former speakeasy, now re-stored to its Jazz Age glory. Big-name jazz acts top the bill, and there's a weekly po-etry slam. *See page 183.*
- **Andy's Jazz Club** Jazz combos of every style and the occa-sional blues band take the stage for evening and afternoon sets at this longtime jazz joint near the Magnificent Mile. *See page 157.*

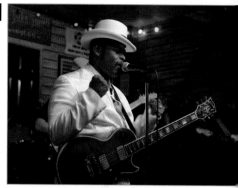

**ABOVE:** Kingston Mines. **LEFT:** "Sue" at the Field Museum.

## 3est Museums

Art Institute of Chicago With more han 30,000 works panning 5,000 years, ne of the world's reat museums is an omage to artistic en-eavor, with iconic vorks by Grant Wood, Edward Hopper, Pi-asso, and others. *See ages 130–133.*
Museum of Science nd Industry Walk ırough a human eart, explore a coal nine, tour a Ger-nan submarine, nd marvel as uffy, yellow hicks peck heir way into ne world at this un, interactive exploration of human ingenuity. *See pages 239 and 242–243.*
- **Field Museum of Natural History** The star of the show is a natural-born killer named Sue – the largest T-rex ever found – but this sprawling facility also houses Egyptian mum-mies, ancient artifacts, wildlife dioramas, and dinosaur fossils. *See pages 226–229.*
- **Chicago History Museum** The city's development from frontier outpost to vibrant metropolis is chronicled in lively exhibits. *See page 174.*

## Free Chicago

- **Chicago Cultural Center** The world's largest Tiffany dome crowns this Beaux Arts temple, which is host to a myriad of free exhibitions, con-certs, and theatrical performances. *See pages 115–116.*
- **Lincoln Park** This lakefront park is home to the oldest zoo in the country, a boating lake, white sand beaches, and a conservatory — all free and only a stone's throw from cosmopolitan cafés and chichi boutiques. *See pages 169–171.*
- **The Lakefront** Join thousands of Chicagoans who cy-cle, walk, jog, or rollerblade on miles of lakefront paths, or hit the beach for vol-leyball, sunbathing, and swimming. *See page 164.*
- **Millennium Park** The city's showcase park is centered around the Jay Pritzker Pavilion, site of free classical concerts and other events all sum-mer long. *See pages 136–137.*

**LEFT:** sculpture at the Art Institute. **BELOW:** North Avenue Beach.

**Above:** Green City Market. **Lower Left:** Chicago River cruise **Bottom Left:** Chicago Children's Museum.

## Food Favorites

- **Taste of Chicago** Sample hundreds of Chicago eateries at a 10-day gastronomic extravaganza in Grant Park. *See page 135.*
- **Chicago Red Hot** True to the city's blue-collar roots, the humble hot dog is the quintessential taste of Chicago. If you can stand the good-hearted abuse, try the Wiener's Circle, or stop for lunch at Hot Doug's on Friday or Saturday for duck-fat fries and a full dose of hip Chicago in its hot dog seeking glory. *See pages 177 and 187.*

- **Al's #1 Italian Beef** For an authentic taste of Chicago, head to Little Italy and try an Italian beef sandwich: a split roll piled with thin slices of juicy beef and *giardiniera* or roasted peppers. Order it "wet" and the whole thing is dunked in gravy. *See page 80.*
- **Green City Market** The city's biggest farmers' market is a source of fresh, regional produce, cheese, meats, and baked goods; local chefs often drop in for cooking demonstrations. *See page 175.*
- **South Side Barbecue** No culinary tour is complete without a foray to the South Side for barbecue, whether Lem's, Barbara Ann's, or someone's backyard. *See pages 240–41.*
- **Deep Dish Pies at Pizzeria Uno** Sure its touristy, but this is the place that put Chicago pizza on the map. *See page 157.*
- **Mexican Food** From River North's Frontera Grill to the tamale guys who haunt local bars, the city is exploding with regional Mexican specialties. *See pages 157.*
- **Alinea** Go for the full, 24-course "tour" at this culinary laboratory – so many dishes, so expensive, so worth it. *See page 176.*

## Best Tours

- **Architecture Cruise** Cruise the Chicago River as knowledgeable docents from Chicago's Architectural Foundation provide an intelligent and engaging commentary on the city's landmark buildings. *See pages 127 and 286.*
- **Historic Skyscrapers Walking Tour** This fast-paced tour is a visual timeline of Chicago's architectural history, from Daniel Burnham's prototype skyscrape to the Modernist masterpieces of Mi van der Rohe. *See page 286.*
- **Untouchables Tour** A lighthearted romp through the city's Pr hibition-era underbe as gangster imperso ators lead bus tours the onetime haunts Al Capone and the s of the infamous St Valentine's Day Ma sacre. *See page 175.*

## Chicago for Families

- **Chicago Children's Museum** This interactive playground is best for the very young. *See page 151.*
- **Lincoln Park Zoo** Visit rare and endangered wildlife and feed the animals at the Farm in the Zoo. *See pages 170–71.*
- **Navy Pier** A Ferris wheel and carousel are among the classic amusement park rides at Pier Park. *See page 151.*
- **Court Fountain** Kids love getting drenched at this sculpture composed of two glass-brick towers that project t faces of Chicagoans who pucker up and "spit" a jet of water. *See pages 136–37.*
- **Morton Arboretu** This sprawling park suburban Lisle has garden and maze ju for kids. *See page 2*
- **Notebaert Nature Museum** A thousar butterflies flit arour this hands-on natur center. *See page 17*

## )NLY IN CHICAGO

**The El** The elevated rains that encircle the _oop are a fast and onvenient way to get round town and a retty good way for ewcomers to acquaint emselves with the ity. *See page 266.*

**Second City** This aucous improv com-dy club launched the areers of Bill Mur-ay, Dan Aykroyd, Mike Myers, and a ost of other *Saturday Night Live* regulars nd is still a fertile raining ground for some of the nation's most promising comedic talent. *See page 173.*

- **Ravinia Festival** OK, so it's not actually in Chicago, but packing a picnic and heading north to Highland Park for a romantic night of classical music under the stars is a long-standing Chicago tradition. *See page 258.*
- **Wrigley Field** The Chicago Cubs may not win very often, but they play at one of America's most hallowed and beloved ballparks. It's worth taking in a game even if you're not a baseball fan. *See page 180.*
- **Chicago Blues Festival** More than 750,000 blues lovers come to Grant Park to hear an unmatched lineup of both established and upcoming blues musicians in a four-day, open-air jam. *See page 135.*

**ABOVE:** the Blue Line stops at Damen and North Avenues.
**LEFT:** Chicago Blues Festival.

## BEST PLACES FOR A KISS

- **Promontory Point** Offering outstanding views of the skyline from a southern vantage point, it's no wonder this Hyde Park outlook is a perennially popular spot for weddings. *See page 238.*
- **Hancock Center Observatory** The panorama from "Big John's" 94th-floor observatory is intoxicating. And having a cocktail or two at the 96th-floor Signature Lounge will enhance the mood. *See pages 147–48.*
- **North Pond** The banks of this Lincoln Park lagoon are an intimate green space rendered uniquely urban by the Loop skyline visible just a mile or two away. In inclement weather, head to the warm and leafy Conservatory at the south end of the pond. *See page 171.*

## ONEY-SAVING TIPS

**count Lodging** Booking accom-dations through discount travel osites can provide huge rack rate ings, often as much as 50%. Be e to ask for weekend or corporate s and package deals.

**ecial Passes** Most museums, uding the Art Institute, Museum of temporary Art, and the Museum Science and Industry, designate a admission day (check in ad-ce as they are constantly chang-as well as discounts for students seniors. The Chicago CityPass offers discounted admission to five attractions – the Shedd Aquarium, Field Museum, Adler Planetarium, Hancock Observatory, and Museum of Science and Industry.

**Eat Smart** Many downtown restaurants offer affordable, pre- and post-theater dinner menus. Restaurants in the outer neighborhoods are attractively priced and of comparable quality to their upscale peers in the Loop and Near North. Opting for a BYOB restaurant can be much cheaper than choosing a restaurant that serves alcohol (beware of high corkage charges).

**Theater tickets** Many theaters offer two-for-one discounts, notably the Steppenwolf (call at 11am on the day of the performance). There are scores of free concerts and performances in Grant and Millennium parks, the Chicago Cultural Center, and neighborhood street festivals. Check the Chicago Office of Tourism (egov.cityofchicago.org) for a listing of events.

**Events Listings** Check the *Chicago Tribune* (www.chicagotribune.com), its entertainment website (http://chicago.metromix.com), and the free *Chicago Reader* (www.chicagoreader.com).

Prude

WESTIN

Huron CONSULTING GROUP

# MASTER OF REINVENTION

**The Windy City, Second City, Hog Butcher for the World, the City that Works, a City on the Make — Chicago's been called a lot of different names over the years, which just goes to show how resilient the place really is**

From its birth as a frontier trading post to its postindustrial future, Chicago is a master of reinvention. Its unexpected contra-ctions and improbable successes spring from e sort of can-do spirit that both gets the Sears wer built and keeps the hopes of Cubs fans oat year after year. Its ruthless ambition has ıde the city's political machine as much a ›me-grown specialty as deep-dish pizza. An ernational center of finance and trade on par th Los Angeles and Hong Kong, Chicago has en, correspondingly, the site of labor activism d unrest that shook and reshaped the modern ›rld. It's black and white, rich and poor; the thplace of both the blues and the skyscraper.

## ›ul of a new city

the last century Chicago's streets and parks ve been the canvas for visionary urban signers like Louis Sullivan and Daniel Burn-

> *hopeless for the occasional visitor to try to up with Chicago… She is always a novelty; he is never the Chicago you saw when you ed through the last time." – Mark Twain*

m. But for the visitor it has a lot more to fer than just fascinating history. It's home to ›rld-class music and theater, and a cutting-ge restaurant scene that's shaking up the linary establishment. A controversial plan to transform public housing has brought unprecedented reinvestment to once-distressed neighborhoods, while downtown sees its own residential building boom. And with more than 100 miles (160 km) of new bike paths and an aggressive beautification program, it's on its way to fulfilling a mayoral vision as the greenest city in the country.

"It is not Paris and buttermilk," wrote critic H.L. Menken of Chicago in the 1920s. "It is American in every chitling and sparerib. It is alive from snout to tail." Many years later, author Norman Mailer expressed a similar thought when he described Chicago as "perhaps the last of the great American cities." ❑

**ECEDING PAGES:** Jay Pritzker Pavilion; Chicago River. **FT:** Sears Tower. **RIGHT:** Chicago Blues Festival.

# THE MAKING OF CHICAGO

**With characteristic Midwestern resilience, Chicago rose originally from marshland and then again from the ashes of a great conflagration**

We have to keep reminding ourselves just how "new" things are over here in the New World. Take, for example, icago. This great American megalopolis, sconced at the center of the US heartland, was t so long ago – in the grand sweep of history ttle more than a swamp, a marshland not far noved from prehistoric muck and mire.

The first outsiders to stumble upon the place re a couple of Frenchmen named Jolliet and arquette. The year was 1673. Louis Jolliet s searching for gold; Jacques Marquette – rt Jesuit missionary, part adventurer – was rching for souls. Representing two strains restless seekers, they were the first Euro- ans to set eyes on the place that became our icago. And they were prototypical in setting pace for all the movers and shakers who in ars to come would do their bit to carve out great city and make history on a grand scale.

*et and Marquette were dispatched to the t Lakes region by Louis XIV to prop up the ch claim on the vast Mississippi River valley een New France and New Orleans.*

Man of plunder (Jolliet) meets man of prayer ather Marquette). It's a kind of contradiction ilt into the genetic makeup of this particular tropolis. Jolliet and Marquette were models

for the people whose doggedness succeeded in raising Chicago out of marsh and meadow, in the process overcoming such vicissitudes as cholera, fire, and financial collapse.

## Meat and merchandise

Jolliet was the forefather who begat meat-packer barons and merchant princes and condominium kings. Marquette was the forefather who begat social workers and community organizers and advocates for the street-curb poor. At worst, they worked at cross-purposes, the men on the make trampling all. At best, they joined in common cause, cash and compassion working together. A pretty park, for

**T:** Chicagoans flee the Great Fire of 1871.
**HT:** Jacques Marquette and Louis Jolliet, missionary lorers, traveling with Native Americans, 1672.

example, can soothe men's souls and increase a real estate agent's profits. These are the types who built Chicago, transforming marshland into Big Shoulders.

Chicago is, above all, an American city, a mid-continental Uncle Sam of gold coasts and slums, of babbling tongues, of punch clocks and blues and verve. It owes that verve to generations of strong backs, to its precious few visionaries, and to a few scoundrels, too. Lovely on its lakefront, shabby on its back streets, Chicago is a cauldron bubbling with contrasts, like the nation itself.

## Out of the swamp

Twelve thousand years ago, Lake Chicago, a larger version of today's Lake Michigan, covered much of what is now the Midwest. As the great glacial lake receded, it left behind vast, waving prairies and a shoreline swamp. America's native people – the Indians who were Chicago's first immigrants – embraced the swampland. They

*The son of a French pirate and an African slave, Jean Baptiste Point DuSable was educated in France before returning to the New World, where he married a Potawatomi woman and lived the life of a frontiersman.*

called it Checagou or Checaguar, or something close. It meant "wild onion" or "skunk," apparently a reference to the smell of rotting marshland onions that permeated the air. The name implied – and still implies – great strength.

From the beginnings of human habitation, the swamp was a place of action, a dealing and swapping ground. The Potawatomis, traveli by canoe, traded furs and skins there. T swamp linked North America's two gr waterways: the Mississippi to the southw – via the Des Plaines and Illinois rivers – a the Great Lakes to the north and east.

During spring rains, shallow-bottom Indian canoes traversed the swamp, traveli about 8 miles (13 km) from the Des Plair River to Lake Michigan to deliver their occ pants to trading powwows.

Jolliet, the entrepreneur, saw the big to coming. Paddling along, coasting past hi prairie grasses, he predicted to Marquette: "H some day will be found one of the world's gr cities." And a later explorer, named Robert C alier, Sieur de La Salle, saw the future too. "T will be the gate of an empire," he comment "The typical man who will grow up here m be enterprising. Each day, as he rises, he w exclaim, 'I act, I move, I push.'"

## Trappers and traders

Only a few hundred miles to the west w farmers and trappers and hunters who litera lived off the land and might go weeks withc

·ing a neighbor. Many believed that the ıntry was getting too crowded if they could smoke from the next farm. For what scant ›plies and companionship they needed, these f-sufficient frontiersmen depended on all, scattered settlements and trading posts. ıere they would swap their vegetables or ns culled from the local animals for food d luxury items that they didn't grow or ke for themselves.

Chicago was one such gathering place, ›wing from trading post to village to city gely because of a geographical location that owed easy transport in all directions. Many those who came to Chicago in the early ys were not farmers or frontiersmen themselves. Some were misfits drawn by the prospect of fewer social and legal constraints in what was at that time the "Wild West." Many were dreamers who believed the West was going to grow dramatically, and then went west themselves to realize those prophecies. They came to Chicago to be big fish in a little pond, and then to make the pond bigger.

**R LEFT:** an allegorical "America" leads pioneers stward in a 19th-century painting designed to inspire tlers. **LEFT:** frontier couple. **TOP:** Jean Baptiste Point Sable (left) and a Potawatomi chief (right). **ABOVE D ABOVE RIGHT:** hunters on the Illinois frontier.

## The house that Jean built

It was a black man who led the way. Jean Baptiste Point DuSable, a tall Haitian-born fur trapper, established a trading post in 1779 on the north bank of the Chicago River at what is now Michigan Avenue. He erected Chicago's first permanent house. Later, he sold the house to another trader, John Kinzie.

Meanwhile, the white man's government began to force out the native people – in the name of progress, of course. General "Mad Anthony" Wayne in 1795 overran the Indians and forced the Potawatomi tribe to cede huge tracts of Midwestern land, including "six miles square at the mouth of the Chickago River." It was prime real estate even then, a speculator's dream as swamps and forestland turned

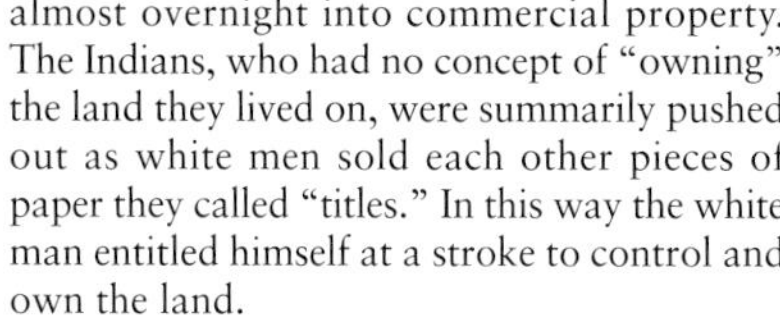

almost overnight into commercial property. The Indians, who had no concept of "owning" the land they lived on, were summarily pushed out as white men sold each other pieces of paper they called "titles." In this way the white man entitled himself at a stroke to control and own the land.

## Flight from the fort

Blue-coated US soldiers arrived from Detroit. In 1803, they built Fort Dearborn at what is now Lower Wacker and Michigan. Ordered to evacuate Fort Dearborn during the War of 1812 against the British, settlers and soldiers fleeing the fort were ambushed by Indians allied with the British. Fifty-two men, women, and children from the fort were slain in what became known as the Fort Dearborn Massacre.

But the pioneering deluge was checked only briefly: the soldiers returned, Fort Dearborn was rebuilt, and 5,000 Potawatomis were booted out for good. Scattered like bungalow dwellers in the path of a coming expressway, some Indians were relocated or drifted to government reservations, often hundreds of miles away; others tried to eke out a living on the edge of the white world, doing menial labor.

## The big boom

Things happened fast after that. In 1825, the Erie Canal was opened, creating a new water route between Chicago and the East to transport furs, grain, lumber, and livestock. The Illinois Legislature plotted a course for the Illinois-Michigan Canal that would connect Lake Michigan and the Mississippi. Federal dollars paid for dredging a harbor. Chicago boomed, though it was less a town than a real-estate lottery. A chunk of Lake Street property bought for $300 in 1833 was sold

one year later for more than $60,000.

New wagons rolled in daily. Settlers fr
the East swelled the population from 50
1830 to 4,170 in 1837. Buoyed by immigra
from Ireland and Germany, within 30 years
population had topped 40,000. Traders a
merchants came. So did saloon keepers a
prostitutes. As with Jolliet, the lure was mon
An early mayor, newspaper publisher "Lo
John" Wentworth, recalled in the 1880s: "
had people from almost every clime, a
almost every opinion. We had Jews and Chr
tians, Protestants, Catholics and infide
Among Protestants there were Calvinists a
Armenians. Nearly every language was rep
sented. Some people had seen much of t
world, and some very little."

## A city is born

Everything was new. Anything was possib
Audacious men blustered like the prairie win
On March 4, 1837, in Vandalia, the southe
Illinois community that was later replaced
Springfield as the state capital, the Legislat
approved a charter that formally recogniz
Chicago, previously a village, as a city. T
tallest building in the city was a lofty two s

;. Nobody owned a basement. Nobody had ess to gas. Nobody had a paved street.

n New York, the *Chicago American* orted that day, picketers were protesting inst bread prices. In Washington, DC, con- outions were being accepted for the con-

*dian uprising known as Pontiac's Rebellion t the Great Lakes country in the 1760s, g hundreds and slowing the pace of ment for years to come.*

iction of the Washington Monument. Out he brand-new city of Chicago, meanwhile, inessmen were advertising 4,000 pounds of chains, bushels of garden seed, Brandreth etable Pills ("known to benefit persons of ilious or costive habit of body") and even moting the virtues of smaller Midwestern towns ("Albion – One of the Healthiest Spots in Western America").

Two months later, in an election marred by brawls, a former New York state legislator named William B. Ogden defeated the early settler John Kinzie to become Chicago's first mayor. Ogden first stomped into town in the 1830s, steaming mad because one of his relatives had purchased, sight unseen, a muddy tract along State Street for $100,000. All Ogden wanted to do was get rid of the useless land.

But after selling a third of the land for the same amount he had paid for the whole lot, Ogden changed his mind. He stuck around. And got rich. He was made for this town. He was part Jolliet and part Marquette, part money man and part civic man, a getter and a giver. In the course of piling up his fortune, he built the city's first drawbridge and also its first railroad – which these days is called the Chicago & North Western.

**LEFT:** hunters return to a frontier cabin, circa 1867. **T TOP:** Fort Dearborn, 1856. **LEFT BOTTOM:** the h Street Bridge spans the Chicago River, 1861. **VE:** a view of Chicago from Lake Michigan 892, about 20 years after the Great Fire.

## Aspirations and action

Chicago's early history is replete with the doings of men with huge egos and boundless ambition. They left personal imprints on an impressionable city. When "Long John" Went-

worth, elected mayor in 1857, became fed up with dogfights and sex shows in the red-light district, he personally led a posse of 30 cops and hundreds of citizens on a cleanup crusade. They demolished every bordello in town.

When Chicagoans tired of slopping around in the mud, a sanitation engineer named Ellis Sylvester Chesbrough proposed raising the level of the entire city. Sidewalks were promptly boosted up, turning ground floors into basements. George Pullman, the railroad man, then used armies of workmen to jack up the buildings themselves. And when Chicagoans tired of contracting cholera and dysentery from foul shoreline drinking water, city workers dug a 2-mile (3-km) tunnel out into the lake to tap clean water. For good measure, Chicago amazed the world in 1900 by making its river run backward. That feat, aimed at using fresh lake water to flush away the polluted, disease-carrying river, was an engineering marve locks and channels that is still studied toda

Chicago was leaving the provinces beh and emerging as America's crossroads. 1856, Chicago was the hub of 10 railr trunk lines. Raw materials brought by wag barge, ship, and train were turned into pr ucts to build and feed the country – lum

## The Verdict Is in: The Cow Is Innocent

In the fall of 1997, the Chicago City Council rewrote history. It passed a resolution exonerating Mrs O'Leary's cow for starting the Great Chicago Fire of 1871. The work of amateur historian Richard Bales inspired the action. Bales used real estate records to piece together a map of what Mrs O'Leary's neighborhood would have looked like, then used the map to argue against the account of the fire's origins given by witness Daniel "Peg Leg" Sullivan.

At a hearing Peg Leg claimed he saw the fire from two doors away and hobbled 193 ft (59 meters) to Mrs O'Leary's barn to rescue her animals. Other buildings would have obstructed Peg Leg's view of the bla and he could not possibly have ho bled the distance on a wooden leg such short time, Bales argued. Co clusion: Peg Leg caused the fire a concocted the story to save face. T City Council agreed.

Lending weight to the "not guil verdict for Mrs O'Leary's cow is account given over half a century a by Chicago importer Louis M. Cohn. Cohn, who died in 1942 at the age 88, claimed that on the fateful night was with a group of boys, includi Mrs O'Leary's son, who were amusi themselves by shooting dice. It w the boys, he said, who knocked ov the lamp that started the conflagratic

n nearby forests, iron ore from Minnesota, stock and produce from some of the rich- farmland in the world. Chicago led the rld in the transportation of cattle, grain, l lumber. Grain elevators, jabbing the sky- , were the Sears Towers of the day.

## anufacturers and merchants

surely as one clever manufacturer knew v to turn out a product, someone else knew v to sell it. The mail-order giants Sears, ebuck & Co. and Montgomery Ward & . were born in Chicago. Legendary mer- nts, whose names are still in evidence not y on Chicago hotels and department stores in branches scattered across America's ail landscape, included Marshall Field, lliam Wieboldt, Potter Palmer, Samuel Car- , and John Pirie. And if the soul of Mar- tte was sometimes conspicuously absent, if rascals sold spoiled beef and defective apons to the Union Army, if the political oster boys seemed all too forgiving of City ll corruption and 400 brothels – well, hell, quote a future alderman, "Hinky Dink" nna: "Chicago ain't no sissy town."

## e Great Fire

en came the fire. That would be the Great icago Fire of 1871, started, as legend has it, October 8 in Mrs O'Leary's barn, now the of the Chicago Fire Department Training ademy. O'Leary's cow got the rap; it kicked a lantern, they said. The fire spread fast, an eyewitness describing it as "a vast ocean of flames, sweeping in mile-long billows and breakers over the doomed city." Three hundred people died; 100,000 were left homeless, and 18,000 buildings were destroyed. Chicago's first city was in ashes.

So they built a second: a sturdier town of fireproof brick. Two days after the fire, W.D. Kerfoot, a spunky real-estate agent, posted a sign on a shack: "All gone but wife, children and energy." Money was there to be made. No time to mourn. Chicago warn't no sissy town.

## Up from the ashes

A civic ripening emerged out of the Great Fire's ashes. Architects from all over the world, sensing unlimited creative and financial opportunity, flocked to Chicago. They endowed the city with a touch of New World class, a skyline of state-of-the-art office buildings. Many of the post-fire classics, particularly those in the range of 14 to 18 stories high along South Dearborn Street, remain the relatively earthbound bulwarks of the steel-frame construction process that led to today's skyscrapers.

Because it was continuing to grow so

**LEFT:** the Great Fire laid waste to the city in 1871.
**VE:** designed by architect Louis Sullivan in 1899, Carson Pirie Scott and Company department e was a sign of the city's business prowess.
**VE RIGHT:** retail magnate Marshall Field.

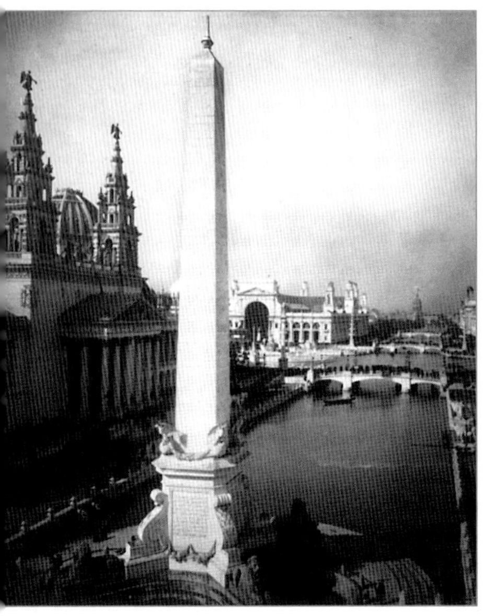

quickly as an industrial and commercial center, downtown Chicago needed big buildings. Thus it was that ambitious architects with powerful new designs were allowed free rein to build toward the clouds.

Three masters led the charge: John Root, designer of the graceful Rookery and Monadnock buildings; Louis Sullivan, designer of the elegant Auditorium and Carson Pirie Scott buildings; and Sullivan's peerless protégé, Frank Lloyd Wright.

Brilliant innovators, they established Chicago's tradition of architectural leadership. Mies van der Rohe, the father of unadorned steel-and-glass modernism, nailed it down. Helmut Jahn, iconoclastic creator of the hotly disputed State of Illinois Center and Xerox building, helped to ensure its strength today.

## Cultural cachet

By 1890, Chicago was struggling out of an era of cutthroat Social Darwinism into an age of social reform. In the City Council, the avaricious "Gray Wolves," the bribery-wizened councilmen, still divvied up the boodle. But more civic-minded Chicagoans demanded social justice, a bit of high culture, and such

public amenities as spacious parks and uncluttered lakefront. The 1890s saw the est lishment of the Art Institute, stocked with Du Masters paintings; the University of Chica founded with Rockefeller money on Marsh Field real estate; the Columbian Museum Chicago (forerunner of the Field Museum), a the Columbian Exposition of 1893, a fabulou successful world's fair that introduced the Fe wheel and the "shake" dancer Little Egypt. I "exotic" bumps and grinds were undoubte modest by today's standards, but Little Egy act nonetheless drew condemnation from m alizing newspaper editors and clergymen w warned that she was arousing lust in the hea and minds of her many male fans.

The Chicago Symphony Orchestra made debut, although the conductor, Theod Thomas, recruited from the New York Ph harmonic, dared not offer many symphonie first. Chicago's musical taste was too undev oped; "light music" had to suffice as cultu Asked why he had bothered to settle in Chica at all, he explained: "I would go to hell if th would give me a permanent orchestra."

> *Turned away by the organizers of th 1893 World's Columbian Exposition, Buffalo Bill Cody leased a nearby pro for his hugely popular Wild West Sho thus benefiting from the fair's notori without having to share the revenue.*

## Men of vision

Thomas was one of those rare men of scope a vision who made Chicago what it is tod There were others such as A. Montgom Ward, a stoical money man in the Jolliet m

who revealed the heart of a Marquette when he launched his 13-year court battle to save Grant Park from public buildings. City Hall, the press, and the business community ganged up on the merchant, calling him an "obstructionist." But in the end, Ward won and established the principle that Chicago's entire lakefront should be preserved "forever open, clear and free."

There was the architect Daniel H. Burnham, who enshrined the concept of a pristine lakefront in his famous city plan of 1909. No other plan has so influenced Chicago's growth. The Burnham plan of 1909 resulted in the creation of a string of lakefront parks and beaches, including Jackson Park and Washington Park; the acquisition of a greenbelt of forest preserves on the city's periphery; the construction of Chicago's main post office; and the siting of the Eisenhower Expressway.

In many ways, it could be said that Chicago's renowned social consciousness was a reaction to the city's equally renowned and legendary greed. In this town of extremes, with its unofficial "Where's mine?" motto, it made a lot of sense for the backlash against rampant capitalism to be a particularly selfless, far-reaching brand of humanitarianism. Whatever the dynamics at work, the city goes on benefiting.

**ABOVE LEFT AND RIGHT:** known as the White City, the stately Beaux Arts structures of the World's Columbian Exposition were designed by Chicago architect Daniel Burnham and his partner Charles Atwood with such prominent East Coast architects as Charles F. McKim.

## Civic conscience

Social reform by 1890 was, in part, a survival tactic. Chicago seethed with labor unrest, and the city became an incubator for a nationally organized labor movement, then in its infancy. Class warfare, fueled by the loose alliance of young unions that were committed to better working and living conditions for all laborers, spooked the millionaires of Prairie Avenue. In the 1880s and 1890s, a nationwide campaign for the eight-hour day and the minimum wage triggered bloody confrontations. Thirteen men were killed in Chicago during one week. The National Guard was called out to quell a workers' riot outside Pullman's railcar plant. Seven policemen were killed in the Haymarket Riot of 1886. No one saw who threw the bomb, but four anarchists went to the gallows.

Pressures for social reform came from other

quarters. From an emerging professional class came such questioning upstarts as social worker Jane Addams, attorney Clarence Darrow, and muckraking journalist Upton Sinclair.

Addams, a proper young woman from Rockford, Illinois, walked among the shabby sweatshops and immigrant tenements on the city's West Side and decided to devote her life to helping the people there. Chicago's population had reached one million by 1890, including hundreds of thousands of Irish, Italian, and Eastern European immigrants living in conditions of squalor within a whiff of the stockyards.

Addams's Hull-House, a settlement house tending to the needs of immigrants at Blue Island and Halsted, became a model for the nation, fighting for an end to child labor, for factory inspections, and for a minimum wage. Jane Addams was some kind of crazy lady, according to the mavens of La Salle Street – Chicago's Wall Street – but, they had to admit, she was effective. Addams and her followers at Hull-House and other settlement houses established throughout Chicago provided fresh milk for babies, taught immigrants English, and set up day-care centers. They provided a range of care and comfort that became a model for inner-city social welfare programs, from prescribing balanced diets for young families to describing how to open a bank account, enroll children in school, or apply for a better job. These early social workers helped instill a sense of self-esteem and hope in an

### HAYMARKET: DAY OF RECKONING

Wearing white robes and hoods and defiantly singing the revolutionary *Marsellaise* anthem, four men went to the gallows in late 1887 as retribution for the sensational Haymarket Square riot that marks one of the darkest moments in Chicago's history.

In the midst of a rally on March 4, 1886, by workers and anarchists who were seeking an eight-hour workday, someone threw a bomb that wreaked havoc – seven policemen and at least four workers mortally wounded plus scores of injuries. It was not long afterward that the penalty (a fifth participant committed suicide in prison) came to be generally regarded as a serious miscarriage of justice – three other men who had been sentenced to life in prison were set free in 1893 by the governor of Illinois.

Haymarket Square was an open market near Des Plaines Avenue and Randolph Street. In the latest of a series of commemorations that have been attempted over the years, a monument by Chicago artist Mary Brogger was dedicated in September 2004.

exploited, downtrodden class of laborers.

Others have followed in Addams's footsteps. In the 1950s and 1960s, Saul Alinsky, the patriarch of militant community organizers, fought City Hall with his Back of the Yards Council and the Woodlawn Organization.

In later years Douglas Dobmeyer, president of the Chicago Coalition of the Homeless, led ragged demonstrations outside the yuppie high-rises that displaced the Skid Row poor.

## Back of the Yards

Upton Sinclair was crazier still. In his book *The Jungle*, his muckraking exposé of the stockyards, he wrote of "the secret rooms where the spoiled meats went to be doctored." He told of workmen whose feet were eaten away by acids in the fertilizer rooms. And he repeated dark tales of workers who had fallen into steaming vats and emerged as beef lard.

But there was much more to the stockyards than the horrendous working conditions. There were the living conditions, often no more sanitary. Families, many of them immigrants from Europe, were crowded into narrow wooden row houses in the neighborhood known as Back of the Yards. Many of the workers were rural Europeans who spoke little or no English. Many were unfamiliar with life in America, knowing only what they had heard from friends and relatives about how easy it was to get a high-paying job and how wealthy Chicago was.

What the immigrants didn't learn until they arrived was how hard they had to work, often in reprehensible conditions; how much daily living cost, and how quickly those seemingly high wages disappeared; and how Chicago's vast wealth was accumulated and hoarded by a relative few who profited from the backbreaking labor of the new arrivals.

**LEFT:** a Chicago playbill advertises a popular musical comedy in 1899. **ABOVE LEFT:** social reformer Jane Addams was the founder of the American settlement house movement. **ABOVE RIGHT:** Mordecai "Three Finger" Brown pitched for the Cubs in the early 1900s.

The Back of the Yards was a ghetto. Its "inmates" were never free of the stink of animal manure, slaughterhouses, and rendering plants. In hopes of raising enough money to escape, or merely to meet the rents charged for their substandard housing – often owned by the companies using the stockyards – men and women worked long, grueling hours, sometimes taking on more than one job. They often kept their children out of school in order to put them to work, too, so that the whole family might have enough money to move to a new neighborhood and find better jobs.

## The Great Migration

After World War I, the "Great Migration" of poor African-Americans from the Southern states provided a new source of inexpensive labor to be exploited by the stockyards and other industries. Almost overnight, it seemed, much of Chicago's South Side became a predominantly black neighborhood. The rise of the "Black Metropolis," as the area came to be known, witnessed a flourishing of African-American culture, including a string of jazz clubs along a stretch of South State Street known as "The Stroll," where legendary musicians such as King Oliver and Louis Armstrong gave New Orleans jazz a Chicago flavor.

## Crime and corruption

After World War I, Chicago's focus of power shifted from industrialists to politicians. While heirs to Chicago's great retailing and meat-packing fortunes ensconced themselves on the North Shore, crooked politicians and bootleggers plundered the city. The handful of social reformers were too focused on good works to worry about the corruption of an entire political system, and they would probably have been no match for men with machine guns and briefcases anyway. So the bootleggers shot it out and more than 400 gangsters were killed over five years, including seven in the 1929 St Valentine's Day Massacre.

Bestriding the city during the Prohibition years – from 1920 to 1933 when a constitutional amendment outlawed alcoholic beverages of any sort throughout the United States – was that colossus of crime, Al Capone.

A one-time speakeasy bouncer who graduated to running houses of prostitution, Capone built a vast bootlegging empire that included importing whisky from Canada and operating

**FAR LEFT AND TOP:** scenes from the Chicago stockyards. **LEFT BOTTOM:** Al "Scarface" Capone in a 1931 mugshot. **RIGHT BOTTOM:** Joe "King" Oliver and his Creole Jazz Band in Chicago about 1922; the band boosted the career of Louis Armstrong (fourth from right).

his own breweries right in the middle of Chicago. To keep his operations going, he made the bribery of officials at every level, from City Hall to cops on the beat, an everyday fact of life that still plagues Chicago.

Capone, whose business card identified him as a "Second-hand Furniture Dealer," was short and pot-bellied and not particularly physically imposing. He was brilliant and brutal in equal measure and knew how to dole out both punishment and reward. Those who did what he wanted could get rich quickly. Those who didn't could become extinct even more quickly.

He often made his points in a most dramatic way, sending out carloads of gunmen with nonmusical violin cases or interrupting a black-tie banquet to kill a fellow diner, a disloyal lieutenant, with repeated blows to the back of the head with a baseball bat.

> *In 1922 the Illinois Vigilance Association in Chicago reported that its "representatives have traced the fall of l,000 girls in the last two years to" the "pathological, nerve-irritating, sex-exciting music of jazz orchestras."*

Chicago boomed during the Roaring Twenties. Fortunes were made in the stock market. More big buildings went up. Flappers danced on speakeasy tables. Most people tolerated crime as a part of everyday life, as long as it wasn't one of their relatives or friends who was cut down in the crossfire among rival hoodlums.

Capone was finally brought down by a group of federal agents led by Eliot Ness and known as "The Untouchables" for their determined refusal to take bribes.

Unable to pin murder or even bootlegging directly on the guilty Capone, Ness and his men cleverly went after the gangster for failing to pay taxes on his millions in illicit profits. In 1931 Capone was convicted and sentenced to 11 years in prison (he actually served eight). He died in 1947, quietly, in bed, of syphilis.

But Capone didn't invent political corruption in Chicago. Back in 1837, on the very day Chicago voted to become a city, wagonloads of non-resident Irish canal diggers, technically ineligible to vote, were lugged to the convention hall to cast their ballots. Consider just two stealing mayors. When Fred A. Busse died, he left behind a safe-deposit box full of stock in a company that sold the city its manhole covers. And when Prohibition-era Mayor William Thompson died, he left behind safe-deposit

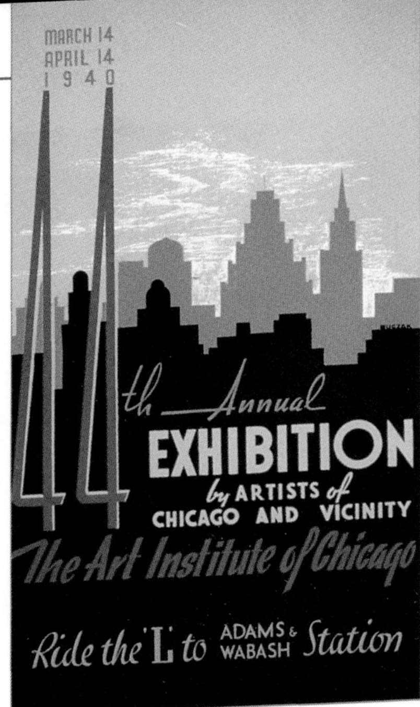
MARCH 14
APRIL 14
1940
44th Annual
EXHIBITION
by ARTISTS of
CHICAGO AND VICINITY
The Art Institute of Chicago
Ride the 'L' to ADAMS & WABASH Station

boxes containing $1,578,000 in cash, stocks, bonds and certificates. No one knows exactly how the mayor got so rich, or where that money came from. However, Al Capone always liked Thompson, to the point of keeping Big Bill's picture on his office wall.

## Hard times

As a great big factory town, Chicago was hit especially hard when Wall Street crashed late in 1929 and the Depression ensued. Bankers and manufacturers battened down their hatches while jobless Chicagoans seeking redress marched forlornly on State Street. This did not stop the city, however, from putting on another world's fair in 1933, this one marking a "Century of Progress" and providing an opportunity for an exotic dancer named Sally Rand to more or less steal the show with a titillating act.

Taking to the stage adorned with little beyond

### TONY CERMAK: UNLUCKY MAYOR

Since it became a city in 1837, Chicago has experienced the loss of four of its mayors while they were in office. Two of them – Richard M. Daley and Harold Washington – died of natural causes, while two succumbed to homicide.

In 1893 a disgruntled job-seeker gunned down Carter H. Harrison at Harrison's home, causing the assassin to undergo the hangman's noose. Forty years later, Chicago Mayor Anton Cermak was unlucky enough to be sitting with President-elect Franklin D. Roosevelt in the back seat of an open car in Miami, Florida, in February 1933, when a deranged assassin struck. The assassin, an unemployed Italian-born bricklayer named Giuseppe Zangara, shouted "Too many people are starving!" before discharging his gun. Cermak was fatally wounded, for which Zangara was put in the electric chair.

But was FDR really the target? Or was it in fact Cermak? Doubts have been raised, not surprisingly considering the kind of people Cermak had dealt with over the years in a Chicago replete with gangsters. Born in Bohemia, he was an earthy, colorful type who raised himself by the bootstraps from coal miner's son to mule-skinner to political wheeler-dealer adept at melding together various "ethnics" in pursuit of wealth and power – and at the risk of intruding on gangster turf. He reportedly boasted that he would seek mob support and then "boot them out of town" after the election campaign.

Known by various sobriquets such as "Pushcart Tony" and "Ten Percent Tony," Cermak was elected mayor in 1931, giving Democrats control of city government for the first time. He won a smashing victory over "Big Bill" Thompson, an equally skillful political operative, by a record margin.

a large fan, a feather boa, and a ball, she teased the fantasies of male voyeurs eager for glimpses of bare flesh as she cavorted provocatively.

The city's economic fortunes picked up as the nation entered World War II and assembly lines buzzed again. In the interim, a team of physicists at the University of Chicago achieved success in 1942 in America's effort to build a nuclear reactor, first of its kind, and help bring about Japan's surrender three years later. Directed by the Italian-born physicist Enrico Fermi, the scientists toiled in strict secrecy on their "atomic pile" in a mundane basement beneath the athletic stadium. The university has produced more Nobel Prize winners than any other institution in the world.

## Race and ethnicity

In the second half of the 20th century, various social stresses tugged at Chicago's political landscape. Chief among them was a growing racial tension that grew out of the large influx of African-Americans from the South who flocked to the city for economic opportunity. Thousands had come in the wake of World War I, and World War II provided even greater stimulus – some 65,000 blacks settled in Chicago between 1941 and 1945.

Poor housing conditions in black neighborhoods, already overcrowded, was exacerbated, and the impact on the public schools and their ability to accommodate children from poor, rural Southern backgrounds was profound. Race came to replace the ethnic factor as the dominant political issue, and the unbending nature of the Democratic apparatus that took control of the city's government in 1933 did not help. Politicians seemed clueless about how to achieve any kind of reform, and not until the election of a black mayor, Harold Washington, in 1987 were African-Americans able to wield much power.

Inevitably, violence erupted over the years, as for example in August 1965 when a swerving fire truck killed an African-American girl on the West Side and two nights of resulting violence caused injury to scores of residents. A year later, Dr Martin Luther King Jr, the

**FAR LEFT:** Sally Rand titillated audiences during the 1933 World's Fair. **LEFT:** a poster for a 1940 exhibit at the Art Institute of Chicago. **ABOVE LEFT:** World War II recruitment poster. **ABOVE RIGHT:** Chicago women were encouraged to work in the city's factories during World War II.

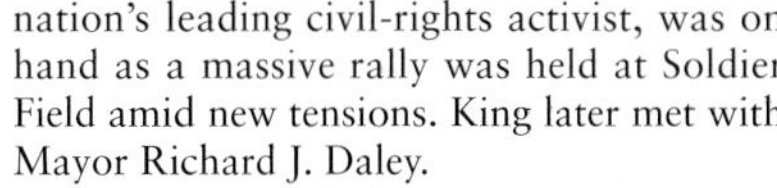

nation's leading civil-rights activist, was on hand as a massive rally was held at Soldier Field amid new tensions. King later met with Mayor Richard J. Daley.

Daley, strong-willed and capable, dominated the city's political life from 1955 to his death in 1976 – he was Chicago's mayor for six terms. But he seemed never to achieve any deep-down grasp of the black community's needs and aspirations – as Dr. King himself told reporters following the meeting with "Hizzoner" at City Hall. Daley, for his part, was given to denouncing "outsiders" for stirring up trouble.

The mayor's impact on Chicago public life was huge and often controversial. During his regime, whole communities were bulldozed for expressways, plazas, and universities. He plowed ghettos and built segregating walls of high-rise public housing, and he ran expressways toward the Loop. The business center thrived, although the Loop's once-glittering nightlife did not.

Daley was a kingmaker, supposedly even playing a crucial role – as many believe – in getting John F. Kennedy elected president over Richard M. Nixon in 1960 by sitting on the Chicago results until the right moment. Daley's winning margin in the mayoral elections went from 49 per cent in 1955 to as high as 75 per cent in later years.

It helped, of course, that a lot of middle-class voters had long ago abandoned the city for

## THE WHOLE WORLD WAS WATCHING

All hell broke loose in the politically turbulent year of 1968, and Chicago was ground zero for much of the fallout. North Vietnam ratcheted up the war with its Tet Offensive, which seemed to help turn America's favorite TV newsman, Walter Cronkite, against the conflict. A dispirited Lyndon B. Johnson gave up on seeking another term as President. And the man who might have bested him, Senator Robert M. Kennedy, was gunned down in a Los Angeles hotel.

Chicago Mayor Richard M. Daley, not happy about the rioting that had occurred in his city, as elsewhere, upon the assassination of Dr Martin Luther King Jr, vowed to crack down on the antiwar troublemakers publicly conspiring to make things uncomfortable for complacent Democrats at their upcoming national convention in the Windy City.

They did indeed, those rambunctious Hippies and Yippies, chanting and taunting and carrying on before and especially during that memorably divisive August week of the convention, incurring retribution from Daley's police augmented by National Guardsmen who confronted the protestors on Michigan Avenue and around the Loop and in public parks. Meanwhile, inside the Amphitheatre where the Democrats were convening, things outside reached such a fevered pitch that Senator Abe Ribicoff of Connecticut felt constrained to denounce the "Gestapo tactics" on the streets. Mayor Daley snarled back at him from the floor in decidedly ungenteel language. All this on prime time national television.

There would be spectacle in the courtroom afterwards as the "Chicago 7" antiwar instigators – including the irreverent Abbie Hoffman and Jerry Rubin – were put on trial. An associate, Bobby Seale, was ordered bound and gagged as the trial ensued. None of the convictions that resulted lasted beyond the appeal stage.

greener pastures. The last hurrah for Republicans had come and gone with the Prohibition-era mayor William "Big Bill" Thompson.

## Mayoral sweepstakes

Chicago has had three other mayors of special note since Daley's demise in 1976, one of them being his son, Richard M. Daley. The others were Jane Byrne and the late Harold Washington.

Byrne, a protégé of the first Mayor Daley, seemed to have come out of nowhere in winning a surprising victory in the Democratic primary in 1979. She went on to victory in the general election as Chicago's first, and thus far only, female mayor. Much was expected in the way of various necessary reforms in municipal administration until Byrne got bogged down in various political flaps and controversies and lost the support of a goodly number of blacks and white ethnics alike.

Harold Washington was a popular state legislator who asserted in 1983, on behalf of fellow African-Americans, that it was finally "our turn" to rule over Chicago's municipal government. He defeated Byrne and Richard M. Daley in the Democratic primary before besting his Republican opponent in the general election in a most divisive contest. Washington was lionized by blacks both for his election victory and his early administrative promise, and his death of a massive heart attack in 1987 caused great disappointment. Hopes that Democratic fragmentation would be overcome also were dashed.

**FAR LEFT:** Chicago railroad worker, 1943. **LEFT:** members of the Chicago 7 speak to the press after the 1968 Democratic Convention. **ABOVE:** Richard J. Daley campaigns with presidential candidate Jimmy Carter in 1976. **ABOVE RIGHT:** Mexican Independence Day parade.

Richard M. Daley, son of the legendary six-time mayor, is on track to outdo the senior Daley in tenure. First elected in 1989, he has been returned to the office by voters five times successively, the last time in 2007. He is generally regarded as having instilled a new sense of hope and enterprising spirit in Chicago's administration.

There has been major development activity downtown, and a number of large-scale projects pushed by Daley are receiving public support – not the least of which is Millennium Park, a 24-acre (10-hectare) public space for concerts, recreation, and oversize modern sculptures that has won kudos from Chicagoans despite cost overruns and construction delays. Cuts in taxes have been made to benefit business interests, trees have been planted throughout the city, and efforts have been made to put more police officers on active duty.

Post-industrial Chicago is competing again in a service-oriented economy, and there has been an upsurge in recent years in residential activity – people moving back to the city. In general, things appear to be upbeat for the city by the lake. ❑

# LAW AND DISORDER

**Chicago's gangland history includes some of the most colorful and notorious episodes in the annals of crime**

Two moments resonate with special force in Chicago's crime-laden historical memory: the morning of February 14, 1929, and the evening of July 22, 1934. The scene of the crimes: the city's Lincoln Park district on the North Side.

The first is of course the infamous St Valentine's Day Massacre wherein seven men were lined up against a garage wall and summarily sprayed with a barrage of bullets by a foursome of killers, two of them posing as policemen. It was Al Capone's way of letting rival mob leader Bugs Moran who was crime boss around here. (Capone conveniently arranged to be in Florida at the time.)

The other less than shining moment, five years later, involved John Dillinger, bank robber extraordinaire and Public Enemy No. 1 in those lowdown Depression days. On that occasion the 31-year-old Dillinger met his end, after a night of moviegoing with a couple of lady friends, in an alley outside the Biograph Theater – the feature film, appropriately, was a gangster flick, *Manhattan Melodrama*, starring Clark Gable. Waiting in the wings were FBI agents and police guns intent on writing "Finis" to the Dillinger saga.

*The Chicago Daily News estimated that at his peak Al Capone controlled 6,000 speakeasies, 2,000 bookmakers, and scores of bordellos. His weekly revenue was roughly $6 million.*

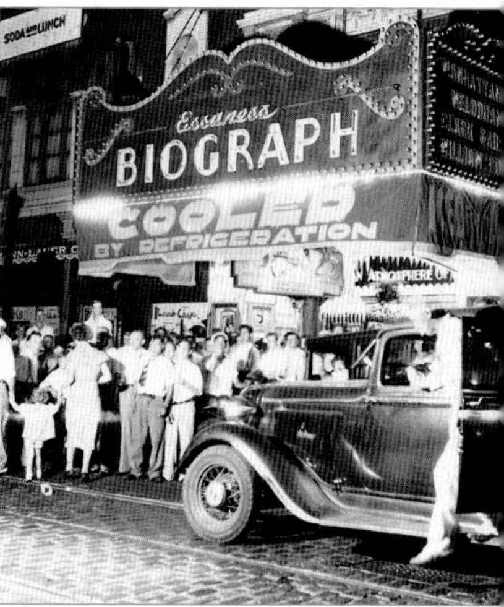


**LEFT:** Al Capone in 1932.

**RIGHT:** notorious bank robber John Dillinger was shot and killed outside the Biograph Theater in 1934.

## Polishing the image

For a time, Chicagoans were none too thrilled about the inconvenient truth of their city's link to crime and tried to sweep it under the rug. In the 1950s and '60s, Mayor Richard J. Daley and others attempted to downplay the image of "Scarface" Capone, Tommie guns, and all that Roaring Twenties jazz. But that began to change as the city learned to live with, if not love, its gangland reputation through tours, exhibits, and restaurants.

Ironically, the structure with the strongest link to gangster lore – the Biograph Theater, at 2433 North Lincoln Avenue – has nothing to do with the infamous Capone. As for Dillinger, he himself was not part of any crime syndicate but rather a freelancer who resembled Humphrey Bogart and came across as a regular guy.

Hard-core gangster enthusiasts can join the John Dillinger Died for You Society, a tongue-in-cheek fan club started in 1966 for followers of gangster lore. Applicants to the Society receive a membership card, a history of the group, a catalog of gangster accoutrements and notices of meetings where an empty chair is always left for the club's namesake. And loyalists remember to mark their calendar each July 22 to commemmorate "John Dillinger Day."

## A history of violence

Chicago's oldest crime structure stands at Dearborn and Hubbard streets. It is the old Criminal Courts Building, a gray stone fortress that has been renovated for private offices.

### The Untouchables

Al Capone and his mob were pursued relentlessly by federal Prohibition agent Eliot Ness and his handpicked team of nine agents, who tried to destroy Capone's thriving bootlegging empire. After banding together, Ness and his men quickly grabbed Capone's attention by raiding 18 of the mobster's Chicago warehouses in one night.

Initially reluctant to have the members of this federal team killed, Capone had his men offer the agents bribes, which were refused. One mobster threw an envelope stuffed with cash into an agent's car as he passed on the road. The agent caught up with the car and threw back the envelope. When the press learned of the failed bribe attempts, Ness and his men were dubbed "The Untouchables."

Ness and his men continued to damage Capone's illegal business, and an enraged Capone made unsuccessful attempts to knock off members of the team, including Ness himself.

Ness got a break in the case when, during a routine raid, his agents stumbled across Capone's accounting records. In the end, the misdeeds that sent Capone to the slammer weren't murder or bootlegging but the far more prosaic crime of tax evasion. He was convicted of 22 counts of tax evasion in 1931 and sentenced to 11 years in prison, although he was released three years early for good behavior. Ness had the satisfaction of personally escorting his elusive quarry to the train that took him to the penitentiary. Prohibition was repealed during Capone's incarceration, and his health and criminal organization deteriorated.

Behind it, where a firehouse now stands, was the old jail where executions were carried out.

In all, 92 prisoners were hanged in the old jail between 1882 and 1929. It would have been 93, but in 1921 "Terrible" Tommy O'Connor, condemned to hang for murdering a police detective, escaped four days before his date with the hangman's knot.

The perpetrators of gangland murders were rarely arrested by the police, however, let alone sentenced to death. Instead, their courtrooms were the smoke-filled headquarters of gangster bosses, and their executions were carried out by gunmen whose own days were probably numbered.

**LEFT:** a police re-creation of the St Valentine's Day Massacre, 1929. **ABOVE TOP:** gangsters Earl Weiss (left) and Dion O'Banion (right). **ABOVE BOTTOM:** Eliot Ness. **ABOVE RIGHT:** actor Robert Stack portrayed Eliot Ness in the popular TV series *The Untouchables*.

## Turf war

During the 1920s, most of the death sentences delivered by gangsters were the result of territorial wars that began over bootlegging and quickly expanded to extortion, gambling, prostitution, labor racketeering, and corruption of public officials. The methods of punishment were swift and often ingenious, such as rubbing the bullet tips with garlic so that if they happened to miss a vital organ the victim could still die of gangrene.

At first, the gangs were content to keep to their own sides of town, but eventually greed got the best of them and entrepreneurs sparked open warfare.

In July of 1921, independent businessman Steve Wisniewski hijacked a beer truck belonging to Dion O'Banion. "Deanie," as close friends knew him, had been an altar boy and a singing waiter. But by 1921, O'Banion was the undisputed crime boss of the city's North Side. His top lieutenant, Earl Weiss, forced Wisniewski into a car at gunpoint at the corner

of Halsted and 14th streets. Wisniewski got his brains blown out and made history by being the first victim to be "taken for a ride."

O'Banion ran his operation from a flower shop at 738 North State Street, now a parking lot. He had become a thorn for South Side crime boss Johnny Torrio. On November 10, 1924, Capone – who at the time was Torrio's top lieutenant – sent a trio of killers into O'Banion's flower shop to silence the Irish tenor forever.

Weiss took over O'Banion's gang, but not for long. On October 11, 1926, Weiss and his driver, Sam Peller, died in a storm of machine gun bullets on the steps of Holy Name Cathedral at 735 North State Street. Both Weiss and O'Banion were taken to a mortuary at 703 North Wells Street, now an art gallery. Back then, it was the site of some of Chicago's most lavish gangster funerals. O'Banion's funeral procession included 122 cars and 26 trucks loaded with flowers.

## Scarface surfaces

By now, Al Capone had taken over from Torrio, who survived an assassination attempt and decided to retire amid the city's longest running gang war. Its violence was so blatant that Tony Lombardo, Capone's consigliere, was gunned down on a Friday afternoon, September 7, 1928, walking east on the south side of Madison, between Dearborn and State. At the time, State and Madison was known as "the world's busiest corner."

And then came the most notorious of all gangland attacks, the one that would forever burn Capone into Chicago's history – the St Valentine's Day Massacre. Capone, whose estimated income surpassed an astonishing $105 million in 1927, was at last convicted in 1931 of income tax evasion and sentenced to 11 years in prison (he served only eight of them).

Capone died in 1947 in Florida, his body ravaged by syphilis because, for all his ruthlessness and savagery in dealing with those who got in his way, he himself had a fear of needles, even those filled with penicillin. His body was transported back to Chicago and buried in the family plot at Mount Carmel Cemetery in the western suburb of Hillside, about a 40-minute car drive from downtown.

As for "Machine Gun Jack" McGurn, who masterminded the St Valentine's Day Massacre, his life ended on the seventh anniversary of the event. In 1936, two remnants of the Moran gang wreaked revenge and mowed McGurn down with Tommy guns. As a parting gesture the hitmen left a seasonal calling card in inimitable gangster style – a blood-red valentine pressed into McGurn's lifeless left hand. ❑

**ABOVE:** Chicago police officers survey the aftermath of gangland warfare.

## Murder Castle

As the 19th century wound down, the young and restless everywhere were flocking to the cities in pursuit of happiness and escape from the mundane ways of town and country. Chicago was very much an urban magnet, attracting such as Carrie Meeber, the fictional heroine of Theodore Dreiser's debut novel *Sister Carrie* whose wholesome vitality helped her to overcome the cruel realities of impersonal urban life and find a measure of success, if not happiness.

For many, the city could be a tough nut to crack as young males and females got swallowed up in the madding crowds of anonymous city life. Social observers noted that many lives seemed to become vanishing acts in the metropolis.

There was no more gruesome example of this than the poor souls who fell victim to one of the most notorious serial killers in American history. The perpetrator's name was Herman Webster Mudgett, also known as Dr. H. H. Holmes.

Holmes carried out his monstrous crimes in the three-story, block-long World's Fair Hotel he erected at 701 63rd Street in the Chicago suburb of Englewood. Neighbors had dubbed the place a "Castle," and after an investigation in 1895 exposed its ghastly residue – bones, vertebrae, a hip socket, a vat of acid holding ribs – it came to be known as the "Murder Castle." His victims were young women, mostly, but his murder spree in the 1893-95 period also took the lives of children and men in Chicago and elsewhere.

The building was equipped with labyrinthine corridors, soundproof and windowless rooms, escape-proof vaults and, most awfully, gas jets that rendered a slow death to the hapless victims he lured there. Holmes chose his victims from among his women employees, many of whom had been required to contract life insurance policies that named him as beneficiary, as well as female lovers and hotel guests. Many suffered agonizing deaths by asphyxiation through gas or other means of suffocation. Victims' remains were melted down in kilns, cadavers skinned, skeletons sold to medical schools.

Holmes ultimately confessed to 27 murders and six attempted murders. It is thought that the actual number may have been over 200. The sordid happenings occurred against the backdrop of the World's Columbian Exposition, held at nearby Jackson Park. The six-month exposition in 1893 was a tremendous success, attracting many young men and women to settle in Chicago.

**RIGHT:** serial killer Herman Webster Mudgett may have claimed more than 200 victims; the story of his crime spree is recounted in Erik Larson's best-selling book *The Devil in the White City*.

Born in New Hampshire in 1860, Holmes graduated from the University of Michigan Medical School, where he stole bodies from the laboratory in a scheme involving fraudulent insurance claims. He moved to Chicago, proceeded to acquire a drugstore through fraud and murder, and erected his hotel.

Inquiries by relatives of his victims, combined with suspicions arising out of various discrepancies in his insurance claims, led to his arrest in Philadelphia, where, at the age of 35, he was hanged on May 7, 1896. ❑

# THE WINDS OF POLITICS

**In a balkanized place like Chicago, it's necessary to be experienced at political gamesmanship – just ask whoever happens to be mayor!**

When the winds blow in Chicago, politically speaking, they pretty much emanate from the fifth floor of City Hall on North LaSalle Street, which since 1911 has been ground zero for everything that goes on in town. In Chicago, the mayor behind the desk there sits firmly in the catbird seat, to a degree matched in few other cities.

## Seat of power

Heaven help the political wannabes who, without first checking in with the major-domo on North LaSalle, attempt to sally forth into the precincts on any kind of mission. And that goes for presidential hopefuls, gubernatorial aspirants, legislators, and favor-seekers of all stripes. Here in the Windy City the mayor tends to speak loudly and also carry a big stick – a tendency most famously exemplified by the irrepressible Richard J. Daley, who ruled the roost for an unprecedented six terms from the 1950s through the 1970s. His son Richard M. Daley, mayor since 1989, is exhibiting the same staying power.

*Richard J. Daley, Chicago's Democratic boss, was initially elected to the Illinois legislature as a Republican. The Republican encumbent died before the election, so Daley took his place on the ballot.*

Both Daleys are standouts in a line of over four dozen mayors who have served ever since Chicago formally became a city back in the 1830s. First to hold the office was William B. Ogden, a businessman with railroad connections. Businessmen were the major players as the city began rapidly developing as a trade mecca and transit hub in the 19th century – Ogden helped bring about America's first transcontinental rail line.

Among others who became mayors in the city's formative years were a watchmaker, a brick manufacturer, a sawmill operator, a meatpacker, and an enterprising physician named Levi Boone – a descendant of Daniel Boone, the pioneer trailblazer.

**LEFT:** "Hizzoner" Richard J. Daley.
**RIGHT:** Jimmy Carter campaigns in Chicago in 1976.

## Rise of the politicians

The duties of mayors and aldermen – representing that other vital force in Chicago government, the City Council – were solidified in 1872 when the city was granted increased governmental powers by the Illinois state legislature. This happened during the mayoral term of Joseph Medill, the famed editor-publisher of the influential *Chicago Tribune*. Gradually, the businessman-as-mayor model faded in favor of the professional politician. In 1907, for example, the mayor's post went to a German-American saloonkeeper named Fred Busse – the first Chicagoan with a non-British ancestry to hold the office.

More than a few larger-than-life characters have emerged to make Chicago history. Few were as brash and disputatious as William Hale Thompson, better known as "Big Bill." He was mayor from 1915 to 1923 and again from 1927 to 1931, turbulent years when the city was a virtual haven for gangsters and bootleggers – à la Al "Scarface" Capone.

Thompson achieved a measure of fame by asserting that he would be pleased to sock the King of England on the nose if His Highness ever so much as set foot in Chicago, a provocation that would not at all hurt the mayor's standing with the city's large Irish-American voting bloc. Thompson died in 1944, after which he was found to have stashed away the princely sum of \$1½ million in safety-deposit boxes. And why not? The mayor was said to have no compunction about accepting campaign funds from Capone, who reciprocated by keeping Thompson's framed photo displayed on his wall. "Big Bill" and "Scarface" seemed to get along just fine.

## Hooray for Lincoln

Chicago has had a longstanding affinity for politics. Democrats and Republicans have held two dozen national conventions here, with much wheeling and dealing going on in those proverbial smoke-filled backrooms. The first such convention took place in the momentous year of 1860, when the fledgling Republican Party met here to chose as its nominee for president of the United States a dark-horse candidate named Abraham Lincoln. Glory and martyrdom lay ahead for this Illinois "native son."

A handful of governors and US senators from Chicago have gained fame and sometimes notoriety against the backdrop of the

mayor's office. Adlai Stevenson was a former Chicago lawyer and Illinois governor who was twice nominated as presidential candidate by Democrats in the 1950s. Otto Kerner was a popular governor who as a judge would be brought down for accepting bribes – the prosecutor in Kerner's 1973 trial was James "Big Jim" Thompson, who himself went on to become a long-serving governor.

The city's most famous non-elected politician has been Jesse Jackson, the civil-rights activist who twice (1984 and 1988) sought the Democratic nomination for president, unsuccessfully. An ordained minister, Jackson joined Martin Luther King, Jr., in demonstrations protesting Chicago's heavily segregated white neighborhoods in the mid-1960s, and he was a prominent minority voice in denouncing Mayor Richard J. Daley's "shoot to kill" order in the wake of the rioting that was touched off by Dr. King's assassination in 1968. Jackson was the driving force behind voter-registration campaigns and boycotts that eventually brought to power Harold Washington, the city's first African-American mayor, in 1983.

> *"I too wish to defend my city from people who keep saying it is crooked," streetwise author Nelson Algren wryly commented. "In what other city can you be so sure a judge will keep his word for $500?"*

**FAR LEFT:** Abraham Lincoln. **LEFT:** William B. Ogden, the New York state legislator who became Chicago's first mayor. **ABOVE:** Jesse Jackson.
**ABOVE RIGHT:** a political cartoon from a 1900 edition of *Harper's Weekly* comments on corruption in Chicago.

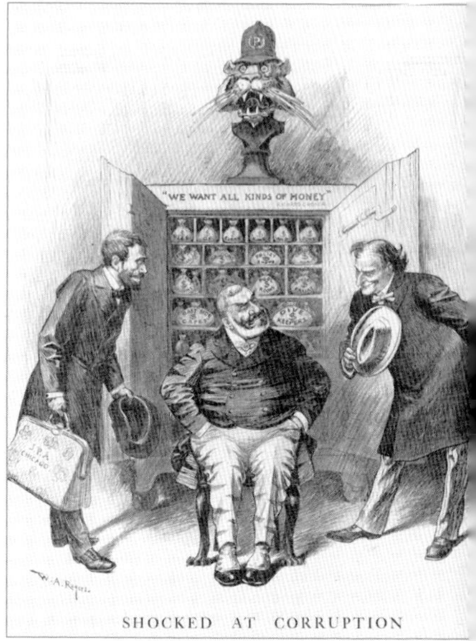


## Welcome to the machine

Chicago has some 1½ million registered voters, and they are overwhelmingly Democratic in party allegiance. The city has been a Democratic stronghold ever since Franklin D. Roosevelt and his New Deal style of government was swept into office in the wake of the Great Depression – the last Republican mayor was "Big Bill" Thompson. But as strong and well-oiled as the Democrats' legendary "machine" has been, plenty of divisions have tugged away at party unity over the years.

Anton Cermak, elected mayor in 1931, overcame Irish-American domination of the party by melding together a Democratic coalition largely composed of white ethnic immigrants and African-Americans – black voters traditionally had been loyal to the Lincoln legacy and the Republicans' Grand Old Party mystique.

Following the fatal shooting of Cermak in Miami Beach, Florida, in 1933 – the mayor was accompanying FDR at the time and took a bullet presumably intended for the president-elect – a new generation of largely Irish-American political operatives managed to recapture control of the Democratic apparatus in Chicago. They produced four mayors in

succession – Edward Kelly, Martin Kennelly, Richard J. Daley, and Michael A. Bilandic. The key figure was Daley, who would dominate Chicago's public affairs for years.

## The Daley era

Richard J. Daley's career in public service began in 1936 when he was elected to the Illinois state legislature as, anomalously, a Republican. He was first elected mayor of Chicago in 1955, the third in succession to emerge from the heavily Irish Catholic working-class neighborhood of Bridgeport on the city's South Side. He went on to win re-election on five successive occasions, his margins of victory growing wider as middle-class Republicans left the city in heavy numbers for suburban lifestyles.

*Chicago has 50 wards, each represented by an alderman. Neighborhoods within the wards have precinct captains who report to committeemen, who in turn report to their party chiefs.*

Known familiarly to Chicagoans as "Hizzoner," Daley exerted firm leadership of the city's fortunes at a time of social and economic change that was sapping the vitality of the Midwest's so-called "rust belt" cities. Imperious as he was, Daley was an enabling force in pushing through major construction projects during his term in office. These included O'Hare International Airport, the Sears Tower, various expressways, subway projects, Chicago landmarks, and more. His long reign ended on December 20, 1976, when he succumbed to a heart attack while visiting a doctor.

## Making history

As the 20th century progressed, Democratic hegemony over the city's public affairs was mitigated by racial division, which kept tearing away at the old ethnic-black accommodation. Daley may have been effective in treating the needs of selected groups within Chicago's polity, especially his own white-majority constituency, but he was criticized for neglecting the aspirations of other segments – most notably the African-American community. He was seen by critics as exploiting divisions in race and class for his own ends.

A decline in the fortunes of the old-line Democratic machine came in 1979 when Jane Byrne was elected as Chicago's first female mayor. Although welcomed by liberals and reform-minded activists for her promises to effect a change in attitudes and practices of municipal government, Byrne and her administration fell short in achievement.

History was made again four years later, in 1983, with the election of Harold Washington as Chicago's first black mayor. Washington's victory was assured when, in the Democratic primary, the vote among white citizens was split between Mayor Byrne and Mayor Daley's

son, Richard M. Daley. Washington's winning coalition was built on a strong black turnout and a sufficient showing among Hispanics and "lakefront liberals" to capture 52 percent of the vote. He did well again in a 1987 primary rematch with Byrne.

The strong hand which so many of Chicago's mayors have had in stirring the political pot is mitigated by the solidity of the city's unwieldy aldermanic structure. Mayors here have to deal with a City Council that is comprised of 50 aldermen, each of whom oversee fiefdoms containing phalanxes of ward-heelers, precinct captains and varied favor-seekers.

Mayor Washington's term was marked by incessant struggle between his office and the City Council. It was a Hobbesian struggle wherein both sides were at constant odds and, hence, little could get accomplished. His untimely and unsettling death in 1989 necessitated a special election that succeeded in launching a new Daley era in Chicago. The protagonist now was Daley the younger.

Richard M. Daley began his tenure by shunning the trappings of bossism that his father had worn so eagerly. Exhibiting a more pragmatic-minded approach, Daley has generally been awarded high marks for his dealings with various constituencies, and he quickly consolidated Hispanic and liberal support. Hispanics constitute the city's fastest-growing minority, some elections in recent years turning on a combination of their numbers and those of the so-called lakefront liberals. Daley was re-elected in 1991 and again on four successive occasions.

**FAR LEFT:** Barack Obama campaigns for the Democratic nomination for president in 2008. **LEFT:** Harold Washington. **ABOVE:** National Guardsmen at the 1968 Democratic Convention. **ABOVE RIGHT:** Richard M. Daley.

## Ups and downs

Chicago's changing political landscape in recent times, especially as it affects Democrats, is probably best exemplified by the fortunes of two major players: Dan Rostenkowski and Barack Obama. A product of the powerful Cook County machine, Rostenkowski was the son of a Chicago precinct leader who was elected to Congress in 1959 and long wielded power in tax and trade issues as chairman of the House Ways and Means Committee. His career went down in flames following his indictment for mail fraud in 1994.

Obama, the biracial offspring of a Kenyan father and a Kansan mother who had met in Hawaii, was an honors graduate of the Harvard Law School who had been a community organizer in Chicago from 1985 to 1988. He moved to his wife's hometown of Chicago and became a lecturer at the University of Chicago Law School before serving with distinction in the Illinois Senate and then winning election to the US Senate in 2004 by a huge margin.

The young legislator became a rising star on the national political scene by virtue of his early stand against the US military initiative in Iraq as well as a skillfully delivered keynote speech at the 2004 Democratic National Convention in Boston that brought him wide acclaim and thrust him into a leading position in the 2008 presidential sweepstakes. ❑

# DECISIVE DATES

**ABOVE:** Jacques Marquette.

## Formative Times

### 9000 BC

Lake Chicago, covering much of what is now the American Midwest, recedes with the glaciers, leaving swamps separating the prairies and Lake Michigan.

### AD 1600

Potawatomi Indians use swamps that link the Great Lakes and the Mississippi River as a place for trading; the land comes to be known as "Checagou" – for the stink of rotting wild onions.

## A City Takes Root

### 1673

A Jesuit and an explorer, guided by native inhabitants of the region, steer their canoe into the marshland that becomes Chicago. The priest is Jacques Marquette; the gold-seeking explorer is Louis Jolliet.

### 1779

Jean Baptiste Point DuSable establishes a trading post on the Chicago River.

### 1795

Troops led by General "Mad Anthony" Wayne overcome resistance by Native Americans and force them to give up tribal lands, including much of what is now downtown Chicago.

### 1803

Federal soldiers arrive from Detroit and erect Fort Dearborn. Nine years later it is the site of the tragic Fort Dearborn Massacre, a Native American uprising that costs the lives of 52 men, women, and children.

**BELOW:** bombs rip through Haymarket Square during the labor unrest of 1886.

## Growth and Prosperity

### 1825

Chicago's emergence as a Midwestern trading center is triggered by the opening of the Erie Canal.

**ABOVE:** Chicago Cubs, 1907.

### 1831

A bridge goes up over the Chicago River, linking the town's north and south sides.

### 1833

Population soars and so does property value. In just a year, the sale price for one downtown plot goes from $300 to $60,000.

### 1837

Having grown in just seven years from 50 residents to 4,170, Chicago is incorporated officially as a city. Elected as its first mayor is William B. Ogden.

### 1848

The city is launched as a world center for trading in commodities with formation

of the Chicago Board of Trade, ranking today as the world's oldest and largest futures exchange.

**1860**
Organizers of the upstart Republican Party convene in Chicago to put forth, as their choice for president, a new force on the national political scene – Abraham Lincoln.

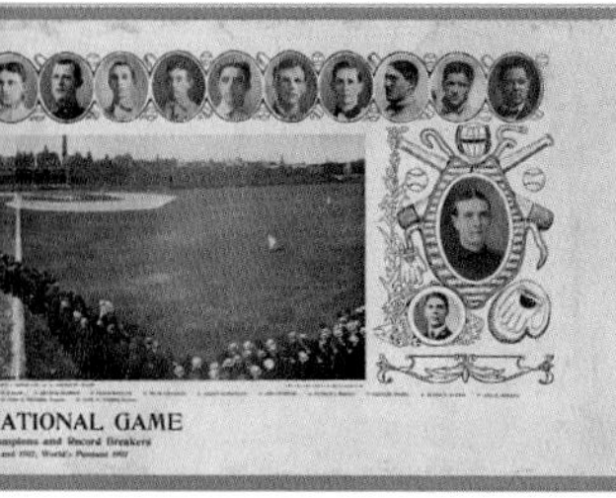


## Fire and Immigration

**1871**
America's most infamous conflagration, the Great Chicago Fire, destroys 18,000 buildings and renders 100,000 people homeless. The toll: 300 dead.

**1886**
Seven policemen are killed by bombs during the infamous Haymarket Riot brought on by worker discontent. A landmark event in American labor history, it reaches its climax with the hanging of four anarchists.

**1889**
A promising young architect named Frank Lloyd Wright designs a home-studio in the Chicago suburb of Oak Park that prefigures his reputation as master builder, while the reform-minded Jane Addams jump-starts the nation's welfare movement by founding Hull-House, prototype of the urban "settlement houses" that serve a floodtide of immigrants to America.

**1890**
Bolstered by a wave of newcomers from Europe, Chicago's population climbs past the million mark.

**1893**
Chicago is host as the World's Columbian Exposition celebrates the 400th anniversary of Columbus's landing in the New World – and America's debut as a global power.

## Dawn of a New Century

**1900**
Engineers complete a massive project that reverses the flow of the Chicago River and stops waste from polluting Lake Michigan.

**1906**
A shocking new book by Upton Sinclair – *The Jungle* – exposes the unsanitary conditions prevalent in Chicago's stockyards.

**1909**
Architect Daniel Burnham unveils the *Plan of Chicago*.

**ABOVE:** World War I bond drive.

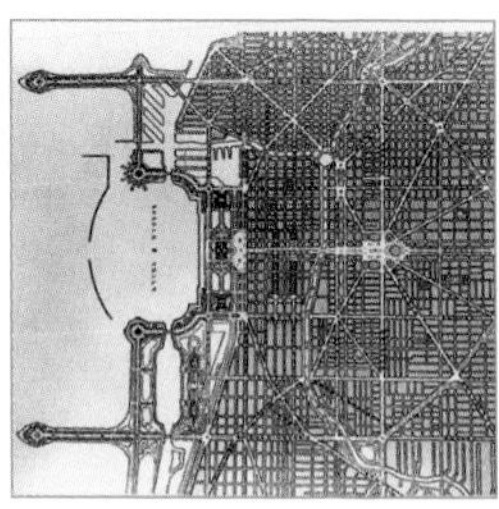

**RIGHT TOP:** Daniel Burnham's *Plan of Chicago*. **RIGHT:** Columbian Exposition.

**ABOVE:** the aftermath of the St Valentine's Day Massacre.

**1919**
Race riots triggered by the drowning at a public beach of an African-American boy exact a toll of 38 dead.

**ABOVE:** Al "Scarface" Capone.

**1919**
A bribery scandal involving eight members of the White Sox during the World Series causes them to be banned from professional baseball. Among them is "Shoeless Joe" Jackson.

**1920**
Opening of the Michigan Avenue Bridge.

## Crime and Punishment

**1929**
Gang warfare shifts into high gear as seven people are gunned down in the St Valentine's Day Massacre; the stock-market crash on Wall Street hurtles the city into economic Depression.

**1931**
Chicago's powerful crime boss Al "Scarface" Capone is indicted for evasion of the federal income tax. He spends years in prison before his death in 1947, at his Miami Beach estate, of syphilis.

**1934**
Tipped off by "The Lady in Red," federal agents gun down the notorious bank robber John Dillinger as he emerges from a movie theater.

**1942**
The first nuclear chain reaction is accomplished by a group of physicists at the University of Chicago.

**RIGHT:** Mayor Richard J. Daley.

**1951**
The writer Nelson Algren publishes, to much acclaim, his prose poem *Chicago: City on the Make*.

**1952**
Hugh Hefner, impish offspring of strict Methodist parents, borrows $1,600 to launch a racy publication he calls *Playboy*, with his native Chicago as home base.

**1955**
Richard J. Daley becomes Chicago's strong-arm mayor, proving himself such a vital force as to swing the presidential election in favor of fellow Democrat John F. Kennedy in 1960 via questionable "late" vote tallies.

## Rage and Reform

**1966**
Founding of the Chicago Freedom Movement by the Rev. Martin Luther King Jr.

**1968**
Rage against the Vietnam War pits hippies, yippies, and assorted radicals against Chicago police in violent street battles that are set against the backdrop of the Democratic National Convention.

**1969**
The world's attention is focused on antiwar demonstrations and the trial of the militant Chicago Seven.

**1972**
The Chicago Mercantile Exchange, begun in 1919 as a tiny butter-and-egg market, is the pioneer force in creation of the financial futures markets.

**1973**
Completion of the 110-story Sears Tower, the world's tallest (until 1996) office building.

**1976**
Saul Bellow, native Canadian and longtime Chicagoan, wins the Nobel Prize for literature.

**1979**
In the mayoral race, Chicagoans irate over ineffective government choose Jane Byrne over Michael Blandic, the successor to Mayor Daley.

**1987**
Chicago's first black mayor, Harold Washington, dies after four years in office.

**RIGHT:** marathon runners pass under the BP Bridge in Millennium Park.

## Another Daley

**1989**
Richard M. Daley, son of the first Mayor Daley, becomes mayor.

**1991**
Powered by superstar athlete Michael Jordan, the Chicago Bulls win the first of several championships and become a dominant force in the National Basketball Association.

**1992**
Chicago native Carol Moseley Braun becomes the first black woman elected to the US Senate. A construction mishap causes massive flooding in the Loop.

**1996**
Chicago again plays host to the Democratic National Convention.

**1998**
The Chicago Bulls win the NBA title for the third straight year.

**1999**
The city is paralyzed by record-breaking blizzards.

**ABOVE:** Mayor Richard M. Daley.

**2004**
Millennium Park opens to warm reviews despite construction and cost overruns. US Senator Barrack Obama – a former Illinois state senator from Chicago – delivers a rousing address at the Democratic National Convention, fueling speculation of a presidential bid.

**2007**
Obama enters the contest for the Democratic presidential nomination.

**2007**
The US Olympic Committee chooses Chicago as a candidate for the 2016 Olympic Games.

# LITERARY CHICAGO

## Champions of the underdog, the downtrodden, and the working class, Chicago writers thrive far from the centers of literary power

Poke a Chicago writer, editor, or publisher and you'll likely dislodge strong opinions as to the health of the local literary scene. Chicago is scorned as flyover country by the New York publishing establishment, they cry, and, worse, the city can't support it's own talent. To be taken seriously, they say, a writer needs to move to New York City – or stick it out here and be prepared to fight twice as hard for a piece of the literary pie.

To a degree, this is true. Chicago doesn't have the publishing infrastructure of New York City, and while many young writers cut their teeth here, they often move on to kinder, greener pastures. But, taken on its own merits, Chicago's literary culture is distinctly alive and well.

In fact, it's thriving, thanks in large part to the fact that it's *not* in New York. Far from the madding crowd, Chicago writers have the freedom to take risks, experiment, and offend without worrying that the editor of Knopf will be watching if they fail.

*The Chicago Tribune awards the Heartland Prize to the authors of an outstanding novel and work of nonfiction. The Literary Prize is awarded to an author for lifetime achievement.*

**PRECEDING PAGES:** Vic Theatre.
**LEFT:** Studs Terkel won a Pulitzer Prize in 1985 for *The Good War*, an oral history of World War II.
**RIGHT:** Richard Wright, author of *Native Son*.

### Working-class voices

Chicago's literary reputation has long been founded on the sort of gritty, working-class sentimentality and acerbic wit popularized by legendary columnist Mike Royko. His *Boss: Richard J. Daley of Chicago*, a withering account of the reign of King Richard the First, remains perhaps the best book ever written about 20th-century Chicago. Royko died in 1997, but he's only the most recent embodiment of a distinctive literary voice that has been evolving for more than a century. It's a voice that springs from neighborhood streets far from downtown corridors of power to champion the underdog and give a loud raspberry to the Man.

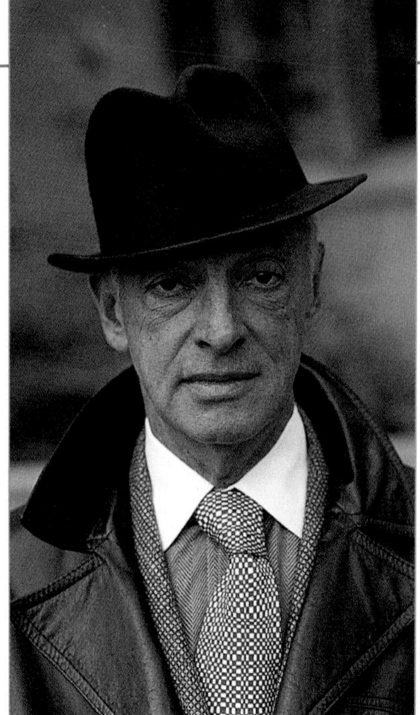

Before Royko there was Nelson Algren, best known for his novel *The Man With the Golden Arm*, a piece of street-smart, bloody-knuckles realism for which he won the first National Book Award for fiction in 1950. Before Algren there was that master of the short story, Ring Lardner, who developed his style as a Chicago sportswriter and is best remembered for his two collections of baseball stories, *You Know Me Al* and *Alibi Ike*.

And before Lardner there was the syndicated Chicago newspaper columnist Finley Peter Dunne, whose literary alter ego, Martin J. Dooley, an Irish immigrant saloonkeeper of droll wit, entertained readers across the nation. Dooley had a knack for slicing through pretense, much in the manner of Royko's own wiseacre alter ego, Slats Grobnik. It was Dooley who first said, "Trust iv'rybody, but cut the cards."

## Literary hub

From about 1890 to 1925, Chicago was a national hub of literary bustle. H.L. Mencken, writing in 1917, declared Chicago "the literary capital of the United States" and insisted that all the great American writers of his day had lived at least for a time in Chicago.

"Chicago has drawn them in from their remote wheat towns and far-flung railroad junctions, and it has given them an impulse that New York simply cannot match – an impulse toward independence, toward honesty, toward a peculiar vividness and naivete."

As examples of such independent voices, Menken held up Sherwood Anderson, Theodore Dreiser, Edgar Lee Masters, Carl Sandburg, and George Ade. He might have added Upton Sinclair, whose 1906 masterwork, *The Jungle*, was a muckraking tour de force that exposed the brutally oppressive, nauseating conditions of the Chicago stockyards and inspired sweeping, industry-wide reforms.

## Paper tigers

Chicago's reputation as a pull-no-punches writer's town is in part rooted in the newspaper circulation wars of a century ago. Then, many of the major papers attempted to cater to their expanded readership by adopting a more democratic editorial tone, courting writers who had an engaging, vernacular style. But Chicago newspapers did more for literature than allow plain speech to get down on paper. In an age before writers' conferences

and creative writing fellowships, the papers offered a sort of hardball literary apprenticeship. Dreiser, Sandburg, Eugene Field, Edna Ferber, and Ben Hecht were among those who put in time on Chicago newspapers, happy for the paycheck and camaraderie.

Sandburg covered the 1919 Chicago race riots for the *Daily News* and wrote a book about the tragedy. He later won Pulitzer Prizes – two for poetry and one for his biography of Abraham Lincoln – and wrote the poem that would become a Chicago cliché: "Hog Butcher for the World, Tool Maker, Stacker of Wheat, Player with Railroads and the Nation's Freight Handler, Stormy, Husky, Brawling, City of the Big Shoulders." The stockyards are gone and the big shoulders now wear Brooks Brothers, but the image sticks.

Hecht worked at the *Daily News* alongside

*A highlight of any literary tour of the Chicago area.is the Ernest Hemingway Birthplace and Museum in suburban Oak Park, though "Papa" left town after high school and rarely returned.*

Sandburg and immortalized this high-spirited era of Chicago journalism in his smash play *The Front Page*, which later became a movie that has been remade several times since. His *1,001 Afternoons in Chicago*, a collection of slice-of-life columns from the same era, remains a benchmark of literary journalism.

**FAR LEFT:** Sinclair Lewis. **LEFT:** 1976 Nobel laureate Saul Bellow **ABOVE:** Ring Lardner (second from right) with US president Warren Harding (far left) outside the White House. **ABOVE RIGHT:** Carl Sandburg was an accomplished folk musician in addition to being a writer.

## The power of poetry

Outside the newsrooms, Chicago's literary scene during the 1910s and 1920s was anchored by the poet and editor Harriet Monroe. The magazine she founded, *Poetry*, was the official organ of the American Modernist movement and the first to publish T.S. Eliot, Marianne Moore, William Carlos Williams, and Ezra Pound. (In a turn of fate worthy of great literature, after years of shoestring existence a staggering 2002 bequest from Lilly Pharmaceuticals heiress Ruth Lilly turned *Poetry*, overnight, into one of the wealthiest and most influential literary organizations in the world.)

Later, another woman came to dominate Chicago poetry – Gwendolyn Brooks, whose second collection, *Annie Allen*, a series of poems about a young girl growing up in Bronzeville, won her the Pulitzer Prize for poetry in 1950, the first bestowed on an African-American writer. Brooks was later named poet laureate of Illinois.

## Midcentury stars

In midcentury, while the nation struggled through the Great Depression and a second world war, Chicago produced several more nationally important novelists, including

Algren, Richard Wright, and James T. Farrell, all of a proletarian bent.

Wright, who moved up to Chicago from Mississippi in the 1920s, worked as a postal clerk by day and wrote by night. His best works, including the novel *Native Son*, were strongly influenced by Dreiser's naturalistic fiction. Farrell, a second-generation South Side Irishman, wrote more than 50 books. His brutally realistic Studs Lonigan trilogy, about an aimless youth growing up in Chicago from the early 1900s to the Depression, remains a classic of Chicago realism.

Chicago's other enduring Studs, Pulitzer Prize-winning oral historian and broadcaster Studs Terkel, took his nickname from Farrell's hero. He shot to national acclaim in 1974, with the publication of *Working*, a collection of interviews exploring American attitudes toward their jobs. More than 40 years later, Terkel – in his signature red socks and gingham shirt – is still one of the city's most beloved and idiosyncratic figures. He signed off his famed WFMT radio show in 1997, but 10 years later, at the age of 95, published his 17th book, the memoir *Touch and Go*.

## A Nobel laureate

Chicago's undisputed literary superstar, Saul Bellow, who won the Nobel Prize in 1976, found inspiration in the city's working-class

### CHICAGO NOIR

From Richard Wright's *Native Son* to Ernest Hemingway's short story "The Killers" about a pair of two-bit thugs who plot to kill a washed-up boxer, many of Chicago's most celebrated literary works speak to the seedier side of urban life. And real life Chicago is certainly not lacking in crime fiction's building blocks of greed, lust, and corruption. So it's no surprise that some of the best-known Chicago writers built their careers on the darker side of the genre.

Attorney Scott Turow is a best-selling master of intricate legal thrillers. Sara Paretsky's V.I. Warshawski series puts a uniquely feminist spin on the private eye. More recently, newcomers like Kevin Guilfoile, author of the dystopian cyberthriller *Cast of Shadows*, has joined forces with Paretsky and others as members of the Outfit, a collective of Chicago crime writers that takes its name from the city's notorious crime syndicate.

What binds these disparate writers together may actually be their shared lack of glitz and glamour. In lieu of the sexy LA cool of Dashiell Hammett is, more often than not, a bleak, beaten-down pragmatism borne of mean Midwestern streets and long, cold winters.

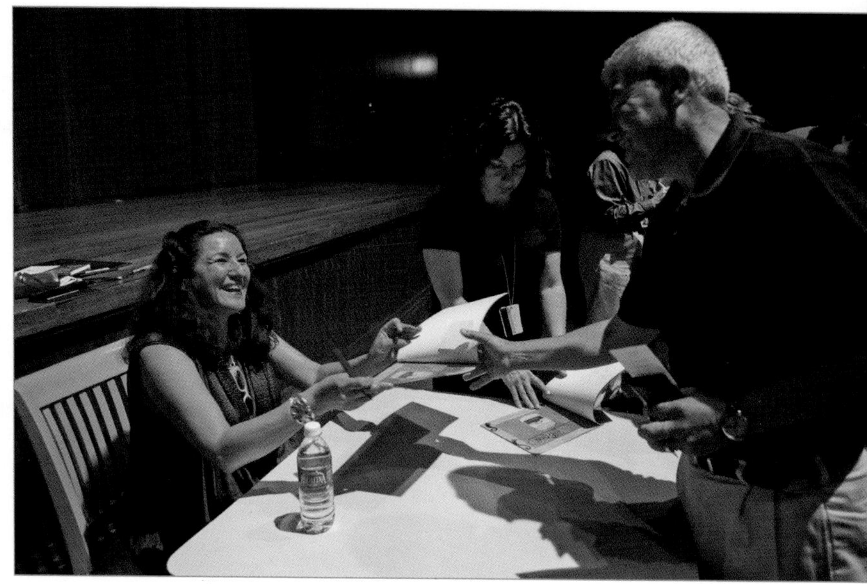

streets as well. His larger-than-life characters, dreamers and thinkers, struggle for meaning against a quintessentially Midwestern backdrop of brash urban hustle and bustle. Read the opening lines of his 1953 breakthrough *The Adventures of Augie March*, "I am an American, Chicago born – Chicago, that somber city – and go at things as I have taught myself, freestyle, and will make the record in my own way: first to knock, first admitted; sometimes an innocent knock, sometimes a not so innocent."

## Chicago today

Nowadays many acclaimed writers call Chicago home and muse, among them National Book Award recipient Larry Heinemann, Harry Mark Petrakis, mystery novelists Sara Paretsky and Scott Turow, Jeffrey Eugenides, and Stuart Dybek – a 2007 winner of a MacArthur "genius" grant whose lyrical short stories draw on his childhood in Pilsen and Little Village. Bosnian writer and adopted Chicagoan Aleksandar Hemon writes wryly of the contemporary immigrant experience in *Nowhere Man*; printmaker-turned-novelist Audrey Niffenegger wove her years in the city's art and music scenes into a best-selling love story, *The Time Traveler's Wife*.

Others have, as ever, moved away, but their memories of Chicago provide an abundance of material: Sandra Cisneros based *The House on Mango Street* on her own formative years in the Pilsen barrio; Adam Langer's *Crossing California* gives a humorous spin to his own childhood in the Jewish enclave of Rogers Park in the 1970s.

But across town young writers continue to emerge to remake literary Chicago in their own image, starting magazines, self-publishing their work, and staging irreverent literary events in the back rooms of bars. Some succeed, some fail, and some become the new heroes of the local scene – like Columbia College Chicago teacher Joe Meno, an indie success story whose edgy, irreverent work puts a punk spin on Chicago's distinctive, streetwise aesthetic, bringing it sharply into the 21st century. ❑

**FAR LEFT:** bookstore browsing. **LEFT TOP:** the Harold Washington Library is the site of numerous literary events. **LEFT BOTTOM:** vintage books for sale in the Printers' Row district. **ABOVE:** author Sandra Cisneros chats with readers at a book signing.

# CHICAGO IN THE MOVIES

**The Windy City's association with the movie business dates to the silent era, and both the city and its actors have been lighting up the silver screen ever since**

From the earliest days of film, when silent stars such as Gloria Swanson and Charlie Chaplin appeared in shorts by Essanay Studios on the North Side, Chicago has been both the subject and setting of memorable movies. In many cases, the films are driven by Chicago-area writers and directors such as David Mamet, whose short play *Sexual Perversity in Chicago* was turned into the 1986 romantic comedy *About Last Night* with a young Demi Moore and Rob Lowe, and John Hughes, maker of comedy hits like *Ferris Bueller's Day Off* and *Home Alone* set mostly in the affluent suburbs of the North Shore. The madcap 1980 comedy *The Blues Brothers* climaxed with stars John Belushi and Dan Aykroyd crashing their car, the Bluesmobile, into Daley Plaza.

Other notable movies filmed in and around Chicago include *Looking for Mister Goodbar* (1977), Oscar-winner *Ordinary People* (1980), the Tom Cruise-Paul Newman vehicle *The Color of Money* (1986), the bittersweet Julia Roberts' comedy *My Best Friend's Wedding* (1997), and the 2002 musical blockbuster *Chicago*.

**ABOVE:** Charlie Chaplin.
**LEFT:** George Clooney's breakout role in the television drama *ER*, set in a Chicago hospital, launched his career as a Hollywood heartthrob.

**ABOVE AND RIGHT:** Chicago's gangland history has inspired numerous films, including *Little Caesar* (1931), in which Edward G. Robinson plays a street punk who claws his way to the top of the mob before coming to a bloody end, and *Road to Perdition* (2002), an atmospheric drama featuring Tom Hanks as a morally conflicted hitman.

## CHICAGOANS IN HOLLYWOOD

Chicago theater has proven to be a fertile training ground for the Hollywood star machine. Known for topical, hard-hitting drama, Steppenwolf Theatre numbers big-screen names such as John Malkovich, John Mahoney, Gary Sinise, and Joan Allen among its ensemble of actors. John Cusack and sister Joan Cusack started acting at a theater in suburban Evanston. He later starred in numerous movies set in and around Chicago, including the adaptation of the Nick Hornby novel *High Fidelity*, relocated to the Wicker Park neighborhood for the film. No company has been more successful as a stepping stone to Hollywood than Second City, the improv comedy troupe that launched the careers of television and movie stars Alan Arkin, Bill Murray, Mike Myers, and Stephen Colbert.

**ABOVE AND RIGHT:** winner of six Academy Awards, including best picture, *Chicago* (2002) starred Catherine Zeta-Jones and Renée Zellweger as singing-dancing Jazz Age killers and Richard Gere as their sleazy lawyer. The story is based loosely on real-life Chicago murders.

**ABOVE:** Jack Lemon and Walter Matthau starred in *The Front Page* (1974), one of many movies based on Ben Hecht and Charles MacArthur's comedy about Chicago newspapermen in the 1920s.

**BELOW:** Second City alumni John Belushi and Dan Aykroyd as Jake and Elwood Blues in the 1980 comedy *The Blues Brothers*, which, in addition to some classic comic bits, features musical performances by James Brown, Aretha Franklin, and Ray Charles.

# CHICAGO BLUES

**Singers and shouters and soulful stylists have added a distinctive zest to the city's mélange of cultural and artistic outpourings**

Chicago and the blues. At first glimpse, the pairing may seem incongruous – subtle African-derived musical art form meets mid-American metropolis. But then, of course, that's how so many urban centers are wont to take shape, deracinated people and traditions thrown together in helter-skelter style.

A whole other dimension was appended to Chicago's social landscape by the mighty wave of black migration from the Mississippi Delta and elsewhere that began flowing at the end of the 19th century. Restless and with little to lose, countless souls gravitated north in quest of jobs and a new shot at life. Inevitably, blues troubadours heeded the same liberating call and implanted their cultural seeds on the mean streets and alleys of the Windy City, adding zest to the city's other flavors.

Gravitating here too were the practitioners of the irresistible new musical concoction known as jazz, conceived in New Orleans out of a mélange of cross-cultural influences, and with the blues as dominant component. They would make musical history here – Joe Oliver, Louis Armstrong, and all the others. Over the years to come, scads of standout blues performers would do their thing here as well – Muddy Waters, Buddy Guy, John Lee Hooker, Willie Dixon, Etta James, and so many more – implanting their art on Chicago's cultural psyche.

*"The Blues are the true facts of life expressed in words and song, inspiration, feeling, and understanding" – bassist, songwriter, and Chess Records producer Willie Dixon*

**LEFT AND RIGHT:** the Chicago Blues Festival, reputedly the world's largest free concert, features performances by blues greats and up-and-coming talent.

## Blue notes

The Chicago blues hold a secure niche in both the annals of American music and today's popular entertainment, as much a part of the town as Dixieland jazz is to New Orleans. It is a loud, showy, rocking style of music that takes traditional blues themes, chords, and bent notes, and juices them up with amplification. Musicologists

could go on and on about the characteristic 12-bar, three-chord schematics and "the dominant seventh," with split quarter tones.

To scholars, blues music refers to the so-called "blue" notes that exist between tones, created, for example, by bending guitar strings. To non-experts, however, the overriding feature of the Chicago blues is that the music is guitar-driven.

It would be difficult to overstate the influence of the Chicago blues on today's popular music, particularly mainstream rock 'n' roll. Anyone who listens to a set of live blues anywhere in Chicago is sure to recognize it as the root of rock. "Musicians treat the blues like gospel; it's a kind of honesty meter, a measure of belief," according to the Paris-based music critic Mike Zwerin. "'He can't even play the blues', is to say he's hopeless. Chicago remains the point of reference – a mecca."

## Hymns and spirituals

The blues grew out of the "field hollers" of slave times, when workers in the cotton fields communicated with each other in long slow chants and songs. Many owners refused to let their slaves talk to each other but didn't mind them singing while they worked. For many, the holler messages passed from field to field, from plantation to plantation, were the only way of keeping in touch with their African traditions, and sometimes the only way of tracking down family members.

As African rhythms melded with European styles of harmony, the field hollers led to classic African-American spirituals and hymns that looked toward happiness some day but not in this lifetime. The early blues, often referred to as the "down-home" or "country" blues, were rooted in the Mississippi Delta, and featured songs that were typically more personal than spiritual. They were songs about loving and leaving, about loyalty and betrayal, about desire and temptation. They were sung for friends at home, for cellmates in prison, or for tips on the street.

Accompanied at first by finger-snapping, stomping, "hambone" thigh-slapping, and other simple forms of percussion, country blues ultimately became associated with the

### MOJO MAN

How blue can you get? There was none greater in that department than McKinley Morganfield, who became a musical legend not long after his arrival in Chicago by train one May morning in 1943, suitcase in one hand and guitar in the other. This 28-year-old erstwhile farmhand had been known since childhood as "Muddy Waters" back in rural Mississippi, and it was by that name that he would become legendary – "the father of Chicago blues."

In 1948 one of his first recordings, "I Can't Be Satisfied," released by the Chess brothers at Aristocrat Records, struck a chord with his transplanted black peers on the teeming South Side, and there would be much more to come. The titles are famous: "Rollin' Stone." "Hoochie Coochie Man." "Got My Mojo Workin'."

The end of a distinguished career came in 1983 when Muddy Waters, at the age of 70, succumbed to cancer at his home in the suburb of Westmont. He was one of the most influential music makers of the 20th century.

acoustic guitar, particularly the homemade "bottleneck" style. Some black freemen became wandering minstrels, taking the field hollers and early blues on the road to perform for slaves and masters alike.

## Moving north

In the post-slavery era, the expanding mills and factories of the North attracted many poor African-Americans up the Mississippi River to Chicago. The migration was a steady stream for much of the first half of the 20th century, but after World War II it became a positive flood as young African-Americans sought higher-paying jobs in the North. The Southern musicians, naturally, followed their audience.

One of the men who acted as a bridge between the Delta and the city, from down-home to urban blues, was Big Bill Broonzy, who came to Chicago from Mississippi in 1924. He was also one of the first Americans to take the blues to Europe, where the music was warmly received. To this day, Chicago performers often bracket dates in small clubs in their hometown with tours of big halls in Europe, and a handful of Chicago blues expatriates have resettled overseas to take advantage of enthusiastic audiences. The famous guitarist Luther Allison was based in Paris before he died. In Chicago, visiting Europeans often seek out blues bars and clubs, and the annual Chicago Blues Festival has become a pilgrimage for many foreign fans.

**FAR LEFT:** Muddy Waters. **LEFT:** a "harp" player at the Chicago Blues Festival. **ABOVE:** John Lee Hooker was known for stripped-down tunes of one or two chords; "I don't play a lot of fancy guitar," he said. **ABOVE RIGHT:** singer and harmonica player Junior Wells.

## Sex and sorrow

Though still popular after World War II, the rural, relatively simple country blues – typically one man with a guitar, singing about lost love and other personal woes – eventually gave way to a faster, more raucous, and often more joyful music. When the electric guitar came into wide use in the 1950s, it was embraced wholeheartedly by Chicago musicians, who soon "fattened" the sound with electric bass, drums, amplified harmonica (or "harp"), and saxophone. The Delta bluesmen who defined the new style in the 1950s included J.B. Lenoir, Jimmy Reed, Little Walter, Howlin' Wolf, Sonny Boy Williamson, John Lee Hooker, and Muddy Waters, who became the one performer most closely identified with the "heavy sound and rough intensity" (to quote blues author Charles Keil) of the Chicago style.

Waters's songs, such as "Hoochie Coochie Man," "Got My Mojo Workin'," "I'm Ready," and "Tiger in Your Tank," epitomize the rollicking sexual bravado that often replaced the theme of sorrow and helplessness so common in country blues.

## The Chess brothers

One of the cornerstones of the Chicago blues in the 1950s and 1960s was Chess Records, the recording company operated by Leonard Chess, his brother Phil, and Leonard's son Marshall. Many of the leading talents in blues cut records with the Chess family. Muddy Waters was with them for years with no contract beyond a handshake. Willie Dixon, who was an accomplished upright bass player as well as a songwriter, was a Chess stalwart who often used his basement to audition new talent for the Chess family.

Today, more than 35 years after guiding light Leonard Chess died and the studio was closed, there's still some question in music circles as to the role of the Chess family. Were they whites who exploited black talent? Would the Chicago blues have become as popular if they hadn't given so many new artists a chance to record?

## English invasion

One thing not in doubt is that many of the architects of modern rock 'n' roll made formative pilgrimages to the tiny Chess studio on South Michigan Avenue. Prominent rock singers and guitarists, particularly the leaders of the 1960s "English invasion" like the Rolling Stones, paid personal homage to Chess's blues artists. For a time, Marshall Chess managed the Rolling Stones, who took their name from a Muddy Waters song. They and other rock stars not only re-recorded a good many Chicago blues tunes but often "borrowed" well-worn guitar riffs, lyrics, and melodies.

When Howlin' Wolf recorded Willie Dixon's "Little Red Rooster," for example, it sold 20,000 copies, a big hit for a local blues record. When the Rolling Stones re-recorded the song in a nearly identical manner, it sold more than 500,000 copies. Tom Marker, a longtime Chicago blues disc jockey, recalled that the English rockers, especially the Stones, were "just crazy" about the blues. "Those guys were big fans of the Chicago sound when they were getting their blues thing together themselves," he said. "They were just trying to copy the stuff. Sometimes they would copy the song lick for lick." Black bluesmen made the music; white rockers made it famous.

## Living on a shoestring

Many blues performers literally sang for their supper and not much more. Even name performers often lived on a shoestring – and still do. "Musicians all over Chicago are working hard, but they're working for almost nothing,"

singer Koko Taylor told the *Chicago Tribune*.

"You sing the blues, die and they have a benefit to bury you. That's the pattern," added Valerie Wellington, who, until she herself died in 1993, at the premature age of 33, was one of the city's brightest young blues singers. Wellington and a number of other performers had formed the Chicago Blues Artists Coalition, a sort of blues-rights organization that aimed to assist performers in their business and financial affairs. Blues Heaven – the de facto blues museum that Willie Dixon's family opened in the old Chess Records building – was started with the goal of also helping blues artists handle their affairs.

## New guard

Sadly, many of Chicago's finest blues musicians and singers have passed on in recent years, including Johnny Littlejohn, Luther Allison, Johnny Copeland, Fenton Robinson, Jimmy Walker, Muddy Waters, and Junior Wells. The good news is that their work has been preserved on CDs. It is also encouraging that a number of younger blues artists have emerged to keep the tradition alive.

The new guard includes such youthful spirits as Deitra Farr, Fruteland Jackson, and Wayne Baker Brooks. In the meanwhile, legends like Buddy Guy – named by no less than Eric Clapton as the world's greatest blues guitarist – continue to uphold and expand the tradition of Chicago blues as both performers and promoters of the music. His nightclub, Buddy Guy's Legends, features blues acts seven nights a week, from superstars like Clapton and the Rolling Stones to local up-and-comers.

For blues fans seeking out the music, an added benefit is meeting the musicians, even the headliners, who typically mingle with the crowd before and after shows. They are often happy to have a chat and maybe a drink. More than any other music, the Chicago blues remain of and for everyday people, with all the highs and lows and worries of everyday life. As Guy put it at his 2005 induction into the Rock and Roll Hall of Fame, "If you don't think you have the blues, just keep living." ❑

**FAR LEFT:** Janiva Magness belts out a song during a tribute to legendary blues vocalist Koko Taylor. **LEFT:** Nellie Tiger Travis performs at the House of Blues. **ABOVE:** guitarist and singer Deborah Coleman carries on the tradition of Chicago bluesmen like Buddy Guy.

PIXIES

# ART AND CULTURE

**No slouch in the diversity department, Chicago is a vibrant place with a peculiar Midwestern bent when it comes to culture**

Chicago may be smack dab in the middle of the American heartland, but don't let that fool you. It ranks right up there with the coastal urban meccas – Los Angeles, San Francisco, Boston, New York – when it comes to cultural richness. For one thing, the Windy City is blessed with the kind of social diversity often associated with artistic distinction, thanks to its own peculiar set of demographics.

There are African-Americans, with origins in the blues-tinged rural South, who brought with them their distinctive aesthetic genius. There's the polyglot mix-and-match of immigrant "ethnics" drawn here originally by the stockyards and meatpacking plants. And, too, there are the aspiring artists attracted to the city's various schools, theaters, and institutions.

The art spectrum in Chicago is as broad as the palate of its people and neighborhoods – the South Side with its hip-hop scene, the North Side's fringe theater, Pilsen and its artist lofts, the Loop's stately Lyric Opera House. The city has been an incubator of early jazz, urban blues, indie rock, improv comedy, and more.

*The Chicago Arts District is host to Second Fridays, monthly openings at galleries and studios around South Halsted and 18th streets in Pilsen East.*

**LEFT:** artists Liz Tuckwell and Joseph Sikora in their Wicker Park studio.
**RIGHT:** street theater in Millennium Park.

## Art in action

The arts and their promoters have from time to time received a good share of help from civic boosters, as for example in 1967 when Mayor Richard J. Daley unveiled a work of sculpture by the renowned modernist Pablo Picasso. Known simply as "the Picasso," the enigmatic sculpture is 162 tons of steel that stands 50 ft (15 meters) in height. Whatever its meaning, youngsters love its playful potential.

Not to be outdone by his father, Mayor Richard M. Daley in 2004 opened Millennium Park. It is filled with (critics like to say crammed with) prominent works of public art, including the high-tech Crown Fountain by

Spanish artist Jaume Plensa and the now-iconic sculpture *Cloud Gate* by Anish Kapoor, a work known affectionately as "The Bean."

Attracting both tourists and locals, Millennium Park emits a sense of the character of Chicago in action. Here you'll find people from every neighborhood, every economic and racial group, leaving their fingerprints on The Bean, watching their kids frolic in the fountain, and enjoying a free concert at the Jay Pritzker Pavilion designed by noted architect Frank Gehry.

## A city of treasures

Chicago has no lack of world-class art. In the city's vibrant center, visitors will find the most prominent of the Loop's cultural institutions: the Art Institute of Chicago. With a central location on Michigan Avenue and a pair of stone lions at the entrance, the Art Institute is impossible to miss. It is both a museum and an art school whose graduate program is rated as one of America's most outstanding.

Among the famous works here are Grant Wood's *American Gothic*, painted in 1930, and Georges Seurat's 1886 pointillist masterpiece *Sunday on La Grande Jatte* and the effusions of such Impressionist luminaries as Manet and Monet, Renoir and Degas, Van Gogh and Caillebotte, many to be housed in a new Modern Wing scheduled to open in 2009.

On the city's Magnificent Mile, you'll find Chicago's other major art museum, the Museum of Contemporary Art. The institution's current building is situated between the landmark Water Tower and Lake Michigan, and the modern design takes full advantage of the light and space that the location affords. The touring exhibits are uniformly impressive, bringing retrospectives of major modern artists to the city.

### Comedy Guru

Charismatic, brilliant, and often infuriating, improv guru Del Close, who inspired comedy greats from John Belushi to Tina Fey, was as notorious for his prodigious appetites as his talent. When, after years of hard living, he succumbed in 1999 to emphysema, he directed partner Charna Halperin to donate his skull to the Goodman Theatre, to be used as a prop in a production of Hamlet – and for years Halperin maintained that she had followed through. The hoax wasn't disclosed until 2006, when she confessed in the *New Yorker* that she'd substituted a skull from a medical supply house. Even in death Close knew how to raise a ruckus.

Smaller art spaces in the Loop can't be ignored. The Chicago Cultural Center houses gallery spaces. Now a venue for lectures, concerts, films, and dance, it was once the city's main public library. The Neoclassical structure, built in 1897, has the world's largest Tiffany stained-glass dome. Also inside the Loop, Columbia College houses the Center for Book and Paper Arts and the Museum of Contemporary Photography.

In the South Side neighborhood of Hyde Park, the University of Chicago has the small but dynamic David and Alfred Smart Museum of Art and the Oriental Institute, which houses an impressive collection of art from the ancient Near East. Also outside the Loop is the National Museum of Mexican Art in Pilsen.

## The gallery scene

The gallery scene is centered in the River North district. This neighborhood has been a nexus for small and cutting-edge galleries since 1976, when the Zolla/Leiberman Gallery moved west, away from Michigan Avenue, to take advantage of the cheap rents and plentiful warehouse spaces left behind after a century of light manufacturing.

A similar transformation is taking hold in the West Loop, which now claims more than half the city's galleries. There are established art dealers like Catherine Edelman and Jean Albano, but don't miss the collection of "outsider art" at Carl Hammer Gallery, the architectural collections of ArchiTech, or the avant-garde work at I Space, which is run by the University of Illinois at Urbana-Champaign.

**LEFT:** a classical concert at the Jay Pritzker Pavilion in Millennium Park; the pavilion was designed by architect Frank Gehry. **ABOVE:** local and touring bands are featured at the Vic Theatre in Lakeview. **ABOVE RIGHT:** *Cindy* by Chuck Close at the Museum of Contemporary Art.

## Stage craft

Mayor Richard M. Daley has made an effort to revitalize the city's downtown theater venues. The "Broadway in Chicago" program brings touring shows to these grand old halls, including the Cadillac Palace and the majestic Auditorium Theatre, an architectural masterpiece celebrated for its famously perfect acoustics.

The Goodman and Steppenwolf theatres often turn the tables by sending performances to Broadway. Steppenwolf, in Lincoln Park, has been creating provocative work since its incorporation in 1975. The theater's strength is its ensemble cast, which numbers screen stars such as John Malkovich, Gary Sinise, John Mahoney, and Joan Allen among its members.

Midlevel theaters add to the talent pool. Victory Gardens nurtures new writers; Congo Square Theatre focuses on African-American issues and claimed August Wilson as a friend, donor, and board member. A signature Chicago theater style – think dance crossed with circus and film – is developed at Look-

ingglass Theatre Company, housed in Chicago's historic Water Tower Water Works. The House Theater, Redmoon Theater, and 500 Clown company practice their own takes on this highly physical style in off-Loop venues.

Chicago's improv comedy scene is legendary and has spawned some of the best comic performers of the last few decades. Second City, still the best place to see live improv, launched its Old Town location in 1959. A short list of its alumni includes Joan Rivers, John Belushi, Gilda Radner, John Candy, and Stephen Colbert.

## Listen to the music

Musically, Chicago is best known for the electric blues and legendary bluesmen like Muddy Waters, Howlin' Wolf, and Buddy Guy. The Chicago Blues Festival attracts more than 750,000 fans to Grant Park every year, and small labels like Alligator Records continue to discover new talent and record such old masters as Koko Taylor and Lonnie Brooks. To experience the blues firsthand, try Buddy Guy's Legends or Rosa's Lounge.

*The Jazz Institute of Chicago sponsors free concerts in city parks, school programs, and the annual Jazz Fair and Chicago Jazz Festival.*

For a night of live jazz, check out the tried-and-true Velvet Lounge on the South Side. Another storied venue, the Green Mill, on the North Side, was partly owned by one of Al Capone's henchmen. The current owner has restored the club to its former speakeasy-era glory.

The words "rock" and "Chicago" might bring to mind the band Chicago, which had a string of hits in the 1970s. But the city has witnessed more than its share of pivotal rock moments, such as Chuck Berry and Bo Diddley recording at Chess Records and the MC5 playing for protestors during the tumultuous 1968 Democratic Convention.

## Rock renaissance

There was a resurgence of rock energy in the 1990s when artists like The Smashing Pumpkins, Veruca Salt, Urge Overkill, and Liz Phair emerged from the city's underground. Nowadays, Chicago boasts critically adored Wilco and a robust network of small record labels devoted to the indie rock scene. Venues such as the Empty Bottle, the Hideout, and Schuba's are showcases for new talent.

Chicago hip-hop has come a long way from the house parties and illegal loft shows that characterized the scene in the 1980s and 1990s. Chicagoans like R. Kelley, Common, Kanye West, and Lupe Fiasco have been taking the Chicago sound international.

Chicago classical music is anchored by traditionalists like the Chicago Symphony Orchestra and Lyric Opera, both with outstanding international reputations. The Symphony has summer digs at the Jay Pritzker Pavilion in Millennium Park and suburban Ravinia Park. The Ravinia Festival has been

held in the park since 1911 and is an easy Metra commute from downtown Chicago. Bring a blanket and a picnic, but don't let the elaborate wine and cheese spreads distract you from the music.

## Dance, film, and radio

Dance companies flourish. Chicago is home base for the Joffrey Ballet, which moved here in 1995 after four decades in New York City. Other companies include innovators Hubbard Street Dance and Thodos Dance Chicago, Latin-influenced Luna Negra Dance Theater, and Balanchine-style teaching company Ballet Chicago.

For Chicagoans, it is no surprise that the nationally syndicated film review program *Ebert and Roper at the Movies* is produced in their city. Events such as the Chicago International Film Festival and Chicago Underground Film Festival showcase screen talent from around the world.

For the serious cinephile, the Gene Siskel Film Center and Facets Multimedia offer showings of international films, past and present. And don't miss the art house Music Box, one of only a few vintage movie palaces still in operation. Visit on a weekend and you'll catch live performances on the theater's original organ.

Radio has also played an influential role in the city's artistic life. Among the many radio programs with a national audience is WBEZ's *This American Life*, hosted by Peabody Award-winner Ira Glass, and often featuring writers such as David Sedaris and Sarah Vowell. Chicago radio was long the home of the city's bard of art and civics, the venerable author and broadcaster Studs Terkel. He still takes pains to point out that art and work are forever linked in this city by the lake, and that's just the way it should be. ❑

**FAR LEFT:** Museum of Contemporary Art. **LEFT:** Ukrainian Institute of Modern Art. **ABOVE TOP:** Green Mill jazz and blues club. **ABOVE BOTTOM:** art student at work at the Art Institute of Chicago. **ABOVE:** Schuba's Tavern brings up-and-coming rock acts to the North Side.

# CHICAGO EATS

**Hog butcher to the world no more, Chicago is now home to a diverse culinary scene exploding with creativity and civic pride**

Food writers have spilled buckets of ink over the last few years heralding Chicago's emergence as a player on the world's culinary scene. "Meat and potatoes no more!" they cry. Now it's all about foamed squash and sous-vide organic bison, with a dusting of freeze-dried pomegranate jus. But while cutting-edge restaurants like Alinea (1723 North Halsted Street; tel: 312-867-0110), Moto (945 West Fulton Market; tel: 312-491-0058), and Avenues (108 East Superior Street; tel: 312-573-6754) deserve the headlines they've garnered for their restless, relentless culinary and technological innovations, the revolution didn't happen overnight.

## Breaking out

In the late 1980s, when fine dining in Chicago meant white tablecloths and veal en croûte, a cocky kid from Wilmette opened his namesake restaurant in a Lincoln Park town house. Charlie Trotter's (816 West Armitage Avenue; tel: 773-248-6228) took fine dining out of the 19th century. Trotter revolutionized local cuisine by eschewing the use of heavy cream and slabs of meat in favor of light, vegetable-based sauces and meticulously constructed multi-course tasting menus. A polarizing figure, he was once dubbed the second-meanest person in town (after Michael Jordan) by *Chicago* magazine, and he's currently public enemy number one in some quarters for throwing his weight behind the city's foie gras ban. But his notoriously exacting standards for both raw materials and performance undeniably raised the bar for restaurateurs across town and beyond. Grant Achatz, Homaro Cantu, and Graham Eliot Bowles – the envelope-pushing

*In 2006 the city council voted to ban the sale of foie gras – making Chicago the first city in the country to outlaw the luxury liver. Some indignant chefs flout the law by offering "free" foie as garnish on suspiciously expensive salad.*

**LEFT:** a chef at work in Charlie Trotter's restaurant, regarded as one of the finest in Chicago.
**RIGHT:** Opera is luring diners to the South Side.

chefs at the aforementioned Alinea, Moto, and Avenues – and breakout stars like Hot Chocolate's Mindy Segal (1747 North Damen Avenue; tel: 773-489-1747), Trotter's former pastry chef, and Boka's Giuseppe Tentori (1729 North Halsted Street; tel: 312-337-6070), his longtime chef de cuisine, are just some of the many chefs who graduated from his culinary boot camp.

That same year Rick Bayless arrived in River North fresh from six years south of the border studying regional Mexican cuisine and writing his now-classic *Authentic Mexican: Regional Cooking from the Heart of Mexico*. His cheery, award-winning Frontera Grill and its sibling, the more upscale Topolobampo (both at 445 North Clark Street; tel: 312-661-1434), brought rich complex moles and exotica like huitlacoche enchiladas to an audience previously stuck on steak tacos. His empire has expanded to include a TV show, more cookbooks, a line of salsas, and other products as well as the Frontera Farmer Foundation, dedicated to supporting small farmers in the surrounding region, and the Rick Bayless Organic Garden, located on two city lots in Bucktown; tours and classes are offered during the summer (see www.urbanedible.blogspot.com).

> *Most Chicago bars shut down at 2am, 3am on Saturdays, but a handful with special licenses serve till 4am during the week, 5am on Saturdays.*

## Destination dining

Outside the kitchen, few have done more to lay the groundwork for Chicago's current restaurant boom than Richard Melman. His Lettuce Entertain You restaurant group reinvented the idea of "destination dining" in 1971 with the Lincoln Park burger joint R. J. Grunt's (2056 North Lincoln Park West; tel: 773-929-5363) and schticky theme restaurants like Ed Debevic's (640 North Wells Street; tel: 312-664-1707), a 1950s diner complete with rude waitresses. Critics accuse Melman of being formulaic, but almost 40 years later the Lettuce empire has expanded to more than 30 restaurants in Chicago and elsewhere, from fast food concepts like Wow Bao (three downtown locations) to the fine-dining temples Tru (676 North St Clair Street; tel: 312-202-0001) and Everest (440 South LaSalle Street; tel: 312-663-8920), plus a host of successful mid-range outfits like Brasserie Jo (59 West Hubbard Street; tel: 312-595-0800), which showcases the casual Alsacian cuisine of Everest chef Jean Joho, and Osteria Via Stato (620 North State Street; tel: 312-642-8450), a family-style Italian collaboration with Tru's Rick Tramonto.

Other visionaries have left their marks on the culinary landscape. In the 1990s, outsize entrepreneur Jerry Kleiner was almost single-handedly responsible for the transformation of West Randolph Street from a desolate indus-

trial stretch to the booming restaurant row it is today. His flashy, theatrical concept restaurants like the French Marche (833 West Randolph Street; tel: 312-226-8399) and pan-Asian Red Light (820 West Randolph Street; tel: 312-733-8880) are still going strong. Kleiner has moved on to the South Side, first Gioco (1312 South Wabash Avenue; tel: 312-939-3870) and Opera (1301 South Wabash Avenue; tel: 312-461-0161) and now Room 21 (2100 South Wabash Avenue; tel: 312-328-1198), luring the chic and stiletto-heeled to points beyond Roosevelt Road with the promise of $15 martinis.

## Independent spirit

Meanwhile, independent chef-owners across town have claimed their own pieces of Chicago's culinary pie. Paul Kahan, *Food and Wine*'s best new chef of 1999, has carved out a niche at the east end of the Randolph Street strip with his innovative contemporary American spot Blackbird (619 West Randolph Street; tel: 312-715-0708), whose sleek steel-on-white design and dedication to fresh, locally sourced ingredients have kept it in the top tier of the Chicago restaurant scene since it opened in 1997. A few doors down is his rustic, communally tabled Avec (615 West Randolph Street; tel: 312-377-2002), where the kitchen, helmed by former Blackbird sous chef Koren Grieveson, turns out toothsome, Mediterranean small plates like chorizo-stuffed madjool dates with smoked bacon and piquillo pepper-tomato sauce. In 2007, Kahan turned over the Blackbird kitchen to Mike Sheerin, a vet of Wylie Dufresne's WD-50 in New York, to focus on his new project, a 4,000-sq-ft (370-sq-meter) beer-focused "gastropub" in the Fulton Market district.

**FAR LEFT:** pastries and coffee at Russian Tea Time. **LEFT:** delis serve up thick sandwiches. **ABOVE TOP:** Charlie Trotter entertains guests at his restaurant. **ABOVE BOTTOM:** Brasserie Jo. **ABOVE RIGHT:** sushi is served with a Brazilian twist at Sushi Samba Rio.

## Seasonal, sustainable

Blackbird and other restaurants across town also bear testament to a quieter Chicago revolution – one that transcends genre and geography and may have more traction than Moto's edible menus. Uniquely situated in the heart of farm country, Chicago chefs have

taken up the banner of local, seasonal, sustainable cooking. In Logan Square, Jason Hammel and Amalea Tschilds have turned the neighborhood spot Lula (2537 North Kedzie Avenue; tel: 773-489-9554) into a national destination, with Monday night prix fixe dinners sourced exclusively from local farms. Michael Altenberg's mod flatbread-pizza joint Crust in Wicker Park (2056 West Division Street; tel: 773-235-5511) is the country's first certified all-organic restaurant, with produce for salads and toppings grown in boxes on the restaurant's back patio. And in Lincoln Park (the park, not the neighborhood), Bruce Sher-

## ITALIAN BEEF

Hot and wet. Dry and sweet. Combo, wet and sweet. The uniquely Chicago creation known as the Italian beef sandwich has its own peculiar lingo. A mound of beef sliced tissue-thin is loaded onto an Italian roll, then topped with tangy *giardiniera* (if you order it "hot") or roasted green bell peppers ("sweet"). Order it "dry" and you're good to go; ask for it "wet" and the whole shebang is dunked into gravy before being wrapped in butcher paper. Feel like living dangerously? Ask for a combo and a grilled Italian sausage will be stuffed in with the beef.

The origins of Italian beef are a bit murky. It's generally believed to be a product of the Depression, when workers in the stockyards took home leftover scraps of meat and roasted them slowly to achieve maximum tenderness. Nowadays, most Italian beef starts with meat from Scala Packing Company and rolls from Gonnella Bread, both venerable Chicago institutions.

As with deep-dish pizza or barbecue, Chicagoans can be fiercely partisan about their beef. Some swear by River North's Mr. Beef (666 North Orleans Street; tel: 312-337-8500); others are devoted to Al's #1 Beef in Little Italy (1079 West Taylor Street; tel: 312-226-4017) or the local chain Portillo's (100 West Ontario Street; tel: 312-587-8910); suburbanites crow over Johnnie's in Elmwood Park (7500 West North Avenue; tel: 708-452-6000). Wherever you go, don't expect four-star service. Beef stands tend to be bare-bones outfits offering at most a window counter and picnic table. None of this matters to the legions of hungry customers who crowd them for lunch. And it shouldn't matter to you. Just remember to grab extra napkins if you order it wet.

man's North Pond (610 North Cannon Drive; tel: 773-477-5845) is an Arts-and-Crafts gem celebrating Chef Sherman's dedication to seasonal cuisine. His deceptively complex dishes are often built upon products from the nearby Green City Market, widely regarded as one of the country's finest farmers' markets.

## Local flavors

But don't let this focus on national-magazine-worthy dining obscure the fact that Chicago's got some strong indigenous foodways of its own. In fact, at times it seems the whole city's gone food crazy. Talk to anyone in town and you'll likely discover passionately held opinions on all manner of local delicacies, from deep-dish pizza and Italian beef to the true definition of a Chicago hot dog – which, for the record, is a boiled or steamed natural-casing beef frank on a steamed poppy seed bun garnished with yellow mustard, Day-Glo green relish, "sport peppers," chopped onions, tomato wedges, celery salt, and a dill pickle spear. No ketchup. Ever.

The popular public television show *Check, Please!*, hosted by former Everest sommelier Alpana Singh, features regular Chicagoans waxing rhapsodic about their favorite restaurants. And the local online food board LTH Forum (lthforum.com), has more than 4,000 members and is regularly mined by local food editors for tips and talent. Visit and you'll tap into heated, often eloquent debates as to the etymology of the uniquely Chicago creation called a "mother-in-law," a tamale in a hot dog bun topped with chili, or the relative merits of Memphis- and Kansas City-style barbecue.

**LEFT:** fresh, local bread and produce are available at the Green City Market at the south end of Lincoln Park. **ABOVE:** a classic Chicago hot dog at the Taste of Chicago festival. **ABOVE RIGHT:** expect dishes made with regional, seasonal ingredients at North Pond in Lincoln Park.

## Hometown favorites

If the city gave prizes for fan favorites, Hot Doug's (3324 North California Avenue; tel: 773-279-9550) would probably sweep the competition. On any given day, lines stretch out the door and around the corner of this cheery "sausage superstore and encased meat emporium," Doug Sohn's staggeringly successful business in an industrial no-man's-land on the West Side. On the menu: classic Italian sausage and bratwurst, exotica like rabbit sausage with apricot-vodka cream and Port Derby cheese, and – on Friday and Saturday – duck-fat French fries.

Recent runners-up in word-of-mouth popularity include the friendly Smoque BBQ (3800 North Pulaski Road; tel: 773-545-7427), whose brisket was an instant hit in the unlikely far-northwest neighborhood of Old Irving Park, and West Town's Coalfire (1321 West Grand Avenue; tel: 312-226-2625), a New Haven-style pizzeria (with, naturally, a coal-burning oven) that's the dream of J. Spillane, a longtime bartender at the Matchbox just up the street.

## Ethnic eats

The success of all three speaks to Chicago's defining quality. This is famously a city of ethnic neighborhoods, and to taste the full range of what the city has to offer you need to venture beyond downtown. Visit Pilsen and Little Village (the largest Mexican community in the US outside Los Angeles) for tamales and *carne en su jugo*. With a Polish population second in size only to Warsaw, there's no shortage of hearty Polish cooking. Check out the all-you-can-eat Polish buffet at Red Apple (3121 N. Milwaukee Ave; tel: 773-588-5781) on the northwest side.

In the Middle Eastern neighborhood of Albany Park, you can nosh on *koubideh* and *baba ghannoush* at Noon-O-Kabob (4661 North Kedzie Avenue; tel: 773-279-8899). On Devon Avenue on the North Side, you'll find Indian and Pakistani restaurants serving *naan* and *chana masala*. Try Khan BBQ (2401 West Devon Avenue; tel: 773-274-8600) for tender chicken *boti* and lamb kabobs or Arya Bhavan (2508 West Devon Avenue; tel: 773-274-5800) for a 20-ft-long (3-meter) vegetarian buffet. Hit Argyle Street for Vietnamese cuisine and North Lincoln Avenue's Koreatown for *bi bim bop*. And don't forget the soul food meccas of the South and West Sides.

In fact, that peculiar Chicago hot dog, with it's Italian *giardiniera*, Polish pickles, Greek peppers, and German mustard, is itself a tidy representation of the city's culinary influences. Trek out to the Superdawg drive-in (6363 North Milwaukee Avenue; tel: 773-763-0660) for one of the best. ❑

### PIZZA, THREE WAYS

Chicago is justifiably famous for its deep-dish pizza. The gut buster invented by Pizzeria Uno's Ike Sewell in 1943 is a uniquely decadent concoction: dense, flaky crust and pounds of mozzarella wrapped around sausage or other fillings and topped with chunky tomato sauce, the flavors fusing together to create an artery-clogging one-dish meal. But not everyone is a fan. There's a vocal faction of thin-crust aficionados who swear by the crispy, cracker-thin pies found in taverns and elsewhere. Cut into signature squares rather than wedges, for years these pizzas were the closest you'd get to authentic Italian 'za. But in recent years oven-fired Neapolitan-style pizza has become the rage. Nowadays, there's a pie for every palate.

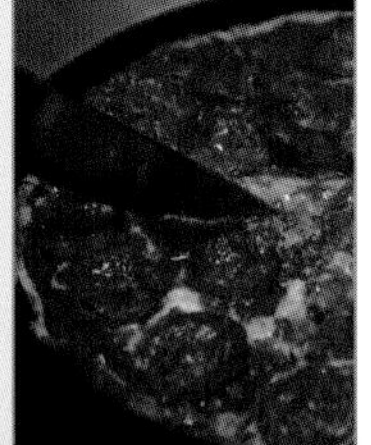

## Built on Beer

Walk the streets of any Chicago neighborhood and one thing is clear: this city loves its beer. In fact, two taverns were among the city's first buildings, and today terra-cotta detailing on some vintage pubs speaks to their history as "tied" houses selling only Schlitz, Blatz, or Pabst. Less lovely but no less iconic are the Old Style signs that glow outside corner bars advertising "Cerveza fria" in Spanish, "Zimne piwo" in Polish, or just plain "Cold beer."

In its 19th-century heyday, Chicago was a brewing powerhouse. Many of the city's founding fathers – including William Lill, Michael Diversey, and Charles Wacker – were in the beer business. By 1857, Lill and Diversey's business was the largest brewery west of the Atlantic coast, producing more than 45,000 barrels a year. Housed in a four-story tenement, it loomed over the Water Tower at the corner of Pine (now Michigan) and Chicago until it, and everything else in town, was leveled in the Great Fire.

After the fire, Chicago's beer needs were met by Milwaukee breweries as the city struggled to rebuild. The local brewers who were able to bounce back were hit again 40 years later when Prohibition effectively ended Chicago beer production – at least legally. Bootleggers Johnny Torrio and his protégé Al Capone somehow managed to keep the taps flowing at thousands of Chicago speakeasies. Following the repeal of Prohibition, the brewing industry faltered due to the combined pressures of World War II and the subsequent rise of large national brands; the Peter Hand Brewery, creators of Meister Brau and the last of the small local outfits, closed up shop in 1978.

Nowadays, craft brewing is back in the spotlight, thanks in large part to the breakout success of the Goose Island Beer Company in the 1990s. The city's first brewpub, Goose Island is now available nationwide. Production has been moved to a larger facility, but visitors to the original Clybourn Avenue brewpub can still watch small batches of beer being made daily, and the company's Honker's Ale and 312 Urban Wheat dominate beer taps around the city.

Distribution problems and the high cost of real estate still make it difficult for anyone smaller than the Goose to set up shop in the city, but many small regional breweries have staked a claim to the Chicago market, including Two Brothers, from Warrenville, and Indiana-based Three Floyd's. Flossmoor Station, in suburban Flossmoor, was named "Best Small Brewpub Brewer in America" in 2006. Closer to the urban core, the Wicker Park pizzeria Piece brews award-winning beers available only by the jug or 64-ounce "growler." Meanwhile, students from all over flock to the world-famous Siebel Institute of Technology. Founded in 1868, this acclaimed brewing academy now uses classrooms at Goose Island to train the next generation of brewers.

Chicago beer may never again hit its 19th-century apex, but beer culture still thrives. Pubs like the Map Room, Quenchers, and the Hopleaf, with dizzying lists of imported and niche brews, are nirvana for beer geeks. Even the corner tavern is likely to have more than Old Style on tap. ❑

**FAR LEFT:** fried plantains at a Washington Park festival. **LEFT TOP:** Bende & Son Salami Co. **LEFT BOTTOM:** Greektown bakery **RIGHT:** Hopleaf Bar.

ILLINOIS
19
adidas
WALK
32
91

# GOOD SPORTS

**Win or lose, larger-than-life figures dominate the games in a town fiercely loyal to its teams**

Chicago is a broad-shouldered sports town, devoted to big, brawny heroes like Bronko Nagurski, Dick Butkus, Sammy Sosa, and Bobby Hull. It's not that Chicagoans are unable to appreciate the finesse of a Gale Sayers or Michael Jordan, but over the years they've shown a predilection for tough, bruising play, regardless of the sport.

### The Bears

That's partly why Chicago is first and foremost a Bears town. Through thick and thin, the football team has been the city's top sports franchise. From the time the squad reports to training camp in downstate Bourbonnais in July to the last game of the season in midwinter, the Bears dominate the sports pages and sports-talk radio, and it takes something exceptional – like the White Sox's World Series win in 2005 – to break through their grip on media coverage.

*The Northwestern University Wildcats are charter members of the Big Ten Conference and winners of eight Big Ten championships.*

Even in lean years, the Bears can be counted on to deliver a bone-crushing defense that lives up to the team's nickname, "The Monsters of the Midway." The moniker was particularly apt for the 1985 team widely considered the best in NFL history after it trounced the New England Patriots 46-10 in Super Bowl XX.

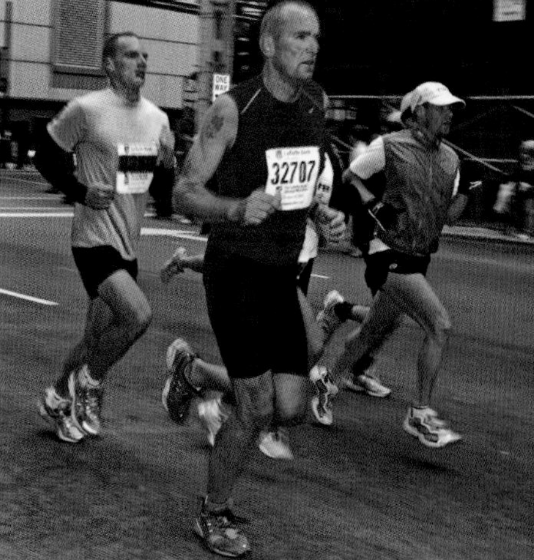


**LEFT:** the Northwestern University Wildcats.
**RIGHT:** about 45,000 runners participate in the annual Chicago Marathon.

The Bears were one of the original NFL franchises, and their signing of superstar running back Red "The Galloping Ghost" Grange from the University of Illinois in 1925 helped prop up the fledgling pro league. Since then the Bears have been known for running backs like Nagurski, Sayers, and Walter Payton, who long held the career record for rushing yardage. They also have a tradition of great middle linebackers – Butkus, Mike Singletary, and Brian Urlacher – befitting the town's love of powerful and aggressive players.

The Bears play at Soldier Field on the lake-

front south of the Loop. In a city that takes pride in its architecture, the recently refurbished stadium is something of an ugly duckling. The structure's original columns have been retained, with the new stadium built inside. Some critics say it looks as if a spaceship has landed on the site. Inside, however, it's a surprisingly intimate and comfortable venue, with the upper decks looming over the field. Fans show up early on Sundays in all kinds of weather for pregame tailgate parties in the parking lots.

### THE BILLY GOAT CURSE

As a promotional stunt, William Sianis, owner of the Billy Goat Tavern, brought a goat to the 1945 World Series at Wrigley Field, but it had to be removed due to complaints about the smell. Sianis supposedly cursed the Cubs, and when the team lost to the Detroit Tigers he sent a telegram reading, "Who stinks now?" Today, the story is considered an apocryphal creation of *Tribune* sports columnist David Condon, but there's no denying some strange things have happened to the Cubs – missed catches during critical games, black cats on the field, and not a single trip to the World Series since 1945.

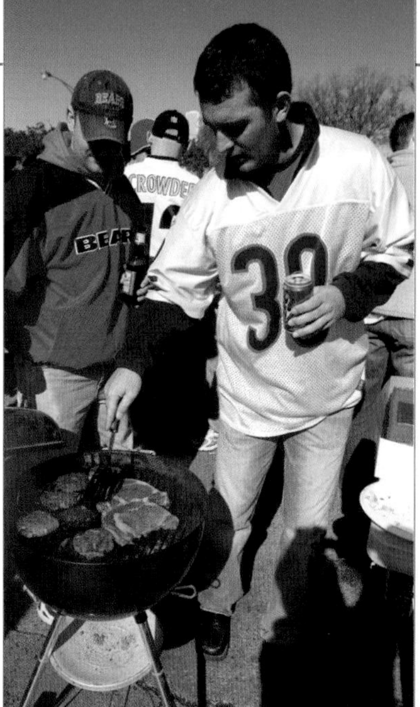


## Lovable losers

If the Bears are the team the city's sports fans most closely identify with, then the Cubs are the most beloved. That's partly due to the fact that the baseball team plays at Wrigley Field, the oldest and arguably most beautiful ballpark in the National League. The "Friendly Confines" – as the stadium is sometimes known – are renowned for the ivy on the outfield wall, the hand-operated scoreboard, the sun-worshipping "Bleacher Bums" who crowd the outfield stands, and the numerous home-field traditions such as tossing back homerun balls hit by the opposing team. In fact, the franchise is so traditional it was the last in the major league to add outdoor lights, in 1988, and only then over the objections of a good many fans.

Although the Cubs haven't reached the World Series since 1945, they've had more than their share of big-time, matinee-idol ballplayers over the years. Sammy Sosa, Ryne Sandberg, Mark Grace, and Ron Santo all established themselves as Chicago favorites, as did the ebullient Ernie Banks, known to fans as "Mr Cub."

But somehow, for all their talent, the Cubs always manage to mess it up in the end, as in

their heartbreaking stumble before the post-season in 1969, the disappointing 1984 and 2003 playoffs, and the 2007 shut out in the division series.

In 2008, the Cubs will commemorate the 100th anniversary of their last World Series championship. Nevertheless, Cubs fans remain loyal, filling Wrigley Field from spring to fall, with many games selling out soon after tickets go on sale in February.

## The Sox

On the working-class South Side, fans of the White Sox tend to be more demanding. The Sox are one of the charter members of the American League and a powerhouse in the League's early history. Sox fans point with pride to the way their "Hitless Wonders" upset the Cubs in Chicago's only city series in 1906. The Sox won it all again in 1917 led by "Shoeless" Joe Jackson, then suffered four decades of failure after the 1919 "Black Sox" scandal, when Jackson and seven other players conspired to throw the World Series to the Cincinnati Reds (see box, page 89).

*Looking for tickets to a sold-out game? Try state-licensed ticket brokers or online sites like StubHub and Craig's List. Scalping tickets at a game is illegal but not uncommon.*

**Left Top:** fans of the Chicago Bears gather at Soldier Field for tailgating parties before the game. **Left:** Cubs fan, loyal but disappointed. **Above:** Wrigley Field is a storied ballpark famous for its ivy-covered outfield wall, manually operated scoreboard, and the fans' "colorful" chants.

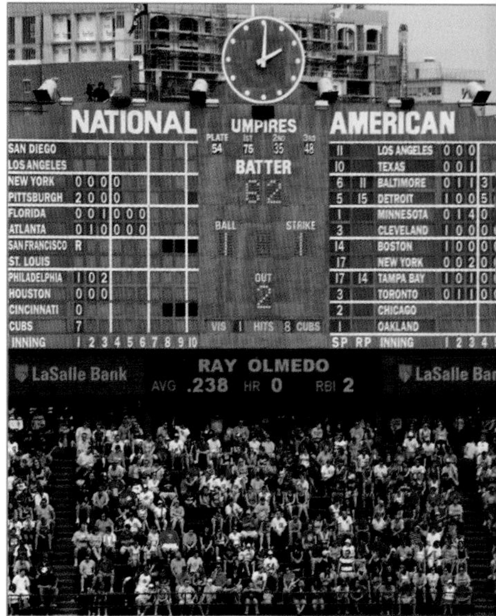


Even when the team's fortunes were revived in the 1950s and 60s, the White Sox usually found their way blocked by the New York Yankees. They also found that, unlike the Cubs, they had to win games in order to attract fans, as they did with the homer-happy "South Side Hit Men" of 1977 and the "Winning Ugly" division champs of 1983. Otherwise, the franchise has experienced more than a few lean years.

In 1990, the Sox moved from the old Comiskey Park across 35th Street to the new Comiskey Park, a larger and more utilitarian facility if not exactly more charming. Renovations over the years have included the addition of a roof and an outfield deck. They even planted a little ivy. It's now called US Cellular Field, although fans usually refer to it as the Cell or simply Sox Park.

In 2005, the Sox broke through for the city's first World Series championship in 88 years, led by a cast of characters including manager Ozzie Guillen and players Paul Konerko, A.J. Pierzynski, Joe Crede, Bobby Jenks, Mark Buehrle, and Jose Contreras. That brought many Sox fans back for good and engendered loyalty for years to come.

## Hardwood heroes

Led by Michael Jordan – regarded by many observers of the sport as the single greatest basketball player of all time – the Bulls won six NBA championships in the 1990s. Their winning streak was a source of much late-spring celebration and civic pride. Fans in Chicago and elsewhere respected the team's consistent play and mental toughness as well as the skill and beauty of players like Scottie Pippen and Horace Grant and role players such as Dennis Rodman, John Paxson, and Steve Kerr.

The team has had to labor under the shadow of those glory days ever since, trying to live up to the leaping Jordan statue outside the arena – the United Center – that he practically built. Still, Bulls fans have remained loyal, filling the United Center even in losing seasons.

> *The University of Chicago football team were the original "Monsters of the Midway," a nickname later adopted by the Bears.*

## Ice men

The NHL Blackhawks have had a bit more of a roller-coaster ride. Chicago used to be a prime hockey town, with the Hawks one of the original six NHL franchises, and the old Chicago Stadium routinely crammed with screaming fans. Bobby "The Golden Jet" Hull led the team to its last Stanley Cup championship in 1961. The Hawks suffered for decades under the ownership of Bill Wirtz, who let Hull go in the 1970s and watched as the fan base dwindled in the 1990s. With the move to the United Center, some essential life seemed to go out of the team. Wirtz's son Rocky took over the reins in 2007 and immediately arranged for an influx of talent, starting with teen phenoms Patrick Kane and Jonathan Toews, and reawakening the hopes of Chicago hockey fans.

## It's how you play the game

Those aren't the city's only spectator sports. The Fire soccer team thrived at Soldier Field, then moved to Toyota Park in Bridgeview. Mixing spectator sports with participant sports, the Chicago Marathon has become an annual October event, attracting a field of top runners, as well as some 40,000 not-so-elite entrants. Likewise, the Golden Gloves boxing tournament fills the St Andrew's gym on the North Side in late winter.

In summer, the city's fans become avid players of their own, whether sailing on the lake in preparation for the Mackinac Island race, playing volleyball at North Avenue Beach, or softball in Grant Park. Just remember, in Chicago they don't play with a conventional 12-inch softball and gloves, but barehanded with a 16-inch Clincher softball. It's a big ball for a big game, in a city that has always prided itself on big, burly shoulders. ❑

## 'Say It Ain't So, Joe'

Chicago is unfortunately the place that bred the infamous "Black Sox" scandal of 1919 in which the White Sox (founded in 1900, on the South Side) became embroiled in a bribery conspiracy that shook professional baseball to its core.

The team had arrived in Cincinnati in October 1919 to engage the Reds in the first World Series after World War I. Fans across the nation were highly engaged. The White Sox were the overwhelming favorites. Pitcher Eddie Cicotte had won 29 games, and the legendary "Shoeless" Joe Jackson, an illiterate former cotton-mill worker from the South, sported an impressive batting average of .356.

The bribery plot, as most accounts have it, was initiated by White Sox first baseman Arnold "Chick" Gandil, who met with a bookmaker in a Boston hotel three weeks before the series began. For $80,000 to be provided by a group of gamblers, he agreed to arrange for the White Sox to lose. Gandil recruited Cicotte and other White Sox players, including Jackson, and the payoff was raised to a princely sum of $100,000.

Ultimately, the White Sox lost five games to three in contests marred by bobbled catches and bad throws. The team reportedly won their three games only out of anger when the gamblers were slow in making their bribe payments. A year later, under the relentless goading of newspaper reporters, a Chicago grand jury indicted eight White Sox ballplayers on nine counts of conspiracy to defraud. The scandal had a devastating effect. Team owners, under pressure to clean up the game, appointed Judge Kenesaw Mountain Landis as the first commissioner of baseball.

The scandal also triggered a wave of bitterness and cynicism. A Chicago newspaper reported that a young boy clutched desperately at Joe Jackson's sleeve as the fallen hero left the grand jury hearing and pleaded with him, "Say it ain't so, Joe. Say it ain't so."

"Yes, kid, I'm afraid it is," Jackson is said to have replied.

Like so many good, overinflated Chicago newspaper stories of the era, this one turned out to be a fabrication by a reporter. But the bitterness was real (and "Say it ain't so, Joe" became an enduring epithet). Although the players were acquitted of criminal charges, they were banished for life from standard professional baseball.

It took a charismatic New York Yankees slugger named Babe Ruth, with a penchant for swatting baseballs long distance into the stands, to recapture fan loyalty and rescue the game from the depths of the "Black Sox" scandal. ❑

**FAR LEFT:** a marathon runner approaches the finish line. **LEFT:** biking past the Art Institute. **ABOVE:** Arnold Gandil **RIGHT:** "Shoeless" Joe Jackson.

Hotel 71

# CHICAGO ARCHITECTURE

**After the Great Fire, Chicago re-invented itself as a center of architectural innovation – an identity that continues to the present day**

As cities go, Chicago is still wet behind the ears. It's oldest surviving building, the Clarke House, now at 1855 South Indiana Avenue, dates only to 1836, about a year after the region's Indian population, having just bartered away 5 million acres (2 million hectares) of land, paraded out of Chicago for the last time.

"Building, breaking, rebuilding," is how poet Carl Sandburg described the city's relationship to its architecture, and there's no better place to get a feel for this than in the Prairie Avenue Historic District, where the Clarke House was moved in 1977. In the 1880s, this was where the city's most prosperous citizens built their mansions, from meatpacker Philip Armour to railroad tycoon George Pullman, who built his own company town and named it after himself.

Prairie Avenue's heyday was brief, and over time most of the grand mansions were demolished. The Glessner House (1800 South Prairie), a brawny, 1887 Romanesque edifice that's among the best works of Boston architect Henry Hobbs Richardson, was turned into a museum.

*The Chicago Architecture Foundation offers more than 50 tours focusing on various styles, neighborhoods, architects, and other themes. Go to www.architecture.org*

**LEFT:** the Loop encompasses some of America's most significant urban architecture.
**RIGHT:** the Clarke House is Chicago's oldest building.

It became one of only a handful of survivors, cast adrift in a sea of rubble-strewn lots.

Then, in the last decade, Prairie Avenue became hot again. Walk down the street today and you'll see the old mansions handsomely restored, the once-vacant lots filled with elegant new buildings designed in the style of their older neighbors. From royalty to bum to royalty again – as Sean Connery explained in the movie *The Untouchables*, "that's the Chicago way."

## Chicago School

There's no better example of Chicago's talent for re-invention than the architecture of the Loop, where, in less than a square mile, you'll

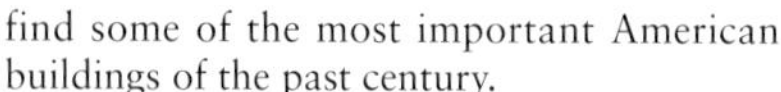

find some of the most important American buildings of the past century.

Take the Auditorium Building (430 South Michigan Avenue), for instance, an 1886 masterpiece by the firm of Adler and Sullivan. Dankmar Adler laid out the huge theater so that a person speaking in a normal voice can be heard in the farthest row. Louis Sullivan designed the cascading interior arches, ablaze with warm, incandescent light, that outline the ceiling. A young Frank Lloyd Wright helped with the ornamentation.

While New York architects were creating towers that looked like wedding cakes with layers of floors stacked upon each other with little regard for creating an articulated whole, Louis Sullivan saw clearly that the skyscraper must be "every inch a proud and soaring thing, rising in sheer exultation ... without a single dissenting line." Although many of Sullivan's best buildings were wantonly demolished in the 1960s and 70s, his ideas are reflected in several turn-of-the-century skyscrapers designed by his contemporaries.

Among the finest examples are Daniel Burnham's 1896 Fisher Building (343 South Dearborn); the 1894 Old Colony Building by the firm of Holabird and Roche; and the 1891 Manhattan Building (431 South Dearborn) by William LeBaron Jenney, who's known as "the father of the skyscraper" due to the now-demolished Home Insurance Building, often cited as the first time a steel (and cast-iron) skeleton was used to support a tall building. The standout of this era is the 1891 Monadnock Building (53 West Jackson) by Daniel Burnham and John Wellborn Root. One of the

### THE BEST LAID PLANS...

Daniel Burnham's influential *Plan of Chicago* didn't always materialize as the author intended. As he recommended, the city's lakefront has been almost entirely reserved for public parks, but when, in 1965, the city finally got around to building a new civic center, it wasn't the Beaux Arts palace Burnham envisioned. Instead, the city built the Richard J. Daley Center (50 West Washington Street), a handsome skyscraper faced in warm brown Cor-Ten steel. It's amusing to imagine what Burnham would have made of the sculpture that dominates the site's bustling plaza – not a heroic figure in the classical mode but an enigmatic work by modernist hero Pablo Picasso that is sometimes likened to the head of an Afghan hound. And what became of the site Burnham chose for his proposed city center? Since the 1960s, it's been occupied by a tangle of highway ramps known with some derision as the Spaghetti Bowl.

tallest buildings of its time, its load-bearing walls are 6 ft (2 meters) thick at the base. There's no external ornamentation, only curved brick walls.

Together, these firms created what came to be known as the Chicago School of Architecture, which eschewed the slavish recycling of classical Greek and Roman motifs in favor of a distinctly American architecture – unfussy and direct.

## Burnham's plan

Ironically, one of the Chicago School's most prominent figures was also the least representative of the movement's pared-down style. Daniel Burnham was a man of big ideas and the energy to see them through. "Make no little plans; they have no magic to stir men's blood," he famously declared, and he put that ambition to work as the director of the 1893 World's Columbian Exposition. To the millions who visited the fair, Burnham's White City, as it came to be known, was the epitome of classical splendor, and it later served as a model for the City Beautiful movement that sought to reform the squalor of congested, coal-blackened cities with rational planning and Beaux Arts architecture. In 1905, Burnham was commissioned to create plans for the cities of San Francisco and Manila. Working with his assistant Edward H. Bennett, he applied what he had learned to the 1909 *Plan of Chicago* – the Magna Carta of urban planning, with sweeping proposals for transportation, recreation, and culture.

**FAR LEFT:** Auditorium Building. **LEFT:** Manhattan Building. **ABOVE:** the Glessner House on Prairie Avenue was designed by Boston architect Henry Hobson Richardson. **ABOVE RIGHT:** at 1,451 ft (442 meters), the Sears Tower was the world's tallest building for more than 25 years.

## Mies: less is more

So clear and powerful was the vision of the Chicago School that its influence reached all the way to Europe, where a young architect, Ludwig Mies van der Rohe, would later return the favor. After fleeing from Nazi Germany in 1937, Mies settled in Chicago, where he took a position as director of the architecture program at the Illinois Institute of Technology. There he created a second Chicago School. His redesign of the campus culminated in 1956 with the construction of Crown Hall, all glass and black steel, with the roof hung from two huge steel trusses, leaving the interior free of internal columns – the world's largest one room schoolhouse.

Mies was famous for reducing architecture to its essentials. "Less is more," and "God is in the details" are among his famous dictums. On Dearborn Street, just north of the Monadnock Building, those values find expression in Mies's Federal Center, two glass and jet-black steel skyscrapers and a single story post office set around a grand plaza, itself centered around a soaring metal sculpture by Alexander Calder, *Flamingo*. Painted fire engine red, it's a flamboyant counterpoint to Mies's austere design.

Mies died in 1969, but his legacy is evident throughout the city. It was in that year that the John Hancock Center (875 North Michigan Avenue) was completed. The Sears Tower (233 South Wacker Drive) may be taller, but "Big John" is Chicago's true romantic skyscraper, a gently tapering modernist obelisk whose grid-like facade is enlivened with X-shaped braces.

## Postmodern visions

In the hands of less talented architects, Mies's style had the unfortunate tendency to degenerate into a mere formula, and it wasn't long before architects rebelled against the proliferation of "glass boxes." Bertrand Goldberg led the way in the early 1960s with his Marina City (300 North State Street). Built at a time when much of the middle-class was fleeing to the suburbs, Goldberg's "city within a city" pioneered the concept of downtown living. Where Mies offered only straight lines, Goldberg celebrated curves. The twin 60-story towers are round in shape, and with their petal-like balconies have been compared to corncobs. Each contains 900 apartments, with about the same number of parking spaces in the open spiral garages that occupy the first 20 floors. The complex's large auditorium, now home to the House of Blues, is capped with a distinctive, saddle-shaped roof.

Other Chicago architects responded to Mies with a fusion of high technology and classical references. Perhaps the best example is Helmut Jahn's 1985 Thompson Center (100 West Randolph Street), a glass-walled, spaceship of a building that garnered worldwide notoriety when it was completed in 1985. Looking like an overgrown erector set, the building's 17-story atrium is surmounted with a glass rotunda and has elevators speeding up and down open shafts. A more graceful expression of the postmodern sensibility is the curved

### A Dalliance with Deco

Art Deco is usually associated with iconic New York skyscrapers like the Chrysler and Empire State buildings, but Chicago had a brief fling with Art Deco style, too. Perhaps the most impressive example is the sleek Board of Trade Building (141 West Jackson Boulevard), completed in 1930 and capped with a 31-ft (10-meter) statue of Ceres, the goddess of grain, by sculptor John Storrs. Its graceful setbacks, bathed in floodlights, dominate the view down canyon-like LaSalle Street, while the polished marble and silver trim of the recently restored lobby gleams like a flapper in sequins. Up the street, the elegant Art Deco Field Building, completed in 1931, was the last skyscraper built in Chicago for a quarter century after the onset of the Great Depression.

glass face of 333 West Wacker, designed in 1983 by the firm of Kohn Pedersen Fox.

## The new frontier

The generation of buildings now taking shape in Chicago draws upon a wide range of references and often reflects their designers' distinctive, sometimes idiosyncratic, sensibilities. Rising along the Chicago River just a block from Marina City, the Trump International Hotel and Tower represents a pendulum swing back to traditional modernism. At 1,362 ft (415 meters), it is among the tallest buildings to be constructed in Chicago since the Sears Tower in 1974. Architect Adrian Smith, then of Skidmore, Owings and Merrill, has taken the classic glass box and reshaped it into a cascading series of massive trapezoid setbacks.

Trump Tower is only one of several skyscrapers reaching ambitiously to the heavens, evincing an architectural swagger that has taken on a certain poignancy after the 9/11 terrorist attacks. Studio/Gang's 82-story Aqua (255 North Columbus) will have balconies of varying sizes, creating an undulating facade of swells and valleys. Also under construction is Santiago Calatrava's 150-story Chicago Spire (400 North Lake Shore Drive), a spiraling, drill-bit-shaped tower that is destined to be the tallest structure in North America.

Elsewhere in the city, architects are putting a new spin on established styles and employing familiar construction materials in novel ways. At the University of Chicago, Rafael Vinoly's 2004 Graduate School of Business pays homage to the cubist masses of Frank Lloyd Wright's Robie House, which is just across the street. On the IIT campus, Rem Koolhaas's McCormick Tribune Campus Center is a pinball machine of orange-tinted glass and lively interiors. Running along the roof is a 530-ft-long (161-meter) elliptical, stainless steel tube with bright orange trim that muffles the noise of the El trains that pass through it.

In the Grand Crossing neighborhood, John Ronan's Gary Comer Youth Center (7200 Ingleside Avenue) is clad in red, blue, and white asphalt panels that bring a splash of exuberant

**FAR LEFT:** Art Deco style at the Chicago Board of Trade. **LEFT:** the glass facade of the Spertus Institute is composed of 726 windows in 556 different shapes. **ABOVE:** Marina City's rounded balconies contrast sharply with the angularity of the city's many boxy, glass buildings.

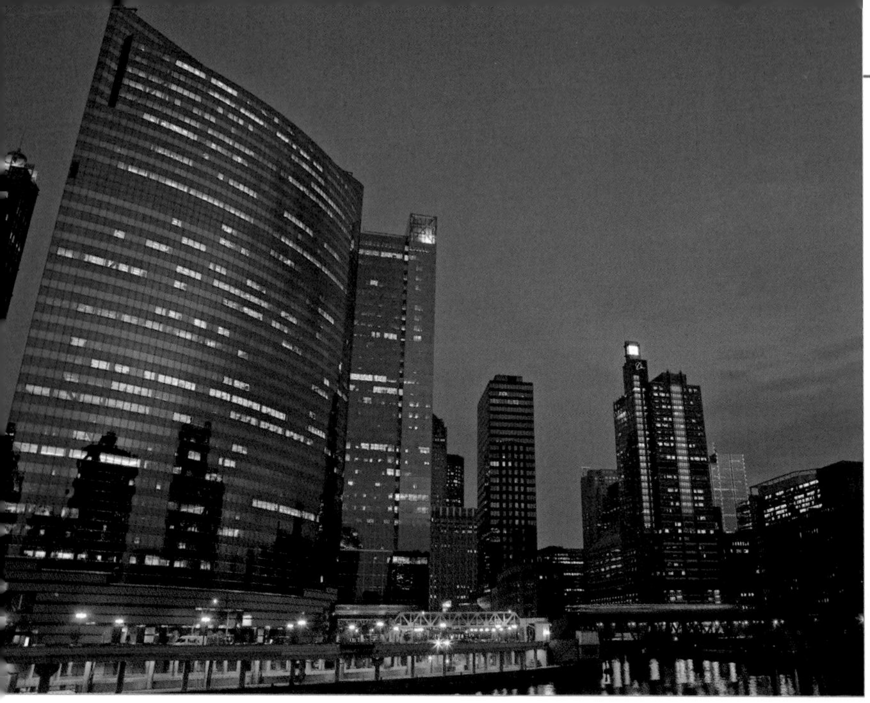

color to this often troubled community. In dazzling Millennium Park, Frank Gehry's Jay Pritzker Pavilion features a concert stage framed in swirling stainless-steel scallops. On South Michigan Avenue, the faceted, glass face of the new Spertus Institute adds a welcome modernist counterpoint to the boulevard's classic facades.

*Despite his genius as an architect, Louis Sullivan died poor and lonely in a downtown hotel, bitter that his vision of an authentically American architecture had been dashed by the resurgence of Neoclassical style.*

## The Wright legacy

Ironically, Chicago's most influential architect did the vast majority of his work outside the city. Unlike most other prominent architects of his time, Frank Lloyd Wright (1867–1959) didn't care all that much for big cities. Early in his career (just before Louis Sullivan fired him for secretly taking commissions on the side), he chose to settle in suburban Oak Park, where visitors can still view some of his finest work, including his own home and studio.

Instead of the thrusting verticality favored by his contemporaries, Wright built close to the ground. The Prairie School, as his style later came to be known, emphasized horizontal planes, organic materials, and integration with the landscape. Instinctively forward-thinking, Wright anticipated the proliferation of automobiles and the sprawling suburbs it would engender. His so-called Usonian houses presaged the modern-day interest in "green" architecture with its emphasis on natural light and energy-efficient heating and cooling.

As with Burnham, Wright's most idealistic visions weren't always realized precisely as he had hoped, but his hand is evident in virtually every suburban subdivision in America. In a larger sense, Sullivan, Burnham, Mies, and all architects who cling to a faith in the centrality of the urban experience have been fighting a rear-guard action against suburban sprawl. The houses, offices, and communities occupied by most Americans owe far more to Wright's prophetic vision. ❑

**ABOVE:** 333 West Wacker towers over the Chicago River.

## Egos in the White City

Daniel Burnham and John Wellborn Root enlisted some of the East Coast's most prominent architects to assist them with the design of the 1893 World's Columbian Exposition, though perhaps none was as formidable as Charles F. McKim, principal of the New York firm McKim, Mead, and White.

Initially, Root wanted the fair to reflect an "American style," eclectic and colorful. But McKim had other ideas. He had already persuaded his colleagues that the fair should revert to the classical style that was the stock in trade of firms like his own. Root died suddenly of pneumonia in 1891 and was replaced as Burnham's partner by Charles Atwood, an architect known for his facility with classical details.

With Burnham's penchant for thinking big, the fair's design veered toward the monumental. Just as America was exerting itself as a world power, the fair's classically inspired buildings evoked an architecture of empire.

The fair was an overwhelming success, drawing more than 27 million visitors over six months. "These visitors were astonished," wrote Louis Sullivan, who decried the resurgence of classical style as a bankrupt rehashing of the "bogus antique." What the masses beheld as "an amazing revelation of the architectural art" Sullivan saw as a virus spreading "a violent outbreak of the Classic and Renaissance in the East, which slowly spread westward, contaminating all that it touched. The damage wrought by the World's Fair will last for half a century."

Although the fair's buildings gave the appearance of immortal landmarks, most were constructed of white plaster "staff" placed over wood and iron frames. Nearly all were destroyed by fire less than a year after the fair closed. Only Atwood's Neoclassical Palace of Fine Arts survived, having been built with brick under the plaster to protect the precious works of art that were housed inside. In the 1930s, the original plaster facade was re-created in stone, and the building was taken over by the Museum of Science and Industry. Stand at the far side of Columbia Basin, its water gently lapping against the steps leading to the museum's south entrance, and you can almost imagine you're back at the White City in 1893.

Atwood's partnership with Burnham reached its zenith in the 1895 Reliance Building at Washington and State streets. The skyscraper's gleaming, terra-cotta facade harkens back to the White City, but the large plate glass windows anticipate the steel-and-glass towers that wouldn't be built for another five decades. After long years of neglect, the Reliance has been beautifully restored as the Hotel Burnham, with an elegant restaurant, the Atwood Café.

**RIGHT:** the Columbian Exposition inspired the City Beautiful movement of the early 20th century.

Atwood, secretly an opium addict, was fired by Burnham shortly after the Reliance Building was completed. He died nine days later, at the age of 46. Never again would Burnham have such a talented designer as his partner. With exceptions like the elegant Santa Fe Building (224 South Michigan Avenue) and the Flatiron in New York, Burnham's designs became increasingly monumental, even pompous. He was, to the end, the architect of ambition. ❑

# SHOPPING

## Classy department stores, chichi designers, quirky boutiques – Chicago shopping is a many splendored thing

Variety is the essential ingredient of Chicago shopping. Whether it's haute couture or shabby chic, there are plenty of opportunities to make a purchase. Michigan Avenue is to Chicago what Fifth Avenue is to New York, a parade of high-end designers punctuated by flagship chain stores and sleek malls. In the Loop is Macy's, formerly Marshall Field's, the legendary department store, a shopping mecca with eight floors of fashion and furniture. Oak Street is where the gilded and glamorous shop, a confection of boutiques and antique stores popular with ladies who lunch. Farther north, the leafy streets of Lincoln Park and Old Town harbor charming, idiosyncratic shops, interspersed with cosmopolitan cafés and restaurants. For a more raw experience, the sprawling Maxwell Street Market on the West Side is quintessential Chicago, right down to the live blues bands and Polish sausage.

**BELOW:** farmers sell fresh, regional produce, flowers, honey, cheese, and baked goods at the farmers' market in Federal Plaza, held weekly May to October. Federal Plaza is just one of several markets that cater to a growing demand for local, seasonal foods. Others are at Daley Plaza, the Museum of Contemporary Art, and Lincoln Square. The biggest is Green City Market in Lincoln Park, which has about 50 vendors and a full schedule of guest chefs.

**ABOVE:** On the northern end of the Magnificent Mile, Water Tower Place features more than a hundred fashion and interior design stores around a glitzy, eight-story atrium.

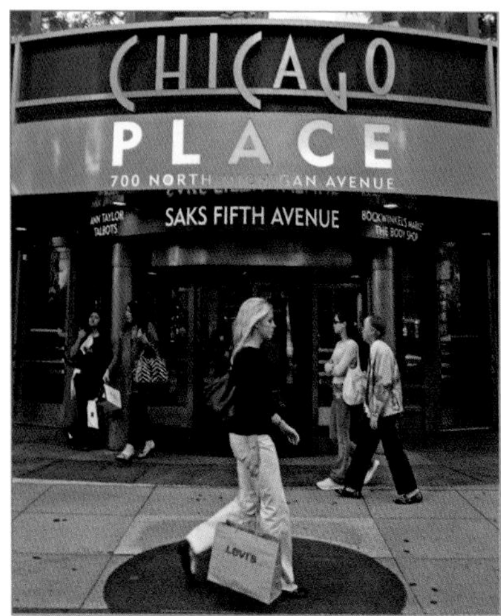


**ABOVE:** Chicago Place on the Magnificent Mile is a sleek, contemporary shopping mall with more than 45 shops and restaurants on eight floors, including upscale department store Saks Fifth Avenue.

**RIGHT:** Formerly Marshall Field's – a Chicago tradition for more than a century – Macy's on State Street is the country's second-largest department store, with designer boutiques, three floors of furniture, gourmet eateries, and much more.

**BELOW:** artists, dealers, and collectors gather at Navy Pier for the annual Sculpture Objects & Functional Art, or SOFA, show.

The Maxwell Street Market has more than 400 vendors selling used household goods, vintage clothing, CDs, jewelry, and produce.

Young shoppers visit the American Girl Place, a doll "salon" with a café, theater, doll hospital, and thousands of dolls and accessories.

Music fans search vintage vinyl at a record shop near the intersection of Damen, Milwaukee and North avenues in artsy Wicker Park.

**BELOW:** the Magnificent Mile is the place for haute couture, with high-end department stores such as Bloomingdale's, Nordstrom, and Neiman Marcus.

Abercrombie
& Fitch

Hampton Inn & Suites

OF FAME

ANDY'S

*Wrigley Field*
page 180

*Blues Clubs*
pages 65–9

*Magnificent Mile*
pages 143–48

*John Hancock Center*
pages 147–48

*Navy Pier*
page 151

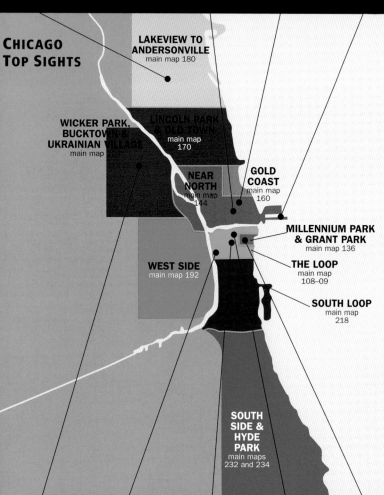

# Chicago Top Sights

LAKEVIEW TO ANDERSONVILLE
main map 180

LINCOLN PARK & OLD TOWN
main map 170

WICKER PARK, BUCKTOWN & UKRAINIAN VILLAGE
main map 204

NEAR NORTH
main map 144

GOLD COAST
main map 160

MILLENNIUM PARK & GRANT PARK
main map 136

WEST SIDE
main map 192

THE LOOP
main map 108–09

SOUTH LOOP
main map 218

SOUTH SIDE & HYDE PARK
main maps 232 and 234

*Wicker Park*
pages 203–10

*Sears Tower*
pages 114–15

*Art Institute*
pages 112–13

*Macy's*
pages 116–17

*Millennium Park*
pages 136–37

# PLACES

**The cutaway map opposite shows the neighborhoods of Chicago, while the Places section to follow details all the attractions worth seeing, arranged by area. Main sites are cross-referenced by number to individual maps**

Chicago's city limits encompass a wildly diverse swath of urban geography, from the immigrant gateways of Pilsen and Uptown to the jazz clubs of historic Bronzeville, the boutiques of trendy Bucktown, and the bungalows of far northwest Mayfair. What unites them all is Chicago's rigorous street grid, which stretches north, south, west, and occasionally east with a clockwork regularity that makes getting around town a snap. For this, credit an unsung civic hero: onetime building superintendent Edward P. Brennan, who in 1909 standardized street names and addresses citywide.

Capitalizing on the flat prairie landscape, early surveyors laid out main streets along straight lines that ran from one end of the city to the other, but numbering was inconsistent and many streets were known by multiple names. The "Brennan system" simplified things, with addresses radiating from the intersection of State Street (running north-south) and Madison Street (east-west) in the heart of the Loop in a logical formation: addresses progress by 100 per block; eight blocks equal a mile, and every mile there's a major thoroughfare.

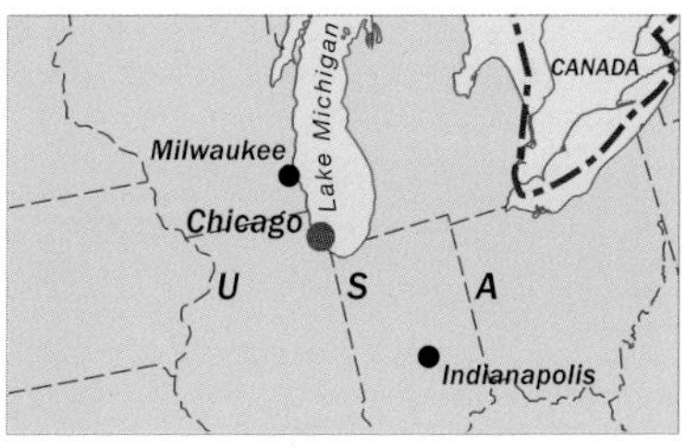


Even-numbered addresses are found on the north and west sides of a street, and odd numbers on the south and east sides. If you know the address and direction of your destination, you can easily figure its distance from the ground zero of State and Madison. In fact, Chicagoans often describe locations in the context of the grid, estimating a destination as "about 1600 West" or "somewhere around 4000 North" of a particular street.

Of course, to every rule there must be an exception or three, and Chicago has those in the form of diagonal streets that cut across the grid, most notable among them Milwaukee, Lincoln, Elston, Ogden, and Archer avenues. These angled streets result in often confusing six-way intersections when they meet up with the major east-west and north-south roads. Grand boulevards with parkways in the center ring the city, connecting the parks of the South and West sides. And the Chicago River, around whose branches cluster the central neighborhoods of the Loop, South Loop, West Loop, and River North, confounds the grid entirely.

For all this tidy structure, Chicago can be quite polarized, with the mostly affluent North Side on one hand and the working-class and sometimes distressed South Side on the other. But of course it's not as simple as all that – not the least because of the overlooked West Side, a once rundown area now seeing a reinvestment boom. At least to the east, things are more constant: to the east is Lake Michigan and Lake Shore Drive (aka US 41), one of the most iconic and beautiful roadways in the world. Take a drive from one end to the other and you'll survey a bit of everything the city has to offer. ❑

**PRECEDING PAGES:** nighttime view; Andy's Jazz Club on Hubbard Street.

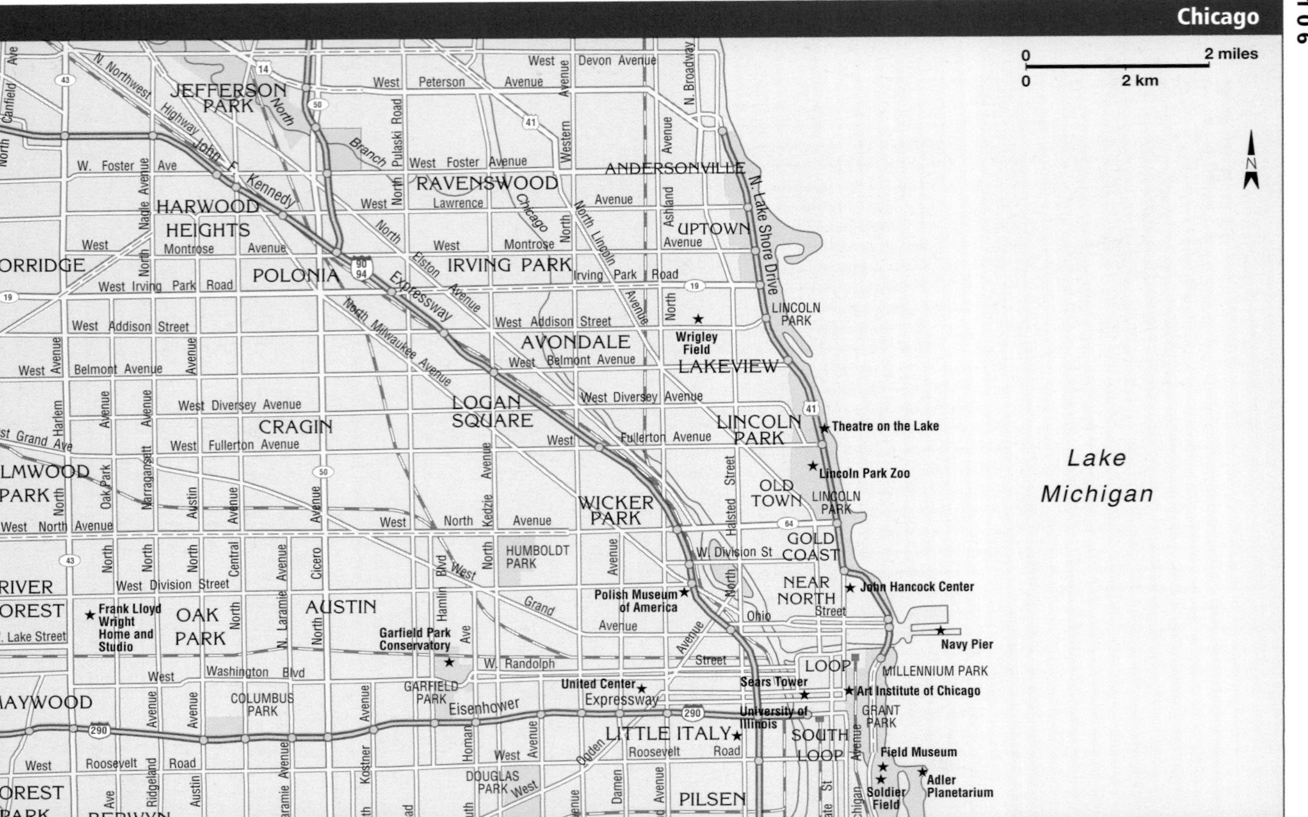
Chicago
0 2 miles
0 2 km
N
Lake
Michigan
N. Lake Shore Drive
Navy Pier
MILLENNIUM PARK
Art Institute of Chicago
GRANT PARK
Field Museum
Adler Planetarium
Soldier Field
John Hancock Center
Lincoln Park Zoo
Theatre on the Lake
Wrigley Field
Sears Tower
United Center
Polish Museum of America
Garfield Park Conservatory
Frank Lloyd Wright Home and Studio
University of Illinois
ANDERSONVILLE
UPTOWN
LINCOLN PARK
LAKEVIEW
OLD TOWN
GOLD COAST
NEAR NORTH
LOOP
SOUTH LOOP
LITTLE ITALY
PILSEN
WICKER PARK
HUMBOLDT PARK
LOGAN SQUARE
AVONDALE
IRVING PARK
RAVENSWOOD
POLONIA
CRAGIN
AUSTIN
GARFIELD PARK
DOUGLAS PARK
COLUMBUS PARK
OAK PARK
JEFFERSON PARK
HARWOOD HEIGHTS
NORRIDGE
ELMWOOD PARK
RIVER FOREST
MAYWOOD
FOREST PARK
BERWYN
N. Broadway
West Devon Avenue
West Peterson Avenue
West Foster Avenue
W. Foster Ave
Lawrence Avenue
West Montrose Avenue
West Irving Park Road
West Addison Street
West Belmont Avenue
West Diversey Avenue
West Fullerton Avenue
West North Avenue
West Division Street
W. Division St
W. Randolph Street
West Washington Blvd
West Roosevelt Road
Eisenhower Expressway
John F. Kennedy Expressway
North Milwaukee Avenue
North Elston Avenue
North Lincoln Avenue
N. Northwest Highway
Grand Avenue
West Grand Ave
Ogden Avenue
North Ashland Avenue
North Halsted Street
North Western Avenue
North Kedzie Avenue
North Pulaski Road
North Cicero Avenue
N. Laramie Avenue
North Central Avenue
North Austin Avenue
North Narragansett Avenue
North Oak Park Avenue
North Harlem Avenue
North Canfield Ave
Nagle Avenue
W. Lake Street
Hamlin Blvd
Homan
Kostner
Damen Avenue
Ridgeland Ave
Ohio Street
State St
Michigan Avenue
Chicago
Branch
North
41
19
50
64
14
43
90
94
290

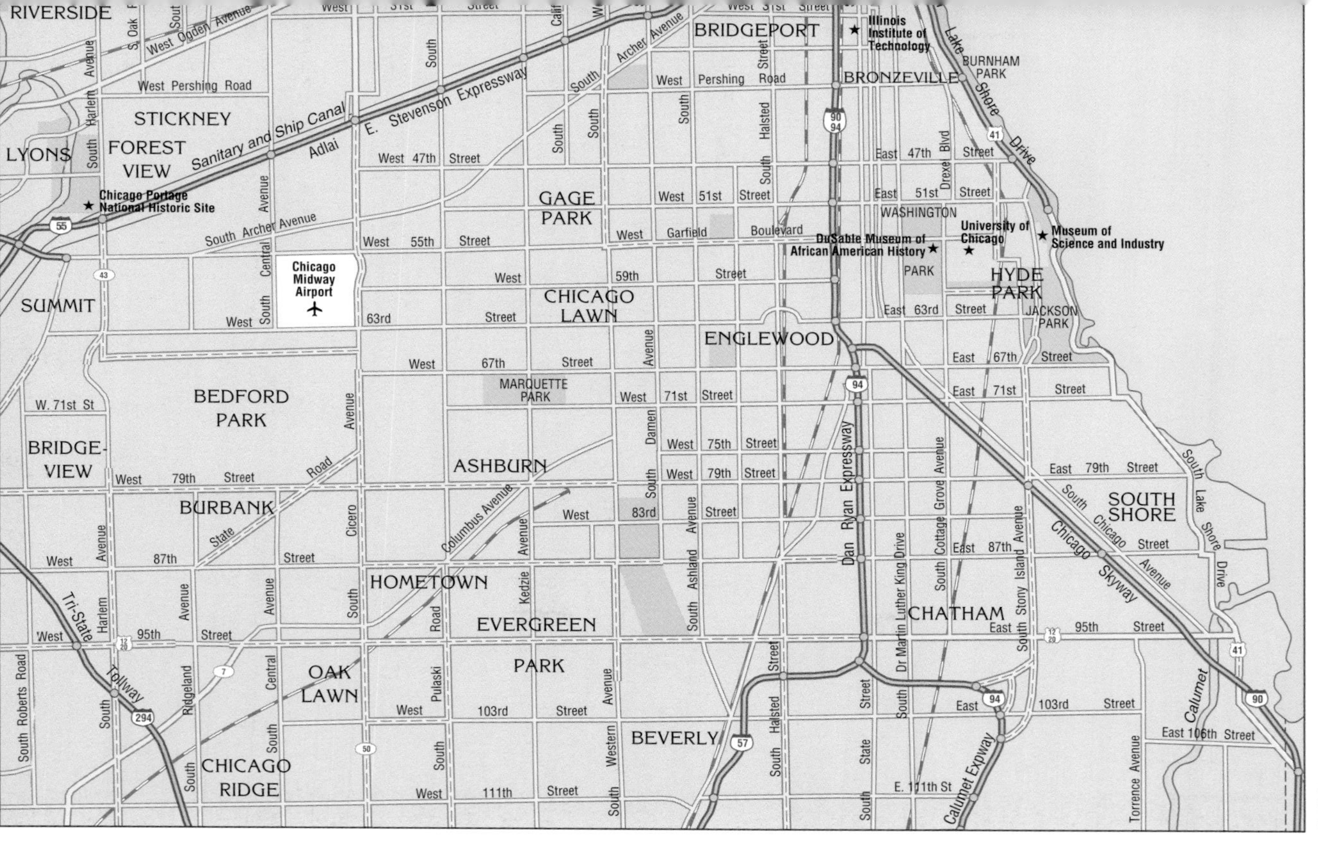
RIVERSIDE
LYONS
STICKNEY
FOREST VIEW
SUMMIT
BRIDGEVIEW
BEDFORD PARK
BURBANK
OAK LAWN
CHICAGO RIDGE
HOMETOWN
EVERGREEN PARK
BEVERLY
ASHBURN
CHICAGO LAWN
GAGE PARK
ENGLEWOOD
BRIDGEPORT
BRONZEVILLE
WASHINGTON PARK
HYDE PARK
JACKSON PARK
BURNHAM PARK
SOUTH SHORE
CHATHAM
MARQUETTE PARK
Chicago Portage National Historic Site
Chicago Midway Airport
Illinois Institute of Technology
DuSable Museum of African American History
University of Chicago
Museum of Science and Industry
Lake Shore Drive
South Lake Shore Drive
Adlai E. Stevenson Expressway
Dan Ryan Expressway
Chicago Skyway
Calumet Expway
Tri-State Tollway
Sanitary and Ship Canal
Calumet
South Chicago Avenue
South Archer Avenue
Archer Avenue
Columbus Avenue
West Pershing Road
Pershing Road
West Ogden Avenue
Garfield Boulevard
South Stony Island Avenue
South Cottage Grove Avenue
South Dr Martin Luther King Drive
South State Street
South Halsted Street
South Ashland Avenue
South Damen Avenue
South Western Avenue
South Kedzie Avenue
South Pulaski Road
South Cicero Avenue
South Central Avenue
South Ridgeland Avenue
South Harlem Avenue
South Roberts Road
Torrence Avenue
Drexel Blvd
West 47th Street
West 55th Street
West 63rd Street
W. 71st St
West 79th Street
87th Street
West 95th Street
West 103rd Street
West 111th Street
East 47th Street
East 51st Street
East 63rd Street
East 67th Street
East 71st Street
East 79th Street
East 87th Street
East 95th Street
East 103rd Street
East 106th Street
E. 111th St
55
94
90
41
57
294
43
50
7

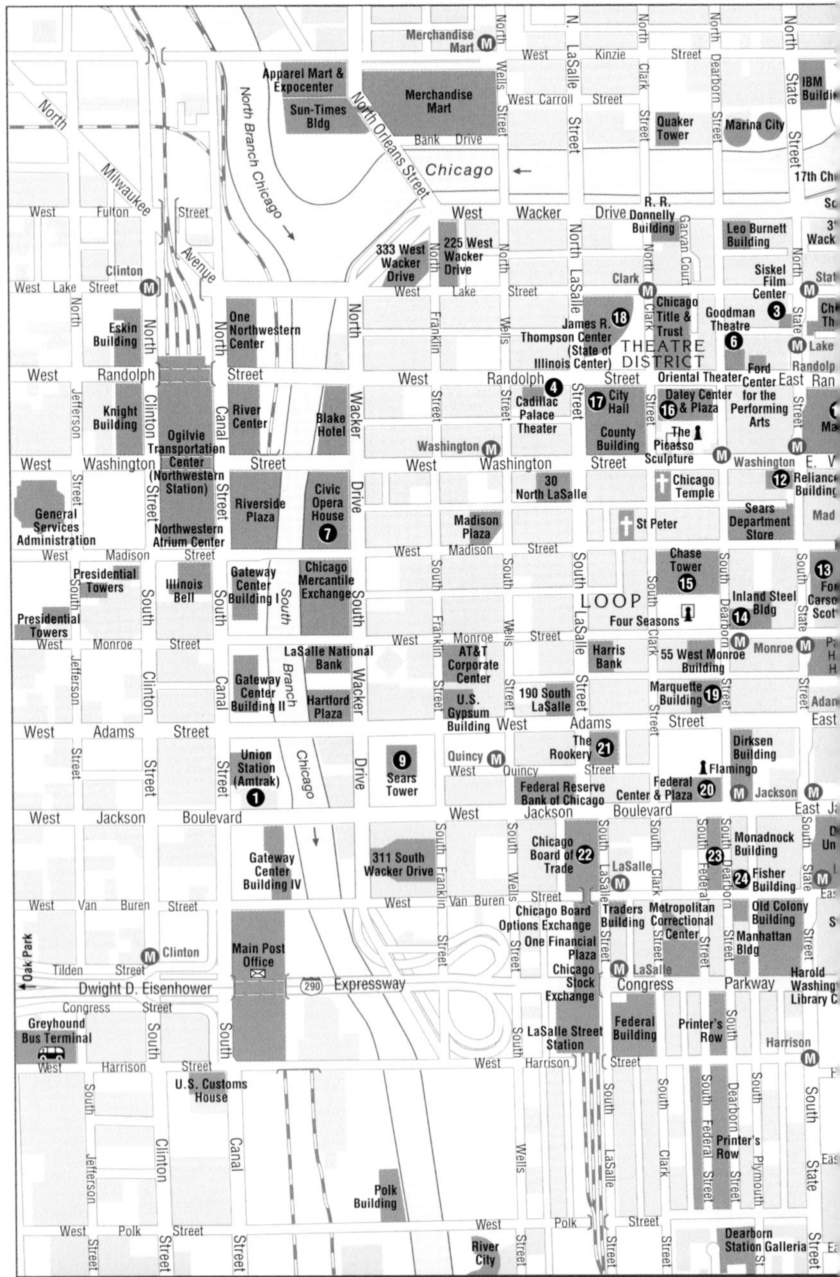

Merchandise Mart
Apparel Mart & Expocenter
Merchandise Mart
Sun-Times Bldg
North Branch Chicago
North Orleans Street
Chicago
West Kinzie Street
West Carroll Street
Bank Drive
Quaker Tower
Marina City
IBM Building
17th Church
North Milwaukee Avenue
West Fulton Street
West Wacker Drive
R. R. Donnelly Building
Leo Burnett Building
333 West Wacker Drive
225 West Wacker Drive
Garvan Court
Clinton
West Lake Street
Clark
Siskel Film Center
Eskin Building
One Northwestern Center
James R. Thompson Center (State of Illinois Center)
Chicago Title & Trust
Goodman Theatre
THEATRE DISTRICT
Lake
West Randolph Street
Oriental Theater
Ford Center for the Performing Arts
Randolph
Knight Building
Ogilvie Transportation Center (Northwestern Station)
River Center
Blake Hotel
Cadillac Palace Theater
City Hall
County Building
Daley Center & Plaza
The Picasso Sculpture
Washington
West Washington Street
General Services Administration
Northwestern Atrium Center
Riverside Plaza
Civic Opera House
Madison Plaza
30 North LaSalle
Chicago Temple
St Peter
Reliance Building
Sears Department Store
West Madison Street
Presidential Towers
Illinois Bell
Gateway Center Building I
Chicago Mercantile Exchange
Chase Tower
LOOP
Four Seasons
Inland Steel Bldg
West Monroe Street
LaSalle National Bank
Gateway Center Building II
Hartford Plaza
AT&T Corporate Center
U.S. Gypsum Building
190 South LaSalle
Harris Bank
55 West Monroe Building
Marquette Building
Monroe
West Adams Street
Union Station (Amtrak)
Sears Tower
Quincy
The Rookery
Federal Reserve Bank of Chicago
Federal Center & Plaza
Dirksen Building
Flamingo
Jackson
West Jackson Boulevard
Gateway Center Building IV
311 South Wacker Drive
Chicago Board of Trade
LaSalle
Monadnock Building
Fisher Building
West Van Buren Street
Chicago Board Options Exchange
One Financial Plaza
Chicago Stock Exchange
Traders Building
Metropolitan Correctional Center
Old Colony Building
Manhattan Bldg
Main Post Office
Clinton
Oak Park
Tilden Street
Dwight D. Eisenhower
290
Expressway
Congress Parkway
Harold Washington Library Center
Greyhound Bus Terminal
LaSalle Street Station
Federal Building
Printer's Row
Harrison
West Harrison Street
U.S. Customs House
Polk Building
Printer's Row
West Polk Street
River City
Dearborn Station Galleria

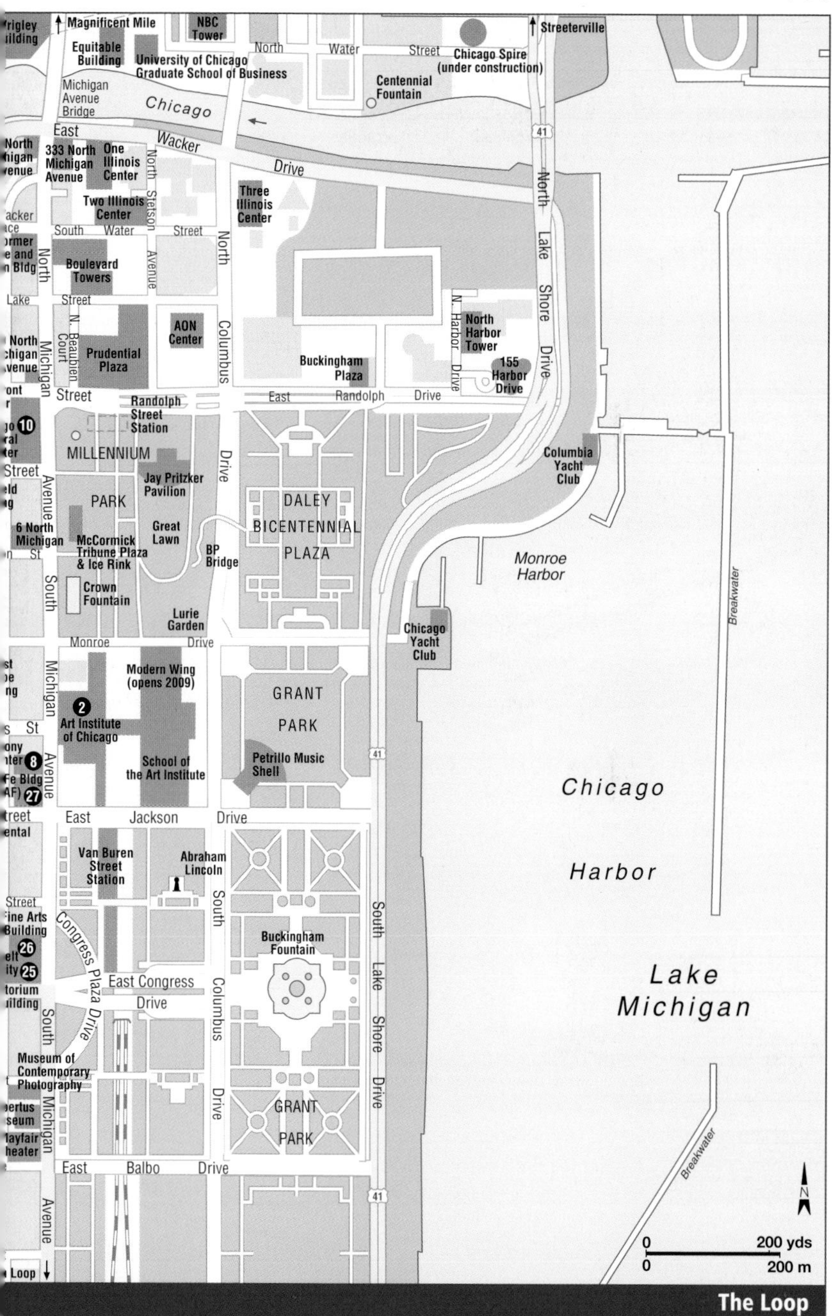
Magnificent Mile
NBC Tower
Equitable Building
University of Chicago Graduate School of Business
North Water Street
Chicago Spire (under construction)
Streeterville
Centennial Fountain
Michigan Avenue Bridge
Chicago
East Wacker Drive
333 North Michigan Avenue
One Illinois Center
Two Illinois Center
Three Illinois Center
North Stetson Avenue
South Water Street
Boulevard Towers
Lake Street
N. Beaubien Court
Prudential Plaza
AON Center
North Columbus Drive
Buckingham Plaza
N. Harbor Drive
North Harbor Tower
155 Harbor Drive
North Lake Shore Drive
East Randolph Drive
Randolph Street Station
MILLENNIUM PARK
Jay Pritzker Pavilion
Great Lawn
McCormick Tribune Plaza & Ice Rink
BP Bridge
DALEY BICENTENNIAL PLAZA
Columbia Yacht Club
Monroe Harbor
Crown Fountain
Lurie Garden
Chicago Yacht Club
Breakwater
6 North Michigan
North Michigan Avenue
South Michigan Avenue
Monroe Drive
Modern Wing (opens 2009)
Art Institute of Chicago
School of the Art Institute
GRANT PARK
Petrillo Music Shell
Chicago Harbor
East Jackson Drive
Van Buren Street Station
Abraham Lincoln
South Columbus Drive
Buckingham Fountain
South Lake Shore Drive
Congress Plaza Drive
East Congress Drive
Lake Michigan
Museum of Contemporary Photography
GRANT PARK
Breakwater
East Balbo Drive
Loop
41
N
0 200 yds
0 200 m

ANNO DOMINI
Free
Evenings
Thursdays
nd Fridays
ART INSTITU
CHICAGO
ART INSTITUTE
CHICAGO

*Recommended Restaurants, Bars & Cafés on pages 128–9*

# THE LOOP

**Encompassing both soaring skyscrapers and ornate palaces of culture, Chicago's legendary Loop is the economic and political heart of the city and a living reminder of its rich architectural legacy**

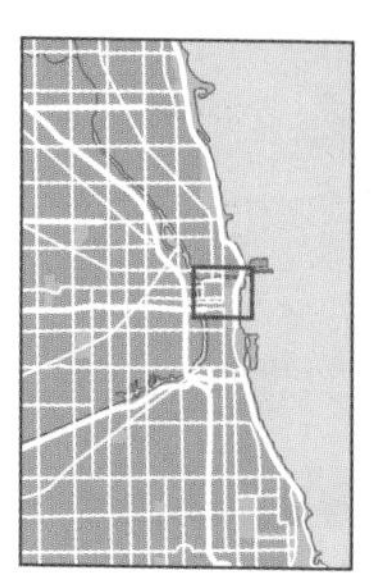

**Main attractions**

- ART INSTITUTE OF CHICAGO
- THEATRE DISTRICT
- SEARS TOWER
- CHICAGO CULTURAL CENTER
- MACY'S
- CARSON PIRIE SCOTT
- CHASE TOWER
- DALEY PLAZA
- CITY HALL
- FINANCIAL DISTRICT
- THE ROOKERY
- CHICAGO BOARD OF TRADE
- AUDITORIUM BUILDING
- MICHIGAN AVENUE
- CHICAGO RIVER

Advertising industry execs and options traders, art students and tourists – all jostle for space on the sidewalks of the Loop. Chicago's central business district is a rich showcase of the city's architectural and cultural history. Bounded by Michigan Avenue to the east, the Chicago River to the north and west, and Congress Parkway to the south, it takes its name from the elevated tracks that ring the central business district and around which CTA trains clatter in, yes, a loop.

Its main north-south arteries are LaSalle, Dearborn and State streets and Michigan Avenue. Ground zero of the street grid is the intersection of State and Madison streets, from which all addresses radiate north, south, east, and west in an orderly way.

Today, a small bronze plaque at the corner of Michigan Avenue and Wacker Drive commemorates the founding of Fort Dearborn on the south bank of the Chicago River in 1803. A swampy frontier outpost, it was demolished in 1812 during what's now known as the Fort Dearborn Massacre but was rebuilt in 1816. For many of the ensuing decades the hub of commercial activity in the growing settlement was Lake Street, just south of the fort, until dry-goods magnate Potter Palmer built the first Palmer House Hotel at State and Monroe in 1871.

## Century of progress

Only 13 days after the Palmer House opened, it was destroyed in the Great Fire of 1871, which virtually leveled all of downtown Chicago. When the smoke cleared, Palmer commissioned architect John

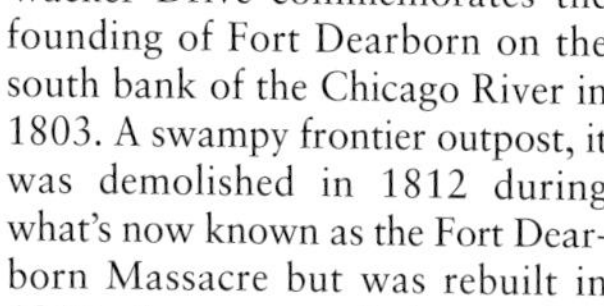

**LEFT:** bronze lions flank the entrance to the Art Institute of Chicago.
**RIGHT:** a shopper finds a colorful bouquet at the Federal Plaza farmers' market.

M. Van Osdel to build what was then the grandest hotel in town, and a host of other architects, engineers, and designers soon followed suit. The building boom that ensued put new ideas about architecture and urban design into practice and paved the way for a period of extraordinary growth and productivity that established Chicago as a major urban center.

## Avant architecture

Over the course of the 20th century, the Loop was the site of one architectural innovation after another, from the country's first skyscrapers and the minimalism of Mies Van der Rohe to the playful postmodern experiments of Helmut Jahn. And while only fragments of Daniel Burnham's sweeping 1909 *Plan of Chicago* were ever implemented, his vision can be seen throughout the Loop – in double-decker Wacker Drive, designed to route truck traffic around the business district and make the waterfront more attractive; in ornate **Union Station** ❶ (225 South Canal Street), intended to secure Chicago's place as the Midwest hub of transportation and shipping; and, most noticeably, in the vast expanse of parkland that separates the skyscrapers from the lakefront, which is maintained, according to his dictum, "Forever open, free and clear."

**ABOVE:** the Theatre District is centered on Randolph and Dearborn streets.
**BELOW:** the grand staircase of the Art Institute of Chicago.

## Power center

The Loop has always been Chicago's seat of finance and government, but it only recently emerged as a cultural and commercial power as well. In the 1970s and 1980s, the streets were desolate concrete canyons after 5pm. Today, thanks to the aggressive efforts of Mayor Richard M. Daley's administration, the Loop is a bustling metropolitan center, with thriving restaurants and shops, hip hotels like the Hard Rock and the W, and a residential population of more than 16,000.

## Art Institute of Chicago ❷

111 South Michigan Avenue 312-443-3600, www.artic.edu/aic
Mon–Wed and Fri 10.30am–4.30pm, Thu 10.30am–8pm, Sat–Sun 10am–5pm charge; free Thu evening

The **Art Institute of Chicago** and its school are the artistic heart of the Loop. While the Institute originally opened as the Chicago Academy of Fine Arts in 1879, the School of the Art Institute was founded much earlier, in 1866, and boasts a roster of world-class alumni, including Grant Wood and Georgia O' Keeffe (who famously didn't graduate).

One of the world's finest art museums, the Art Institute (see pages 130-133 for details) is a repository of more than 30,000 works spanning some 5,000 years. Attempting to see everything in a single visit is a futile and exhausting endeavor. Far

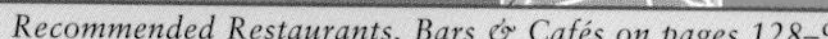

more rewarding is to spend time with a selection of major works, then perhaps choose a few galleries for general perusal.

### Modern Wing

Visitors should note that at the time of this writing a huge expansion was under way that will increase the Institute's capacity by one third. The new Renzo Piano-designed Modern Wing is scheduled to open in 2009. In the interim, many exhibits, including Marc Chagall's vibrant stained glass *America Windows*, are temporarily closed.

## THEATRE DISTRICT

Outside the museum there's plenty to do after dark. The sleek new **Gene Siskel Film Center** ❸ (164 North State Street; tel: 312-846-2800), named for the late co-host of *Siskel and Ebert at the Movies*, books new independent films, foreign imports, and retrospectives of art-house classics. Across the street, the baroque 3,600-seat **Chicago Theatre** – a former movie palace with a soaring five-story lobby and Wurlitzer pipe organ – presents big name acts like Neil Young and Aretha Franklin.

Other restored vintage theaters like the **Cadillac Palace** ❹ (151 West Randolph Street; tel: 312-986-5853) are host to touring Broadway hits, while the **Storefront Theater** ❺ (66 East Randolph Street; tel: 312-742-8497) and new digs for the **Goodman Theatre** ❻ (170 North Dearborn

**TIP**

The Art Institute is host to a lively schedule of lectures, readings, symposia, film screenings, and performances in which actors relate the stories of notable artists and their work.

**LEFT:** Halloween parade on State Street. **BELOW:** a brass band marches past the iconic Chicago Theatre on State Street during the Thanksgiving parade.

Film series at the Gene Siskel Film Center (164 N. State St) focus on various genres, time periods, ethnic groups, and countries, including, in recent years, the Chicago Palestine Film Festival, Asian American Showcase, African-American Auteurs, Hong Kong Film Festival, and more.

**ABOVE:** the landmark clock at Marshall Field's, now Macy's.

Street; tel: 312-443-3800) and **Joffrey Ballet** (70 East Lake Street; tel: 312-739-0120) ensure that the city's homegrown talent has downtown performance space.

For the highbrow, the **Civic Opera House** ❼ (20 North Wacker Drive; tel: 312-419-0033) is home to the sumptuous **Lyric Opera of Chicago**. A masterful 1929 hybrid of Art Nouveau and Deco design, it sits like a throne on the east bank of the Chicago River and is considered one of the most beautiful opera houses in the world.

On the east side of the Loop the internationally acclaimed **Chicago Symphony Orchestra** is in residence nine months of the year at the acoustically stunning **Orchestra Hall** in **Symphony Center** ❽ (220 South Michigan Avenue; tel: 312-294-3333). In summer all this culture spills outdoors, with **Millennium Park** and **Grant Park**, the city's collective "front yard," hosting a myriad of festivals and events, from the crowd-pleasing **Chicago Blues Festival** in June through the wildly diverse **World Music Festival** in September.

## The First Lady

The 1871 marriage of entrepreneur Potter Palmer and socialite Bertha Honoré united two of the most influential Chicago families of the day. Aggressive and visionary, Palmer was single-handedly responsible for developing State Street into the city's principal retail thoroughfare. In 1852, he opened the dry-goods store that became Marshall Field's.

Bertha used her wealth and standing to advance several pet causes. She was an advocate of women's rights and was determined to bolster Chicago's cultural cachet. An astute art collector, Bertha filled her picture gallery with the works of Monet, Renoir, and Cezanne well before they were in fashion in the US. By donating her private collection to the Art Institute, she created the largest body of Impressionist works outside of Paris.

Bertha's taste for the good life wasn't lost on Palmer, who bequeathed a large sum of money to Bertha's future husband, famously stating, "He'll need it."

## Sears Tower ❾

✉ 233 South Wacker Drive ☎ 312-875-96960, www.theskydeck.com ⏲ daily May–Sep 10am–10pm, Oct–Apr 10am–8pm ⓢ charge for Skydeck

Looming above it all is the vertiginous **Sears Tower**. Designed by the firm of Skidmore, Owings & Merrill, it was unveiled in 1973, just three years after construction began. Draped in black aluminum and glistening with bronze-tinted glass, its sleek profile dominates the skyline from just about every vantage point. The **Skydeck** provides exhilarating views of the city and a range of interactive child-friendly exhibits documenting Chicago's history and architectural landmarks.

On a clear day you can see four states: Michigan, Indiana, Wisconsin, and Illinois.

### Race to the top

At 1,454 ft tall (443 meters) and a dizzying 110 stories, the Sears Tower was the world's tallest building until 1996, when it was surpassed by the antennae of Malaysia's Petronas Towers, and is an iconic manifestation of the city's relentless drive to do things bigger and better than anyone else. But, in that very spirit, the

*Recommended Restaurants, Bars & Cafés on pages 128–9*

building that defines Chicago will itself soon play second fiddle to a newcomer. The city that gave birth to the skyscraper is set to become home to the tallest building in the US (and the tallest all-residential building in the world) – Santiago Calatrava's **Chicago Spire**, rising to an expected 2,000 ft (610 meters) at 400 North Lake Shore Drive.

## Chicago Cultural Center ⑩

78 East Washington Street 312-346-3278, www.cityofchicago.org
Mon–Thu 8am–7pm, Fri 8am–6pm, Sat 9am–6pm, Sun 10am–6pm free

The ideal place to start a walking tour of the Loop is the stately **Chicago Cultural Center**, home to the **Chicago Visitor Center**, which provides an abundance of information and maps. Each year, the Cultural Center hosts thousands of free events, ranging from jazz concerts to modern art exhibitions and movie screenings.

This Neoclassical building was constructed in 1897 as Chicago's first public library to house the huge inventory of books sent by Queen Victoria, who was apparently concerned about Chicago's cultural literacy following the Great Fire. The muscular granite and limestone exterior, with 3-ft-thick (3-meter), load-

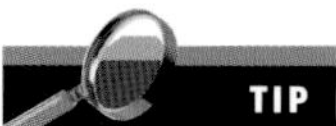


Take a tuneful break from touring at the Chicago Cultural Center, which offers free lunchtime concerts weekdays at 12.15pm as well as a Sunday Salon series.

**LEFT:** Sears Tower.
**BELOW:** runners pass through the Loop during the Chicago Marathon.

*The Atwood Café is named after Charles Atwood, one of the architects responsible for the landmark Reliance Building.*

bearing walls, defied the Chicago School style then gaining in popularity. The bronze-framed doors of the Washington Street entrance are reminiscent of a Roman gateway. Ionic columns and a Romanesque portal lead to a vestibule dominated by a Carrera marble staircase, inlaid with mother-of-pearl mosaics and green marble medallions. The stairs lead in turn to **Preston Bradley Hall**, where the world's largest Tiffany dome, spanning some 38 ft (12 meters), is the Cultural Center's crowning glory. Free, hourlong tours of the building (tel: 312-744-6630; Wed, Fri, Sat at 1.15pm) meet in the Randolph Street lobby; self-guided tour leaflets are available in the Visitor Center.

## Retail temple

Two blocks west of the Cultural Center is **Macy's** ⓫ (111 North State Street; tel: 312-781-1000, www.visitmacyschicago.com; Mon–Thu 10am–8pm, Fri–Sat 10am–9pm, Sun 11am–6pm), formerly Marshall Field's, one of the world's most celebrated department stores. When Marshall Field immortalized the slogan "Give the lady what she wants," he established a Chicago institution with a cult following, and while today it may be Macy's in name (following a 2006 buyout by Federated Department Stores), it remains Field's in spirit. On the first anniversary of the Macy's takeover, scores of activists staged a protest under the store's iconic clocks, mourning the loss of Frango mints, Christmas in

**ABOVE:** the domed mosaic Tiffany ceiling at Macy's, formerly Marshall Field's. **RIGHT:** the grand atrium at Macy's.

the Walnut Room, and other hallowed Field's traditions.

Inside it's a shopping mecca with 13 stories of men's and women's apparel, three floors of home furnishings and interior design, a bridal salon, children's clothing and toys, cosmetics, jewelry, and an upscale food court on the seventh floor. Even if you're not in a shopping mood, the store is worth visiting for a look at the glorious Louis Tiffany ceiling composed of 1.6 million pieces of rare Favrile iridescent glass. The ceiling was completed in 1907 and crowns the southern section's five-story atrium.

## A landmark reborn

Across the street, on the corner of State and Washington, is the **Reliance Building** ⓬. Designed by Daniel Burnham, John Root, and Charles Atwood in 1891 and completed in 1895, it's a precursor of the modern skyscraper and regarded as a paradigm of the Chicago School.

The Reliance was the first building to be supported by an interior iron and steel frame and the first to feature a tripartite "Chicago window" – a large fixed center pane flanked by two smaller double-hung sash windows. With "curtain walls" stretched like skin over the steel skeleton, the building was the direct forerunner of the modernist works of Mies van der Rohe.

After a century of neglect, the Reliance was granted landmark status in the 1970s and restored to its former glory in the 1990s. The exterior granite base was replaced with terra-cotta and limestone, and the interior was faithfully reconstructed with mosaic-tiled floors, marble ceilings, and an ornate iron filigree elevator shaft. It's now home to the Kimpton Group's boutique **Hotel Burnham** (1 West Washington Street; tel: 312-782-1111). If you can't afford a room, stop in for afternoon tea in the hotel's **Atwood Café** (winter only).

## Carson Pirie Scott & Company ⓭

Walk south on State Street, past trendy mass-market retailers like H&M, to Madison Street, where the former **Carson Pirie Scott & Company** department store (1 South State Street; tel: 312-641-7000) is quintessential Louis Sullivan. Completed in 1899, it was Sullivan's last tall building, an arresting vision of extravagant ornamentation and modular structure.

Practical considerations reigned supreme in the architect's vision, not surprising given that it was Sullivan who coined the phrase "form follows function," the mantra of modernists such as Le Corbusier and Mies van der Rohe half a century later. The abundance of organic motifs – interlacing berries, vines, flowers, and geometric symbols that seem to writhe across the building's

**ABOVE:** loyal shoppers protest the conversion of Marshall Field's to Macy's.

**BELOW:** the ornate entrance to the Carson Pirie Scott department store designed by renowned architect Louis Sullivan.

*The plaza at Chase Tower is a pleasant place to take a break from touring.*

**ABOVE:** *The Four Seasons* by Marc Chagall. **BELOW RIGHT:** Chase Tower.

facade – were intended to attract female clientele with money in their purses. The sweeping horizontal sheaths of glass, other fine examples of Chicago windows framed by cast-iron plates, were intended to provide a showcase for the store's merchandise.

Sullivan invited entry from every angle by positioning the arched entrance so that it can be seen from both Madison and State streets. Not known for his modesty, the architect worked his initials into the tracery above the main entrance. The department store closed in February 2007 and the building is currently empty; plans for redevelopment remain open.

## Inland Steel and Chase Tower

One block west, the **Inland Steel Building** ⓮ (30 West Monroe Street) was the first tall structure to be constructed in the Loop after the Great Depression and is notable for pioneering the use of steel pilings and external columns, which maximizes interior space. It was also the first office building to have air conditioning and underground parking.

At the center of the Loop stands the elegantly curved **Chase Tower** ⓯ (10 South Dearborn Street), at 60 stories the seventh-tallest building in town and a foil to the stark, angular geometry of the surrounding structures. The popular public radio quiz show *Wait, Wait ... Don't Tell Me!* tapes Thursdays in the building's **Chase Auditorium**; see www.npr.org/programs/waitwait for ticket information. A sunken plaza at the foot of the structure is dominated by Marc Cha-

### Rage Against the Machine

On Labor Day weekend, 1979, you could be forgiven for thinking that Chicago was a city under siege. Over 200 national guardsmen, three Sherman tanks, three helicopters, several fire trucks, and a SWAT team converged on Daley Plaza to film the climactic scene of the *Blues Brothers*, in which hundreds of police officers and soldiers attempt to capture Jake and Elwood Blues, played by Second City alumni John Belushi and Dan Aykroyd. Costing a record $3.2 million, it was the most expensive movie scene ever filmed in a major metropolis. Anticipating fervent opposition from newly elected Mayor Jane Byrne to their audacious plan to drive a car through the glass facade of Daley Plaza, Belushi and Aykroyd offered to donate $50,000 to charity. For Byrne, however, the timing couldn't have been better. She regarded the scene as a symbol of her pledge to smash the political machine that had dominated city government for years.

*Recommended Restaurants, Bars & Cafés on pages 128–9*

gall's huge, gorgeous mosaic ***The Four Seasons***, and on a nice day it's a great spot for lunch outdoors.

## Daley Plaza ⓰

Two blocks north on Dearborn Street is the imposing **Daley Center and Plaza**, designed by C.F Murphy Associates to house the Circuit Court of Cook County in 1965. Monumental in scale, it occupies an entire block, bounded by Washington, Randolph, Dearborn, and Clark streets. The structure's Miesian attributes are evident (the building's chief designer studied under Mies van der Rohe) in the expansive horizontal spans between each column.

The building's judicial vocation called for spacious courtrooms and soaring ceilings unimpeded by columns that would, at the same time, evoke the grandiosity of a classical structure. Daley Plaza is host to festivals, concerts, and a weekly farmers' market in summer but is most famously the site of the untitled Picasso sculpture that evoked both praise and scorn when it was installed in 1967.

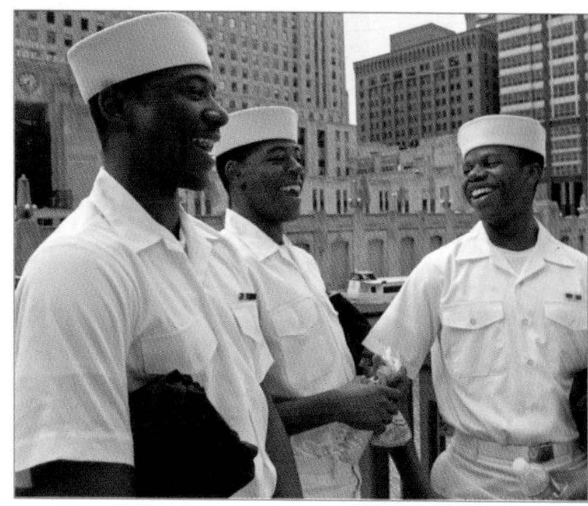

### Picasso and politics

In 1963, Chicago architect William Hartmann traveled to the French Riviera to invite Picasso to produce a maquette for a sculpture that would adorn the plaza. To everyone's surprise, the artist agreed and, refusing the $100,000 fee, produced a scaled-down model (now in the collection of the Art Institute) as a gift to the people of Chicago. The 50-ft-tall (15-meter), 162-ton steel sculpture was produced

**ABOVE:** sailors on shore leave take in the sights.
**BELOW:** the Loop encompasses some of the country's most historic high-rise architecture.

*The roof of City Hall is a testament to Mayor Daley's vision of the city as a leader in green technology. In 2001 a 38,000-sq-ft (3,500-sq-meter) "green roof" was installed – at a cost of $1.5 million – to test the effects of vegetation on temperature regulation and air quality. The roof is planted with native prairie grasses and has beehives and a rainwater collection system.*

**ABOVE:** stained-glass windows at the Chicago Temple Building recount episodes in the city's history. **BELOW:** a cyclist pedals through downtown traffic.

in Gary, Indiana, and unveiled amid a storm of controversy as Chicagoans struggled to relate to the ambiguous form, which has been subsequently described as everything from a woman's head to a bird to Picasso's Afghan hound.

### Nearer my God to Thee

Across Washington Street is the **Chicago Temple Building**, a 1924 skyscraper topped with an eight-story spire. Occupied by the United Methodist Church, the building has a Gothic sanctuary on the ground floor and a smaller **Sky Chapel** in the spire, said to be the world's highest church.

## CITY HALL ⑰

On the next block, Chicago's **City Hall** (121 North LaSalle Street) shares a building with the administrative offices of Cook County. Inside the Classical Revival structure designed by seminal Chicago architects Holabird and Roche, you'll find the

Map on pages 108–9



*Recommended Restaurants, Bars & Cafés on pages 128–9*

offices of the mayor and city clerk, as well as the city's 50 aldermen and various city departments. City Council sessions are free and open to the public if you're interested in seeing how the "city that works" *really* works. Check the city's web site at www.cityofchicago.org for a schedule of meetings and rules for admission.

## Postmodern puzzle

Perhaps no other building symbolizes the excesses of the 1980s like the **James R. Thompson Center** ⓲ (100 West Randolph Street), just north of City Hall. Loved and loathed in equal measure, the postmodern pink and blue UFO or slice of wedding cake, depending on your perspective, was constructed in 1985 by Helmut Jahn, who was commissioned by Thompson, the former Illinois governor, to construct a government building. The 17-story glass facade makes irregular heating and cooling a source of constant frustration for the office workers disgorged into the complex via the subterranean blue line stop.

Still, dazzling or dissonant, the elevators and stairs that cantilever into the atrium are one of the most striking architectural features in the city. Jean Dubuffet's abstract, black-and-white *Monument With Standing Beast* dominates the plaza at the northwest corner of Randolph and Clark streets.

## Chicago School landmark

On the south end of the Loop, the **Marquette Building** ⓳ (140 South Dearborn Street) was designed by Holabird and Roche in 1895. With its terra-cotta exterior, wide horizontal windows, and skeleton steel frame, it

*Cook County shares a grand Neo-classical building with City Hall.*

**LEFT:** *Monument with Standing Beast* by Jean Dubuffet.
**BELOW:** the Loop is named for the elevated train tracks that surround the area.

*Designed by Burnham and Root, the Rookery was the world's tallest building when it was completed in 1888. The interior was later renovated by Frank Lloyd Wright.*

**ABOVE CENTER:** the Chicago Board of Trade is the world's oldest futures and options exchange. **BELOW:** traders at work at the Board of Trade.

is an archetype of Chicago School design. The lavish interior conforms more to classical style than modernism. The two-story rotunda lobby is adorned with magnificent Tiffany mosaics that evoke the life of French explorer Jacques Marquette, who roamed through Illinois in 1674-75.

## FEDERAL CENTER ⑳

Dramatically juxtaposed to the Marquette building, the **Federal Center and Plaza** (219 South Dearborn Street) is a potent symbol of Chicago's transition from the Chicago School to Modernism. The tripartite group, composed of the Dirksen federal court-house on the east side of the street and the 45-story Kluczynski civic office building and a post office on the west, exemplifies the clean, taut lines of the Miesian aesthetic.

Mies van der Rohe's impact upon the urban landscape during the post-war period cannot be understated. He defined the precepts of International Modernism and the concept that "less is more." Mies's perfectionism was renowned – he was reputed to have entered trancelike states as he

contemplated his architectural models. Here the geometrical precision, fluid interior space, and purity of form are characteristic of Mies's discipline; note how the grid lines of the plaza are aligned to the columns. Not surprisingly, owing to the architect's exacting vision, the building took some 15 years to complete and was blighted by budgetary overruns.

The plaza's centerpiece is a 53-ft-tall (16-meter), scarlet, steel stabile by sculptor Alexander Calder. Titled ***Flamingo***, the work's swirling form and vivid color is a startling contrast to the brooding sobriety of the plaza.

## FINANCIAL DISTRICT

One block west of the plaza, the **Rookery Building** ㉑ (209 South LaSalle Street), built in 1885, is a captivating presence in the middle of the LaSalle Street financial canyon. The building took its name from the temporary city hall, located on this spot between 1872 and 1884, which was given the moniker of the Rookery as it was a preferred landing post for the Loop's pigeon population.

With its extravagant design, fluid space, and prodigious ornamentation, no other building quite immortalizes the talents of Burnham and Root. Advancing the concept of the skeleton frame, the architects envisioned a light-filled atrium supported by steel frames around which shops and offices would be harmoniously centered. The muscular exterior is composed of red granite, load-bearing walls framed by graceful columns. The interior, renovated by Frank Lloyd Wright in 1907, invites superlatives. A cantilevered stairway adorned with ornate iron tracery complements the elaborate glass and iron filigree of the domed skylight. Improbably white marble, inlaid with geometric gold leaf designs, glitters in the lobby and atrium.

## BOARD OF TRADE ㉒

The frenetic energy of the city's financial district is reflected in the sublime **Chicago Board of Trade** building (141 West Jackson Boulevard; tel: 312-435-3590), a goose-bump-inducing exemple of Art Deco style designed by Holabird and Root in 1930. Home to the oldest futures and options exchange in the country, the building spews forth hordes of garishly jacketed traders at lunch.

**TIP**

The J. Ira and Nikki Harris Family Hostel (24 E. Congress Prkwy; tel: 312-360-0300; www.hichicago.org) is an affordable option for alternative lodging in the Loop. Spacious and clean, with 500 beds, laundry, wi-fi, and a community kitchen, it was voted "best large hostel in the world" by hostelworld.com in 2006. Rates start at $27 a night for a dorm bed with shared bath.

**BELOW:** enjoying a smoke at a cigar store in the Chicago Board of Trade Building.

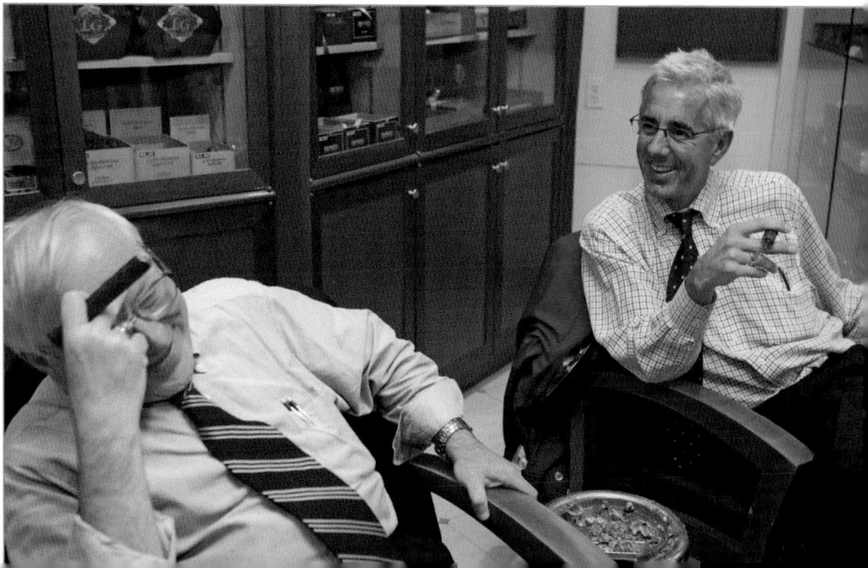

Behind the recessed entrance is a 45-story tower, crowned by an aluminum statue of Ceres, the goddess of grain.

## Toward the lake

The **Monadnock Building** ㉓ (53 West Jackson Boulevard) was constructed in two stages: Burnham and Root completed the northern portion in 1891; Holabird and Roche designed the southern addition in 1893. When completed, the naked slab of the northern section was the city's largest office building, standing 197 ft (60 meters) high and supported only by 6-ft-thick (2-meter) load-bearing walls. For John Wellborn Root, who believed that a building should be a fusion of rich ornamentation and powerful functionalism, the austere design of the Monadnock was anathema, and the building's final "I" shape – an unadorned tower that curves outward at the base and at the cornice – sprang from his disdain.

Despite its lack of wind bracing, the Monadnock stood firm against a violent storm that struck Chicago several years after its completion. As wind gusts reached 88 miles per hour (142 kmh), engineers converged on the building and swung a plumb bob from the top floor through the stairwell, which revealed that the Monadnock barely vibrated in the storm.

**ABOVE:** an ornate cast-iron staircase leads to the top of the Rookery. **BELOW:** actors play the part of 1930s paparazzi during a special event at the Auditorium Building.

## SOUTH DEARBORN STREET

A block south, the 275-ft (84-meter) **Fisher Building** ㉔ (343 South Dearborn Street) is more reminiscent of a gothic cathedral than a modern high-rise. Completed in 1896 by Burnham and Co., it is distinguished from its restrained Chicago School peers by a medley of mythological ornamentation. Eagles and other beasts lurk on the upper stories and marine creatures writhe on the lower stories – evidently a play on the surname of owner Lucius Fisher.

Across the street, in the shadow of the El, is the **Old Colony Building** (407 South Dearborn Street). Revolutionary in many respects, the 210-ft-tall (64-meter) building was one of the first office spaces to feature oriel windows (rounded corner windows that increase light and ventilation). The lobby is a vision of Italian marble and oak woodwork with ornate crests.

Just south, the **Manhattan Building** (431 South Dearborn Street) is the seminal work of William le Baron Jenney, the "father of the steel skyscraper" and the earliest surviving building in the world with an inte-

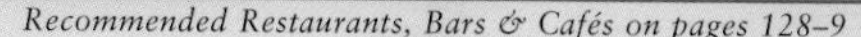

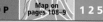

*Recommended Restaurants, Bars & Cafés on pages 128–9*

rior steel frame throughout. One of the Manhattan's most striking features is the assortment of windows, including bow windows and paired windows, as well as large undivided sheaths of flush glass. The building's location, squat on a narrow, built-up street, necessitated a window scheme that would permit maximum natural light.

## Auditorium Building ㉕

One block south and two blocks east, at the corner of Michigan Avenue and Congress Parkway, is Adler and Sullivan's awe-inspiring **Auditorium Building** (50 East Congress Parkway; tel: 312-431-2389, www.auditoriumtheatre.org; tours Mon 10am and 1pm; charge). Constructed in 1889, the theater is a spectacular fusion of Adler's engineering expertise and Sullivan's architectural vision; critics frothed with joy over its state-of-the-art acoustics and sumptuous ornamentation. Frank Lloyd Wright, notoriously restrained in praise of his peers, described it as "the greatest room for music and opera in the world – bar none."

The magnificent granite and limestone building boasts an opulent lobby adorned with gold leaf mosaics and floors of inlaid tesserae marble. Sadly, even the commercial space, occupied by a hotel and offices, could not support such extravagance, and less than a decade after its completion the 4,300-seat Auditorium Building was deemed a fantastic failure.

After the Depression, the theater closed and fell into disrepair, but the building was given a lifeline in 1946 when it was purchased by Roosevelt University. Roosevelt began a campaign to raise money for its restoration and in 1967, after an extensive renovation, it reopened with a sell-out performance by the New York City Ballet. Now home to the Joffrey Ballet, it's a sumptuous, busy venue for dance, music, and touring Broadway musicals.

## Michigan Avenue

Turn the corner and you're back on Michigan Avenue. This entire stretch, from the Auditorium north to the

**Above:** fresh, local produce is sold at the Federal Plaza farmers' market. **Below:** the Auditorium Building by Sullivan and Adler is regarded as a masterpiece of the Chicago School.

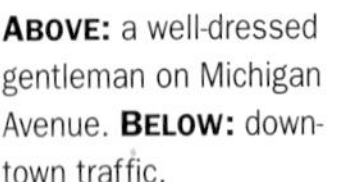


One of the most enjoyable ways to learn more about the Loop and its architecture is to take the Chicago Architecture Foundation's Historic Skyscraper walking tour. Contact the Foundation for the schedule of upcoming tours (tel: 312-922-3432; www.architecture.org).

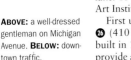

**ABOVE:** a well-dressed gentleman on Michigan Avenue. **BELOW:** downtown traffic.

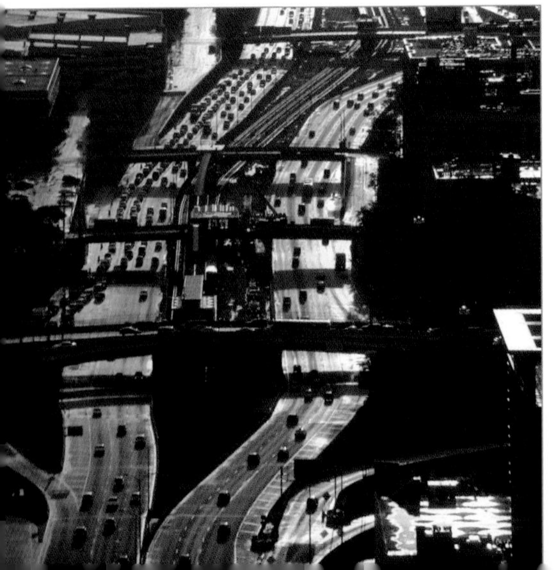

Cultural Center is known to architecture buffs as the **Michigan Avenue "cliff"** – a contiguous wall of buildings that's particularly stunning in the morning, as the sun rises over the lake. To the east are Grant Park, the Art Institute, and Millennium Park.

First up is the **Fine Arts Building** ㉖ (410 South Michigan Avenue), built in 1895 by Solon S. Beman to provide a showroom for Studebaker Carriages. Following a renovation in 1898, the building was transformed into studio space for writers, painters, and musicians; former tenants include Frank Lloyd Wright. Take the manually operated elevator upstairs and the sounds of classical piano and violin mingle with singers practicing arias and guitar students stumbling through the chords to *Let It Be*, nicely embodying the inscription over the entranceway: "All Passes – Art Alone Endures." The **FAB Gallery** (Suite 433; tel: 312-913-0537) is one of several galleries in the building that features the work of local artists.

## Friends of architecture

At the beginning of the 20th century, the 17-story **Santa Fe Building** ㉗ (224 South Michigan Avenue) housed the Railway Exchange, a symbol of Chicago's pivotal position at the crossroads of the nation's railroad network. The Santa Fe Railroad Company had its offices here and erected the sign that has become an iconic reference point. It's now home to the **Chicago Architecture Foundation** (tel 312-922-3432; www.architecture.org), an appropriate use for the building where Daniel Burnham devised his famous *Plan of Chicago*.

The Foundation's galleries present changing exhibits on the city's rich architectural past, present, and future. Step into the **Archicenter** shop for information on the vast array of educational offerings. Knowledgeable docents lead multiple tours daily – from Loop walks organized by theme (Downtown Deco, Louis Sullivan: Lost and Found, among many others) to neighborhood bus tours and the popular Chicago River architecture cruise. There's even a downtown "happy hour" tour that ends with a free drink at a local restaurant, which, after all that walking, you will surely be ready for. ❑

*Recommended Restaurants, Bars & Cafés on pages 128–9*

## The Chicago River

**The waters of this hard-working river connect Chicago to the lake and Chicagoans to their city's history**

When, in 1816, Potawatomi Indians ceded to the United States a swath of land around the mouth of a sluggish, shallow waterway, a city was born. Without the Chicago River, there would have been no reason to settle on this marshy, mosquito-ridden turf. Running from Lake Michigan through the heart of downtown before branching north and south, the whole system is more than 150 miles long (240 km). With the 1848 completion of the Illinois and Michigan Canal linking it to the Des Plaines River, the Mississippi, and, by extension, the Gulf of Mexico, it was a critical factor in establishing Chicago as the shipping and transportation hub of the Midwest.

In the late 19th century, the river was essentially an open sewer; industrial and human waste flowed downriver into the lake, poisoning the city's water and triggering waves of cholera and typhoid that led to hundreds of deaths. The 1900 construction of the Sanitary and Ship Canal reversed the flow of the river and protected the water supply from disease – an unprecedented feat of engineering that's celebrated daily in summer when Centennial Fountain, at the river's mouth, unleashes an arc of water across the channel for ten minutes every hour.

But a scant 15 years after this triumph, the river was the site of one of the city's greatest tragedies, when the *S.S. Eastland*, loaded with 2,500 Western Electric workers bound for a picnic at the Indiana dunes, capsized while moored at the dock. All told, 812 people – including many families – drowned or were crushed to death; a plaque at the Wacker Drive and LaSalle Street bridge marks the spot where the disaster occurred.

Today the river is no longer a shipping thoroughfare, but more than 50,000 commercial and recreational boats still travel its waters annually. In spring, as thousands of pleasure craft head to the lake, the Loop's bascule bridges rise and fall in graceful concert. Canoeists paddle the tree-lined channels of the North Side (rent your own at Chicago River Canoe and Kayak; tel: 773-252-3307). Tour boats offer a perspective on downtown architecture. And, of course, the river is famously dyed green every Saint Patrick's Day.

Best of all, the river is a lot cleaner than it was 20 years ago, thanks to conservation groups like Friends of the Chicago River. More than 60 fish species – not to mention ducks, geese, beavers, turtles, snakes, and frogs – call it home. Look just west of the Michigan Avenue bridge and you'll see a "fish hotel" moored to the bank, installed in 2005 to provide newcomers a refuge from the waterway's never ceasing activity. ❑

**ABOVE AND RIGHT:** tour boats cruise the scenic Chicago River.

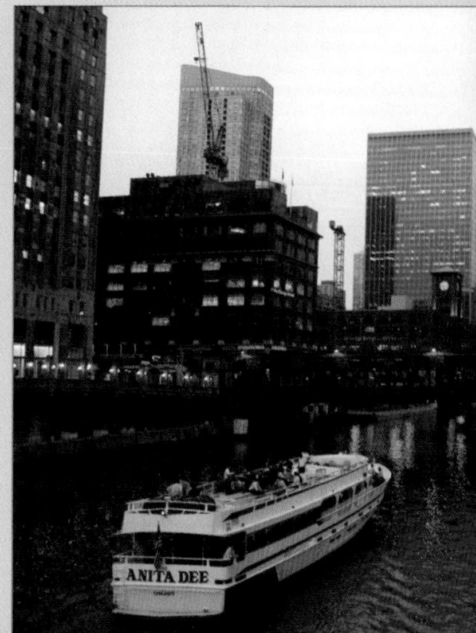

# BEST RESTAURANTS, BARS AND CAFÉS

## Restaurants

Prices for a three-course dinner per person with a half-bottle of house wine:
**$** = under $20
**$$** = $20–$45
**$$$** = $45–$60
**$$$$** = over $60

### 17 West at the Berghoff

17 W. Adams St 312-427-3170 L & D Mon–Sat **$$$** [p307, C2]
The late, lamented Berghoff restaurant – the first spot in town to get a liquor license following Prohibition – closed in 2006 after 107 years in business, but its awkwardly named replacement has done a lot to preserve the historic charm of the space. The food gets mixed reviews, but many beloved German standards are still on the menu, including Wiener schnitzel, creamed spinach, and Black Forest cake.

### Atwood Café

1 W. Washington St 312-368-1900 B, L & D Daily **$$$** [p306, C2]
Expect contemporary American comfort food in a dramatic dining room off the baroque lobby of the Hotel Burnham. In winter a full afternoon tea service is also offered.

### Bombon Café

170 W. Washington St 312-781-2788 B & L Mon–Sat, D Mon–Fri **$** [p306, C1]
The Loop outpost of this Pilsen-based mini-chain is a fun, reliable, affordable stop for savory *tortas*. Try the Yucateca, a tantalizing blend of pork stew with *achiote*, pickled red onions, habañero chiles, avocado, cheese, and black bean spread. Leave room for the extravagant Mexican pastries.

### Catch 35

35 W. Wacker Dr 312-346-3500 L Mon–Fri, D daily **$$$$** [p306, C1]
Offered as 35 daily specials, the fresh fish at this upscale seafood restaurant is as spot-on as ever, though the decor – complete with revolving piano bar – could use a face-lift. Located in the Leo Burnett building, it's a popular after-work stop for ad execs and other industry types.

### China Grill

230 N. Michigan Ave 312-334-6700 B, L & D daily **$$$** [p306, C1]
The setting, inside the Art Deco Carbide and Carbon Building, is part of the attraction of this high-energy Hard Rock Hotel dining room. Expect expertly prepared, if pricey, Asian fusion plates like Shanghai lobster with curry, ginger, and crispy spinach. The adjacent Base bar is a fun, swank spot for a nightcap.

### Everest

440 S. LaSalle St 312-663-8920 D Tue–Sat **$$$$** [p306, C2]
An internationally acclaimed temple of fine dining, Everest floats 40 floors above the Loop atop the Chicago Stock Exchange building. Under the direction of Chef Jean Joho, the menu showcases Alsatian-influenced French classics

**LEFT:** 17 West at the Berghoff.
**RIGHT:** Chef Jean Joho of Everest creates French classics high atop the Chicago Stock Exchange.

and a stupendous wine list in an elegant, romantic setting with views that can't be beat.

### Giordano's

310 W. Randolph St 312-201-1441 L & D daily $ [p306, B1]
Sure it's touristy but – why deny it? – you're a tourist. If you want to sample Chicago deep-dish pizza, this place is as good as any in the Loop.

### Hannah's Bretzel

180 W. Washington St 312-621-1111 B & L Mon-Sat $ [p306, C1]
This cheery organic sandwich shop earned quick fame for its namesake "bretzels" – large, chewy, breadlike pretzels that, with soup, make a meal on their own. Don't pass up the ultrafresh sandwiches on bretzel bread.

### Heaven on Seven

111 N. Wabash St 312-263-6443 B & L Mon–Sat, D third Friday of every month $ [p307, C1]
The original outpost of what's now a trio of festive, Mardi Gras bead-bedecked Cajun spots, this popular restaurant on the seventh floor of the historic Garland Building has been dishing up fried oyster po' boys and sweet potato pie since 1980. Cash only.

### Italian Village

71 W. Monroe St 312-332-7005 L & D Mon–Sat, L, D Sun at the Village only $$ [p306, C2]
A Chicago landmark for more than 80 years, the Village is really three restaurants in one: steakhouse La Cantina, contemporary Vivere, and the traditionally rustic Village, an extravagantly decorated Northern Italian fantasyland on the second floor.

### Miller's Pub

134 S. Wabash Ave 312-263-4988 L & D daily $$ [p307, C2]
This Loop standby, adjacent to the Palmer House Hilton, is classic Old Chicago – steaks, burgers, chops, Greek and Italian specialties, and Canadian baby back ribs.

### Lou Mitchell's

565 W. Jackson Blvd 312-939-3111 B & L daily $ [p306, B2]
This legendary downtown breakfast spot is famed for hefty omelettes, crispy hash browns, and complimentary Milk Duds and doughnut holes while you wait for a table.

### Plymouth Restaurant

327 S. Plymouth Ct 312-362-1212 B, L & D daily $ [p306, C2]
Affordable diner standards and bar munchies make the casual Plymouth a reliable stop for any Loop sojourn. The basement bar is popular with local law students, or grab a beer and head to the roof deck for fantastic skyline views.

### Rhapsody

65 E. Adams St 312-786-9911 L Mon–Fri, D daily $$$ [p307, C2]
This elegant, airy dining room and lovely patio behind Symphony Center serves eclectic takes on classic French cuisine. The kitchen stays open a half hour after the final curtain when the Chicago Symphony Orchestra is in residence; closed Sundays in winter.

### Russian Tea Time

77 E. Adams St 312-360-0000 L & D daily $$$ [p307, C2]
Come to this downtown spot for a bit of old-world glamour and such Russian standbys as blintzes, dumplings, caviar, stuffed cabbage, and as many vodka shots as you can handle, all served by

stern but gracious waiters. An elaborate afternoon tea is served daily from 2.30pm to 4.30pm.

### Shikago

190 S. LaSalle St 312-781-7300 L Mon–Fri, D Mon–Sat $$$ [p306, C2]
This new contemporary pan-Asian fusion comes from chef Kevin Shikami (he also runs River North's Kevin), who is being hailed lately as one of Chicago's breakout chefs.

## Bars

**BIG Bar**, Hyatt Regency Chicago, 151 E. Wacker Dr (tel: 312-565-1234). The 48 oz. cocktails at this hotel lounge are as ludicrously oversized as the bar itself. At 160 ft (49 meters) long, it is reputed to be the longest freestanding bar in North America.

**Cal's Liquors**, 400 S. Wells St (tel: 312-922-6392). Diviest of the dives, tiny, grubby Cal's attracts an eclectic crowd of bike messengers, traders, and garage punks.

**Cardozo's Pub**, 170 W. Washington St (tel: 312-236-1573). This basement bar near City Hall is a favorite lunch and after-work spot for political power brokers and their underlings. The burgers are first rate.

**The Martini Bar**, 401 S. LaSalle St (tel: 312-377-6111). The name says it all: you can toss back concoctions from a list of 30 specialty martinis in the company of brokers coming untucked after a long day in the financial district trenches.

# Art Institute of Chicago

**One of the premier art museums in the country boasts a world-class collection of early modern European paintings, iconic 20th-century American works, and much else**

The Art Institute's holdings range from ancient to modern and represent just about every corner of the globe. Most impressive is the collection of Impressionist and Post-Impressionist paintings built around the works donated to the Institute by socialite Bertha Honoré Palmer in 1924. From the ancient world come Greek, Roman, and Egyptian sculptures and artifacts and a significant collection of Asian art dating back 5,000 years. Some 3,000 pieces of arms and armor illustrate the metal-working skills of Medieval and Renaissance artisans. The decorative arts department encompasses European and American furnishings as well as extensive if somewhat peculiar collections of paperweights and miniature interiors. Scheduled to open in 2009, a new modern wing will house significant works by such latter-day masters as Paul Cézanne, Henri Matisse, Pablo Picasso, Georgia O'Keeffe, and Edward Hopper.

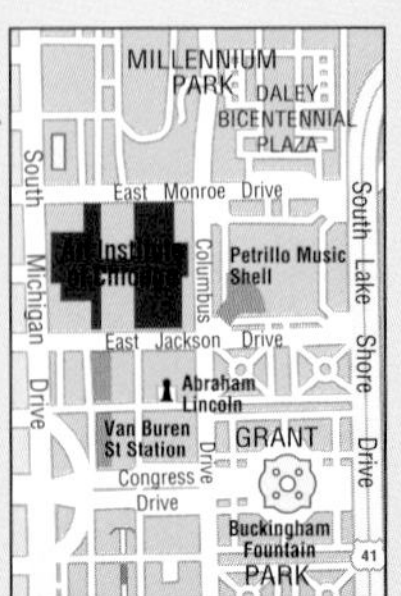


## The Essentials

*111 South Michigan Avenue*

*312-443-3600, www.artic.edu/aic*

*Mon–Wed and Fri 10.30am–4.30pm, Thu 10.30am–8pm, Sat–Sun 10am–5pm*

*charge; free Thur evening*

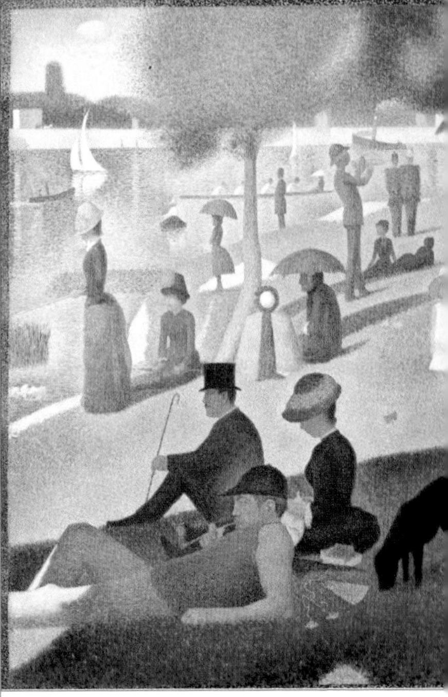

**Above:** *A Sunday on La Grande Jatte* (1884) by Georges Seurat.
**Above right:** *Self-Portrait* (1887) by Vincent van Gogh.
**Below:** *Two Sisters (On the Terrace)* by Pierre Auguste Renoir.

**ABOVE:** a museum-goer takes in Gustave Caillebotte's *Paris Street; Rainy Day*, 1877. In addition to his talent as a painter, Caillebotte was a collector of his fellow Impressionists' work as well as a funder of art exhibits.

## BACK TO SCHOOL

Founded in 1866 as the Chicago Academy of Design – a frontier outpost of European-style art education – the School of the Art Institute of Chicago (SAIC) has since blossomed into one of the top art schools in the country, numbering among its students such illustrious figures as Walt Disney, Edward Gorey, Georgia O'Keeffe, and Claes Oldenburg.

SAIC offers undergraduate programs in creative writing, historic preservation, digital media, fashion, and film as well as the traditional disciplines of painting, sculpting, and drafting. Its graduate program was ranked number one in the country by *US News and World Report* in 2006. It consistently takes top honors in that category, and each year the city is bolstered by an influx of new artistic blood in the form of freshly minted SAIC graduates. You can see what the students and faculty are up to at several venues: the Betty Rymer Gallery (280 S. Columbus Dr.), Gallery 2 (847 W. Jackson Blvd, 2nd fl), and the Student Union Galleries (37 S. Wabash).

**ABOVE:** the grand staircase suggests the Art Institute's opulence. Constructed in 1893 in time for the World's Columbian Exposition, the original building was designed in Beaux Arts style by the Boston firm of Shepley, Rutan and Coolidge.

**TOP:** Edward Hopper's *Nighthawks* (1942).
**MIDDLE:** *Water Lilies* (1906) by Claude Monet.
**BOTTOM:** *America Windows* (1977) was donated by Marc Chagall in memory of Richard J. Daley.
**RIGHT:** Tang Dynasty Buddha (AD 725).

## Second Level

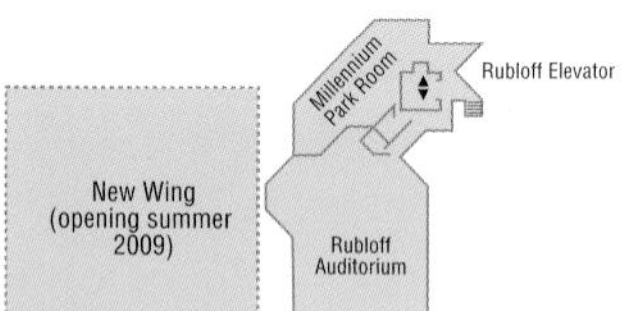


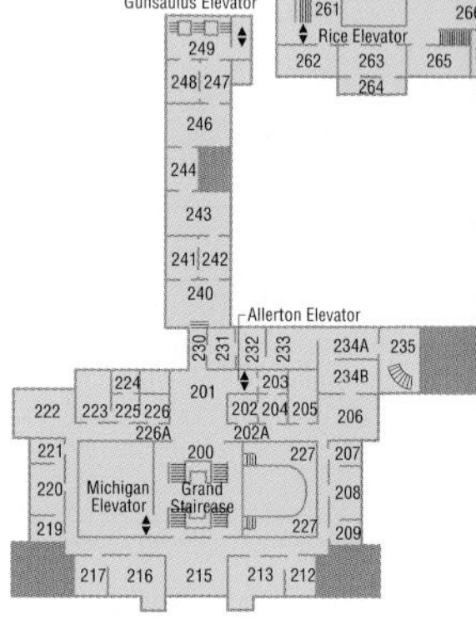

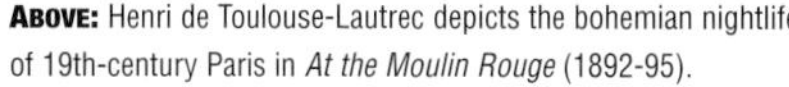

**ABOVE:** Henri de Toulouse-Lautrec depicts the bohemian nightlife of 19th-century Paris in *At the Moulin Rouge* (1892-95).
**RIGHT:** *American Gothic* (1930) by Grant Wood.

## First Level

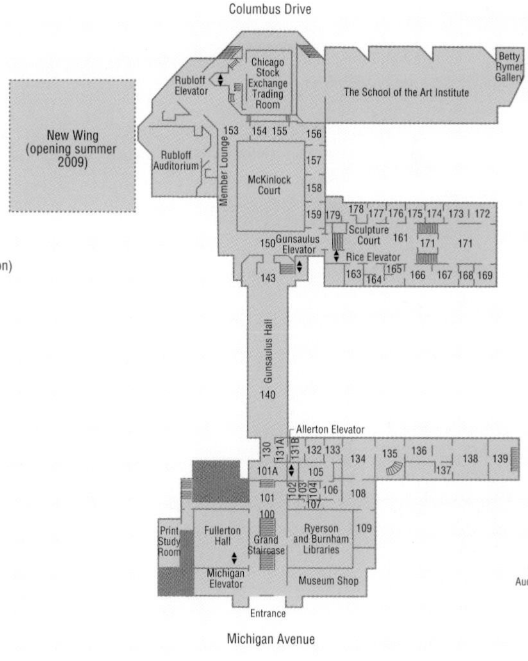

Columbus Drive

Chicago Stock Exchange Trading Room
The School of the Art Institute
Betty Rymer Gallery
Rubloff Elevator
New Wing (opening summer 2009)
Rubloff Auditorium
Member Lounge
153 154 155 156 157 158 159
McKinlock Court
179 178 177 176 175 174 173 172
Sculpture Court 161 171 171
150 Gunsaulus Elevator
Rice Elevator
143
163 164 165 166 167 168 169
Gunsaulus Hall
140
Allerton Elevator
130 131A 131B 132 133 134 135 136 137 138 139
101A 105
101 102 103 104 106 107 108
100
Print Study Room
Fullerton Hall
Grand Staircase
Ryerson and Burnham Libraries
109
Michigan Elevator
Museum Shop
Entrance

Michigan Avenue

## Lower Level

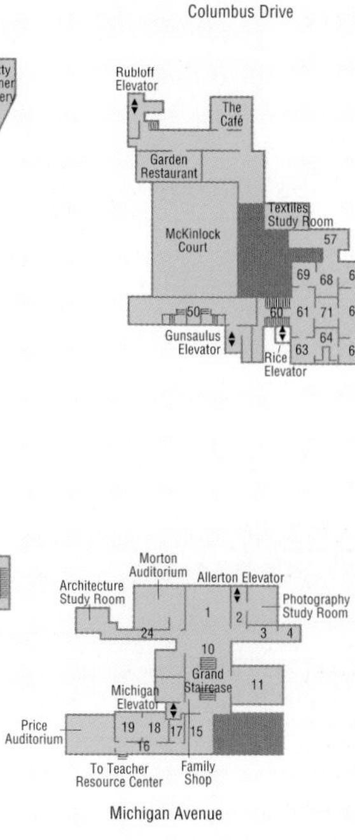

Columbus Drive

Rubloff Elevator
The Café
Garden Restaurant
McKinlock Court
Textiles Study Room
57
69 68 67
50 60 61 71 66
Gunsaulus Elevator
64
Rice Elevator
63 65

Morton Auditorium
Architecture Study Room
Allerton Elevator
Photography Study Room
1 2 3 4
24
10
Grand Staircase
11
Michigan Elevator
Price Auditorium
19 18 17 15
16
To Teacher Resource Center
Family Shop

Michigan Avenue

LYRIC OPERA AT MILLENNIUM PARK

Recommended Restaurants, Bars & Cafés on page 139

# GRANT AND MILLENNIUM PARKS

**"Forever open, clear, and free," Chicago's front yard is a green oasis that's home to music, dance, huge festivals, and the largest T. Rex skeleton in the world**

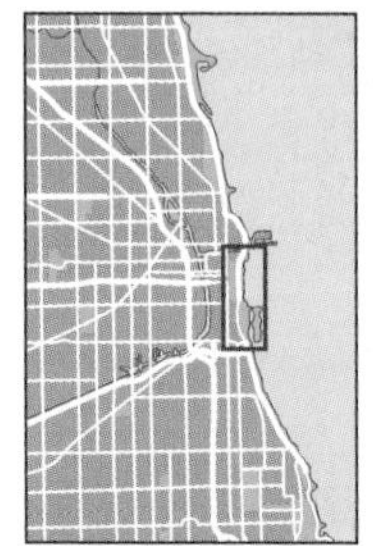

Green, sprawling **Grant Park** ❶ brings Chicago's motto – *Urbs in Horto*, or City in a Garden – to life. Stretching south from Randolph Street to McFetridge Drive and west from Lake Michigan to Michigan Avenue, its 320 acres (130 hectares) are a haven for lunchtime refugees from the Loop as well as the strollers, bicyclists, and joggers who use the paved lakefront path from dawn till after dark.

Grant Park is also the site of some of the city's biggest summer events. The **Chicago Blues Festival** (tel: 312-744-3315, www.chicagobluesfestival.org) draws more than 750,000 music lovers to the park for a peerless lineup of established and up-and-coming performers; the **Taste of Chicago** (tel: 312-744-3315, www.tasteofchicago.us) is a massive food festival with fireworks and live music; and **Summerdance** is an 11-week series of outdoor dance lessons in the park's **Spirit of Music Garden** (601 South Michigan Avenue, between Harrison Street and Balbo Drive).

## Wasteland to parkland

The scene was quite different a little more than a century ago. Back then the area was a stagnant wasteland threaded by railroad tracks and teeming with urban detritus, some of it from the Great Chicago Fire of 1871. Not until 1906, when mail-order magnate Aaron Montgomery Ward began campaigning to force the city to clean up the area and maintain it as a public park, did it begin a gradual transformation into a pleasant recreational and cultural space. The park's metamorphosis was guided by the highly influential 1909 city-planning document the *Plan of Chicago*.

**Main attractions**

- CHICAGO BLUES FESTIVAL
- TASTE OF CHICAGO
- SUMMERDANCE
- BUCKINGHAM FOUNTAIN
- "THE BEAN"
- CROWN FOUNTAIN
- JAY PRITZKER PAVILION
- MCCORMICK TRIBUNE PLAZA AND ICE RINK
- LURIE GARDEN
- BP BRIDGE
- FIELD MUSEUM
- SHEDD AQUARIUM
- ADLER PLANETARIUM
- SOLDIER FIELD

**LEFT:** the Lyric opera performs at the Jay Pritzker Pavilion.
**RIGHT:** Chicago Blues Festival.

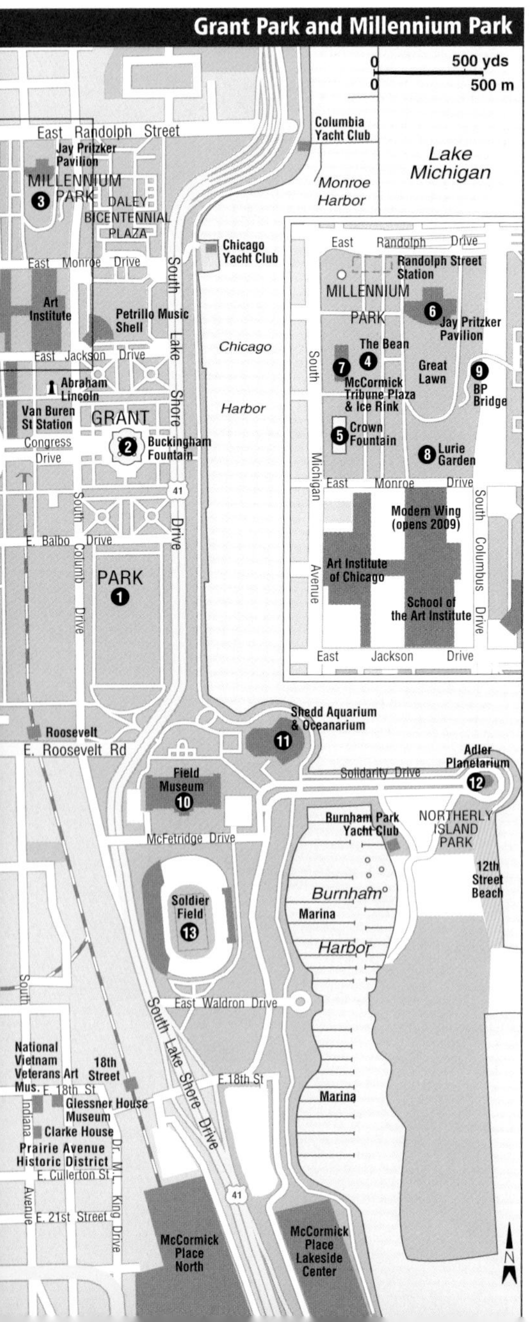


Co-authored by architect Daniel Burnham – the man responsible for the breathtaking buildings of the World's Columbian Exposition just 16 years earlier – the plan called for a string of lakefront parks and beaches. Without Ward and Burnham, modern Chicagoans might be fleeing the lakefront instead of flocking to it.

## BUCKINGHAM FOUNTAIN ❷

To see the park's centerpiece – stately **Buckingham Fountain** – head to the intersection of Columbus Drive and Congress Parkway. Modeled after a fountain at the Palace of Versailles in France, the fountain sends a towering spray 150 feet (45 meters) into the air once an hour from 8am to 11pm, April to October (weather permitting). The fountain's four bronze horses represent the four states that border Lake Michigan: Illinois, Wisconsin, Michigan, and Indiana. After dark, the spray is accompanied by a light and music show.

## MILLENNIUM PARK ❸

For decades after Grant Park's transformation, much of its northern section remained unwelcoming, marred by abandoned Illinois Central Railroad tracks. From 1997 to 2004, the 24½ acres (10 hectares) between Columbus Drive and Michigan Avenue north of Monroe Drive were transformed into the stunning **Millennium Park**. Despite numerous construction delays and cost overruns, the park has become one of Chicago's favorite outdoor venues.

Most visitors start at **"The Bean,"** ❹ the curvaceous, three-story steel sculpture created by Anish Kapoor and properly known as *Cloud Gate* (off Michigan Avenue between Washington and Madison streets). Its curved, reflective surface makes it a cross between a work of art and a funhouse mirror.

Another big draw, particularly on hot days, is the nearby **Crown**

*Recommended Restaurants, Bars & Cafés on page 139*

**Fountain** ❺, which consists of two glass-brick towers bracketing a shallow granite basin. The faces of a thousand Chicagoans alternate on video screens behind the bricks; about every five minutes, the face on the screen puckers up and "spits" a stream of water that shoots out of the tower. In summer, near-constant hordes of children in bathing suits run around the fountain, splashing each other and shrieking with delight whenever they are doused with water.

Over the park's **Great Lawn** (which has what is possibly the lushest grass in Chicago), a vast metal trellis soars. It's part of the eye-catching **Jay Pritzker Pavilion** ❻, an outdoor concert venue that accommodates 11,000 for free classical music performances and other warm-weather events. Designed by architect Frank Gehry, the pavilion is framed with wavy sheets of stainless steel that resemble giant ribbons curling away from the stage.

In winter, skaters whiz around the park's **McCormick Tribune Plaza and Ice Rink** ❼, pausing for a mug of hot chocolate at the adjacent **Park Grill** (11 North Michigan Avenue; tel: 312-521-7275; Sun–Thu 11am–9.30pm, Fri–Sat 11am–10.30pm). Other attractions in Millennium Park include serene, 2½-acre (1-hectare) **Lurie Garden** ❽ and the stainless-steel-sided **BP Bridge** ❾, a serpentine, 925-ft-long (280-meter) pedestrian pathway that leads to nearby Daley Bicentennial Plaza.

## MUSEUM CAMPUS

Abutting Grant Park's southern end, the sprawling, 57-acre (23-hectare) **Museum Campus** is home to three of Chicago's best-known institutions: the Field Museum, Shedd Aquarium, and Adler Planetarium.

### The Field Museum ❿

1400 South Lake Shore Drive
312-922-9410, www.fieldmuseum.org daily 9am–5pm charge

Some people just don't know how to end a party. After the World's Columbian Exposition closed in 1893, the city was left with scores of

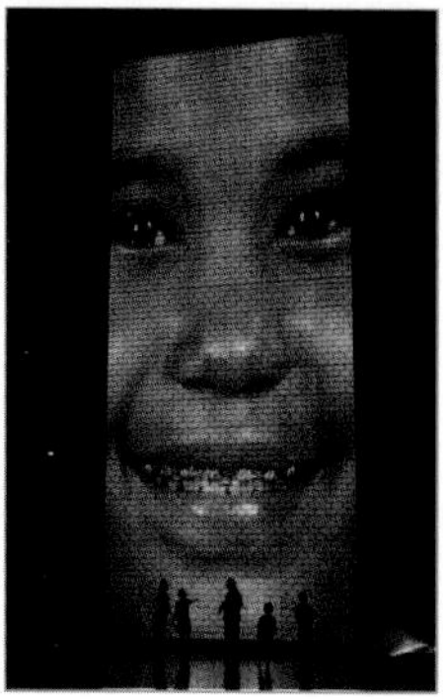

**ABOVE:** children enjoy getting drenched at Crown Fountain. **BELOW:** Field Museum of Natural History.

scientific and cultural artifacts. Backed by $1 million from retail tycoon Marshall Field, the **Field Museum** opened in 1894 at the Palace of Fine Arts in Jackson Park. On opening day, the *Chicago Tribune* reported that the new museum was "like a memory of the fair."

In 1921, the museum left the Fine Arts building (now occupied by the Museum of Science and Industry) and moved into its current home. The marble Neoclassical building may look a bit intimidating on the outside, but inside the Field is downright colorful, with exhibits ranging from the impressive to the odd.

Most museum-goers head straight to Sue, the largest and most complete skeleton of a *Tyrannosaurus rex* ever discovered. All 42 feet (13 meters) of her stand near the north entrance on the main level, though you'll have to climb to the second level to see her skull. Other highlights include the Pawnee Earth Lodge, a life-size Native American dwelling; the stuffed remains of Bushman, the world's first celebrity gorilla; and the bijous in the Grainger Hall of Gems. In the interactive Underground Adventure, kids get an up-close-and-personal look at insect life.

**ABOVE:** a drum circle keeps the beat in Millennium Park.
**BELOW:** Shedd Aquarium.

## Shedd Aquarium ⓫

✉ 1200 South Lake Shore Drive
☎ 312-939-2438, www.sheddaquarium.org ⌚ Mon–Fri 9am–5pm, Sat–Sun 9am–6pm, daily in summer 9am–6pm Ⓢ charge

The Shedd Aquarium is one of the largest of its kind in the world. Though it opened in 1929, it wasn't until 1991 that it acquired its biggest draw – the **Oceanarium**, which houses Pacific white-sided dolphins, sea otters, tide-pool creatures, penguins, and beluga whales. Daily exhibitions in the 1,000-seat amphitheater feature dolphins leaping, somersaulting, and demonstrating other "natural" behaviors under the watchful gaze of their trainers.

Among the other exhibits are **Wild Reef**, with more than 20 sharks; **Caribbean Reef**, where sea turtles and moray eels keep company; and **Waters of the World**, home of the Shedd's oldest resident, an 80-year-old Australian lungfish named Granddad.

The aquarium is extremely popular (especially with groups of schoolchildren); in 2006 it was one of the city's most heavily visited cultural attractions, second only to the Field Museum. Sunday mornings are your best bet for a quiet visit. Or, on other days of the week, arrive just as it opens, spend a couple of hours strolling around, and make your escape before the masses arrive.

## Adler Planetarium ⓬

✉ 1300 South Lake Shore Drive
☎ 312-922-7827, www.adlerplanetarium.org ⌚ daily 9.30am–4.30pm, to 6pm in summer, to 10pm on the first Fri of the month Ⓢ charge

*Recommended Restaurants, Bars & Cafés below*

An easy walk east of the aquarium leads to the **Adler Planetarium**. The Adler sits on a small, artificial island connected to the mainland by a causeway. Its lakefront location affords fantastic views of the Chicago skyline, making it worth a stop even for non-stargazers.

Styling itself "the first modern planetarium in the Western Hemisphere," the Adler was the brainchild of Sears, Roebuck executive Max Adler. On a trip to Europe, Adler encountered the Zeiss planetarium projector – which reproduced images of the night sky inside a domed auditorium – and promptly donated one to the city of Chicago, which built the planetarium to house it in 1930. Journey through the night sky in its Sky Theater, take in a movie about black holes or the big bang in the StarRider Theater, or see exhibits on the Milky Way, the history of space exploration, and more.

## Home of the Bears

Dedicated to American war veterans, 66,944-seat **Soldier Field** ⓭ (1410 South Museum Campus Drive; tel: 312-235-7000, www.soldierfield.net) stands just south of the Museum Campus and is best known as the home of the Chicago Bears. It has also been host to historic events such as the Jack Dempsey-Gene Tunney heavyweight boxing match of 1927 and the Grateful Dead's last concert, in 1995.

The original stadium was built between 1922 and 1928 in the same Neoclassical style as the nearby Field Museum, but a renovation in 2003 altered its appearance so substantially that the field lost its status as a National Historic Landmark.

Guided tours are available but require reservations (tel: 312-235-7244; charge). On non-game days, the public can stroll among the field's massive colonnades for free. ❑

*Skaters flock to the McCormick Tribune Ice Rink on cold winter nights.*

**LEFT:** Bears fans gather for a tailgating party before a game at Soldier Field.

# RESTAURANTS & BARS

### Restaurants

**The Gage**
24 S. Michigan Ave
312-372-4243 L & D daily, Brunch Sat-Sun **$$$** [p307, C2]
This clamorous "gastropub" seats 300 across the street from Millennium Park. Steaks and burgers – and excellent fries – share space with rustic curveballs like roast saddle of elk and crispy chicken livers. There's also a long and interesting menu of specialty cocktails.

**The Green at Grant Park**
352 E. Monroe St
312-987-1818 L & D daily May–Oct **$$** [p307, D2]
One of the city's quirky little gems, this patio restaurant is set in a landscaped 18-hole putting course in the middle of Grant Park. The food is nothing to write home about – mostly sandwiches with a few heartier entrées thrown in – but the setting is delightful.

**Intelligentsia Café**
53 E. Randolph St
312-920-9332 B, L & D daily **$** [p307, C1]
Tank up on gourmet coffee at this slick café near Millennium Park. The baristas are experts, the atmosphere is postindustrial chic, and the java is divine.

**Park Grill**
11 N. Michigan Ave
312-521-7275 L & D daily. **$$$** [p307, C1]
This smart eatery does its best work with grilled meats, but the real attraction is the setting, just across from Millennium Park with winter views of skaters zipping around the ice rink. In summer, the rink is transformed into an al fresco dining area. The adjacent Park Café is good for a quick bite or a take-out picnic.

Prices for a three-course dinner per person with a half-bottle of house wine:
**$** = under $20
**$$** = $20–$45
**$$$** = $45–$60
**$$$$** = over $60

# PUBLIC ART

**Chicago sculpture isn't confined to museums. The city has transformed its open spaces into a public art gallery**

A 1978 Chicago law mandates that 1.33 percent of the cost of constructing or renovating municipal buildings be set aside for the commission or purchase of artworks. The result is a city graced with one of the finest collections of public art in the world. The Percent for Art program, as it is called, also stipulates that 50 percent of the art must be by Chicagoans. During the program's first 30 years, the city acquired more than 160 works for permanent public display, and the success of Percent for Art has inspired over 200 similar programs in cities throughout the US. Private money has played a role, too, as with the use of corporate funds to subsidize much of Millennium Park, the site of two especially prominent works of public sculpture: *Cloud Gate*, better known as The Bean (see above right), and *Crown Fountain*, two glass-block towers with LED screens that project the images of a thousand Chicagoans "spitting" water into a shallow granite basin.

**ABOVE:** a statue of Abraham Lincoln in Grant Park.

**LEFT:** a 22-ft-high (7-meter) bronze sculpture by Henry Moore graces the atrium of Three First National Plaza in the Loop.

**ABOVE:** commonly known as The Bean, *Cloud Gate* is a three-story, 110-ton steel sculpture in Millennium Park. Created by British artist Anish Kapoor, the piece is meant to resemble a drop of mercury. The curved, mirrorlike object reflects the image of visitors, the city, and the sky, and has become one of the most beloved and visited sculptures in the city.

**ABOVE LEFT:** Henry Moore's *Nuclear Energy* at the University of Chicago commemorates the first controlled nuclear reaction, under the direction of physicist Enrico Fermi, in 1942.

**ABOVE RIGHT:** *Garden Variety* by Jonathan Franklin.

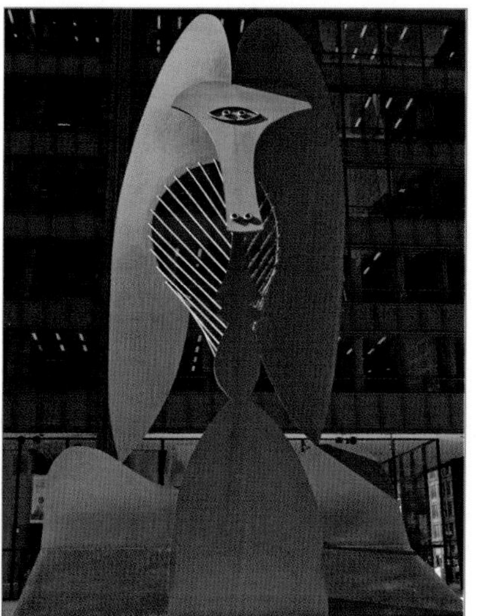

**ABOVE:** a woman's head? An Afghan hound? Chicagoans are still scratching their heads over the untitled sculpture donated to the city by Pablo Picasso in 1967 and known simply as "the Picasso."

## INTERNATIONAL TREASURES

Chicago's collection of public art is international in scope and especially strong in abstract works. The most prominent piece is undoubtedly Pablo Picasso's enigmatic steel sculpture at Daley Plaza. The Spanish master declined the $100,000 commission fee, choosing instead to give the sculpture as a gift to the city. Outside the nearby Chicago Temple Building is a work by another Spanish modernist, Joan Miró, a 39-ft (12-meter) "earth mother" with outstretched arms and a face like a weather vane (above). French artist Marc Chagall's *Four Seasons* stands in the Chase Tower Plaza. The monumental work is a ceramic-and-glass mosaic some 70 ft (21 meters) long and 14 ft (4 meters) high. An admirer of "art brut" produced by so-called outsider artists, French painter and sculptor Jean Dubuffet produced the black-and-white abstraction *Monument with Standing Beast* at the James R. Thompson Center in the Loop.The international collection has expanded in recent years with the addition of *Cloud Gate* by Indian-born British sculptor Anish Kapoor and *Crown Fountain* by Spanish artist Jaume Plensa, both in Millennium Park.

**ABOVE:** dedicated in 1927, Buckingham Fountain in Grant Park was designed by Edward H. Bennett with sculptures by Jacques Lambert. A 20-minute water display starts every hour on the hour. The fountain's four sculpted seahorses represent the four states contiguous to Lake Michigan: Wisconsin, Illinois, Indiana, and Michigan.

Water T wer Plac

# NEAR NORTH

**You can shop till you drop on the Mag Mile, browse the gallery district, or brave the Navy Pier crowds for a ride on the Ferris wheel – this neighborhood has attractions to suit most every taste**

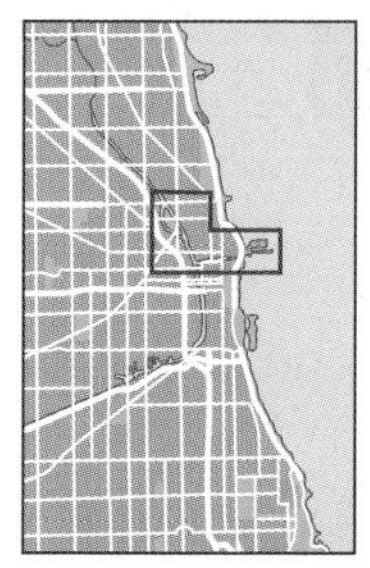

Arguably Chicago's most vibrant and tourist-friendly district, the Near North is in reality three neighborhoods in one. The **Magnificent Mile**, its de facto Main Street, beckons with flower-filled sidewalks and glittering shop windows. To the east, busy **Streeterville**, which has the densest population in the city, is a tightly packed grid of modern towers and high-end condos. While catering mostly to its wealthy residents, the neighborhood does host several major tourist attractions, including the Museum of Contemporary Art and, farther south, the cacophonous urban playground of Navy Pier. To the west of Michigan Avenue, you can see vestiges of the late 19th and early 20th centuries in the surviving Romanesque Revival mansions and converted industrial buildings of **River North**, many now housing art galleries and design showrooms.

## THE MAGNIFICENT MILE 1

State Street may have a song named after it, but there's no doubt that, in the retail arena at least, it's long been superseded by the Magnificent Mile, the nickname given to North Michigan Avenue between Oak Street and the Chicago River. (It's actually more like three-quarters of a mile.) It's come a long way from its humble origins as Pine Street, a residential neighborhood with a smattering of warehouses near the river. Following the recommendations of architect Daniel Burnham in the *Plan of Chicago*, the city transformed Pine Street into a European-style boulevard in 1913 by making it wider and connecting it with Michigan Avenue

**Main attractions**

- MAGNIFICENT MILE
- WATER TOWER
- GARRETT POPCORN
- JOHN HANCOCK CENTER
- DRAKE HOTEL
- MUSEUM OF CONTEMPORARY ART
- NAVY PIER
- CHICAGO CHILDREN'S MUSEUM
- MARINA CITY
- HOUSE OF BLUES
- MERCHANDISE MART
- GALLERY DISTRICT
- HOLY NAME CATHEDRAL
- WASHINGTON SQUARE PARK
- NEWBERRY LIBRARY

**LEFT:** the John Hancock Center rises over the Water Pumping Station, one of the few buildings to survive the Great Fire.
**RIGHT:** House of Blues.

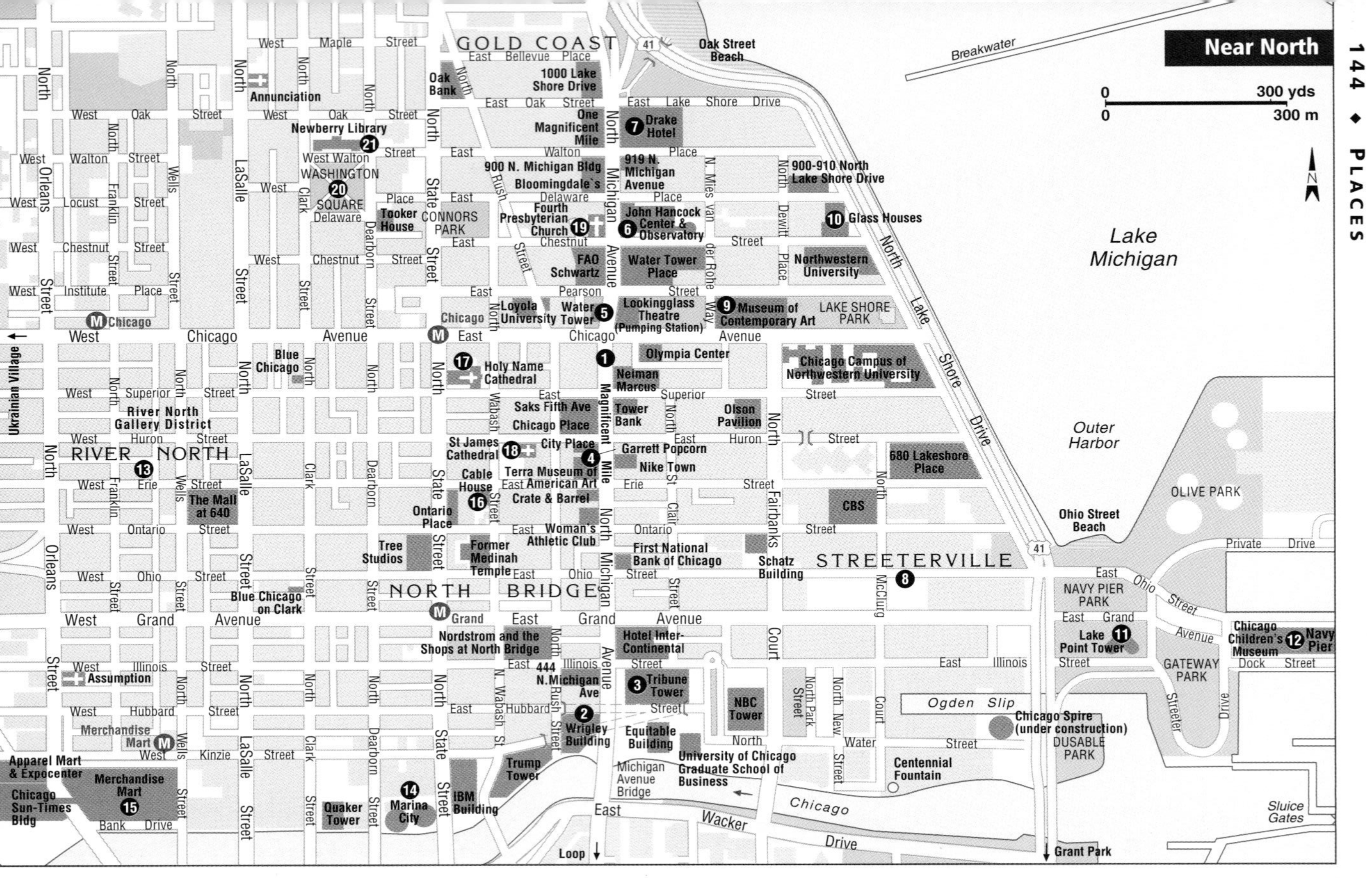

Near North
0
300 yds
300 m
N
Lake Michigan
Breakwater
Outer Harbor
Ohio Street Beach
Oak Street Beach
OLIVE PARK
NAVY PIER PARK
GATEWAY PARK
DUSABLE PARK
LAKE SHORE PARK
CONNORS PARK
WASHINGTON SQUARE
GOLD COAST
STREETERVILLE
NORTH BRIDGE
RIVER NORTH
Chicago Children's Museum
Navy Pier
Lake Point Tower
Chicago Spire (under construction)
Ogden Slip
Centennial Fountain
Sluice Gates
Grant Park
Loop
Ukrainian Village
North Lake Shore Drive
Chicago
Wacker
Drive
Drake Hotel
One Magnificent Mile
1000 Lake Shore Drive
Oak Bank
919 N. Michigan Avenue
900 N. Michigan Bldg
Bloomingdale's
John Hancock Center & Observatory
Fourth Presbyterian Church
900-910 North Lake Shore Drive
Glass Houses
Northwestern University
Water Tower Place
FAO Schwartz
Museum of Contemporary Art
Lookingglass Theatre (Pumping Station)
Water Tower
Loyola University
Chicago Campus of Northwestern University
Olympia Center
Neiman Marcus
Holy Name Cathedral
Olson Pavilion
Tower Bank
Saks Fifth Ave
Chicago Place
City Place
Garrett Popcorn
Nike Town
Terra Museum of American Art
Crate & Barrel
St James Cathedral
Cable House
680 Lakeshore Place
CBS
Woman's Athletic Club
First National Bank of Chicago
Former Medinah Temple
Ontario Place
Schatz Building
Hotel Inter-Continental
Tribune Tower
NBC Tower
University of Chicago Graduate School of Business
Equitable Building
Wrigley Building
Michigan Avenue Bridge
444 N. Michigan Ave
Nordstrom and the Shops at North Bridge
Trump Tower
IBM Building
Marina City
Quaker Tower
Tree Studios
Tooker House
Newberry Library
Annunciation
Blue Chicago
Blue Chicago on Clark
The Mall at 640
River North Gallery District
Assumption
Merchandise Mart
Apparel Mart & Expocenter
Chicago Sun-Times Bldg
Magnificent Mile

on the other side of the river via a double-decker bridge. A building boom followed, during which many of the most prominent structures on the strip were built, including the impossible-to-miss **Wrigley Building** ❷ at the southernmost end. An imposing building whose triangular shape was modeled after the Seville Cathedral's Giralda Tower, it's actually two towers connected by walkways at street level and at the 3rd and 14th floors. Clad in white terra-cotta tiles, the French Renaissance facade looks particularly grand at night, when it's illuminated by floodlights.

Across the street, at 401 North Michigan, there's a plaque set in the pavement in **Pioneer Square** noting the site of the home of Jean Baptiste Point du Sable, who ran a trading post at this location in the late 18th century. The first permanent non-native settler in the area, du Sable – the Haitian-born son of a French sea captain and a slave – is officially recognized as the founder of the city.

At 435 North Michigan is another architectural treasure, the gothic **Tribune Tower** ❸. As its name suggests, this is the headquarters of the *Chicago Tribune*, one of the city's two daily newspapers. It's also the site of WGN Radio, and visitors can watch the broadcast through windows on the first floor. The tower, with its buttressed spire modeled after the cathedral in Rouen, France, was designed by Raymond Hood and John Howell, who won a 1922 competition over the more modern

The Billy Goat Tavern (430 N. Michigan Ave, lower level; tel: 312-222-1525) is a favorite hangout of the ink-stained wretches at the nearby *Chicago Tribune*. Tavern founder Bill Sianis was legendarily responsible for the curse that has dogged the Cubs since 1945. The Billy Goat entered pop culture history via an equally legendary *Saturday Night Live* skit – Cheezborger! Cheezborger! No fries, cheeps!

**ABOVE:** Tribune Tower. **BELOW:** Michigan Avenue Bridge and Wrigley Building.

designs of architects Eliel Saarinen and Walter Gropius. Carvings of Robin Hood and a "howelling" dog near the main entrance are meant to represent the architects themselves.

Incorporated into the lower-level walls are bits of historical buildings from around the world, many of them brought back by *Tribune* correspondents. There are fragments of the Parthenon, Taj Mahal, Colosseum, and, more recently, a piece of steel from the former World Trade Center in New York. The first and second floors house the **McCormick Tribune Freedom Museum** (445 North Michigan Avenue; tel: 312-222-4860, www.freedommuseum.us; Wed–Mon 10am–6pm; charge). Geared toward teenagers, it's dedicated to exploring issues related to personal and political freedoms, especially those related to the First Amendment.

## Art, history, commerce

The main activity along the Magnificent Mile is shopping. Strollers have their choice of high-end boutiques such as **Tiffany, Louis Vuitton,** and **Cartier**; mid-range retailers like the **Gap** and **Pottery Barn**; and department stores, including **Macy's, Bloomingdale's, Saks Fifth Avenue,** and **Neiman Marcus,** some of which are located in indoor malls.

Although some Chicagoans have decried the increasingly big-box, big-brand nature of the strip, a few independently and locally owned businesses survive here and there. **Crate & Barrel,** which has its flagship store at 646 North Michigan Avenue, got its start in Chicago in 1962. **Garrett Popcorn** ❹, at 670 North Michigan, is another beloved local tradition, especially around the winter holidays, when giant tubs of buttered, caramel, and cheese popcorn are a hot commodity. When you smell popcorn and see a line snaking out the door, you'll know you've found the place.

But some of the beautiful things on the Mag Mile are free, including

**ABOVE:** a street drummer keeps time on the Michigan Avenue Bridge. **BELOW:** shopping on the Magnificent Mile.

*Recommended Restaurants, Bars & Cafés on pages 156–7*

the views of the sidewalk planters, which bloom with gorgeous seasonal designs. Quirky city-sponsored art installations – which in the past have included cow sculptures adorned by area artists and fanciful dress forms outfitted by local design students – are also a frequent sight.

It's hard to miss the little square surrounding the historic **Water Tower** ❺, at 806 North Michigan Avenue. Dating from 1869, the 138-ft (42-meter) Gothic Revival tower, constructed of yellow limestone quarried from suburban Joliet, was one of the few buildings to survive the Great Chicago Fire and is one of the city's most beloved landmarks. Inside you'll find a visitor center and the **City Gallery** (tel: 312-742-0808; Mon–Sat 10am–6.30pm, Sun 10am–5pm), which hosts photographic exhibitions with local themes.

Across the street, the matching pumping station is still in use, although it's now also home to the **Lookingglass Theatre Company** (821 North Michigan Avenue; tel: 312-337-0665), a troupe founded in 1988 by Northwestern University students (including David Schwimmer, best known as Ross from the sitcom *Friends*) and acclaimed nationwide for its imaginative productions.

## John Hancock Center Observatory ❻

875 North Michigan 312-751-3681, www.hancock-observatory.com daily 9am–11pm, last ticket sold 10.45pm charge

A block north is another widely recognized symbol of Chicago, the 100-story **John Hancock Center**, completed in 1970 and designed by

*Shoppers break for lunch on Michigan Avenue.*

**ABOVE LEFT:** John Hancock Center.
**BELOW:** Santa Claus drops into the Magnificent Mile Lights Festival, kicking off the holiday shopping season.

**ABOVE:** diners at the Signature Lounge atop the John Hancock Center enjoy sweeping skyline views.
**BELOW:** fireworks illuminate the sky over the lakeshore.

the firm of Skidmore, Owings, and Merrill. Its distinctive X-braces distinguish it as an exponent of structural expressionism, an architectural movement that sought to integrate structural elements into a building's exterior. The **Observatory** is a popular destination for its unparalleled views of the lake and city (which many prefer to those at the taller Sears Tower), although it's just as easy to admire them from the **Signature Lounge** on the 96th floor, where the only fee is for an overpriced cocktail. The building's sunken elliptical plaza is a less dizzying place to stop and catch your breath, with a gently splashing waterfall and a few casual eateries; try the Italian deli **L'Appetito** (tel: 312-337-0691) for a hearty sub or fresh-grilled panini.

Although its entrance is just off Michigan Avenue, the **Drake Hotel** ❼ (140 East Walton Place; tel: 312-787-2200) is indisputably one of the highlights of the Magnificent Mile. Built in 1920 in an Italian Renaissance style with funds from some of the city's most prominent families – including the Palmers, the Armours, and the McCormicks – the hotel has been host to celebrity guests such as Princess Diana, Elizabeth Taylor, and Salvador Dalí. The wooden bar in the Cape Cod Room, one of the hotel's five restaurants, still bears the carved initials of Joe DiMaggio and Marilyn Monroe. A series of extensive renovations over the last several years by the current owner, Hilton International, hasn't detracted from the air of genteel elegance; a highlight is afternoon tea (accompanied by a harpist) in the sumptuous Palm Court.

## STREETERVILLE 8

The area east of Michigan Avenue between Oak Street and the river was once part of Lake Michigan. When it started silting up with sand and garbage in the mid-19th century, the Sands – as the area came to be known – started attracting prostitutes, gamblers, and other undesirable types, much to the dismay of nearby residents who had invested in lakefront property. Then, in 1886, the boat of "Cap" George Wellington Streeter ran aground on the Sands, and he declared jurisdiction over "the district of Lake Michigan." Although his claim never stuck, his legend lives on in the neighborhood's name, Streeterville.

### Museum of Contemporary Art 9

220 East Chicago Avenue 312-280-2660, www.mcachicago.org
Tue 10am–8pm, Wed–Sun 10am–5pm charge

One of the area's main attractions is the **Museum of Contemporary Art**, which sits behind a sprawling plaza that hosts a farmers' market during the summer and, occasionally, giant art installations. The museum's permanent collection includes pieces by Francis Bacon, Alexander Calder, and Andy Warhol, although much of the interior space is dedicated to temporary and touring exhibits. It's not all about what's hanging on the walls; music, dance, plays, and other performances are integral parts of the programming. Admission to the museum galleries

*Choreographer Julia Rhoads directs a dance rehearsal at the MCA performance space.*

**LEFT:** a sand painter demonstrates her work at the Museum of Contemporary Art.
**BELOW LEFT:** MCA's dramatic spiral staircase.
**BELOW:** the Medinah Temple, now Bloomingdale's Home store.

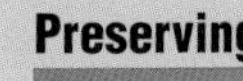

## Preserving the Past

More than a few old and beautiful buildings in the Near North area – some historically significant, others not so much – have been demolished to make way for new developments, endangering the architectural legacy that's one of the city's strongest assets. Protests from residents and preservationists were successful in saving the city block occupied by the Tree Studios (North State Street between Ontario and Ohio streets), graceful Queen Anne and English Arts and Crafts buildings that provided studio and living space to artists, and the Medinah Temple (600 North Wabash Avenue), a fanciful Islamic Revival building housing an ornate auditorium. During a subsequent restoration the studios were converted to retail and office space and the temple to a Bloomingdale's Home store. Many residents consider this a loss, although most find it preferable to the building of yet another faceless tower.

*Artwork of various styles is displayed at the annual Exposition of Sculpture, Objects & Functional Art, or SOFA, at Navy Pier.*

is free on Tuesdays; in the summer you can wrap up a visit with the popular **Tuesdays on the Terrace** cocktail hour, offering live jazz and an opportunity to relax in the lovely terraced sculpture garden facing the lake. The museum store is several cuts above the average gift shop, offering housewares, toys, and fashion for the design conscious.

## Glass houses

In an area brimming with posh high-rises, the twin steel-and-glass apartment towers positioned perpendicular to each other at 860 and 880 North Lake Shore Drive are notable for their sleek, spare design. Known as the **Glass Houses** ❿, they're the work of Ludwig Mies van der Rohe, and they influenced high-rise design for years after their construction in 1949 and 1951. They are the architect's first buildings to be awarded landmark status by the city.

A few blocks south is **Lake Point Tower** ⓫, which owes a debt to Mies in that its architects, his former students John Heinrich and George Schipporeit, were influenced by one of his old sketches. Heinrich and Schipporeit took Mies's glass-and-steel skeleton and gave it three curving wings with a 120-degree angle between each. Completed in 1968, Lake Point Tower draws attention for its height (it was the tallest residential building in the world until 1993), its extraordinary design, and its status as the only skyscraper east of Lake Shore Drive, which allows for unimpeded views of the lake and skyline.

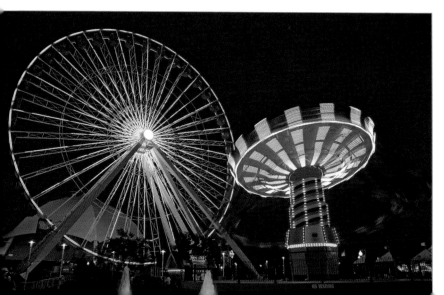

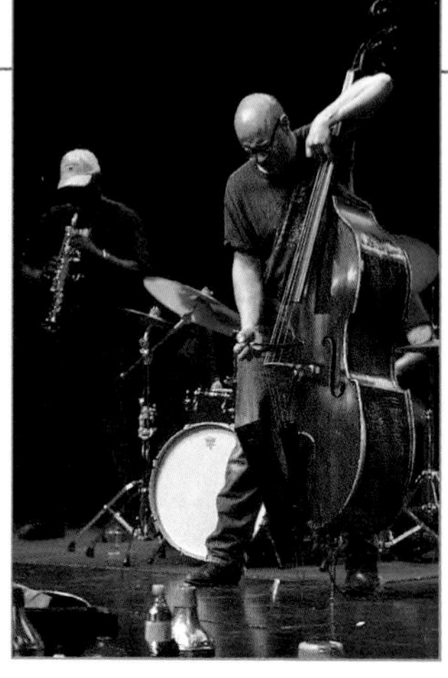

**ABOVE RIGHT:** live jazz at the MCA. **BELOW:** amusement park rides at Navy Pier.

*Recommended Restaurants, Bars & Cafés on pages 156–7*

## NAVY PIER ⓬

Just east of Lake Point Tower is the 3,000-ft-long (900-meter) **Navy Pier,** which has undergone many incarnations since its construction in 1916. Originally called Municipal Pier, it was designed by architect Charles Summer Frost following plans laid out by Daniel Burnham and was meant to serve the day-to-day requirements of industrial shipping and provide a place for public entertainment and leisure. Renamed Navy Pier in 1927 in honor of World War I sailors, it later served as a convention site, Navy training center, and a facility for the University of Illinois.

After a $200 million restoration in the 1990s, it is now the Midwest's most-visited tourist destination thanks to a wide range of attractions that include a 148-ft (45-meter) Ferris wheel (modeled after the original Ferris wheel built for the 1893 Columbian Exposition), a carousel, an IMAX theater, a miniature golf course, and the **Chicago Children's Museum** (700 East Grand Avenue; tel: 312-527-1000, www.chicagochildrensmuseum.org; Sun–Wed and Fri 10am–5pm, Thu and Sat 10am–8pm; charge), which is housed in the **Headhouse,** a Neoclassical building with two towers that originally held water tanks to feed sprinkler systems. At the east end of the pier, the auditorium houses the beautifully restored **Grand Ballroom** with a half-dome ceiling. Several lakefront cruises leave from the pier, and there's a fireworks display every Saturday night during the summer. Although it tends to be very crowded in warm weather and residents often grumble about the traffic, its success is undeniable.

**ABOVE:** Japanese cuisine meets Brazilian style at Sushi Samba Rio, a popular River North restaurant.
**BELOW:** Chicago Children's Museum at Navy Pier.

**EAT**

Set in the gallery district, elegant MK (868 N. Franklin St; tel: 312-482-9179) is one of River North's big draws. The sophisticated seasonal menu draws inspiration from France and Italy and is notoriously vegetarian-unfriendly.

**ABOVE RIGHT:** Irma Thomas at the House of Blues. **BELOW:** Marina City.

## RIVER NORTH ⓭

Heading several blocks west on Grand Avenue takes you to **River North**, an area with fewer splashy diversions – with the exception of a handful of chain theme restaurants – but plenty to entice architecture buffs, art lovers, admirers of fine furniture, and anyone who likes to stroll through interesting neighborhoods.

On the river at State Street are the two 60-story towers of **Marina City** ⓮ (300 North State Street), affectionately known as "the corncobs" for their cylindrical shape and rounded "petal" balconies. Completed in 1959 and designed by Bertrand Goldberg (yet another student of Ludwig Mies van der Rohe), the project was intended to combat the flight of professionals to the suburbs by offering a "city within a city," with on-site amenities like restaurants, a gym, a theater, and even a skating rink. Today the complex is the site of the **House of Blues** (329 North Dearborn Street; tel: 312-923-2000), part of a chain of nightclubs and restaurants with a packed schedule of blues, rock, and hip-hop acts.

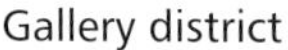

Farther west along the river is the sprawling Art Deco **Merchandise Mart** ⓯ (300 North Wells Street; tel: 800-677-6278, www.mmart.com), once the largest building in the world with 4 million sq ft (370,000 sq meters) of floor space. Built by the Marshall Field family in 1930 to consolidate its wholesale business, the facility was sold to Joseph Kennedy in 1945 and owned and managed by the Kennedy family for the next 53 years.

While most of the space is used as wholesale design and furniture showrooms and for conventions, the first two floors are dedicated to retail. On the plaza facing the river are eight bronze busts of such retail magnates as Marshall Field, Aaron Montgomery Ward, and Frank Winfield Woolworth, as well as 17 murals by Jules Guerin depicting scenes of commerce in world history.

### Gallery district

North of the Merchandise Mart is a cluster of design and furniture shops stocked with luxe home furnishings and ethnic antiques, many with quadruple-digit price tags. When

*Recommended Restaurants, Bars & Cafés on pages 156–7*

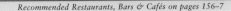

you hit Erie, Huron, and Superior streets, the design showrooms give way to art galleries. This is the **River North gallery district**, and it reputedly has the highest concentration of art galleries outside of Manhattan, many in converted warehouses. Galleries here specialize in everything from contemporary photography to folk and outsider art.

## A vanished era

The spate of new condominium towers east of the gallery district makes it difficult to imagine the neighborhood during its 19th-century heyday. One of the few remaining buildings from that era is the fortresslike **Cable House** ⓰ at 21 East Erie Street, former home of Ransom R. Cable, president of the Chicago, Rock Island & Pacific Railway Company. Built in 1886, the house is a beautiful example of the Romanesque Revival style, with round arches and rough-cut stone walls.

It is now owned by another prominent Chicago businessman and philanthropist, Richard H. Driehaus, whose company, Driehaus Capital

Management, is headquartered in the building. It isn't open to the public, but you can peek at the pretty side courtyard through the fence.

## Let us pray

The entire area between LaSalle Street and Michigan Avenue has been dubbed the **Cathedral District**, thanks to the presence of three towering religious institutions. The Gothic Revival **Holy Name Cathedral** ⓱ (735 North State Street; tel: 312-787-8040) is the seat of the Catholic Archdiocese of Chicago. Check out the massive bronze doors leading into the

**ABOVE:** Gallery district. **BELOW:** the House of Blues at the Marina City complex.

vestibule and nave: each weighs 1,200 pounds (540 kg), but they can be opened with the touch of a finger thanks to some crafty hydraulic engineering. **Saint James Cathedral** ⓲ (65 East Huron Street; tel: 312-787-7360) is the home of the Episcopal Diocese of Chicago. Built, like the Water Tower, from Joliet limestone, the church's tower, the foundation, and parts of the facade are among the only structures in the area to survive the Great Chicago Fire. The **Fourth Presbyterian Church** ⓳ (112 East Chestnut Street; tel: 312-787-8425) is the second-oldest surviving structure on Michigan Avenue north of the river.

**ABOVE:** Chicago River. **BELOW:** Pizzeria Uno, home of Chicago deep dish pizza.

## WASHINGTON SQUARE PARK AND NEWBERRY LIBRARY

North of Chicago Avenue, **Washington Square Park** ⓴ looks like just another peaceful patch of greenery, albeit with the palatial mass of the Newberry Library rising over it. Most days there is little sign of its raucous past as "Bughouse Square," where from the 1910s to the mid-1960s left-leaning intellectuals, poets, and eccentrics addressed the crowds from soapboxes.

Some of the famous orators who said their piece here include anarchist Lucy Parsons and attorney Clarence Darrow. The park relives its past one weekend every summer during the "Bughouse Square Debates," a free-speech free-for-all that attracts advocates, activists, and agitators of every stripe. Heckling is encouraged.

The atmosphere is more decorous inside the **Newberry Library** ㉑ (60 West Walton Street; tel: 312-943-9090, www.newberry.org; Mon, Fri and Sat 8.15am–5.30pm, Tue, Wed and Thur 8.15am–7.30pm; free), a private research institution with a world-class collection of rare books (including a Shakespeare first folio and a first edition of *Moby-Dick*), maps, sheet music, and other printed material. It's also a rich source of genealogical information, with a vast collection of local histories, census information, and birth and marriage records from all over the country.

The reading rooms are open only to those who apply for a reader card, but a selection of manuscripts, photographs, and other items from the collection are exhibited on a rotating basis, and the library schedules touring exhibits, author readings, lectures, and plays.

Free tours of the library building – designed by Henry Ives Cobb in the fashion of a Renaissance palace – are offered Thursday at 3pm and Saturday at 10.30am. ❑

*Recommended Restaurants, Bars & Cafés on pages 156–7*

# The Gallery Scene

**Art dealers in River North have transformed a post-industrial no-man's land into a vibrant gallery district**

A common complaint about Chicago's art world is that despite all the artists spit out by the School of the Art Institute and other institutions every year, it's hard to get them to stick around once they've achieved a level of success. It's a strange paradox, because for all the painters and photographers packing up for New York and Los Angeles, Chicago boasts a gallery scene to rival either of the coastal heavyweights. Nowhere is this more obvious than in River North, which boasts as many as 60 galleries, most of them crowding Huron and Superior streets between Wells and Orleans.

The area was a desolate landscape of warehouses and former industrial buildings in the late 1970s, when pioneering art dealers like Bob Zolla and Roberta Lieberman staked their claims. Others soon followed, and by the mid-1980s an art community to rival New York's SoHo (or, today, Chelsea) had coalesced. Since then, the area has become a thriving dining and nightlife hub, and though a 1989 fire destroyed a dozen galleries and rising rents have driven emerging and avant-garde galleries – and even some of the old guard – to set up shop in the West Loop and elsewhere, it remains a critical part of Chicago's independent art scene.

There's something for everyone in River North, and unlike far-flung neighborhoods, it's easily accessible by public transportation via the #66 Chicago Avenue bus or the brown line El (get off at Chicago and Franklin).

Here you will find abstract painting and sculpture at **Zolla/Lieberman** (now run by Roberta Lieberman's son, William, at 325 West Huron Street; tel: 312-944-1990) and **Roy Boyd** (739 North Wells Street; tel: 312-642-1606), another area pioneer. **Stephen Daiter** (311 West Superior Street; tel: 312-787-3350) specializes in vintage experimental photography, and **Zygman Voss** (222 West Superior Street; tel: 312-787-3300) showcases museum quality work by the masters. **Judy Saslow** (300 West Superior Street; tel: 312-943-0530) and **Carl Hammer** (740 North Wells Street; 312-266-8512) champion the often unclassifiable creations of outsider artists like Lee Godie, an enigmatic, often homeless woman who for years sold her French Impressionist-inspired paintings on the steps of the Art Institute. And while the focus of area dealers is resolutely international, hometown heroes ranging from Chicago Imagist Ed Paschke to cartoonist Chris Ware are well represented.

The best thing about all this artistic bounty is that, unlike most museums, it's all free – at least to look. Exhibits traditionally open the first Friday of the month, and on those nights the streets swarm with chic Chicagoans hopping from one gallery to the next, cheap wine in hand. For a more mellow scene, try one of the free gallery tours offered every Saturday by the Art Dealers Association of Chicago (www.chicagoartdealers.org). Tours meet at the Starbucks at 750 North Franklin Street at 11am and visit four different galleries each week. ❑

**RIGHT:** art lovers can visit dozens of galleries in the River North district.

# BEST RESTAURANTS, BARS AND CAFÉS

## Restaurants

Prices for a three-course dinner per person with a half-bottle of house wine:

**$** = under $20
**$$** = $20–$45
**$$$** = $45–$60
**$$$$** = over $60

### Aigre Doux

230 W. Kinzie St 312-329-9400 L Mon–Fri, D daily **$$$$** [p304, B4]

Chef Mohammad Islam met his wife and future pastry chef Malika Ameen at Chicago's four-star Dining Room at the Ritz-Carlton. The pair later returned from LA to open this contemporary American newcomer in early 2007. French for "sour and sweet," Aigre Doux offers savory dishes like artichoke soup with bay scallops and some truly staggering desserts – think sticky toffee pudding with candied kumquats and Devonshire ice cream.

### Avenues

108 E. Superior St 312-573-6754 D Tue–Sat **$$$$** [p304, C3]

The foie-gras-and-Pop-Rocks lollipop is off the menu – a casualty of Chicago's foie gras ban – but this luxurious Peninsula Hotel dining room remains a standard-bearer for experimental American cuisine. Award-winning chef Graham Elliot Bowles goes for broke with a tasting menu loaded with tricks like lavender-infused marshmallows and lamb dressed with mint jus made from crushed Altoids.

### Bin 36

339 N. Dearborn St 312-755-9463 B, L & D daily **$$$** [p304, C4]

A wine shop, bar, and fine dining room under one roof, Bin 36 is all about the grape, with 50-odd wines by the glass and another 300 bottles, and pairings suggested on the menu. The food is solid contemporary American bistro fare, and the space – part of Bertrand Goldberg's Marina City complex – is a little piece of modernist history.

### Café Iberico

739 N. LaSalle St 312-573-1510 L & D daily **$$** [p304, B3]

Loud, crowded, and a little down at the heels, this popular tapas bar caters to a diverse crowd with cheap wine, plates of classic Spanish snacks, and efficient, if not terribly solicitous, service.

### Cyrano's Bistrot, Wine Bar, and Cabaret

546 N. Wells St 312-467-0546 L Mon–Fri, D Mon–Sat **$$** [p304, B4]

Chef Didier Durand has become something of a celebrity as the leader of the campaign to overturn Chicago's ban on foie gras. His cheery bistro delivers duck à l'orange, cassoulet, and other bistro classics. There's music in the downstairs cabaret most nights.

### De La Costa

465 E. Illinois St 312-464-1700 L Mon–Fri, D daily **$$$** [p305, D4]

A ceviche bar, curtained cabanas for private dining, and miles of brocade are just some of the over-the-top flourishes that distinguish this huge Nuevo Latino hot spot near Navy Pier. But Chef Douglas Rodriguez, a James Beard Award winner, delivers the goods on the plate.

**LEFT:** Shaw's Crab House.

### Frontera Grill

445 N. Clark St 312-661-1434 L & D Tue–Sat **$$** [p304, B4]

Chef Rick Bayless is almost single-handedly responsible for introducing gringo Chicago to regional Mexican cuisine, and while nowadays he may be busier shooting TV segments and hawking salsa than actually cooking, his flagship Frontera Grill remains an essential stop on any dining tour. Head to sibling and neighbor Topolobampo for a pricier, more formal meal.

### Gene and Georgetti

500 N. Franklin St 312-527-3718 L & D Mon–Sat **$$$** [p304, B4]

Unapologetically old-school, Gene and Georgetti is the quintessential Chicago steakhouse: no-frills ambience, gruff service, and monster hunks of meat. Local politicos and other bigwigs get the royal treatment; everyone else can lump it.

### Osteria Via Stato

620 N. State St 312-642-8450 D daily **$$$** [p304, C3]

Show up hungry, because you're going to have to roll yourself home. For a flat $36, diners get a choice of entrée and an avalanche of antipasti, pasta, and sides, all served family style. An à la carte menu is also available, as is lunch, in the enoteca next door. Opt for the "Just Bring Me Wine" plan and you'll get a flight of three 4-ounce tastes picked by sommelier Belinda Chang.

### Pizzeria Uno

29 E. Ohio St 312-321-1000 L & D daily **$** [p304, C4]

Expect long waits and lots of tourists at this birthplace of Chicago-style deep-dish pizza. The quarry: a buttery, cornmeal-dusted crust loaded with meat and about a pound of cheese.

### Quartino

626 N. State St 312-698-5000 L & D daily **$$** [p304, C3]

The specialty here is small, shared plates of classic Italian bites: house-cured salumi and other antipasti; brick-oven pizza; toothsome pastas (try the gnocchi with arugula pesto); and entrées like roasted Tuscan sausage and braised lamb. Wine is available by the quartino for as little as $4, the kitchen is open late, and overall it's a fun, if loud, option that ardent fans say is the closest you'll get to Italy on the North Side.

### Shaw's Crab House

21 E. Hubbard St 312-527-2722 L Mon–Fri, D daily **$$$$** [p304, C4]

Classic 1940s glamour and excellent, pricey seafood make Shaw's a perennial special-event destination. The jazzy, more casual Oyster Bar offers selections from the main menu. Bartenders mix serious martinis.

### Spiaggia

980 N. Michigan Ave 312-280-2750 D daily **$$$$** [p305, C3]

Perched above Michigan Avenue, with an unparalleled view of the lake, four-star Spiaggia is a luxurious showcase for Tony Mantuano's exquisite Italian cooking. Don't have $165 to drop on the tasting menu? Neighboring Café Spiaggia offers a selection of more affordable lunch and dinner options in casual digs.

### Sushi Naniwa

607 N. Wells St 312-255-8555 L Mon–Fri, D daily **$$** [p304, B4]

Owner Bob Bee is also the brains behind Wicker Park's sleek Bob San, but this established, traditional spot delivers the same fresh, expertly prepared fish, minus the glitz.

### Tru

676 N. Saint Clair St 312-202-0001 D Mon–Sat **$$$$** [p305, C3]

Rick Tramonto and Gale Gand's whimsical gastronomic temple may be the best place in Chicago to pretend to be rich for a night, with luxuries ranging from the sublime – the $250 glass "caviar staircase" – to the ridiculous. Do women really need separate stools for their purses? But Gand's justly acclaimed desserts may well steal the show: order the three-course tasting and you'll be showered with truffles, madeleines, macaroons, lollipops, and miniature pastries on top of main events like hazelnut napoleons and chocolate-port semifreddo. Add impeccable service and you've got a finely-tuned hospitality machine.

## *Bars*

**Andy's Jazz Club**, 11 E. Hubbard St (tel: 312-642-6805). Stop in for dinner, a late-night drink, Friday lunch, or Sunday brunch. Andy's has primo jazz seven days a week.

**Pops for Champagne**, 601 N. State St (tel: 312-266-7677). This classy joint moved from Lakeview to this historic Tree Studios location in 2006. In addition to more than 100 bottles of bubbly, Pops offers a raw bar and assorted small plates, plus selected cheeses and cured meats. There's live jazz five nights a week in the basement club.

**Signature Lounge**, 875 N. Michigan Ave (tel: 312-787-9596). The drinks are overpriced and there's usually a mob, but there's no better place for nighttime views than this spot on the 96th floor of the Hancock Building.

*Recommended Restaurants, Bars & Cafés on pages 166–7*

# GOLD COAST

**Genteel luxury defines this elegant lakeshore neighborhood, one of the city's oldest and loveliest and – not coincidentally – most expensive**

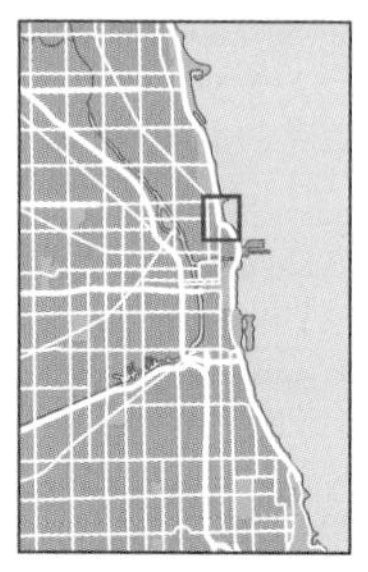

The Gold Coast doesn't have many museums or notable tourist attractions, but for those who want to imagine the city as it was a century ago, there's no better neighborhood to visit. Clustered in the northeast corner are the historic mansions and town houses of Astor Street, many designed by the most notable architects of the day for the city's wealthiest families.

As well as architectural masterpieces, the Gold Coast includes the luxury boutiques of Oak Street, a strip of nightclubs and restaurants on Rush Street, and one of the city's most popular beaches. Here the past and the present coexist with grace and style.

## ASTOR STREET

On a fine day, there are fewer activities more enjoyable than a walking tour of residential architecture in the **Astor Street District** ❶. Here, thick canopies of trees create a hushed atmosphere that makes it easy to ignore the noisy intrusions of modern urban life and imagine the sound of horse-drawn carriages and the sight of uniformed servants whisking in and out of side entrances.

The foundation of the Gold Coast was laid down in the 1880s when dry-goods magnate Potter Palmer moved his family from the posh South Side into a mansion in what was then the no-man's land of North Lake Shore Drive. The rest of the city's elite soon followed, decamping from their once fashionable digs on Prairie Avenue and building their own mansions in the area – often buying land from Palmer, who had shrewdly snapped it up.

**Main attractions**
- ARCHBISHOP'S RESIDENCE
- PATTERSON-MCCORMICK MANSION
- MADLENER HOUSE
- INTERNATIONAL MUSEUM OF SURGICAL SCIENCE
- CHARNLEY-PERSKY HOUSE
- PLAYBOY MANSION
- PUMP ROOM
- FISHER STUDIO HOUSES
- OAK STREET SHOPPING
- OAK STREET BEACH
- RUSH STREET NIGHTLIFE
- LASALLE TOWERS

**LEFT:** sunbathers relax on Oak Street Beach, a favorite summer destination of winter-weary Chicagoans.
**RIGHT:** Gold Coast cocktail party.

On a fine day, the patio at Melvin B's Truck Stop (1114 N. State St; tel: 312-751-9897) is a lively spot for a drink and decent pub grub.

## Magnificent mansions

Most of the early mansions (including Palmer's) have been demolished. One notable exception is the **Archbishop's Residence** ❷ (1555 North State Parkway), a magnificent brick mansion bristling with turrets and towers and set on a wide landscaped lawn. Built in 1885 for the first Catholic archbishop of Chicago, it has been the residence of the city's archbishops ever since.

Pope John Paul II stayed here during a visit in 1979. Although the mansion isn't open to visitors, it offers a glimpse of the Gold Coast's opulent 19th-century origins, not least for the rear alley, which is paved with cedar blocks treated with creosote, a method used until the 1930s because it was cheaper than brick and safer for horses. The house and alley are both listed in the National Register of Historic Places.

Just off Astor Street is the **Patterson-McCormick Mansion** ❸ (20 East Burton Place), built in 1892 as a wedding present from *Chicago Tribune* publisher Joseph Medill to his daughter. Designed by Gilded Age architect Stanford White, the ocher-toned structure has a gracious columned entrance and balcony and reflects the resurgence of Neoclassi-

**ABOVE RIGHT:** the Gold Coast stretches north from Oak Street Beach to Lincoln Park. **BELOW:** a friendly face on the lakeshore.

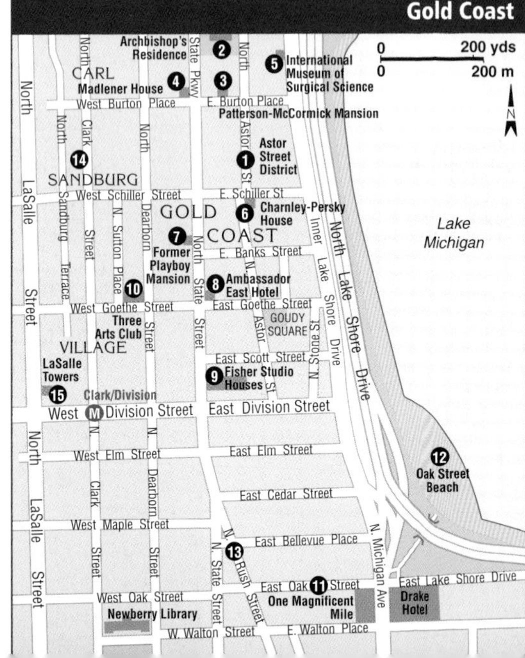

*Recommended Restaurants, Bars & Cafés on pages 166–7*

cal design in the late 19th century. It was later sold to Cyrus Hall McCormick II, president of the International Harvester Company, who enlarged the north end of the building. It is now divided into condominiums.

### Modern influence

A few steps west, the **Madlener House** ❹ (4 West Burton Place), shows what a difference a decade can make. Built in 1902 by architect Richard E. Schmidt and designer Hugh M.G. Garden, the limestone-and-brick cube combines modern elements from the Chicago and Prairie schools with the stateliness of the Renaissance Revival style. Of particular note is the off-center entrance, which, with its incised limestone frame and bronze grillwork, is a nod to the work of Louis Sullivan. The interior displays the influence of the Arts and Crafts movement that inspired Sullivan, with a characteristically simple design executed in natural materials like wood and glass. The courtyard contains architectural fragments of the many notable Gold Coast buildings that have been demolished. The house is now occupied by the offices of an arts foundation but is open to tours in conjunction with the nearby Charnley-Persky House (see below); for information, call the Society of Architectural Historians, tel: 312-573-1365.

High-rises dominate North Lake Shore Drive just a few blocks away, though one mansion has managed to survive: a graceful 1917 structure designed by famed architect Howard Van Doren Shaw and modeled after the Petit Trianon, Marie Antoinette's hideaway at Versailles.

## International Museum of Surgical Science ❺

✉ 1524 North Lake Shore Drive, www.imss.org ☎ 312-642-6502 ⏲ Tue–Sun 10am–4pm, closed Sun in winter ⓢ charge

This splendid structure now houses the International Museum of Surgical Science, which chronicles medical practices through the ages. For the

*A familiar sight in the Gold Coast – high-rise condos towering over fine old mansions.*

**BELOW:** the Archbishop's Residence is a stately Queen Anne-style mansion built in 1885, one of the few grand 19th-century houses that remain.

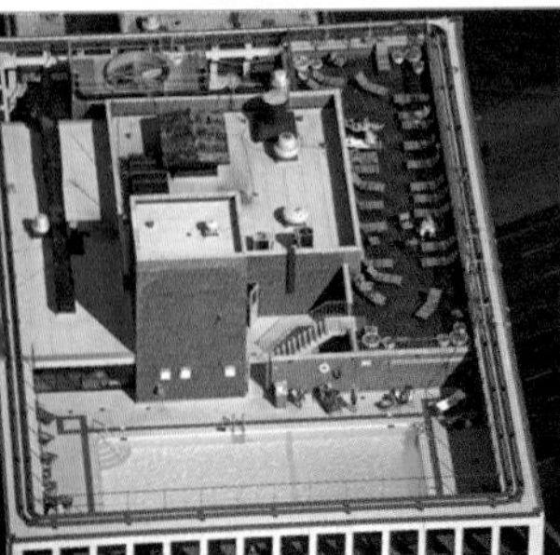

most part, this is a museum in the old-fashioned sense. There are numerous oddities and artifacts displayed under glass and painted depictions of such gruesome scenes as an amputation in the 17th century and a caesarian section in the 19th. Other holdings include drills used by ancient Incans to bore holes in a patient's skull (apparently this was thought to release evil spirits), a working iron lung, and a plaster cast of Napoleon's death mask. The ground floor houses an old-fashioned apothecary stocked with a variety of snake-oil remedies.

More contemporary attractions include exhibits on the history of nursing and advances in spinal surgery as well as rotating exhibits of artwork with a medical theme called "Anatomy in the Gallery." Many of the original interior features have survived, including marble fireplaces and the grand, gilded staircase.

**ABOVE:** enjoying the high life around a rooftop pool.
**BELOW:** dinner at a Gold Coast fund-raiser.

## Charnley-Persky House ❻

1365 North Astor Street, www.charnleyhouse.org 312-915-0105 tours Wed and Sat charge Sat, free Wed

The Charnley-Persky House, originally known as the James Charnley House, injected a shot of modernity into the neighborhood when it was completed in 1892. Architect Louis Sullivan and his draftsman, a young Frank Lloyd Wright, discarded the heavy ornamentation of the day in favor of more abstract forms. With the exception of a wooden, loggia-like balcony, the brick and limestone exterior has few decorative details, and the structure's horizontality presages Wright's Prairie School.

The interior is built around a rectangular atrium leading up to a third-floor skylight, punctuated by carved oak railings. Other features include gleaming oak paneling and molding around arched entryways and intricate mosaic tiles around the fireplace. On the front door is an example of Sullivan's flair for intricate ironwork. The house, one of the

*Recommended Restaurants, Bars & Cafés on pages 166–7*

few Sullivan residences that remain close to its original condition, is now the headquarters of the Society of Architectural Historians.

## Bring on the bunnies

About a block away is the former **Playboy Mansion** ❼ (1340 North State Street), home and headquarters of *Playboy* magazine publisher Hugh Hefner. The "Bunny Hutch," as it was known, was notorious for wild parties and Hef's swinging lifestyle. Since Hefner's departure in the early 1970s, the building has been put to more mundane uses: first as a dormitory for the School of the Art Institute, then as upscale condominiums.

## Celebrity zone

At the corner is the **Ambassador East Hotel** ❽ (1301 North State Street; www.theambassadoreasthotel.com; tel: 312-787-7200), site of the **Pump Room** restaurant, a favorite haunt of celebrities such as Humphrey Bogart, Lauren Bacall, and Liza Minnelli. The restaurant has since lost much of its cachet, and the only famous faces you're likely to see are in the photos on the walls. A planned renovation may restore the hotel to its former station.

Walk a block down North State Street for a look at the **Fisher Studio Houses** ❾ (1209 North State Street), a rare example of pre-World War II Art Moderne style. This modern jewel, with its characteristic rounded edges and glass-block windows, was designed by architect Andrew Rebori, with additional touches by artist Edgar Miller, including hand-painted windows that sadly were damaged during a rehab some years ago. The 12 residential units are clustered around a narrow central courtyard.

A jog northwest is the **Three Arts Club** ❿ (1300 North Dearborn Street), built in 1914 by the firm of Holabird and Roche to provide affordable housing for young female art students. The building, which resembles a Tuscan villa with a central brick-lined courtyard and fountain, features mosaics celebrating painting, drama, and music as well as bas-relief figures set between the exterior arches.

The club, which counted Jane Addams among its founders, ceased its residence program in 2003 and sold the building in 2007. It will most likely be converted into a luxury hotel.

**ABOVE:** Hugh Hefner inspects a lineup of "bunnies" at the Playboy mansion in 1966. **BELOW:** pleasure boats crowd a lakeshore harbor south of Oak Street Beach.

**EAT**

For a convenient (but pricey) bite on the beach, the Oak Street Beachstro (tel: 312-915-4100) serves burgers, sandwiches, pizza, and salads.

**ABOVE:** fine art and antiques at an Oak Street boutique. **BELOW:** a family outing at Oak Street Beach.

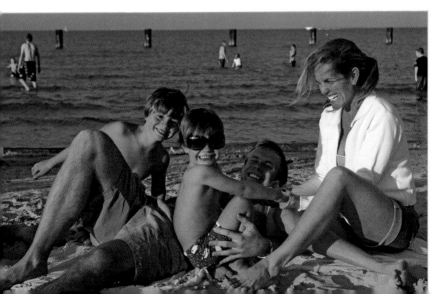

## OAK STREET ⓫

Oak Street between Michigan and Rush is the address of some of the city's most luxurious boutiques and salons. Prada, Hermes, Yves St Laurent, and other high-end designers maintain outposts here, though you will also find a few independent boutiques such as **Ultimo** (114 East Oak Street; tel: 312-787-1171), a longtime presence that offers a discriminating selection of fashions by well-known and up-and-coming designers. Even if all you can afford is a bottle of shampoo at **Bravco** (43 East Oak Street; tel: 312-943-4305), a beauty supply store that stocks nearly every hair-care product known to woman, the pretty tree-lined street is pleasant for window-shopping, with most shops set in attractive old town houses.

### Oak Street Beach

At the eastern end of Oak Street is **Oak Street Beach** ⓬. Connected to Oak Street by a pedestrian tunnel that passes under North Lake Shore Drive, this popular beach is crowded with summer sun worshippers, who come for the convenient location and stunning skyline backdrop.

The lakefront path is often crowded with bicyclists, joggers, dog walkers, and in-line skaters, who breeze past ice cream and hot dog stands while people-watchers on the concrete steps eye the tanned and oiled bodies on the sand. While there's a certain amount of posing, families are a frequent sight, and on warm summer days there are plenty of people frolicking in the water.

## RUSH STREET ⓭

Turn right on Rush Street, and you'll be on the bar and nightlife strip

known far and wide in the 1970s for its swinging singles bars. These days Rush Street is downright posh, with elegant restaurants (many with sidewalk seating in summer), chic bars, and expensive nightclubs.

Popular stops include **Jilly's Piano Bar** (1007 North Rush Street; tel: 312-664-1001), an old-school place with a Rat Pack feel (it's named after Frank Sinatra's onetime manager); **Le Passage** (937 North Rush Street; tel: 312-255-0022), an upscale lounge and dance club; and such swanky steakhouses as **Gibson's** (1028 North Rush Street; tel: 312-266-8999) and **Grotto** (1030 North State Street; tel: 312-280-1005).

Up on West Division Street is where you'll find the rowdier "party hearty" atmosphere of yore. Bars like **The Original Mother's** (26 West Division Street; tel: 312-642-7251), **Bootlegger's** (13 West Division Street; tel: 312-266-0944), and **Shenannigans** (16 West Division Street; tel: 312-642-2344) have an informal sports bar or pub vibe and attract mainly young crowds. If imbibing excessive amounts of beer and shots isn't your thing, these may not be the places for you.

## North of Division

North of Division, the architecture is of more recent vintage. Between North Dearborn and LaSalle streets is **Carl Sandburg Village** ⓮, a series of high-rises and town houses built in the 1960s as a buffer against urban blight encroaching from the west.

Often overlooked are the **LaSalle Towers** ⓯ (1211 North LaSalle Street), which are adorned with a trompe l'oeil by mural artist Richard Haas, who transformed the featureless rear wall of a former apartment hotel by painting the distinctive terra cotta cladding, projecting bay windows, and other architectural features employed by the Chicago School. On one side Haas created a rendering of Louis Sullivan's arched "Golden Door," which the architect constructed for the 1893 World's Columbian Exposition. Above the "door" is a "reflection" of the Chicago Board of Trade Building, which stands some two miles to the south. ❑

*The area around Rush and State streets is known as the Viagra Triangle, owing to the aging lotharios who troll the once-swinging singles clubs.*

**ABOVE:** beach volleyball. **BELOW:** a speedboat slices through the waters of Lake Michigan.

# BEST RESTAURANTS, BARS AND CAFÉS

## Restaurants

Prices for a three-course dinner per person with a half-bottle of house wine:

**$** = under $20
**$$** = $20–$45
**$$$** = $45–$60
**$$$$** = over $60

### Adobo Grill

1610 N. Wells St 312-266-7999 D daily, L Sat–Sun **$$** [p304, B1]
If you're hungry for Mexican food, it's worth strolling down North Avenue toward Old Town to this stylish cantina, where waiters mash up fresh guacamole in a stone mortar at your table and a tequila sommelier will help you choose among a hundred different labels. After a rough start, the kitchen is turning out a fine array of regional Mexican specialties, ranging from old favorites like enchiladas and chile relleno to unexpected dishes such as venison, steamed trout, bass, and octopus. The margaritas are potent.

### Ashkenaz Deli

12 E. Cedar St 312-944-5006 B, L & D daily **$** [p304, C2]
In business since 1973 and essentially unchanged, this classic Jewish deli – a popular breakfast stop – dishes up corned beef, pastrami, and egg salad sandwiches, bagels and lox, cheese blintzes, and roast brisket, plus gefilte fish and chopped liver by the pound.

### Bistrot Zinc

1131 N. State St 312-337-1131 L & D daily, Br Sat–Sun **$$** [p304, C2]
True to the Parisian source material, Bistrot Zinc's a relatively low-glitz option in this glitz-heavy neighborhood. Expect well-executed bistro standards like duck confit, steak *frites*, and *vol au vent en croute* in a lively room complete with a traditional zinc bar.

### Cru Café and Wine Bar

25 E. Delaware Ave 312-337-4001 L & D daily **$$$** [p304, C3]
Outfitted with chandeliers, fireplaces, and lots of warm, dark wood, Debra Sharpe's Cru Café exudes all the elegance you expect of the Gold Coast. There's an epic wine list, but the menu of artisanal cheese and charcuterie, as well as more substantial sandwiches and entrées, is a draw in its own right. Sharpe's gourmet take-out shop, The Goddess and Grocer, is next door.

### Gibson's

1028 N. Rush St 312-266-8999 L & D daily **$$$$** [p304, C2]
Swanky and expensive, this popular steak house is a perennial hot spot for local politicians and other bigwigs, not to mention well-preserved singles on the prowl. Portions are, unsurprisingly, as outsize as the crowd.

### Il Mulino

1150 N. Dearborn St 312-440-8888 D Mon–Sat **$$$$** [p304, C2]
At $60 a steak you expect a fair amount of excess and ostentation, and Il Mulino – the Chicago incarnation of the New York landmark-turned-chain – delivers, along with oodles of "free" side dishes like fried zucchini and house-cured *salumi*.

**LEFT:** waiting for lunch at the lakeshore.

It functions best, though, as a see-and-be-seen spot for high rollers.

### Le Colonial

✉ 937 N. Rush St ☎ 312-255-0088 ⌚ L & D daily **$$$$** [p304, C3]
Le Colonial serves upscale French-Vietnamese food in a bi-level space evocative of colonial Indochina. Of course, the same grub can be had for much less dong up on Argyle Street; here, you're paying for the ambience.

### Merlo on Maple

✉ 16 W. Maple St ☎ 312-335-8200 ⌚ D daily **$$$** [p304, C2]
A spin-off of Merlo Ristorante in Lincoln Park, this town house restaurant adheres religiously to Slow Food principles of authenticity and seasonality. Everything on the Northern Italian menu – based on family recipes from Emilia-Romagna – is made from scratch with the freshest ingredients, from hand-made tortellini filled with prosciutto, Parmigiano Reggiano, and veal tenderloin to osso buco stewed for eight hours in a bath of cognac and white wine.

### Original Pancake House

✉ 22 E. Bellevue Pl ☎ 312-642-7917 ⌚ B & L daily **$** [p304, C2]
A casual breakfast spot famed for platters loaded with sweet sticky Dutch apple pancakes; it's guaranteed to be packed on weekends.

### Pane Caldo

✉ 72 E. Walton St ☎ 312-649-0055 ⌚ L & D daily **$$$** [p304, C3]
Pane Caldo never seems to get the attention its flashier neighbors command – which is a shame, or a blessing, depending on how you look at it. Serving stylish Northern Italian cuisine in an elegantly muted atmosphere, it's suited equally to a business lunch or leisurely romantic dinner.

### The Pump Room

✉ 1301 N. State Pkwy ☎ 312-266-0360 ⌚ L & D daily **$$$$** [p304, C2]
Frank Sinatra, Bogie and Bacall, Judy and Liza: all held court in the famed Booth One back in the day, but the 70-year-old Pump Room – once the ne plus ultra of jackets-required downtown dining – now traffics mostly in nostalgia. Currently helmed by former Tru chef Nick Sutton, the restaurant is slated for renovations, which may shake off some of the dust.

### Table Fifty-Two

✉ 52 W. Elm St ☎ 312-573-4000 ⌚ D Tue–Sun **$$$** [p304, B2]
This new spot from Art Smith dishes out upscale comfort food to legions of fans hoping to catch a glimpse of Oprah's personal chef, who works the room like the pro he is. Expect Southern-inspired classics like a bubbling crock of three-cheese mac-and-cheese, ancho-crusted Berkshire pork chops, and skillet cornbread spiked with lardoons of Parma ham.

### Third Coast

✉ 1260 N. Dearborn St ☎ 312-649-0730 ⌚ B, L & D daily **$** [p304, C2]
Start the day off with espresso and wind down with a martini without ever leaving this lively bar-café. Menu options range from eggs and scones to salads, sandwiches, and a few entrées like steak fajitas. For those weary of restaurant food, there's even a "boring platter" of chicken, beef, or veggie burger with steamed broccoli and brown rice.

### Tsunami

✉ 1160 N. Dearborn St ☎ 312-642-9911 ⌚ D daily **$$** [p304, B2]
This dark Japanese restaurant excels at artfully presented sushi. The menu ranges from traditional sushi and sashimi to kitchen-sink maki rolls, and wanders into fusion with entrées like peppercorn-encrusted tuna loin with bok choy and a wasabi crème fraîche.

## Bars

**Coq d'Or,** 40 E. Walton Pl (tel: 312-787-2200). All dim lighting and red-leather booths, this Prohibition-era bar in the Drake Hotel – another old-school Chicago landmark – delivers stiff martinis, live piano jazz, and unbeatable vintage ambience.

**Elm Street Liquors,** 12 W. Elm St (tel: 312-337-3200). The name reeks of dive-bar package sales, but it's just part of the concept. With novelty cocktails like the "Trust Fund" and the "Label Whore," this sleek and minimalist new lounge is clearly not for the faint of wallet.

**Original Mother's,** 26 W. Division St (tel: 312-642-7251). Cream and the Velvet Underground once played at Original Mother's, an anchor of the Rush Street party scene in the 1970s. Still huge, loud, and rockin', it now mostly caters to a rowdy crowd of young professionals.

**Underground Wonder Bar,** 10 E. Walton St (tel: 312-266-7761). Run by singer, songwriter, and pianist Lonie Walker, this unpretentious spot caters to a happily mixed crowd of regulars, tourists, jazz fans, and Rush Street bar-hoppers. Open to 4am (5am on Saturday), there's live music every night – jazz, blues, reggae, rock, and funk – and no cover before 9pm Sun–Thu, 8pm Fri–Sat.

Together We Are

# LINCOLN PARK AND OLD TOWN

**Though predominantly residential, these bastions of middle-class prosperity still offer plenty for visitors to do, indoors and out**

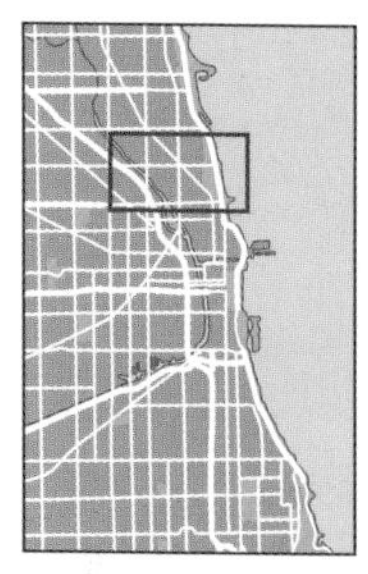

**Main attractions**

- LINCOLN PARK ZOO
- LINCOLN PARK CONSERVATORY
- PEGGY NOTEBAERT NATURE MUSEUM
- THEATER ON THE LAKE
- DEPAUL UNIVERSITY
- BLUES CLUBS
- BIOGRAPH THEATER
- OZ PARK
- ARMITAGE AVENUE SHOPPING
- SECOND CITY
- STEPPENWOLF THEATRE
- CHICAGO HISTORY MUSEUM
- NORTH AVENUE BEACH
- GREEN CITY MARKET

Lincoln Park and Old Town encompass some of the city's most sought-after real estate, and for good reason. Situated to the northwest of the Gold Coast, the neighborhoods are adjacent to leafy, lakefront Lincoln Park and convenient to downtown.

The area was settled by German immigrants in the mid-19th century and remained a solid working-class enclave until just after World War II, when established immigrant families decamped to the suburbs and housing stock began to decline. A resurgence of investment in the 1970s triggered a wave of gentrification, and today once-modest row houses and cottages are occupied by young professionals and affluent families drawn to the area's safe and attractive, if not altogether exhilarating, neighborhoods.

## LINCOLN PARK ❶

On the area's eastern fringe is 1,200-acre (490-hectare) **Lincoln Park**. Designated a cemetery in the mid-19th century in what was then Chicago's northernmost reaches, the park was the first – but not final – resting place of the city's dead, many of whom were carried off by cholera or smallpox. Also buried here were Confederate soldiers who died while in custody at Camp Douglas on the city's South Side during the American Civil War.

It wasn't long before the city fathers, responding to concerns about public health, decided to relocate the bodies and transform the cemetery into a public park. Over the course of the following decades, the borders of the park were altered dramatically as landfill

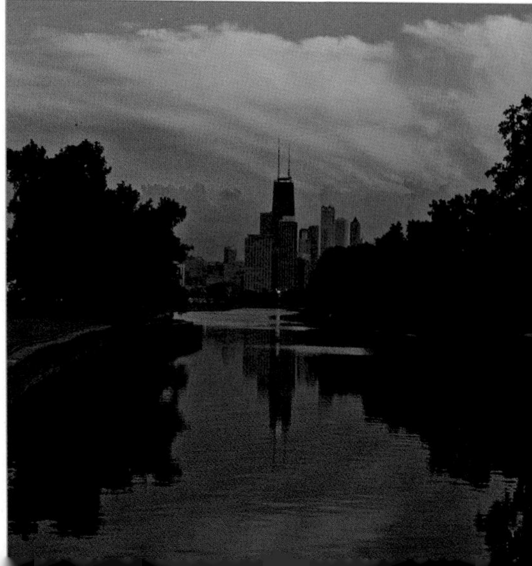

**LEFT:** local farmers sell fresh, seasonal produce at the Green City Market.
**RIGHT:** dusk at Lincoln Park.

**ABOVE:** Lincoln Park Zoo.

was brought in to shore up the coast and canals were dug to drain swampy lowlands, creating the lagoons and ponds that still draw migratory birds and other wildlife. Today, the park's bike paths and trails are a magnet for joggers, bicyclists, and in-line skaters, especially on weekends, when the crowds have to perform a careful dance to avoid crashing into each other.

### Lincoln Park Zoo ❷

✉ 2200 North Cannon Drive ☎ 312-742-2000, www.lpzoo.com ⏲ daily 9am–6pm, to 5pm in winter, to 7pm on summer weekends $ free

The park's main attraction is the **Lincoln Park Zoo**, one of the oldest in the country, established in 1868 with a pair of swans from Central Park in New York City. Nowadays the zoo is quite conscientious about its charges' quality of life, investing in such modern exhibits as an African habitat and a roomy ape house that seek to replicate the animals' native ecosystems. Other

**Lincoln Park and Old Town**

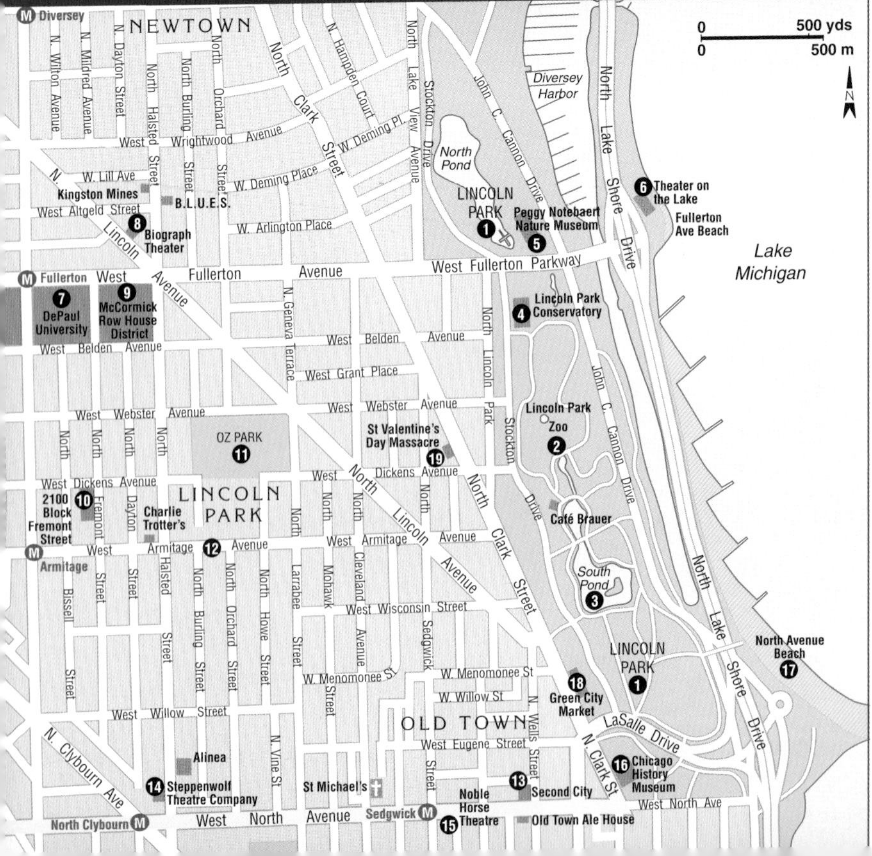

*Recommended Restaurants, Bars & Cafés on pages 176–7*

attractions include a penguin and seabird house, a bear habitat, a primate house, an endangered-species carousel, and the much-loved Farm in the Zoo, with cow-milking demonstrations and opportunities to feed and pet pigs, goats, and other farm animals. At **South Pond** ❸, paddleboat rentals are available right next to the landmark **Café Brauer** (2021 North Stockton Drive; tel: 312-742-2400), an example of early Prairie School architecture.

## Nature centers

Also in the park is the **Lincoln Park Conservatory** ❹ (2391 North Stockton Drive; tel: 312-742-7736; www.chicagoparkdistrict.com; daily 9am–5pm; free), a complex of four iron and glass greenhouses designed by architects Joseph L. Silsbee and M.E. Bell and built between 1890 and 1895. The four structures – the Palm House, Fern House, Orchid House, and Show House – contain a collection of rare and fascinating flora and are especially cozy on a cold winter day; beautifully landscaped outdoor gardens beckon summer visitors.

Across West Fullerton Parkway, the **Peggy Notebaert Nature Museum** ❺ (2430 North Cannon Drive; tel: 773-755-5100; www.chias.org; Mon–Fri 9am–4.30pm, Sat–Sun 10am–5pm; charge) is a big hit with kids for its hands-on exhibits on subjects ranging from recycling and rivers to plant biology and animal "houses." A 2,700-square-ft (250-sq-meter) butterfly haven houses a thousand live butterflies in a re-created tropical forest. A 17,000-square-ft (1,600-sq-meter)

**ABOVE:** the Lincoln Park Conservatory is a warm, green place on a bleak winter day.
**BELOW LEFT:** a volunteer guides visitors through the butterfly haven at the Peggy Notebaert Nature Museum.

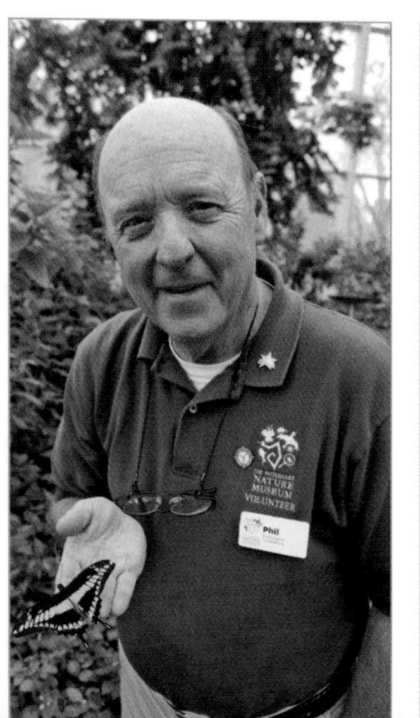


## Tales from the Crypt

Not all of the bodies interred in Lincoln Park were moved when the city decided to relocate the cemetery in the mid-19th century. Construction crews – including one working on an addition to the Chicago History Museum – occasionally unearth human remains in the area, and rumor has it that nearby homeowners have been known to receive a shock during renovations.

The only official vestige of that period in the park's history can be seen just behind the Chicago History Museum: the fenced-off limestone mausoleum of Ira Couch, owner of the Tremont Hotel and Chicago's first millionaire, who died in 1857. When the cemetery was closed, his family successfully argued that the mausoleum would be too expensive to move. Ironically, no one is really sure Couch's remains are inside – records show he was buried in a family plot at another cemetery – or indeed, if there are any remains inside at all. Some historians maintain that the crypt contains the bones of Couch's nephew, also named Ira. The mystery may never be solved, but the mausoleum stands as a curious reminder of what once – and may still – lie beneath the area's carefully manicured lawns.

*Lincoln Park has special DFAs – dog-friendly areas – where dogs can run free and socialize with other canines.*

rooftop garden is part of a green technology project designed to demonstrate eco-friendly building design.

Following Fullerton Parkway east leads to the **Theater on the Lake** ❻ (2401 North Lake Shore Drive; tel: 312-742-7529; www.chicagoparkdistrict.com), which stages performances by theater groups, including Second City and Eclipse Theatre Company. Here, too, is Fullerton Avenue Beach, a low-key strip of sand with a few concession stands and bike rentals.

## Beyond the park

Outside the park, the neighborhood of Lincoln Park lacks a distinct center of gravity, although the area around the 32-acre (13-hectare) campus of **DePaul University** ❼ (West Fullerton and North Lincoln avenues), a Catholic school of some 20,000 students, tends to be a bit livelier than the surrounding residential area.

Shops and restaurants cater mostly to young residents, and there are a few good blues clubs nearby, including **B.L.U.E.S.** (2519 North Halsted Street; tel: 773-528-1012), which books mainly local acts, and the older, larger **Kingston Mines** (2548 North Halsted Street; tel: 773-477-4646) across the street. Farther north is **Delilah's** (2771 North Lincoln Avenue; tel: 773-472-2771; www.delilahschicago.com). There's no live music, but the DJ on duty is likely to be a hot item in the city's music scene, whether the night is dedicated to punk, country, hard rock, or ska, and even the pickiest drinker will find an acceptable tipple among the hundreds of whiskies and ales.

**BELOW:** Kingston Mines is a popular blues club.

### Curtains for Dillinger

Another nearby landmark is the **Biograph Theater** ❽ (2433 North Lincoln Avenue; tel: 773-871-3000), site of the killing of bank robber John Dillinger, declared Public Enemy No. 1 by the federal authorities. On July 22, 1934, federal agents, tipped to Dillinger's presence by the so-called Lady in Red (she actually wore a white blouse and orange skirt), waited for Dillinger to emerge from the theater and shot him six times as he tried to escape. He died in a nearby alley. Listed in the National Historic Register, the Biograph has undergone an extensive renovation and is now operated by the Tony Award-winning Victory Gardens Theater.

### Architectural artifacts

You'll find examples of the area's fine residential architecture in the nearby **McCormick Row House District** ❾ (800 block of West Chalmers Place, 832-58 West Belden Avenue, and 833-927 West Fullerton Avenue), a complex of Queen Anne-style homes constructed in the 1880s by a now-defunct theological seminary.

Also notable are the brick row houses on the **2100 block of Fremont Street** ❿. The houses were built in Italianate style (take note of the tall, narrow windows and incised stone lintels) in 1875 shortly after the Great Fire prompted an ordinance requiring masonry construction.

Recommended Restaurants, Bars & Cafés on pages 176–7

To the east is **Oz Park ⓫** (2021 North Burling Street), named after the fantastical realm imagined by L. Frank Baum, who wrote *The Wonderful Wizard of Oz* while living in Chicago in 1900. The book is said to have grown out of the stories Baum told neighborhood kids. Arranged throughout the park are sculptures by local artist John Kearney: a Tin Man made out of chrome car bumpers and a bronze Cowardly Lion, Scarecrow, Dorothy, and Toto. There's even a yellow brick road, inscribed with the names of donors.

## Armitage Avenue shopping

For shopping in Lincoln Park, start at Halsted Street and head west on **Armitage Avenue ⓬**, where boutiques and salons specialize in trendy styles and high-end lotions and potions aimed mostly at young, well-heeled consumers. The area was awarded landmark status in recognition of its intact, 19th-century commercial architecture, notable for handsome Victorian-era storefronts, decorative masonry, pressed metal ornamentation, corner turrets, and ornate rooflines. Even the El station, with its artful brick and terra-cotta Neoclassical design, reflects the overall look.

This area is also the location of two of the city's finest restaurants: **Charlie Trotter's** (816 West Armitage Avenue; tel: 773-248-6228) and **Alinea** (1723 North Halsted Street; tel: 312-867-0110) both in town houses barely recognizable as businesses save for the valet parking signs in front.

## Old Town

Adjacent to the southern end of Lincoln Park is **Old Town**, a neighborhood of gentrified row houses and frame cottages that still retains a whiff of its hippie past, when artists and actors pioneered the declining housing stock and commercial buildings.

### Second City and Steppenwolf

What brings many visitors to Old Town is **Second City ⓭** (1616 North Wells Street; tel: 312-664-4032; www.secondcity.com), the popular comedy improv company that has nurtured the comic talents of such actors as Alan Arkin, John Belushi, Tina Fey, and Stephen Colbert.

The handprints of famous alums hang outside. On stage, the cast members hone their comedic chops with an all-but-patented mix of scripted and improvised skits.

After a show, head across the street to the **Old Town Ale House** (219 West North Avenue; tel: 312-

**ABOVE:** trim brick town houses are typical of Lincoln Park's residential neighborhoods.
**BELOW:** chefs at work in Charlie Trotter's kitchen, a Lincoln Park restaurant with a large and loyal following.

**ABOVE:**
Old Town is known for quirky independent boutiques that reflect the owner's personality.

944-7020), where Second City performers and students have been meeting for drinks practically since the bar opened in 1958. The exterior has been spruced up, but the inside is still as comfortably rundown as ever. The mural and portraits on the walls – many are the work of one of the owners – are of the bar's many regulars over the years. The jukebox plays only jazz; the former owner, now deceased, wasn't fond of rock and roll, and the current owners have continued the tradition.

Also in Old Town is the highly regarded **Steppenwolf Theatre Company** ⓮ (1650 North Halsted Avenue, tel: 312-335-1650, www.steppenwolf.org), whose ensemble includes John Malkovich, Joan Allen, Gary Sinise, and other actors familiar from film and television.

The annual Old Town Art Fair features the work of more than 200 artists as well as live music, food vendors, and garden tours. The fair is held in summer in the leafy Old Town Triangle District around Wisconsin and Orleans streets.

### Theater on the hoof

Performers of a very different sort are showcased at the **Noble Horse Theatre** ⓯ (1410 North Orleans Street; tel: 312-266-7878; www.noblehorsechicago.com), a riding-academy-turned-theater that features the talents of expert riders and highly trained horses in the tradition of European dressage. The 300-seat theater is set in a handsome 1871 building tucked into a narrow, cobblestone side street.

## Chicago History Museum ⓰

1601 North Clark Street · 312-642-4600, www.chicagohistory.org
Mon–Wed 9.30am–4.30pm, Thu to 8pm, Fri–Sat to 4.30pm, Sun noon–5pm · charge

On the southern edge of Lincoln Park is the **Chicago History Museum.** Renovated in 2006, the museum encompasses three floors of exhibit and research space, with dioramas illustrating the growth of the city from a prairie outpost to a major urban center, including an extensive treatment of the Chicago Fire of 1871. The museum's collection of 22 million artifacts takes in the ordinary and exotic, from common household items of the 19th and early 20th centuries to a 1978

Recommended Restaurants, Bars & Cafés on pages 176–7

Monte Carlo lowrider and Michael Jordan's basketball jersey.

The Studs Terkel Oral History Archive contains interviews conducted by the radio host and historian over the course of his 50-year career. Temporary exhibits reflect the breadth of the city's cultural heritage (a recent show investigated the elements of a classic Chicago hot dog), and a series of lectures, seminars, and movies give visitors a chance to interact with scholars, authors, and other experts.

### A place in the sun

To the east of the History Museum, across a pedestrian bridge over North Lake Shore Drive, is **North Avenue Beach** ⓱. One of the city's liveliest beaches, it attracts a mostly young crowd with summer volleyball tournaments, live music, and bicycle rentals. Those who prefer more intellectual pursuits can head over to the vintage chess pavilion and try their luck with one of the regular players. A beach house resembling a vintage ocean liner has burgers and ice cream on the first level and a casual rooftop restaurant, **Castaway's Bar & Grill** (1603 North Lake Shore Drive, 773-281-1200), with skyline views.

## Green City Market ⓲

✉ Between 1750 North Clark Street and Stockton Drive ☎ 847-424-2486, www.chicagogreencitymarket.org
⏲ Wed and Sat 7am–1.30pm

From May to October, the **Green City Market** takes up residence on Lincoln Park's southwest edge (it moves to the Peggy Notebaert Nature Museum in winter). This is a market for serious foodies. The farmers and vendors are committed to sustainable agriculture, and the products, including fruits, vegetables, cheese, meat, honey, and baked goods, are locally grown or produced. Area chefs forage here for their restaurants and frequently offer cooking demonstrations.

### Massacre site

Farther along North Clark Street, between West Dickens and West Webster avenues, an inconspicuous patch of grass is the site of the **St Valentine's Day Massacre** ⓳ (2122 North Clark Street). At the time of the incident, the lot was occupied by a garage where gangster George "Bugs" Moran kept shipments of bootleg liquor.

On February 14, 1929, six of Moran's henchmen were waiting for their boss when four men (two disguised as police officers) entered the garage. Moran's men, plus an apparently innocent hanger-on, were lined up against a wall and sprayed with machine gun fire. The killers were never identified, but the blame fell squarely on crime boss Al Capone, who claimed to be on vacation in Florida at the time of the murders. ❑

**ABOVE:** Second City has been delighting audiences with improvisational comedy for more than four decades.
**BELOW:** Green City Market.

# BEST RESTAURANTS, BARS AND CAFÉS

## Restaurants

Prices for a three-course dinner per person with a half-bottle of house wine:

**$** = under $20
**$$** = $20–$45
**$$$** = $45–$60
**$$$$** = over $60

### Alinea

1723 N. Halsted St
312-867-0110 D Wed–Sun **$$$$** [p304, A1]

Call it molecular gastronomy or "sci-fi" cooking. When *Gourmet* magazine named Alinea the best restaurant in America in October 2006, the honor only formalized the buzz that the avant-garde restaurant's wunderkind chef, French Laundry-trained Grant Achatz, was the standard-bearer for a revolution in contemporary cuisine. Alinea's menu has been toned down some since then, but it's still full of complicated freeze-dried thises and gelled thats, all impeccably prepared and delivered on custom serving ware that's an integral part of this tightly controlled but still sublimely elegant dining experience. It's not cheap: the 12- and 24-course tasting menus will set you back $135 and $195 respectively, and that's before you've ordered wine.

### Boka

1729 N. Halsted St
312-337-6070 D daily **$$** [p304, A1]

With Charlie Trotter's former chef de cuisine now at the helm, this contemporary American restaurant has quickly become an unheralded star. Look for creative, ambitious dishes like scallop-stuffed squid with black tapioca or a knockout plate of velvety veal cheeks. Known for efficient pre-theater service, Boka is also open late enough for a post-show nosh.

### Charlie Trotter's

816 W. Armitage Ave
773-248-6228 D Tue–Sat **$$$$**

This discreet Lincoln Park town house catapulted Chicago fine dining past fussy French cuisine 20 years ago, and though newbies like Alinea's Grant Achatz have taken the torch, the namesake chef is still a formidable player – as evidenced by the number of hotshot chefs, sommeliers, and servers around town whose résumés proudly tout their Trotter training. Three seasonal tasting menus are offered, including a vegetarian one that many think regularly outshines its meaty counterparts; the wine cellar is considered one of the best in the world.

### Chicago Pizza and Oven Grinder Co.

2121 N. Clark St 773-248-2570 L Sat–Sun, D daily **$**

Offering a unique take on stuffed pizza, this place bakes it in a bowl and flips it upside-down onto the plate: think pizza pot pie. Salads and sandwiches are huge, making dinner a great deal, though the subterranean dining room is often packed.

### Fixture

2706 N. Ashland Ave
773-248-3331 D daily **$$**

This is a cozy lounge with a good beer list and an even better menu of late-night nibbles like meatball-sized buffalo sliders and a smoky mac-and-cheese with bacon and scallops. Try not to laugh at the James Bond-themed wine list.

### Half Shell

676 W. Diversey Pkwy
773-549-1773 L & D daily **$$**

This grungy basement dive serves fresh, tasty seafood. It's not cheap, but it's easier on the wallet than, say, Shaw's. Not in the mood for crab legs? The steak burger is good, too. Cash only.

### Kamehachi

1400 N. Wells St 312-664-3663 L Mon–Sat, D daily **$$** [p304, B2]

A classic sushi spot in Old Town – no saketinis here, just fresh raw fish, expertly prepared. The dining room can be cramped, but there's seating in the upstairs lounge and in the garden, weather permitting.

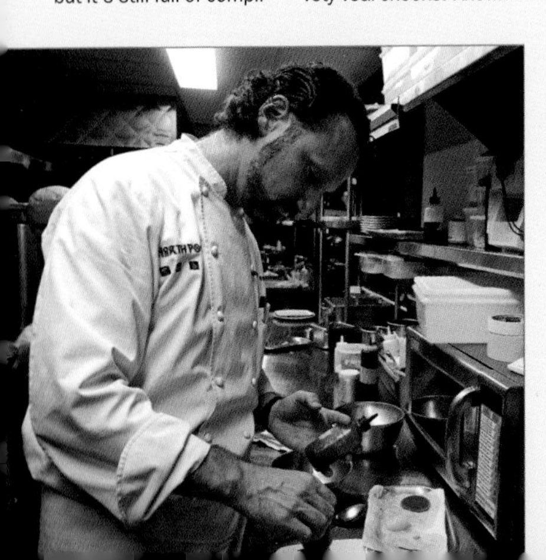

**LEFT:** Chef Bruce Sherman of North Pond.

### Karyn's Raw

1901 N. Halsted St 312-255-1590 L & D daily **$$**

Chicago's most vocal preacher of the raw food gospel, Karyn Calabrese, has spun her passion into a mini-empire offering one-stop shopping for all your holistic needs. Her flagship restaurant isn't for everyone, but initiates swear by dishes like pasta primavera made of julienned vegetable "pasta" tossed with nut sauce and mushrooms.

### Maza

2748 N. Lincoln Ave 773-929-9600 D daily **$**

Order the deluxe appetizer platter at this welcoming Lebanese restaurant and the stupefying array of dishes – smoky *baba ghannoush*, garlicky *ful*, challenging pickled turnips – could well render an entrée superfluous. It's worth forging onward to lamb *shawirma* and couscous, washed down with Lebanese red wine.

### Mon Ami Gabi

2300 N. Lincoln Park West Ave 773-348-8886 D daily **$$**

Gabino Sotelino's charming bistro offers solid French comfort food – onion soup, roast chicken, steak au poivre – in an atmosphere that convincingly replicates a Parisian salon, with lovely views of the Lincoln Park Conservatory.

### North Pond

2610 N. Cannon Dr 773-477-5845 L Tue–Fri, D Tue–Sun **$$$$**

Smack in the middle of Lincoln Park, North Pond is the most beautiful spot in Chicago for a meal, with warm Arts-and-Crafts-inspired interiors opening onto views of the skyline and the eponymous pond. Chef Bruce Sherman sits on the board of the Green City Market, and his daring yet assured cooking reflects a commitment to local, seasonal, sustainable eating.

### Old Jerusalem

411 N. Wells St 312-944-0459 L & D daily **$** [p304, B1]

This long-standing Old Town storefront is a cheap, reliable alternative to the more upscale offerings on this stretch of Wells. No surprises here, just solid Middle Eastern standards and a friendly, low-key scene.

### Riccardo Trattoria

2119 N. Clark St 773-549-0038 D Tue–Sun **$$–$$$**

This intimate, unpretentious restaurant is one of Chicago's best-kept secrets. Chef and owner Riccardo Micchi isn't the type to delegate; he's usually the man in the kitchen dishing up rustic Tuscan standards like farfalle with a venison ragu and a stellar rendition of tripe Florentine.

### Salpicon

1252 N. Wells St 312-988-7811 D daily, Br Sun **$$** [p304, B2]

Rick Bayless acolyte Priscila Satkoff delivers creative regional Mexican dishes inspired as much by her Mexico City childhood as her towering mentor. This festive Old Town spot has drawn steady praise since 1995, a reflection of Satkoff's flair for mixing flavors from both north and south of the border.

### The Wieners Circle

2622 N. Clark St 773-477-7444 L & D daily **$**

Prepare for verbal abuse at this late-night institution. It's a popular stop for those desperately trying to sop up the alcohol in their system before bed, and the staff isn't afraid to put the rowdy crowd in its place. Char-grilled Chicago dogs, thick-cut fries, and chocolate milkshakes make it all deliciously worthwhile.

## *Bars*

**Delilah's,** 2771 N. Lincoln Ave (tel: 773-472-2771). This dark, old-school punk hangout is known citywide for its raucous DJs and owner Mike Miller's staggering selection of whisky – more than 300 bottles, with a bias toward bourbon.

**Goose Island Brewing Co,** 1800 N. Clybourn Ave (tel: 312-915-0071). On any given day this brewpub offers at least ten of its award-winning beers on tap, plus burgers and other pub grub. There's a $5 tour of the brewery every Sunday at 3pm.

**Hideout,** 1354 W. Wabansia St (tel: 773-227-4433). Set in an isolated industrial area, the ramshackle Hideout is one of the city's most eclectic music venues, not to mention a cozy spot to grab a beer or three.

**Old Town Ale House,** 219 W. North Ave (tel: 312-944-7020). Across the street from Second City and open to 4am, the funky, dusty Old Town has been the watering hole of choice for comics, actors, and other neighborhood ne'er-do-wells since 1958. Off-kilter portraits of regulars painted by current owner Bruce Elliot crowd the walls, and the jukebox offers jazz and jazz only.

**Webster's Wine Bar,** 1480 W. Webster Ave (773-868-0608). Offering more than 35 wines by the glass, Chicago's oldest wine bar is a classy but low-key place to sink into a comfy sofa and sip a glass or two.

*Recommended Restaurants, Bars & Cafés on pages 186–7*

# LAKEVIEW TO ANDERSONVILLE

**These North Side neighborhoods stretch along the lake with enclaves catering to gay men, lesbians, foodies, and ever-hopeful Cubs fans**

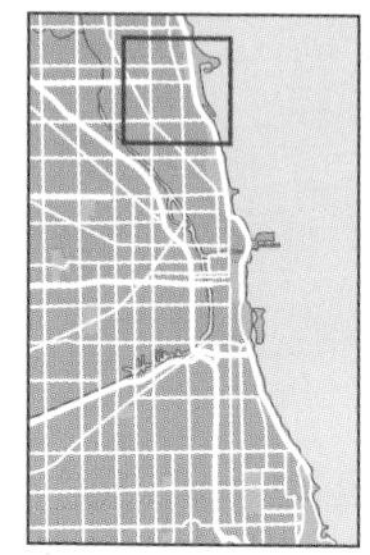

For many Chicagoans, the true heart of the city beats not at the Sears Tower, the Loop, or the lakefront but at Wrigley Field, one of the country's oldest major league ballparks and the home of the ever-hapless, ever-hopeful Chicago Cubs. The ballpark anchors an array of neighborhoods: Lakeview (which includes the Wrigleyville area), Andersonville, and Uptown. Taken as a whole, they're bounded roughly by Diversey Parkway to the south, Ridge Avenue to the north, Ravenswood Avenue to the west, and the lake to the east.

Some Chicagoans consider the entire North Side a white-bread wonderland, but the area is fairly diverse, particularly Uptown and the small gay neighborhood known as Boys Town. It's also rich in history: here you'll find Clark Street, the descendant of a Native American trail that once ran through the area; Graceland Cemetery, the final resting place of Marshall Field and other famous Chicagoans; and the Green Mill, a former mobster hangout and respected jazz venue.

Clark Street cuts diagonally across the street grid and is a convenient base for exploring the area, although traffic is horrendous when the Cubs are playing. It's best to skip driving or even taking the bus in favor of the El's convenient Red Line stops at Addison, Wilson, Lawrence, Argyle, and Berwyn.

## LAKEVIEW

In the early years, Lakeview's chief industry was celery farming, courtesy of the Germans, Swedes, and Luxembourgers who settled here in the

**Main attractions**

- WRIGLEY FIELD
- BOYS TOWN
- SOUTHPORT CORRIDOR
- MUSIC BOX THEATRE
- SCHUBA'S TAVERN
- GREEN MILL
- ARGYLE STREET
- SWEDISH AMERICAN MUSEUM CENTER
- NEO-FUTURARIUM
- GRACELAND CEMETERY

**LEFT:** Schuba's Tavern features top-notch local talent and touring bands.
**RIGHT:** a musical interlude at Wrigley Field, home of the Chicago Cubs.

**ABOVE:** the Pride Parade is a celebration of the gay community.

1800s. After the ritzy (and now demolished) Lakeview House hotel was built near Lake Shore Drive and Byron Street in 1854, wealthy Chicagoans began flocking here to escape the summer heat and periodic outbreaks of cholera. Lakeview was annexed to Chicago in 1889, and Wrigley Field was built in 1914. Today Lakeview is less a neighborhood in its own right than a conglomeration of three smaller enclaves: Wrigleyville, Boys Town (aka Lakeview East), and West Lakeview.

**Lakeview to Andersonville**



## Wrigley Field ❶

⊠ 1060 West Addison Street ☎ box office 773-404-2827, 800-THE-CUBS

If chewing gum magnate William Wrigley, Jr, hadn't bought the ballpark in 1920, baseball fans today would probably by coming to Weeghmanville; the field's original name was Weeghman Park.

Wrigley has seen its share of historic moments during its nine decades of service, including Babe Ruth's legendary "called shot" during the 1932 World Series. Alas, the Cubs nowadays are mostly famous for their less than stellar performance. The last time the team reached the World Series was 1945; the last time they won, 1908.

Still, Cubby fans maintain hope that this year will be the year, and Wrigley's small size, ivy-covered outfield wall, and lake views make it a great place to catch a game. Afterward, head across Clark Street to one of the many bars that cater to the wall-to-wall hordes of Cubs fans who gather for postgame imbibing.

If you can't catch a game, tours of the park are offered during the season (tel: 773-404-2827 for tour schedule; charge) and include a visit to the playing field, clubhouses, dugouts, press box, bleachers, and famous manually operated scoreboard.

## BOYS TOWN

Southeast of Wrigley Field, in the area bounded more or less by Addison and Clark streets, Lake Shore Drive, and Belmont Avenue, is **Boys Town ❷**, the hub of Chicago's gay community. Massive rainbow-ringed pylons line North Halsted Street – the neighborhood's main strip – and no one blinks an eye at the many same-sex couples holding hands.

To get your bearings, start at Belmont Avenue and walk north on Halsted Street past a lively mix of shops, restaurants, and cafés. Night-

Map on page 180

*Recommended Restaurants, Bars & Cafés on pages 186–7*

time action gravitates around several bars here. **Roscoe's Tavern** (3356 North Halsted Street; tel: 773-281-3355) is one of the largest and most popular, with a beer garden, a dance floor, pool tables, and a mostly male crowd, though women are welcome.

**Circuit** (3641 North Halsted Street; tel: 773-325-2233) is a see-and-be-seen dance club strictly for hard partying. There's a pool table and the attached, somewhat quieter Rehab Lounge, but most of the action is on the dance floor. On the first Saturday of every month, Circuit hosts "Girlbar" for lesbians and bisexual women. If you'd rather stay on the sidelines, the **Kit Kat Lounge and Supper Club** (3700 North Halsted Street; tel: 773-525-1111) stages drag shows, with genuinely gorgeous female impersonators lip-syncing pop hits. The food here is skippable, but the large and creative martini menu is worth sampling.

## Stop and shop

If you're in the mood for shopping, **Gay Mart** (3457 North Halsted Street; tel: 773-929-4272) sells anything you can slap a rainbow on, including jewelry, T-shirts, and novelty items of varying degrees of naughtiness. For something more thoughtful, **Unabridged Books** (3251 North Broadway Street; tel: 773-883-9119) is one of Chicago's best independent bookstores, with a large gay and lesbian section as well as plenty of general-interest titles.

## Southport Corridor

Often lumped in with the neighboring Roscoe Village area, West Lakeview doesn't get a lot of respect,

**Above, Left and Below:** Cubs fans take in a game at a neighborhood sports bar and in the stands, including bleachers on town houses across the street from the stadium.

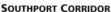

**ABOVE:** preparing for the Pride Parade. **BELOW:** now a highly regarded jazz club, the Green Mill is a former speakeasy once owned by an associate of Al Capone.

except for the stretch of Southport Avenue between Belmont Avenue and Clark Street, which has turned into a shopping and dining destination dubbed the **Southport Corridor**. It's anchored by the historic **Music Box Theatre** ❸ (3733 North Southport Avenue; tel: 773-871-6604), an almost 80-year-old venue for classic, foreign, and independent films. The concession counter puts real butter on the popcorn (a rarity in this multiplex age), an organist sometimes plays jaunty 1920s and 1930s tunes before the show, and the theater ceiling is painted to resemble the night sky, with tiny twinkling lights. In short, it's a classic old-time movie house.

## Sweet stuff

A few minutes' walk south takes you to the **Southport Grocery and Café** (3552 North Southport Avenue; tel: 773-665-0100), widely considered the maker of the best cupcakes in the city. Grab one for a quick sugar rush, then press on to Belmont Avenue. Hang a left, and you'll find yourself at **Uncle Fun** (1338 West Belmont Avenue; tel: 773-477-8223), a souvenir shop, toy store, and "goofatorium" that sells switchblade-style combs, hand buzzers, Mexican wrestling masks, tiny harmonicas, and hundreds of other novelty items. Kids will have a field day here. Few things are priced over $10.

Nearby **Schuba's Tavern** (3159 North Southport Avenue; tel: 773-525-2508) is host to big-name touring musicians as well as top local performers. Shows are in the none-too-big back room, so it's a good idea to book tickets in advance.

## UPTOWN

Uptown's outermost perimeters are roughly Lake Michigan on the east, Irving Park Road on the south, Ravenswood Avenue on the west, and Foster Avenue on the north. In the early 20th century, Uptown was a swanky neighborhood of luxury hotels, swinging speakeasies, and dance halls like the **Aragon Ballroom** ❹ (now a concert venue at 1106 West Lawrence Avenue; tel: 773-561-9500). Then a destination for social dancers from all over the city, the Aragon was famous for its live WGN broadcasts, lavish Mediterranean-inspired interior, and unusually springy dance floor.

### Before Hollywood

Uptown was also the location of Essanay Studios, a powerhouse in the early days of film, with stars like Gloria Swanson, Charlie Chaplin, and studio co-founder G.M. "Broncho Billy" Anderson turning out scores of silent shorts, including the Chaplin vehicle *His New Job*. The studio collapsed in 1918, but its building, at 1333-45 West Argyle Street, still stands. It's now occupied by St Augustine College.

When a housing crisis hit after World War II, Uptown's posh apartments were converted to smaller, cheaper units, the affluent residents left for the suburbs, and the neighborhood slid into squalor. Even the glamorous Aragon fell into disrepair.

There's been evidence of gentrification in recent years. Middle-class Chicagoans are discovering a supply of affordable condos, and new businesses are opening, including the inevitable retail chains. Some longtime residents fear that Uptown will shed its intensely diverse character and become just another yuppie outpost. Time will tell. In the meanwhile, the neighborhood remains a blend of grit, faded glamour, and tentative resurgence.

## Green Mill ❺

4802 North Broadway Street
773-878-5552

Uptown's glamorous past comes to life at the Green Mill, which celebrated its centennial in 2007. The club's notoriety stems mostly from its association with Al Capone, whose associate Jack "Machine Gun" McGurn was a co-owner of the speakeasy during Prohibition.

Underneath the club, a network of underground tunnels hid illicit booze (and, reputedly, the mobsters' regular poker games).

These days, the liquor is in plain sight, and music still pours out of the place. Jazz greats Von Freeman, Kurt Elling, Branford Marsalis, and Patricia Barber have all performed

A few chichi shops have sprung up near Wilson and Magnolia. One is Unique So Chique (4600 N. Magnolia Ave), a combo boutique, tea room, and chocolatier. It looks unassuming, but *Chicago* magazine called its tea service "the best in Chicago."

**ABOVE:** Uptown bar.
**BELOW:** grooving to the music at Schuba's Tavern.

Chicago pizza is not all deep-dish or cut into squares. Spacca Napoli (1769 W. Sunnyside Ave) serves brick-oven Neapolitan pies with a blistered, chewy, ultra-thin crust and light, fresh toppings. The pizza margherita can't be beat.

here. There's music every night of the week; cover charges rarely exceed $12. The Green Mill is also host to the weekly Uptown Poetry Slam, a raucous head-to-head poetry competition.

### Argyle Street

Just off the Argyle El stop (Argyle between Winthrop and Broadway) is a small Vietnamese community. It doesn't really have a name – most people just refer to it as Argyle Street – but the foodies who flock to its many excellent, family-run restaurants are too busy scarfing down *banh mi* (a sort of French-Vietnamese sandwich) and other traditional dishes to notice. If you're new to the area, **Tank Noodle** (4955 North Broadway Street; tel: 773-878-2253) is a good place to start.

## ANDERSONVILLE

Technically a subset of a larger neighborhood called Edgewater, Andersonville stretches from approximately Magnolia to Ravenswood avenues and Winnemac Avenue to Victoria Street. Most of its shops and restaurants are clustered on Clark Street; the intersection of Clark Street and Foster Avenue is a major hub. A few chains, like the inevitable Starbucks, have set up shop, but for the most part this is an enclave of independent businesses and ethnic restaurants.

The remnants of Chicago's Swedish community, once the largest in the United States, survive here, primarily in the form of the small **Swedish American Museum Center** ❻ (5211 North Clark Street; tel: 773-728-8111, www.samac.org; Tue–Fri 10am–4pm, Sat–Sun 11am–4pm; charge). The museum features exhibits drawn from a collection of art and artifacts chronicling the Swedish immigrant experience, a special children's area, a gift shop, and a series of concerts, lectures, films, folk dancing, and other cultural programs. However, most visitors to Andersonville are more interested in another, if only vaguely Swedish, institution: **Ann Sather** (5207 North Clark; tel: 773-271-6677), a neighboring breakfast and lunch spot serving lingonberry pancakes, Swedish waffles, and killer cinnamon rolls.

**BELOW:** an actress prepares to take the stage at a Lakeview theater.

*Recommended Restaurants, Bars & Cafés on pages 186–7*

Along with Boys Town, Andersonville is considered one of the city's gay enclaves. But whereas Boys Town is all about the gentlemen, Andersonville skews lesbian. The friendly, mostly lesbian bar **Star Gaze** (5419 North Clark Street; tel: 773-561-7363) has a pool table, a dance floor, and occasional salsa lessons. The nearby **Women and Children First** bookstore (5233 North Clark Street; tel: 773-769-9299) stocks GLBT (Gay, Lesbian, Bisexual, and Transgender) and feminist books as well as general-interest titles.

You'll find lots of little boutiques on Clark Street north of Foster Avenue, but it's just as much fun, a lot cheaper, and a lot better for your karma to check out the **Brown Elephant** (5404 North Clark Street; tel: 773-271-9382), a thrift shop run by the Howard Brown Health Center, a respected GLBT health care provider. Hidden treasures here have been known to include cashmere coats and Kate Spade purses.

Another of Andersonville's shopping venues, **Scout** (5221 North Clark Street; tel: 773-275-5700), styles itself as an "urban antique shop," with lots of cleverly displayed vintage pieces. Or venture south of Foster Avenue to **The Wooden Spoon** (5047 North Clark Street; tel: 773-293-3190), an upscale cookware shop with cooking classes and a small but thoughtful cookbook collection.

Sitting a block west of the Clark-Foster intersection, the **Neo-Futurarium** ❼ theater collective (5153 North Ashland Avenue; tel: 773-275-5255) puts on quirky, engaging shows like the long-running *Too Much Light Makes the Baby Go Blind*, which features 30 plays performed in 60 minutes. The repertoire changes often, so you'll never see the same show twice. Advance tickets aren't available, and by showtime (11.30pm Fri and Sat, 7pm Sun) the line of hopeful theater-goers is around the block, so get there early or shoot for the Sunday show, when attendance is usually lighter. ❑

**ABOVE:** North Side neighbors get together for a block party.
**BELOW:** the El is fast and convenient, especially on game days when traffic is jammed around Wrigley Field.

## Graceland Cemetery

One of Uptown's loveliest sights is also one of the most historic: Graceland Cemetery ❽ (4001 North Clark Street; tel: 773-525-1105), the final resting place of department store mogul Marshall Field, architects Daniel Burnham, Louis Sullivan, and Ludwig Mies van der Rohe, and other prominent Chicagoans, some with modest gravestones, others with palatial mausoleums and statuary. Also buried here is George Pullman, creator of the Pullman railway car, who was so despised by his workers that his coffin was encased in cement to prevent the body from being desecrated. Visitors are welcome to stroll the grounds on their own, or take a docent-led tour offered by the Chicago Architecture Foundation (tel: 312-922-3432).

# BEST RESTAURANTS, BARS AND CAFÉS

## Restaurants

Prices for a three-course dinner per person with a half-bottle of house wine:

- **$** = under $20
- **$$** = $20–$45
- **$$$** = $45–$60
- **$$$$** = over $60

### Ann Sather

929 W. Belmont Ave 773-348-2378 B & L daily **$**

This beloved Swedish restaurant is owned by alderman Tom Tunney and famed for its rich, gooey cinnamon rolls. There's another one at 5207 N. Clark in Andersonville.

### Anteprima

5316 N. Clark St 773-506-9990 D daily **$$**

Rustic, regional Italian on the Clark Street strip. The antipasti are a standout, full of unusual bites like veal meatballs and some wondrously varied salumi.

### Arun's

4156 N. Kedzie Ave 773-539-1909 D Tue–Sun **$$$$**

The immigrant neighborhood of Albany Park – far west of the lakefront – is home to one of Chicago's most celebrated restaurants. Chef Arun Sampanthavivat (who also has a hand in the French-Asian fusion spot Le Lan in River North) is the Charlie Trotter of Thai food, offering an $85 12-course tasting menu that's tailored to the taste of each individual diner. Critics gripe that for the money you could put together an exhaustive, and better, sampler at any number of fine Thai storefronts, but Arun's is a good choice for a special occasion.

### Ba Le Sandwich Shop

5018 N. Broadway 773-561-4424 B, L & D daily **$**

Chicago's go-to spot for authentic Vietnamese subs: fresh, crusty rolls topped with mayo, cilantro, fish sauce, jalapeños, and pickled daikon, and filled with a variety of meats, from lemongrass sausage to shrimp cake. There's not much room to sit down, so get it to go and head to the lake for a picnic.

### Chicago Diner

3411 N. Halsted St 773-935-6696 L & D daily, Br Sat–Sun **$**

Vegans and vegetarians across the city have been beating a path to this North Side institution since 1983. Service is notoriously sluggish, but if you're looking for tofu and seitan fajitas, or a big bowl of black beans and kale, this is the place.

### Deleece

4004 N. Southport Ave 773-325-1710 L Tue–Sun, D daily **$$**

This unpretentious neighborhood restaurant turns out surprisingly sophisticated globally influenced dishes like caramelized salmon with Chinese black sticky rice. Monday and Tuesday there's a $20 prix fixe dinner.

### Erwin

2925 N. Halsted St 773-528-7200 D Tue–Sun **$$**

Erwin Dreschler's namesake restaurant was an early-adopter of the gospel of seasonal cooking. His streamlined American dishes showcase fresh ingredients and simple techniques. Low-key but classy, Erwin draws a mature crowd of theatergoers and neighborhood regulars.

### Ethiopian Diamond

6120 N. Broadway 773-338-6100 L & D daily **$**

Utterly unglamorous, the friendly Diamond offers delicious, authentic Ethiopian food – mostly *watts*, or stews of beef, chicken, lamb, lentil, and cabbage, on spongy-sour *injera* pancakes. Food is served family-style, and

**LEFT:** Hopleaf serves 200 varieties of beer.
**RIGHT:** Hot Doug's gives Chicago dogs an exotic twist.

the room is huge, making it a great place for a group; there's often music on Friday nights.

### Hot Doug's

3324 N. California Ave
773-279-9550 L Mon–Sat **$**

Catalonian pork sausage with saffron *rouille* and almond-cured Spanish goat cheese, anyone? A couple miles west of Lakeview, Doug Sohn's cheery "encased meat emporium" serves up everything from classic Chicago dogs and brats to exotica like venison or alligator tube steaks. Long lines are common, especially on Friday and Saturday, when Sohn makes his notorious duck-fat French fries.

### Indie Café

5951 N. Broadway Ave
773-561-5577 L & D daily **$**

The Thai and Japanese food at this tiny, spartan Edgewater BYOB has a hard-core following. Devotees laud the beautifully presented, classic dishes and the low prices. The downside: no reservations accepted, which means there's often a wait for a table.

### Jin Ju

5203 N. Clark St 773-334-6377 D Tue–Sun **$$**

Intimidated by *kim chee*? Offering Westernized Korean food in a modern setting, Jin Ju is a gateway to Korean cuisine. Wash your meal down with one of several "soju-tinis," cocktails made with the vodka-like sweet potato spirit that's practically Korea's national drink.

### Marigold

4832 N. Broadway
773-293-4653 D Tue–Sun **$$**

This upscale Indian spot just north of the Green Mill is an Uptown newcomer and indicative of the changing face of the neighborhood. Traditional dishes like lamb *vindaloo* and *sag paneer* are given a creative spin; save room for desserts like ginger crème brûlée.

### Orange

3231 N. Clark St 773-549-4400 B & L daily, D Tue–Sun, Br Sat–Sun **$**

Don't go if you're not prepared to wait; Orange is usually mobbed. Your patience will be rewarded with cutesy-quirky takes on breakfast classics like chai French toast, a "flight" of silver-dollar pancakes in various flavors, and "frushi," or fruit sushi.

### Reza's

5255 N. Clark St 773-561-1898 L & D daily, Br Sun **$**

A bustling Persian institution (there's an even bigger location in River North), Reza's will satisfy a big appetite. Portions are beyond generous; order a combo kabob plate and be prepared to take some dill rice and cubed meat home for breakfast.

### Sola

3868 N. Lincoln Ave
773-327-3868 L Thu–Fri, D daily, Br Sat–Sun **$$**

Chef Carol Wallack (formerly of Deleece) gives contemporary American cooking an Asian-Pacific spin inspired by her Hawaiian roots at this airy, sunny spot. In a hurry? The entire menu is available to go; call in your order, then drive over and it'll be delivered to you curbside.

## Bars

**Big Chicks**, 5024 N. Sheridan Rd (tel: 773-728-5511). Attitude-free gay bar presided over by matriarch Michelle Fire, with patio seating in summer and a free Sunday buffet from sister restaurant Tweet, Let's Eat.

**Cullen's Bar & Grill**, 3741 N. Southport Ave (tel: 773-975-0600). Authentic Irish bar where the bartenders know how to pull a proper pint. There's usually traditional Irish music on Sunday nights, and on Tuesdays the bar hosts an open jam session: BYO fiddle.

**Green Mill**, 4802 N. Broadway Ave (tel: 773-878-5552). The birthplace of the poetry slam and a longtime jazz mecca, the Green Mill is a Chicago institution, restored to its Prohibition-era glory by owner Dave Jemilo in the 1980s. Expect a diverse late-night crowd of hipsters, jazz fans, and overzealous partyers.

**Hopleaf Bar**, 5148 N. Clark St (tel: 773-334-9851). One of Chicago's elite beer bars, the Hopleaf offers an immense, ever-changing selection of beers on tap and bottled. Belgians are the house specialty, many served in elaborate glassware particular to the brand. The rear dining room serves Belgian specialties, including killer mussels and *frites*.

**Long Room**, 1612 W. Irving Park Rd (tel: 773-665-4500). The hip-but-mellow Long Room gets its name from the 60-ft (20-meter) bar stretching the length of the narrow tavern. An outdoor beer garden seats 60.

# FEASTS AND FESTIVALS

**Chicagoans like getting together for a good time, and the city's numerous neighborhood and downtown festivals provide plenty of opportunity**

Chicago is known as the City of Big Shoulders, but it could equally be known as the City of Big Parties. Throughout the year, Chicago residents flock to the city's numerous festivals to enjoy food, drink, entertainment, company, and conviviality. Most of these joyous occasions are held on weekends or holidays, and many of them are held during the summer, but Chicago's festival season is actually 12 months long.

The king of the festivals – and the biggest and most popular of the many annual lakefront celebrations – is the annual Taste of Chicago, a massive food frenzy in Grant Park that takes place in late June and early July. As well as an abundant supply of food, there is also music and entertainment galore. Dozens of the city's restaurants set up stands for the 10-day gorge, and more than 4 million hungry people descend on them.

**ABOVE:** Thanksgiving parade on State Street.
**RIGHT:** a reveler gets into the spirit of the South Side St Patrick's Day celebration.

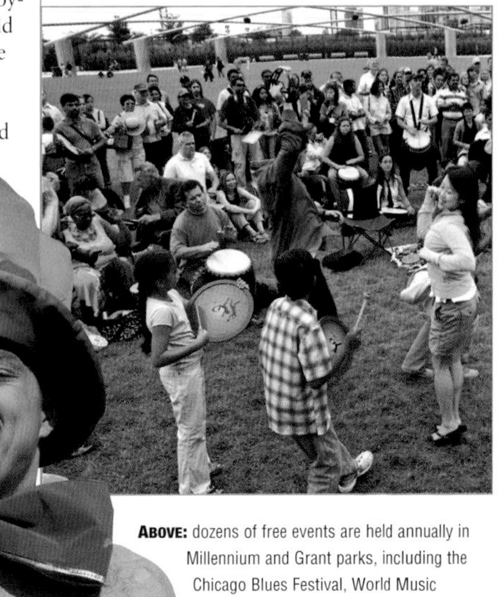

**ABOVE:** dozens of free events are held annually in Millennium and Grant parks, including the Chicago Blues Festival, World Music Festival, Made in Chicago jazz series, and concerts by the Chicago Symphony Orchestra and Lyric Opera Company.

**ABOVE:** a marching band parades down State Street during the Thanksgiving celebration.

**ABOVE:** the Taste of Chicago is held during the last week of June and the first week of July and culminates with Fourth of July fireworks and concerts.

## ROCKETS' RED GLARE

You might think that the inhabitants of a city once destroyed by fire would be wary of pyrotechnics. To the contrary, fireworks are extremely popular in Chicago, and many of the city's festivals end with dazzling fireworks displays.

There are fireworks at Navy Pier every Wednesday and Saturday night during the summer months. On New Year's Eve there are two fireworks shows at Navy Pier – an early one especially for young children and a traditional midnight show for adult revelers. Fireworks are a long-standing tradition at White Sox games, too, even if the team loses.

But the city's biggest and most elaborate pyrotechnics display is the Annual Independence Eve Fireworks Spectacular on July 3 in Grant Park. The show is one of the highlights of the enormously popular Taste of Chicago festival and is usually accompanied by live symphonic music. Some spectators reserve choice spots by pitching tents and camping out long before the show starts.

**ABOVE:** the Mexican Independence Day Parade marches down 18th Street in Pilsen. The event features live music, food vendors, and more than a hundred floats.

**BELOW:** expect flamboyant costumes and wild characters at the Chicago Pride Parade, held in late June in the Lakeview neighborhood. The event caps Gay Pride Month and is attended by as many as 450,000 people.

# WEST SIDE

**Established ethnic enclaves anchor the working-class West Side as it grows and changes with the times**

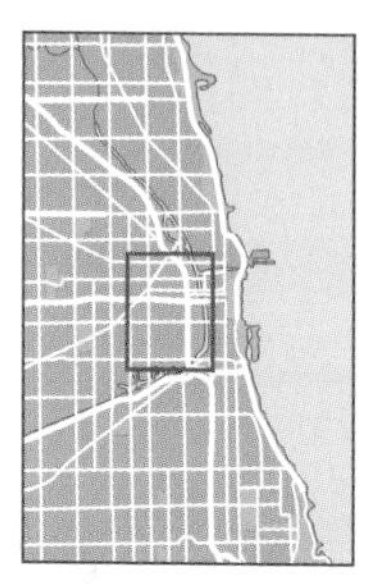

Chicago's West Side is often overlooked by visitors, but those willing to undertake the trek will be rewarded with a view of a city in transition, from the influx of new residents into the formerly desolate West Loop to the thriving Mexican community in Pilsen. The areas around the University of Illinois at Chicago, including Little Italy and the Maxwell Street Market, have also changed dramatically in the last several years, not without complaints from residents unhappy about the rapid rate of change.

Meanwhile, a few pockets of grandeur remain from the days when the West Side was an address with cachet, including the Garfield Park Conservatory, whose restoration has brought renewed attention to the park in which it is set.

## FULTON STREET MARKET ❶

Long a center of the meatpacking industry, the Fulton Street Market neighborhood – Fulton Street west of Halsted Street – is newly chic, with condo developments, stylish nightclubs, design showrooms, and art galleries. You'll have to dodge trucks and forklifts on your way to new businesses like **Pivot** (1101 West Fulton Market; tel: 312-243-4754), a boutique that carries designs made from environmentally sustainable material, and **Jupiter Outpost Café** (1139 West Fulton Market; tel: 312-238-9473), a favorite of area workers and new residents.

Just a few blocks south, on Randolph Street, is a long strip of some of the city's best restaurants, from wine bars like **Avec** (615 West Randolph Street; tel: 312-377-2002) to contemporary French at **one sixty-**

**Main attractions**

- CHICAGO ANTIQUE MARKET
- HARPO STUDIOS
- MUSEUM OF HOLOGRAPHY
- GREEKTOWN
- HELLENIC MUSEUM AND CULTURAL CENTER
- JANE ADDAMS HULL-HOUSE MUSEUM
- MAXWELL STREET MARKET
- LITTLE ITALY
- NATIONAL ITALIAN AMERICAN SPORTS HALL OF FAME
- PILSEN
- UNITED CENTER
- GARFIELD PARK CONSERVATORY

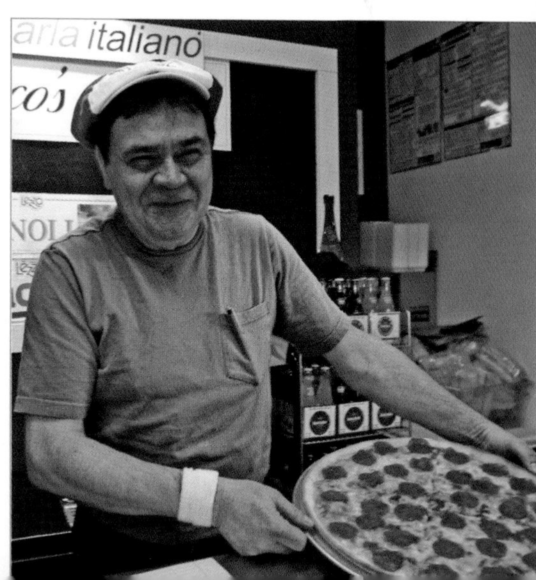


**LEFT:** Old St Patrick's Church is one of the few buildings to survive the Fire of 1871.
**RIGHT:** Franco's Pizza in Little Italy.

*The Jackson Boulevard Historic District around Jackson Blvd and Ashland Ave is full of restored 19th-century town houses and mansions. The 1885 Church of the Epiphany (201 S. Ashland Ave) anchors the block.*

**blue** (160 North Loomis Street; tel: 312-850-0303). On the last weekend of the month from May to October, it's also the site of the huge **Chicago Antique Market** ❷ (1350 West Randolph Street; tel: 312-951-9939, www.chicagoantiquemarket.com; Sat noon–6pm, Sun 9am–4pm).

This is the city's version of the grand flea markets of Paris and London, with less junk and more treasures, including pricey antiques and vintage clothing. There's even a special section where you can peruse the creations of local fashion designers. A few neighborhood restaurants set up stalls, with far more interesting food than the usual greasy street-fest fare.

A short walk south to Washington Boulevard leads you to the home of the *Oprah Winfrey Show*, **Harpo Studios** ❸ (1058 West Washington Boulevard; tel: 312-591-9222, www.oprah.com). Unless you booked far, far in advance, it's unlikely you'll be getting in, unless you luck out with some last-minute tickets, available only via e-mail. The building itself, a former armory, was used as a temporary morgue after the steamship *Eastland* capsized in the Chicago

River in 1915, leading to claims that the building is haunted.

If you can't score seats to the show, consider visiting the little-known **Museum of Holography-Chicago** ❹ (1134 West Washington Boulevard; tel: 312-226-1007, http://holographiccenter.com; Wed–Sun 12.30pm–5pm; charge), which features exhibitions on the art and science of holograms – three-dimensional images created by lasers; workshops are also available.

## GREEKTOWN

The Greektown neighborhood is the last vestige of a close-knit community that was largely displaced by the expansion of the University of Illinois at Chicago and the construction of the Eisenhower Expressway in the early 1960s. What remains is a cluster of restaurants and cafés on Halsted Street between Monroe and Van Buren streets – an area marked by decorative temples at the northern and southern boundaries. Shop for Greek staples at **Athens Grocery** (324 South Halsted Street; tel: 312-332-6737); sample homemade sweets at **Pan Hellenic Pastry** (322 South Halsted Street; tel: 312-454-1886); pick up a gyro at one of the takeout joints; or sit down to a meal of *saganaki* (flaming cheese) and other specialties at one of several good restaurants.

The **Hellenic Museum and Cultural Center** ❺ (801 West Adams Street, 4th floor; tel: 312-655-1234, www.hellenicmuseum.org; Tue–Fri 10am–4pm, Sat 11am–4pm; charge) interprets the Greek cultural experi-

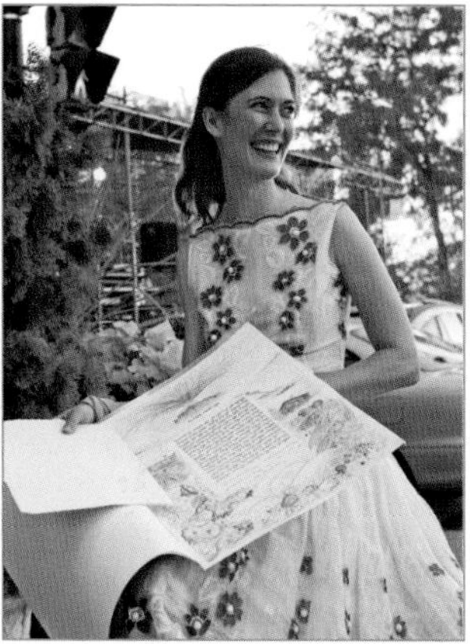

**ABOVE:** a recently married Jewish woman with a *ketubah*, a traditional prenuptial agreement. **BELOW:** local restaurants do brisk business during the annual Taste of Greece festival in Greektown.

Jim's Original (1250 S. Union Ave) is the quintessential Chicago hot dog stand, known for its "Maxwell Street Polish" (Polish sausage with grilled onions and mustard) and pork chop sandwiches.

ence with displays on art, food, and dance, plus educational programs about the myth of Atlantis and other Greek lore.

Perhaps the best way to experience the neighborhood is during one of the many high-spirited festivals, including the annual **Greek Independence Day Parade** (http://chicagogreekparade.org) in March and **Taste of Greece** street fare in August.

## Jane Addams Hull-House Museum ❻

800 South Halsted Street 312-413-5353, www.uic.edu/jaddams/hull
Tue–Fri 10am–4pm, Sun noon–4pm
free

Encompassed within the sprawling campus of the University of Illinois at Chicago, this museum and historic site is dedicated to the life and work of social activist Jane Addams, who founded the settlement Hull-House in 1889 with coworker Ellen Gates Starr. Hull-House attended to the needs of immigrants and other poor West Side residents with a variety of educational programs and other initiatives designed to improve the lot of working people and the urban poor.

Hull-House eventually grew into a complex of 13 buildings. Sadly, all were razed by the university, except the original mansion and dining hall, which were moved about 200 meters to their present location. Permanent exhibits include Addams' office and other rooms decorated with original furnishings; displays chronicle the immigrant experience in Chicago with personal letters, photos, and other artifacts.

## MAXWELL STREET MARKET ❼

Another Chicago institution that was displaced by the university's expansion was the old **Maxwell Street Market**. For more than a century, this was one of the country's largest open-air markets, with just about everything from pearl buttons to pork chops. In order to be heard over the crowd, street musicians began using electric amplifiers, a practice that is said to have given birth to the Chicago blues.

Parts of the West Side are considered high-crime areas. Vigilance is required, especially after dark.

**ABOVE:** Hull-House.
**BELOW:** religious icons for sale in Greektown.

*Recommended Restaurants, Bars & Cafés on pages 200–1*

Relocated to Canal Street and Roosevelt Road, the new Maxwell Street Market (Sun 7am-3pm) is a shadow of its former self but still has hundreds of vendors hawking clothing, antiques, tools, sports memorabilia, seasonal produce, and all sorts of odds and ends. Blues musicians perform on the sidewalks, and there's plenty of cheap and tasty food; the tacos, tamales, and other Mexican street fare are especially good.

Apparently, the market's peregrinations aren't over yet. In 2007 the city announced a plan to move the market yet again, this time to a site three blocks away on Desplaines Street north of Roosevelt Road. The move is expected in 2008, but as of this writing an exact date hasn't been determined.

## LITTLE ITALY

Clustered around West Taylor Street between Ashland Avenue and Halsted Street, Little Italy is Italian in spirit if not in actual fact. Most of the Italian families that settled here in the late 19th and early 20th centuries have since moved on, although there are still a few old-school remnants in the form of the flavored ice at **Mario's Italian Lemonade** (1068 West Taylor Street), the excellent Italian beef sandwiches at **Al's #1 Beef** (1079 West Taylor Street; tel: 312-226-4017), and sandwiches, olive oil, and other Mediterranean delights at the **Conte de Savoia** deli and grocery (1438 West Taylor Street; tel: 312-666-3471). Most of the formal restaurants – such as **Francesca's** (1400 West Taylor Street; tel: 312-829-2828) and **Rosebud** (1500 West Taylor Street; tel: 312-942-1117) – are relatively recent arrivals but nonetheless popular.

The **National Italian American Sports Hall of Fame** ❽ (1431 West Taylor Street; tel: 312-226-5566, www.niashf.org; Mon–Fri 9am–5pm, Sat–Sun 11am–4pm; charge) displays a varied collection of memorabilia, including boxer Rocky Marciano's first World Heavyweight Championship belt and the coat Vince Lombardi wore on his last day as coach

**ABOVE:** a blues band performs at the Maxwell Street Market.
**BELOW:** the Market has more than 400 vendors.

of the Green Bay Packers. Across the street is **Piazza DiMaggio**, a small public space with a statue of the Yankee Clipper, Joe DiMaggio.

## PILSEN

To the south, around **18th Street**, the Pilsen neighborhood has long been an entry point for immigrants, starting with German and Irish workers who settled here in the mid-19th century and, later, Bohemian immigrants (from what is now the Czech Republic) who named the area after the town of Plzen in West Bohemia. Mexican immigrants have been the dominant group since the mid-20th century, and while the neighborhood is a bit rough around the edges it is also one of the most vibrant in the city, with a vital ethnic flavor and a thriving arts community.

The main strip is 18th Street between Western and Racine avenues. The neighborhood's spirit is colorfully expressed at **Casa Aztlan** ❾ (1831 South Racine Avenue; tel: 312-666-5508), a community center adorned with murals. Casa Aztlan puts on the summer **Viva**

**ABOVE AND BELOW:** Pilsen is famous for its many colorful murals.

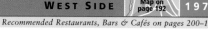

*Recommended Restaurants, Bars & Cafés on pages 200–1*

**Aztlan Festival**, which features live music, food, dancing, artists, and children's activities.

Don't leave the neighborhood without sampling some of the local cuisine. Popular eateries on 18th Street include **Nuevo Leon** (1515 West 18th Street; tel: 312-421-1517), a busy sit-down restaurant known for authentic cuisine, and **Mundial Cocina Mestiza** (1640 West 18th Street; tel: 312-491-9908), which offers Mediterranean dishes as well as Mexican regional cooking. For pastries, cookies, and other sweets, with perhaps an espresso on the side, the cheerful **Bombon Bakery** (1508 West 18th Street; tel: 312 733-7788) is a must.

Here too you'll find numerous art galleries and studios. The **Polvo** collective (1458 West 18th Street 1R; tel: 773-344-1940, www.polvo.org; Sat noon–5pm) features installations, performances, and other work by emerging artists. The **Prospectus Gallery** (1210 West 18th Street; tel: 312-733-6132) shows work by Mexican and local artists. There's another cluster of galleries on Halsted Street in an area called Pilsen East. If you're in town during the second weekend of October, check out the **Pilsen Open Studios** gallery walk (www.pilsenopenstudios.com), which includes stops at galleries and studios around the neighborhood.

## National Museum of Mexican Art ⑩

1852 West 19th Street · 312-738-1503, www.nationalmuseumofmexicanart.org · Tue–Sun 10am–5pm · free

Near the western end of Pilsen, the National Museum of Mexican Art

Artists and musicians jam the comfy booths at the Skylark tavern (2149 S. Halsted St), an oasis of boho cool in Pilsen East. In addition to drinks, the bar serves pretty good burgers and sides of tater tots. Cash only.

**BELOW LEFT:** Pilsen restaurants tend to be small, casual, family-run businesses serving simple but authentic Mexican food.
**BELOW RIGHT:** the former Cook County Hospital.

## Cook County Hospital

At 1901 W. Harrison Street stands a grand Beaux Arts structure that's now dwarfed by the modern offices and buildings of the gleaming Illinois Medical District surrounding it. This is Cook County Hospital ⑪, known as the "Statue of Liberty" of hospitals for its service to immigrants and the poor from 1914 until it closed in 2002, when the hospital moved to a new building. "County" was slated for demolition until preservation groups rallied for it to be saved, citing such architectural flourishes as classical moldings, Ionic columns, and a terra cotta facade festooned with cherubs and lions. A good deal of medical history was made here too, including pioneering work in blood banking, treatment of burns, and trauma management. It also served as the inspiration for the *ER* television series. In 2007, Cook County reversed its decision to raze the building and announced a renovation plan, no doubt prompted by the increasing value of West Side real estate.

Recommended Restaurants, Bars & Cafés on pages 200–1

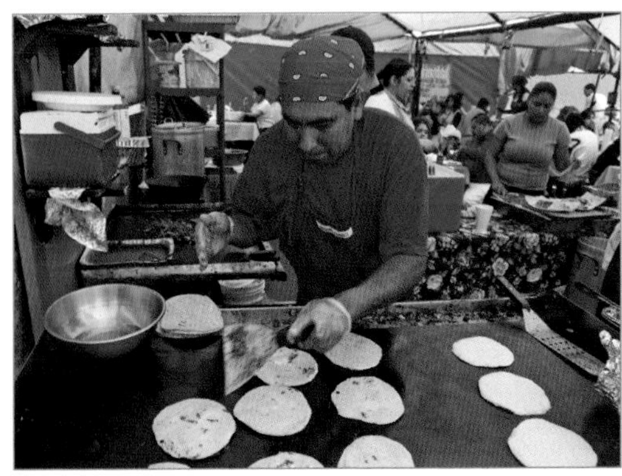

features a wide range of Mexican art and artifacts, encompassing paintings, sculptures, photographs, folk art, textiles, and ancient objects as well as a few works by celebrated muralists Diego Rivera and José Clemente Orozco. A permanent exhibit traces Mexican art from pre-Columbian cultures to the present day. The annual Dia de los Muertos, or Day of the Dead, exhibit usually runs from September to December and presents the work of numerous artists in a variety of media.

**ABOVE:** a cook flips tortillas at the Maxwell Street Market, where vendors sell excellent Mexican food.
**BELOW:** Garfield Park Conservatory.

## UNITED CENTER 12

Farther west is the **United Center** (1901 West Madison Street; tel: 312-455-7000, www.unitedcenter.com), which replaced the old Chicago Stadium in 1994. This huge sports and entertainment complex is the home of the Chicago Bulls basketball team and Blackhawks ice hockey team. It's also the site of a statue of basketball legend Michael Jordan, portrayed in mid-dunk by husband-and-wife artists Omri and Julie Rotblatt-Amrany. The area immediately around the stadium has undergone a change for the better in recent years, but the neighborhood gets dicey as you travel farther out.

## GARFIELD PARK CONSERVATORY 13

300 North Central Park Avenue
312-746-5100, www.garfieldconservatory.org daily 9am–5pm, Thu to 8pm free

A few miles west, in the middle of a pretty rough neighborhood, is one of the jewels of the city's park system, 184-acre (74-hectare) **Garfield Park** (100 North Central Park Avenue). Designed in 1859 by architect William Le Baron Jenney, the park has a lagoon, ball fields, and a playground, but the real highlight is the **Garfield Park Conservatory**. Meant to resemble haystacks, the glass-and-steel structure is arranged around various interior landscapes, including a prehistoric-looking Fern Room, a cactus-filled Desert House, and a children's garden with interactive exhibits and play areas. An outdoor garden is modeled after those of Impressionist master Claude Monet in Giverny, France.

Special events include children's programming, yoga in the Conservatory, gardening clinics, and the annual **Holiday Flower Show** in winter. All in all, this is one of the city's overlooked treasures. ❑

## Oprah: Tough and Tender

**No Chicagoan in our time has risen as much in public esteem as the dynamic Ms. Winfrey – queen of daytime TV, pop culture tastemaker, and lifestyle guru**

Two remarkable careers went into overdrive in 1984, when a couple of newcomers used Chicago as their launching pad to fame and fortune. One was the North Carolina basketball phenom Michael Jordan, who in October made his debut with the Chicago Bulls en route to supersized athletic glory. An even greater success story, in terms of her impact on the public consciousness, was Oprah Winfrey.

Born in 1954 to a poor, unwed teenager in rural Mississippi and a victim of rape at the age of nine (she herself gave birth at 14 to a son who died young), Oprah Gail Winfrey arrived in Chicago in 1983 after stints on radio and television in Nashville and Baltimore. On January 2, 1984, she became the host of a televised talk show with a Chicago-area reach that soon surpassed the dominant Phil Donahue program in viewership and then went national in scope in September 1986. She became renowned as a guru of tough but tender advice in personal relations as well as confidant for such personalities as Jordan and Michael Jackson in television interviews that were watched by millions of viewers.

**ABOVE:** Oprah Winfrey, above with author Toni Morrison and, right, at an awards show.

Nearly a quarter-century old, *The Oprah Winfrey Show* is a TV landmark beamed to zillions of rabidly loyal fans worldwide from a downtown studio courtesy of her own Harpo ("Oprah" backwards) Productions. There's also *O, The Oprah Magazine* as well as the hugely successful Oprah's Book Club she founded in 1996, in addition to other ventures that have made this petite billionaire the leading African-American moneymaker of all time and one of the richest people on earth, with plush lodgings in California, Hawaii, and elsewhere. Her net worth in recent years has been estimated at some $2^{1}/_{2}$ billion.

An actress as well as interviewer, Winfrey made her cinematic debut in *The Color Purple* in 1985, her performance earning her an Academy Award nomination as Best Supporting Actress as well as Golden Globe recognition. Winfrey has been honored by numerous groups, including the National Organization of Women and the National Association for the Advancement of Colored People. A major force in American popular culture, she is widely regarded as one of the most influential women in the US, leading *Vanity Fair* magazine to observe that "Oprah Winfrey arguably has more influence on the culture than any university president, politician, or religious leader, except perhaps the Pope." ❑

# BEST RESTAURANTS, BARS AND CAFÉS

## Restaurants

Prices for a three-course dinner per person with a half-bottle of house wine:

**$** = under $20
**$$** = $20–$45
**$$$** = $45–$60
**$$$$** = over $60

### Artopolis

306 S. Halsted St 312-559-9000 L & D daily **$** [p306, A2]

This cheerful Greektown café specializes in savory "artopitas": phyllo pastries stuffed with combinations like spinach and feta or smoked salmon and Fontina.

### Avec

615 W. Randolph St 312-377-2002 D daily **$$** [p306, B2]

Just west of the Loop proper, this hip, casual spot from Paul Kahan, of neighboring Blackbird fame, offers a small-plates menu strong on lusty Mediterranean dishes and pungent cheese, plus a seemingly endless wine list. It's not for the socially phobic: tables in the narrow, saunalike space are shared and the acoustics can be deafening.

### Blackbird

619 W. Randolph St 312-715-0708 L Mon–Fri, D Mon–Sat **$$$$** [p306, B2]

The minimalist, white-on-white decor can be off-putting, but Blackbird delivers the goods on the plate. The seasonal menu showcases exquisite ingredients prepared with Paul Kahan's hallmark attention to detail and balance. New chef de cuisine Michael Sheerin brings his own experimental sensibility to bear on Kahan's award-winning formula.

### Café Jumping Bean

1439 W. 18th St 312-455-0019 B, L & D daily $

With ever-changing art on the walls and concerts of live flamenco, it's no wonder this sunny corner café has become a Pilsen mainstay. In keeping with the multicultural neighborhood, you can get Mexican hot chocolate and refreshing liquados – fresh fruit milkshakes – along with coffee, tea, sandwiches, and a solid menu of basic café fare. Expect a crowd; cash only.

### Greek Islands

200 S. Halsted St 312-782-9855 L & D daily **$$** [p306, A2]

One of the best of the *saganaki* mills on this stretch of Halsted Street, this traditional Greek restaurant is known for fresh seafood and gruffly efficient service.

### Hashbrowns

731 W. Maxwell St 312-226-8000 B & L daily **$** [p306, A4]

This jumpin' breakfast joint on gutted-and-gentrified Maxwell Street specializes in fried spuds in all their glory, including a gut-busting combo of Idaho potatoes topped with cheddar, onions, sour cream, and crushed Corn Flakes.

### La Sardine

111 N. Carpenter St 312-421-2800 L Mon–Fri, D Mon–Sat **$$$** [p306, A1]

The sleek younger sister of Jean-Claude Poilevey's beloved Le Bouchon, this market-district bistro offers sophisticated French classics – veal kidneys, anyone? – in an atmosphere applauded for being a notch or three less trend-obsessed than its neighbors on the Randolph Street strip. Tuesday's $25 three-course prix fixe menu draws an ardent throng.

### Marché

833 W. Randolph St 312-226-8399 L Mon–Fri, D daily **$$$** [p306, A1]

Designed with owner Jerry Kleiner's trademark theatricality, this industrial-chic brasserie

**LEFT:** Mexican food at a Pilsen restaurant.

in a converted warehouse is known as much for people-watching as the well-executed French fare. If you get bored scoping out the crowd in the dining room, the open kitchen provides entertainment in its own right.

**Moto**
945 W. Fulton St 312-491-0058 D Tue–Sat **$$$$** [p306, A1]
Edible menus. Vacuum-frozen squash foam. Carbonated oranges. Doughnut soup. Homaro Cantu may be the only Trotter-trained chef to appear in both *Gourmet* and *New Scientist*. His molecular-gastronomic fun house is a required stop for anyone fascinated by the cutting edge (or lunatic fringe) of contemporary Chicago cooking. Not everything works, but that'll seem beside the point when the waiter presents you with protective goggles and invites you into the kitchen to see the laser.

**Mundial Cocina Mestiza**
1640 W. 18th St 312-491-9908 L & D daily **$**
The three chef-owners of Mundial have enough fine-dining experience to blanket Pilsen in white tablecloths, but with this homey BYOB storefront they've hit on something more neighborhood friendly. The sophisticated but affordable pan-Latin menu ranges from empanadas and tamales to regional Mexican specialties and creative mainstays like spare ribs in a tamarind-ancho glaze.

**Nuevo Leon**
1515 W. 18th St 312-421-1517 B, L & D daily **$**
A Pilsen landmark for more than 40 years, Nuevo Leon dishes up no-frills regional Mexican fare true to the state that gives the place its name. Housemade flour tortillas are perfect for wrapping around bits of spicy sausage or slow-cooked, chile-spiked pork. And on a cold day nothing beats a cup of foamy, cinnamon-laced Mexican hot chocolate.

**one sixtyblue**
1400 W. Randolph St 312-850-0303 D Mon–Sat **$$$$**
Chef Martial Noguier blends classic French and contemporary American cuisine at this luxurious but understated dining room at the west end of Randolph Street's restaurant row; it's equally appropriate for power dinners and romantic trysts. The wine list is considered one of the best in town, and the service is close to impeccable.

**Rosebud**
1500 W. Taylor St 312-942-1117 L Mon–Fri, D daily **$$**
An anchor of Little Italy whose walls are crammed with photos of Sinatra and Tony Bennett, this old-school northern Italian spot offers gut-busting portions of the classics: think fried *calamari*, *mostaccioli* and *cavatelli*, veal *limone*, and chicken Vesuvio.

**Sushi Wabi**
842 W. Randolph St 312-563-1224 L Mon–Fri, D daily **$$$** [p306, A1]
The wood-and-cement setting makes a starkly minimalist backdrop to the explosions of fresh fish on the plate at this upscale sushi spot. The room's dark and tiny and the crowd can be loud; weekend DJs spin house, techno, and hip-hop.

**Wishbone**
1001 W. Washington Blvd 312-850-2663 B, L & D daily **$** [p306, A1]
In business for almost 20 years, the Wishbone can lay claim to one of the most diverse crowds in town; on any given day the former garage is packed with artists, politicians, sports fans en route to the United Center, and harried staffers from Harpo Studios. They're all here for affordable, ample Southern comfort food: crab cakes, blackened catfish, collard greens, and cornbread.

## Bars

**Beer Bistro**, 1061 W. Madison St (tel: 312-433-0013). This ale house caters to a post-work, pre-sports crowd (the bar runs shuttles to the United Center) and is still a nice alternative to the martini bar scene. With a dozen beers on tap and another 80 or so in bottles, you can't deny the owners know their brews.

**Fulton Lounge**, 955 W. Fulton Mkt (tel: 312-942-9500). This chic cocktail lounge offers a limited menu of wood-oven-fired pizzas and desserts from neighboring Follia, and is full of well-groomed young people sipping mojitos. Outdoor seating, weather permitting.

**Matchbox**, 770 N. Milwaukee Ave (tel: 312-666-9292). Chicago's "most intimate" bar – the tiny Matchbox is about 10 ft wide at its broadest point– is home to some of the best Manhattans in town. There's more spacious sidewalk seating in summer.

**Tasting Room at Randolph Wine Cellars**, 1415 W. Randolph St (tel: 312-942-1313). This elegant but low-key wine bar offers stunning views of the Loop from its loftlike second-floor lounge. Sink into one of the overstuffed leather sofas with a nice little Bordeaux and you may not want to get up again.

Recommended Restaurants, Bars & Cafés on pages 214–5

# WICKER PARK, BUCKTOWN, AND UKRAINIAN VILLAGE

**Something old, something new – hip, trendy Wicker Park and its neighbors, Bucktown and Ukrainian Village, reflect both Chicago's hardscrabble immigrant past and its sleek, modern future**

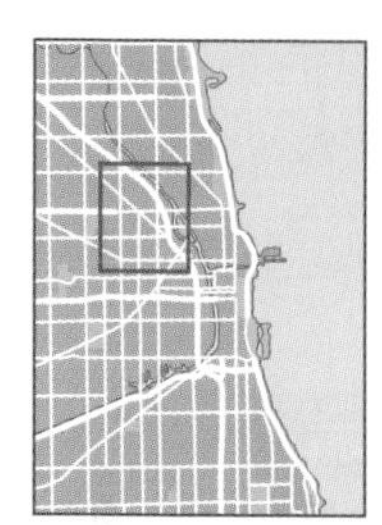

**Main attractions**

POLISH MUSEUM OF AMERICA
NORTH AVENUE BATHS
SHOPS AND NIGHTCLUBS AROUND DAMEN, NORTH, AND MILWAUKEE AVENUES
ART GALLERIES
DIVISION STREET SHOPPING
UKRAINIAN INSTITUTE OF MODERN ART
UKRAINIAN NATIONAL MUSEUM
ST NICHOLAS UKRAINIAN CATHOLIC CATHEDRAL
HOLY TRINITY RUSSIAN ORTHODOX CATHEDRAL
DAMEN AVENUE SHOPPING

Walk around Wicker Park with a local of a certain age and it's hard to shake off the ghost of pop culture gone by. See that strip mall? It once was home to Idful Studios, where Liz Phair recorded her 1993 debut, *Exile in Guyville*. There's the Double Door, where the Rolling Stones played a surprise show in 1997. Here's the once-vacant storefront used for John Cusack's record store in *High Fidelity* in 1999; it's now a 7-11. And over there? That building that's now a Cheetah Gym? That's where they filmed the 11th season of *The Real World* in 2002.

## Changing neighborhood

Of course, urban neighborhoods are constantly changing, but by any measure funky, artsy Wicker Park and neighboring Bucktown and Ukrainian Village have had a roller coaster ride.

At the turn of the 20th century Wicker Park – named after the 4-acre ($1^{1}/_{2}$-hectare) park at its center – was home to some of Chicago's wealthiest German and Scandinavian families, who settled on what was then the western frontier after being snubbed by the WASP establishment on the lakefront. The magisterial brick and stone homes they built between the Chicago Fire of 1871 and 1930 turned Pierce and Hoyne avenues into an architectural showplace of Victorian Gothic and Italianate design; so many German brewery owners lived on Hoyne that the street became known as "Beer Baron Row." Many of the mansions still stand, preserved as part of the **Wicker Park Landmark District**,

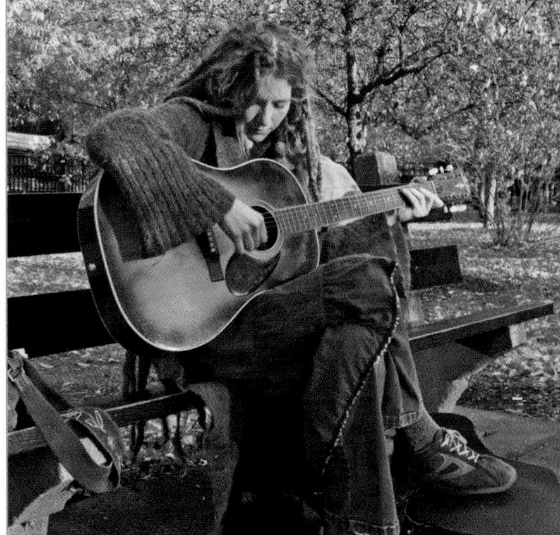

**LEFT:** puppy love in Bucktown.
**RIGHT:** strumming a guitar in Wicker Park, the 4-acre patch of greenery that gives the neighborhood its name.

*A mosaic adorns Saint Nicholas Ukrainian Catholic Cathedral.*

bounded by Bell Avenue and North Leavitt Street to the west, Caton Street to the north, Potomac Avenue to the south, and the Blue line El tracks to the northeast.

## Working-class enclave

But the neighborhood wasn't just the province of the wealthy. Working-class Eastern Europeans and African Americans moved in as well, as did the labor activists later slain in the 1886 Haymarket Affair. Then, during the Depression, the demographics shifted dramatically. The wealthy landowners moved out and the working-class population swelled, with Poles the dominant ethnic group. The **Polish Museum of America** ❶ (984 North Milwaukee Avenue, tel: 773-384-3352, http://pma.prcua.org; Mon–Wed Fri–Sun 11am–4pm; charge), one of the oldest ethnic museums in the country, contains in its collections of folk art, artifacts, and memorabilia a thorough history of the Polish presence in Chicago.

By the 1960s and 70s, Wicker Park was predominantly poor and Hispanic, and marked by blocks of abandoned or derelict real estate – in other words, it was primed for gen-

**Wicker Park, Bucktown, and Ukrainian Village**

0 500 yds
0 500 m

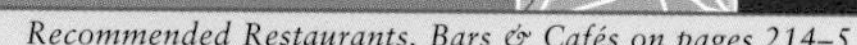

*Recommended Restaurants, Bars & Cafés on pages 214–5*

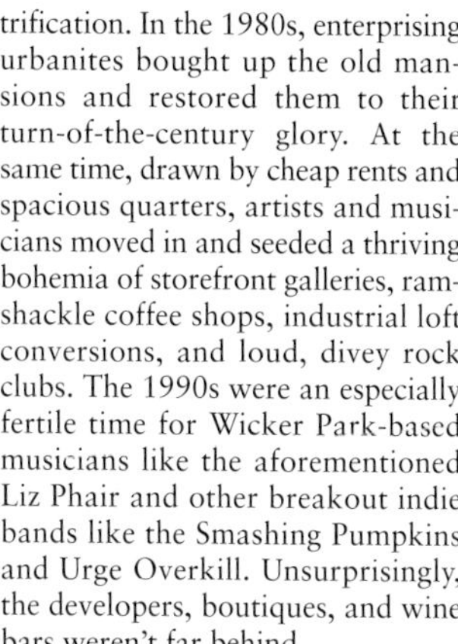

trification. In the 1980s, enterprising urbanites bought up the old mansions and restored them to their turn-of-the-century glory. At the same time, drawn by cheap rents and spacious quarters, artists and musicians moved in and seeded a thriving bohemia of storefront galleries, ramshackle coffee shops, industrial loft conversions, and loud, divey rock clubs. The 1990s were an especially fertile time for Wicker Park-based musicians like the aforementioned Liz Phair and other breakout indie bands like the Smashing Pumpkins and Urge Overkill. Unsurprisingly, the developers, boutiques, and wine bars weren't far behind.

## Resurgence and gentrification

Nowadays, the commercial strips of Milwaukee, North, Division, and Damen are a thriving entertainment district catering to the young, hip, and affluent, with stores purveying vintage and designer clothing, mod home furnishings, and small plates of ahi tuna tartare.

On residential streets, thanks to a ward government that appeared to rubber-stamp any and all requests from developers throughout the 1990s, it's not uncommon to see vintage workingmen's cottages dwarfed on either side by towering cinderblock condos. And though some idiosyncratic neighborhood landmarks like **Earwax Café** (1561 North Milwaukee Avenue; tel: 773-772-4019) have managed to hang in for the long haul, the area now boasts not one but two Starbucks. The artists and other urban pioneers have mostly decamped to more affordable turf in Humboldt Park, Logan Square, and other parts south and west, ceding the sidewalks to young professionals airing their dogs or babies, or both.

**ABOVE:** Earwax Café is a popular Wicker Park hangout. **BELOW:** St Mary of the Angels Catholic Church was established in the early 1900s to serve Polish immigrants.

James Bond-types can stock up on decoder rings, disguise kits, and other spy gear at the Boring Store (1331 North Milwaukee Avenue), a self-described "secret agent supply store" run by 826 Chicago, a tutoring center cofounded by author and native Chicagoan Dave Eggers.

**ABOVE:** The busy intersection of Damen, Milwaukee, and North avenues is known locally as "the crotch." **BELOW:** artist Adam Siegel at his studio in the Flat Iron Building.

### THE CROTCH ❷

The bustling intersection of Damen, North, and Milwaukee avenues – known colloquially as "the crotch" (just north of the Damen stop on the CTA Blue line) – is the best start for a walking tour of the area. On weekend nights, music blares from the bars and clubs ringing the intersection: check out the **Double Door** (1572 North Milwaukee Avenue; tel: 773-489-3160) for touring and local rock bands, **Subterranean** (2011 West North Avenue; tel: 773-278-6600) for up-and-coming hip-hop and indie acts, and **Debonair Social Club** (1575 North Milwaukee Avenue; tel: 773-227-7990) for DJs and a fashion-forward crowd. The three-story terra cotta building that houses Debonair is the **Flat Iron Arts Building** (1579 North Milwaukee Avenue). Creative home to more than two dozen artists and ground zero for the annual **Around the Coyote** arts festival, it's another enduring symbol of Wicker Park and is host to an open studio night on the first Friday of the month.

### Books and baths

Set off east on North Avenue from the intersection and you'll find **Quimby's Bookstore** (1854 West North Avenue; tel: 773-342-0910), a mecca of independent publishing stocked with a dizzying array of zines, art books, comics, erotica, and magazines catering to every imaginable subculture.

Head west of the intersection and you'll pass the beautiful facade of the former **North Avenue Baths** (2039-45 West North Avenue). This was once a communal bathhouse for Russian and Ukrainian immigrants where political power brokers cut deals in the steam room (where it's hard to hide a wiretap).

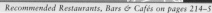

The building fell into disrepair during a stint as a transient hotel and later a brothel and was slated for demolition before being bought by a pair of developers. It's now home to chef Shawn McClain's elegant, award-winning **Spring** (2039 West North Avenue; tel: 773-395-7100), but you can fortify yourself for a lot less at **Sultan's Market** (2057 West North Avenue; tel: 773-235-3072), a grocery store and café that dishes up savory, filling falafel and other Middle Eastern treats.

## MILWAUKEE AVENUE

The entire Milwaukee strip from the crotch to the intersection of Division Street and Ashland Avenue was listed in 2007 as an endangered treasure by the local architectural group Preservation Chicago. Despite the rising tide of gentrification, the handsome storefronts still house numerous bohemian hangouts, including Earwax Café, the excellent **Myopic Books** (1564 North Milwaukee Avenue; tel: 773-862-4882), and **Reckless Records** (1532 North Milwaukee Avenue; tel: 773-235-3727).

Fringe gallery spaces still endure, too. **All Rise Gallery** (1542 North Milwaukee Avenue, 3rd Floor; tel: 773-292-9255) was once a chaotic live-work-party space until owner Lisa Flores took the reins and turned it into a legitimate gallery showing work by local and international artists. Across the hall is **Heaven Gallery** (www.heavengallery.com), and down the street is **Green**

**EAT**

For something quick, inexpensive, and tasty, try Thai Village (2053 W. Division St near N. Damen Ave), a cute neighborhood place with reliably fresh and well-prepared classic Thai dishes and a comfy vibe.

**ABOVE:** Buddhist monks at the Around the Coyote arts fair. **BELOW:** the Division Street Russian and Turkish Baths is a traditional Russian-style bathhouse in Wicker Park.

**Lantern Gallery** (1511 North Milwaukee Avenue, 2nd Floor; tel: 773-235-0936), both showing work by emerging artists of all stripes.

## Shop with style

One thing there's no shortage of around here is clothing. At the high end is the "lifestyle boutique" **Hejfina** (1529 North Milwaukee Avenue; tel: 773-772-0002), which sells cutting edge designs with sometimes shocking price tags. The two-in-one shoe stores **Niche** and **City Soles** (1566 North Damen Avenue; tel: 773-489-2001), at the intersection of North and Damen avenues, stock one of the city's best selections of hip shoes and offer a dangerously tempting sale room.

Although Milwaukee Avenue now has a Levi's Store and an Urban Outfitters, there's still plenty of vintage and secondhand shopping to be found. Check out the **Brown Elephant** (1459 North Milwaukee Avenue; tel: 773-252-8801) for bargains benefiting the GLBT-focused Howard Brown Health Center, or **US #1 Vintage Clothing and Denim** (1460 North Milwaukee Avenue; tel: 773-489-9428) for a dizzying selection of women's boots, leopard fun furs, and wool plaid logging jackets. **Una Mae's Freak Boutique** (1422 North Milwaukee Avenue; tel: 773-276-7002) blends vintage finds from the 1960s to the 1980s with new but affordable pieces reflecting current trends.

Just south of the intersection of Damen, North, and Milwaukee avenues is the park that gives the neighborhood its name. Triangular

**ABOVE:** sidewalk diners on Division Street.
**BELOW:** a local Polish-language newspaper; there are approximately 185,000 Polish speakers in the Chicago area.

**Wicker Park** ❸ was donated to the city in 1870 by brothers Charles and Joel Wicker, businessmen and developers who owned much of the surrounding land. Today softball teams hit the diamond and dogs frolic in the dog run while parents swing their toddlers on the playground and chess players face off at one of several built-in tables. On summer Sundays residents converge on the park for the **Wicker Park Farmers' Market**.

## THE POLISH TRIANGLE ❹

At the intersection of Ashland, Division, and Milwaukee is a plaza-cum-bus stop known as the Polish Triangle. The **Nelson Algren Fountain** at the center honors Wicker Park's favorite son (see box). The inscription encircling the base, from his prose-poem *Chicago: City on the Make*, reads: "For the masses who do the city's labor also keep the city's heart."

Across the street is the **Chopin Theatre** (1543 West Division Street; tel: 773-278-1500). Polish expat Zigmunt Drykacz rents the two stages to edgy local companies when he's not bringing in experimental work from Europe. Stop in next door at the homey diner **Podhalanka** (1549 West Division Street; tel: 773-486-6655) for a steaming bowl of borscht before the show.

### Tacos, vinyl, art

South on Ashland Avenue you'll hit one of Wicker Park's odder landmarks: a trio of bright yellow taquerias, all named **La Pasadita** (1140-42 North Ashland Avenue). Opinions vary as to which is the best, but all are good and open till 3am. Just down the road is **Dusty Groove** (1120 North Ashland Avenue; tel: 773-342-5800), the best source in town for Latin music, funk, and classic soul, as well as an impressive collection of used vinyl. Upstairs is the gallery **Corbett vs. Dempsey** (tel: 773-278-1664), specializing in mid-century American art and Chicago painting in particular.

## DIVISION STREET

To the west, Division Street is a dining and retail artery with a slightly scruffier edge than points north. Old-school outposts like the European-style **Alliance Bakery** (1736 West Division Street; tel: 773-278-0366) and **Phyllis's Musical Inn** (1800 West Division Street; tel: 773-486-9862), a ramshackle dive where the beer is cheap and the music is loud – and the beer garden is one of the

**ABOVE:** having a drink at a Wicker Park bar. **BELOW:** browsing through vintage vinyl at a Milwaukee Avenue record shop.

neighborhood's best kept secrets – coexist with up-and-comers like the funky boutique **Penelope's** (1913 West Division Street; tel: 773-395-2351) and chic sushi spot **Mirai** (2020 West Division Street; tel: 773-862-8500).

Just south of Division on Damen Avenue, a bright neon sign marks the **Rainbo Club** ❺ (1150 North Damen Avenue; tel: 773-489-5999), a longtime haunt of musicians, art students, and other boho types. In business since the 1930s, it was one of Algren's favorite watering holes. Come early to snag one of the battered, red-vinyl booths, the better to people watch.

**ABOVE:** Ukrainian Institute of Modern Art.
**BELOW:** Mass at St Nicholas Ukrainian Catholic Cathedral.

## Humboldt Park

At Western Avenue a large red-and-blue steel sculpture arcs over **Division Street** ❻ in the shape of the Puerto Rican flag. This marks the beginning of the Humboldt Park neighborhood and what's known as the Paseo Boricua. It's a symbolic marker for Chicago's Puerto Rican community, many of whom were displaced west as gentrification swept through Wicker Park and Bucktown. The strip between Western and California avenues (where there's another flag) is home to thriving panaderias, cafés, and community centers serving the Spanish-speaking population.

## Ukrainian Village

Division Street is the nominal boundary between Wicker Park and Ukrainian Village, which is bounded by Grand Avenue on the south, Damen Avenue on the east, and Western Avenue on the west. Anchored by several orthodox

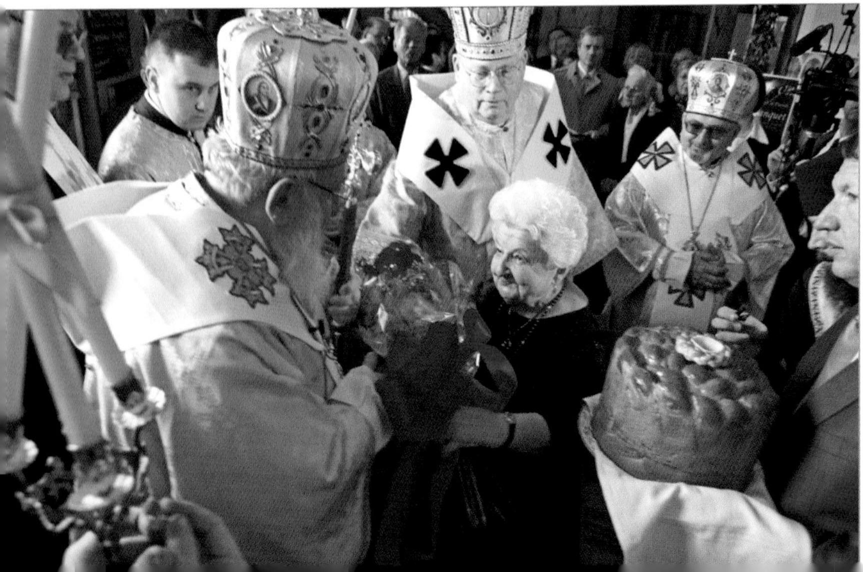

*Recommended Restaurants, Bars & Cafés on pages 214–5*

churches and populated for decades by families of Ukrainian ancestry, the area remained a relatively safe, middle-class neighborhood while surrounding areas became impoverished and dangerous in the 1970s and 80s. It has stayed relatively stable during the development frenzy of recent years, though gentrification may finally be catching up.

Thanks in large part to the insularity of the Ukrainian community, housing stock in the neighborhood is remarkably well preserved. The **Ukrainian Village District**, delimited by Haddon Avenue, Leavitt Street, Augusta Boulevard, and Damen Avenue, was named a Chicago landmark district in 2002. Walk the quiet, tree-lined side streets and you'll get a comprehensive look at residential building styles through the years, from tidy brick cottages to blocky apartment buildings, all characterized by unpretentious design and fine craftsmanship.

## Ukrainian art and artifacts

The corner of Chicago Avenue and Oakley Street gives a good glimpse of the neighborhood's past. On one corner is **Sak's Ukrainian Village** (2301 West Chicago Avenue; tel: 773-278-4445), a dimly lit restaurant and lounge where hearty plates of varenyki and bratwurst are dished up amid Ukrainian folk art. Down the street is the **Ukrainian Institute of Modern Art** ❼ (2320 West Chicago Avenue; tel: 773-227-5522, www.uima-chicago.org; Wed–Sun, noon–4pm; free), a small museum boasting a diverse collection of contemporary painting, sculpture, and mixed-media work.

A block away, the **Ukrainian National Museum** ❽ (2249 West Superior Street; tel: 312-421-8020, www.ukrainiannationalmuseum.org; Thu–Sun 11am–4pm; charge) houses more than 1,400 artifacts, plus decorated eggs and other folk art and archival materials documenting the history of Ukrainians and Ukrainian-Americans.

From the corner you can see the verdigris spires of **St Nicholas Ukrainian Catholic Cathedral** (2238 West Rice Street; tel: 773-276-4537), founded in 1915, to the north. To the south is the gold dome of **Sts Volodymyr and Olha Ukrainian Catholic Church** (2245 West Superior Street; tel: 312-829-5209), founded in 1973 by a faction of tradition-minded St Nicholas parishioners and designed in the Byzantine style of 11th- to 13th-century Ukraine. A few

**ABOVE:** a mural on Division Street in Humboldt Park, hub of Chicago's Puerto Rican community.

**BELOW:** Jeremy Brutzkus and Erika Panther of Coco Rouge, a gourmet chocolate shop on Division Street.

blocks away is the stucco **Holy Trinity Russian Orthodox Cathedral** (1121 North Leavitt Street; tel: 773-486-6064), one of only two churches designed by Chicago architect Louis Sullivan.

## BUCKTOWN 9

North of North Avenue, Wicker Park gives way to Bucktown, generally agreed to be bounded by the North Branch of the Chicago River to the east, Fullerton Avenue to the north, and Western Avenue to the west.

The line between Bucktown and Wicker Park is fluid, with some arguing that Cortland Street is the frontier and others marking turf at the viaduct that runs east-west along Bloomingdale Avenue, an unused rail line that green-space advocates are working to turn into an elevated park and bike path.

Bucktown, one of the earliest settlements west of Fort Dearborn, got its name from the goats that supposedly wandered the streets in the 19th century, when the area was a predominantly working-class Polish neighborhood of small farms, cottages, and, later, light industry. Today it's considerably more chic.

**ABOVE:** a stained-glass panel at St Nicholas Ukrainian Catholic Cathedral, a masterpiece of neo-Byzantine architecture.
**BELOW:** an artist shows her work at a Bucktown arts festival.

### Damen Avenue boutiques

Walk north up Damen Avenue and you're in boutiqueville USA, where au courant ateliers like **P.45** (1643 North Damen Avenue; tel: 773-862-4523) hawk $300 cashmere tunics alongside big designer names like BCBG Max Azria and Marc for Marc Jacobs. Farther north, Art Institute grad **Robin Richman** (2108 North Damen Avenue; tel: 773-278-6150) has carved out her own retail niche with an eponymous boutique specializing in one-of-a-kind pieces, including knitwear of her own design. Menswear is well represented at **Apartment Number 9** (1804 North Damen Avenue; tel: 773-395-2999), and full-figured women can find sexy, trendy pieces in sizes 12 to 24 at Stephanie Sack's friendly **Vive La Femme** (2048 North Damen Avenue; tel: 773-772-7429).

Off the main drags, Bucktown is primarily residential. West of Damen, you can take a break from ogling beautifully restored cottages and "two flats" with a stop at the homey **Charleston** tavern (2076 North Hoyne Avenue; tel: 773-489-4757) or one of Chicago's best beer bars, the **Map Room** (1949 North Hoyne Avenue; tel: 773-252-7636).

Or go east on Cortland and you'll hit a small commercial district anchored by **Jane's** (1655 West Cortland Street; tel: 773-862-5263), where a recent expansion accommodates the dinner and brunch crowds. Tucked behind the restaurant, almost hidden from the street, is **Trap Door Theatre** (1655 West Cortland Street; tel: 773-384-0494), acclaimed for its skillful staging of challenging and often obscure work from the European and American avant-garde. ❑

*Recommended Restaurants, Bars & Cafés on pages 214–5*

## Nelson Algren

**Chicago's poet of the streets explored the grimy underbelly of the city he loved**

Nelson Algren was for decades Chicago's reigning poet of the slums – a maverick, impassioned voice for the voiceless. Born in 1909 and raised in working-class neighborhoods on the south and northwest side, he settled in Bucktown after serving as a private in World War II. His breakout 1950 novel, *The Man With the Golden Arm* (recipient of the first-ever National Book Award), chronicled the broken lives of the pimps, prostitutes, junkies, and gamblers who congregated at the Tug & Maul, a seedy bar said to be inspired by the Rainbo Club.

In 1947 Algren met French feminist and writer Simone de Beauvoir, the longtime partner of existentialist philosopher Jean-Paul Sartre, and charmed her by showing her around the Polish bars of Wicker Park. From his $10 a month walk-up at 1523 West Wabansia (which Beauvoir found "refreshing, after the heavy odour of the dollars in the big hotels and the elegant restaurants"), the unlikely pair launched a torrid affair that ultimately spanned 17 years and three continents before ending bitterly. Rough-and-tumble Algren wanted to marry the coolly intellectual de Beauvoir, who called him her "Division Street Dostoyevski," but she refused to leave both Sartre and France. She later portrayed Algren as Lewis Brogan in her novel *The Mandarins*. At her death in 1986, she was buried in Paris wearing the ring Algren gave her.

In 1956 *The Man With the Golden Arm* was made into a film starring Frank Sinatra as the morphine-addicted hero, Frankie Machine. But the disastrous Hollywood experience (he wound up suing producer Otto Preminger) soured Algren forever on commercial success – and he ultimately soured on Chicago as well, leaving town for Long Island in New York in 1980. He never returned. Algren died of a heart attack the following year.

By 1989 Algren's books were out of print, so his buddy Studs Terkel and others formed the Nelson Algren Committee to try and keep his work alive. Today, all his novels are again available, as are numerous biographies exploring his life and art. And, though an attempt to rename West Evergreen (site of his last Wicker Park apartment) in his honor was aborted, he's left his mark on the neighborhood. In addition to the fountain at the Polish Triangle, there's a Frankie Machine Community Garden at Haddon and Wood, and every year the Committee celebrates his birthday with a public program of songs, performance, readings, and cake.

In his 40-odd years walking Chicago's streets Algren penned numerous novels and short stories – among them *The Neon Wilderness* and *A Walk on the Wild Side* – but he's perhaps best known for the prose-poem *Chicago: City on the Make*, a ferocious indictment of corrupt city government and a love song to the city's grimy underbelly. "Like loving a woman with a broken nose," he wrote of his hometown, "you may well find lovelier lovelies. But never a lovely so real."

**RIGHT:** Nelson Algren portrayed Chicago's gritty working-class neighborhoods.

# BEST RESTAURANTS, BARS AND CAFÉS

## Restaurants

Prices for a three-course dinner per person with a half-bottle of house wine:

**$** = under $20
**$$** = $20–$45
**$$$** = $45–$60
**$$$$** = over $60

### Bongo Room

1470 N. Milwaukee Ave
773-489-0690 B & L Mon–Fri, Br Sat–Sun **$**

Popular brunch spot for treats like chocolate French toast and cranberry-cornmeal flapjacks with *crème anglaise.* Worth it if you can wait up to an hour for a table.

### Crust

2056 W. Division St
773-235-5511 L & D daily **$**

Chicago's first certified-organic restaurant. The slick, cafeterialike atmosphere belies the fresh and sophisticated fare: wood-oven pizza (here called "flat-breads") topped with everything from pepperoni to béchamel sauce, caramelized onions, bacon, and caraway seeds. There's also outdoor seating for 120.

### Earwax Café

1561 N. Milwaukee Ave
773-772-4019 B, L & D daily **$**

A funky neighborhood mainstay since before Starbucks moved in, Earwax Café offers light vegetarian-friendly fare: salads, soups, sandwiches, quesadillas, and specialties like a seitan reuben sandwich with vegan Thousand Island dressing. Breakfast is served all day (try the breakfast burrito), and there's rarely a wait.

### Handlebar

2311 W. North Ave
773-384-9546 B, L & D daily **$**

This casual, cycling-themed restaurant peddles a creative yet reliable vegetarian-friendly menu that includes killer mac-and-cheese and many daily specials, not to mention an excellent list of craft beers.

### Hot Chocolate

1747 N. Damen Ave
773-489-1747 L Tue–Fri, D Tue–Sun, Br Sat–Sun **$$$**

Sleek, trendy, and often jammed, Hot Chocolate offers a short, ever-changing menu of contemporary American specials and a masterful array of desserts courtesy of owner Mindy Segal, a veteran pastry chef. The titular drink shows up in multiple manifestations. Don't miss the devastating black-and-tan: two-thirds hot chocolate, one-third hot fudge.

### Irazu

1865 N. Milwaukee Ave
773-252-5687 L & D Mon–Sat **$** Cash only

This is a casual and authentic Costa Rican joint just a bit up the road from the buzzing hub of Wicker Park. In addition to standards like burritos, tortas, and tostones, there's an extensive selection of shakes in exotic flavors like tamarind and oatmeal.

### Le Bouchon

958 N. Damen Ave
773-862-6600 D Mon–Sat **$$**

This slice of Paris has been a Bucktown anchor since 1994. There are no surprises on the menu, just solid bistro standards like *tarte a l'oignon*, steak *frites*, and *cassoulet*. Tuesday nights there's a popular three-course prix fixe for $22.

### Letizia's Natural Bakery/Enoteca Roma

2144-46 W. Division St
773-342-1011 B, L & D daily **$**

This bakery and coffee shop offers a vast array of pastries plus pizza and panini. The adjacent tiny wine bar is refreshingly unpretentious and welcoming, with a rustic menu of bruschetta,

**LEFT:** Earwax Café.
**RIGHT:** Chicago Avenue takeout joint.

antipasti, and other savory bites. Ample outdoor seating.

**Lula Café**
2537 N. Kedzie Blvd
773-489-9554 B, L & D Sun–Mon, Wed–Sat **$$**
Beloved by its at-times hipper-than-thou clientele, Lula is about a mile northwest of Wicker Park in gentrifying Logan Square. Chef-owners Amalea Tschilds and Jason Hammel emphasize local, seasonal ingredients on an eclectic menu that's half affordable standards like a perfect roast chicken and half daily specials priced a bit higher. There's a popular three-course "farm dinner" on Monday nights, and brunch is guaranteed to be a zoo.

**Piece**
1927 W. North Ave
773-772-4422 L & D daily **$$**
This cavernous and at times cacophonous pizzeria and award-winning microbrewery was one of the first in town to reject Chicago-style pizza in favor of thin-crust, wood-oven "New Haven" style pies. Open late, with live-band karaoke on Saturday nights.

**Pontiac Café and Bar**
1531 N. Damen Ave
773-252-7767 L & D daily **$**
Sure they serve food (sandwiches, mostly) and you could sit inside, but the best way to enjoy the Pontiac – a converted produce stand – is to squeeze in with the young, boisterous crowd on the spacious cement patio in the summer, frosty drink in hand. The bar offers a range of nightly entertainment, from DJs to Sunday night Honky-Tonk Bingo.

**Rodan**
1530 N. Milwaukee Ave
773-276-7036 D daily, Br Sat–Sun **$$**
Hipster central, this high-tech, minimalist restaurant and lounge morphs into a nightclub after about 10pm. For all the slick decor, the globally-inspired food – from fish tacos and pot stickers to steak with chimichurri sauce – is surprisingly good, and the mojitos are a knockout. But it's often easier to just watch the scene than try to actually talk to your date.

**Spring**
2039 W. North Ave
773-395-7100 D Tue–Sun **$$$$**
Award-winning chef Shawn McClain launched his mini-empire (now up to three restaurants) with this Asian-inspired seafood spot in a renovated 1923 bathhouse. Classy and sophisticated, the space matches the food, which emphasizes creative twists on clean, unadulterated flavors.

## Bars

**Danny's Tavern**, 1951 W. Dickens Ave (tel: 773-489-6457). A warren of cozy, candlelit rooms and nooks leads back from the front bar of this established Bucktown hangout. DJs spin most nights but the scene is more living-room dance party than nightclub. Look for the glowing red Schlitz sign.

**Davenport's Piano Bar and Cabaret**, 1383 N. Milwaukee Ave (tel: 773-278-1830). Looking to class up your act? This is the place, with a piano bar up front and a cozy cabaret in the back room. There's no cover in the lounge except after 10pm Saturday.

**Empire Liquors**, 1566 N. Milwaukee Ave (tel: 773-278-1600). Almost tragically hip new bar decked out in Gothic splendor with equal parts mod and vintage accoutrements. Signature cocktails made with flavored syrup are a hallmark; DJs spin nightly.

**Map Room**, 1949 N. Hoyne Ave (tel: 773-252-7636). Billing itself as a "traveler's tavern," the lively and unpretentious Map Room is really the promised land of beer, with 26 brews on tap and five times that many in bottles from around the world.

**Rainbo Club**, 1150 N. Damen Ave (tel: 773-489-5999). The original Wicker Park bar, in business since 1936 and allegedly one of Nelson Algren's old haunts. A bohemian oasis in the pre-gentrification days and still the preferred watering hole of local musicians and artists, the bar has attracted a noticeably more well-heeled crowd in recent years.

**The Violet Hour**, 1520 N. Damen Ave (no telephone). Credited with bringing cocktail culture to Chicago, the Violet Hour was dubbed by *Food and Wine* the "most exciting new bar in America" scant weeks after its 2007 opening. Classic pre-Prohibition tipples – all $11 – are meticulously constructed by bartenders who can wax eloquent on the merits of handcrafted bitters and twice-filtered ice. The polite doorman allows only as many patrons inside as there are seats.

MEN

*Recommended Restaurants, Bars & Cafés on pages 224–5*

# SOUTH LOOP

**Gracious mansions have given way to condos and conventions, but this up-and-coming neighborhood still reflects its colorful history**

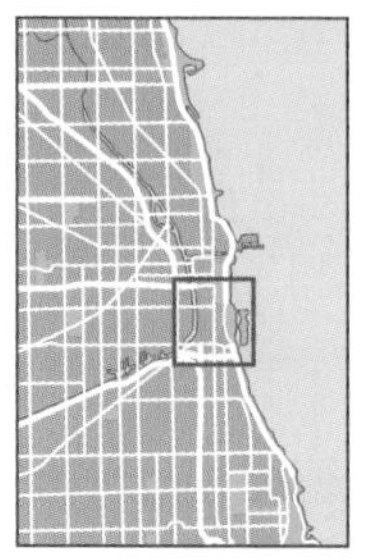

For decades, the South Loop was a no-man's-land full of parking garages and abandoned buildings. But in the 1990s, developers rediscovered the neighborhood, which has the advantage of a prime location near the Loop and lakefront. Shops and restaurants started springing up, and young professionals and families began settling in. It's still not as lively a neighborhood as, say, Lincoln Park, but it appears to be well on its way.

## War and remembrance

The South Loop's boundaries vary, depending on who you ask, but it lies roughly between Congress Parkway to the north, Cermak Road to the south, Lake Shore Drive to the east, and the Chicago River to the west. One of the most notorious events in Illinois history, the Fort Dearborn Massacre, took place here during the War of 1812. British-allied Native Americans ambushed 95 American soldiers and settlers as they tried to make their way from nearby Fort Dearborn to safety. The massacre is believed to have taken place at the site where 18th Street and Calumet Avenue now intersect, though today there's little to mark the spot.

## Good times

Beginning in the 1850s, the South Loop became a railroad hub, drawing commerce to the area. After the Civil War, it turned into a partially residential neighborhood, as many wealthy Chicagoans settled on South Prairie Avenue, drawn by its proximity to the Loop proper. But by the late 1880s, they had mostly moved

**Main attractions**

- HAROLD WASHINGTON LIBRARY
- PRINTERS' ROW
- DEARBORN STATION
- MUSEUM OF CONTEMPORARY PHOTOGRAPHY
- SPERTUS MUSEUM
- NATIONAL VIETNAM VETERANS ART MUSEUM
- PRAIRIE AVENUE HISTORIC DISTRICT
- GLESSNER HOUSE
- BLUES HEAVEN FOUNDATION
- CHINATOWN
- CHINESE AMERICAN MUSEUM OF CHICAGO

**LEFT:** maintaining sartorial standards. **RIGHT:** the El passes overhead; the CTA Red, Green, and Orange lines provide service to the South Loop.

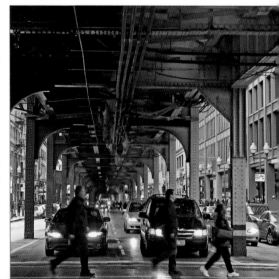

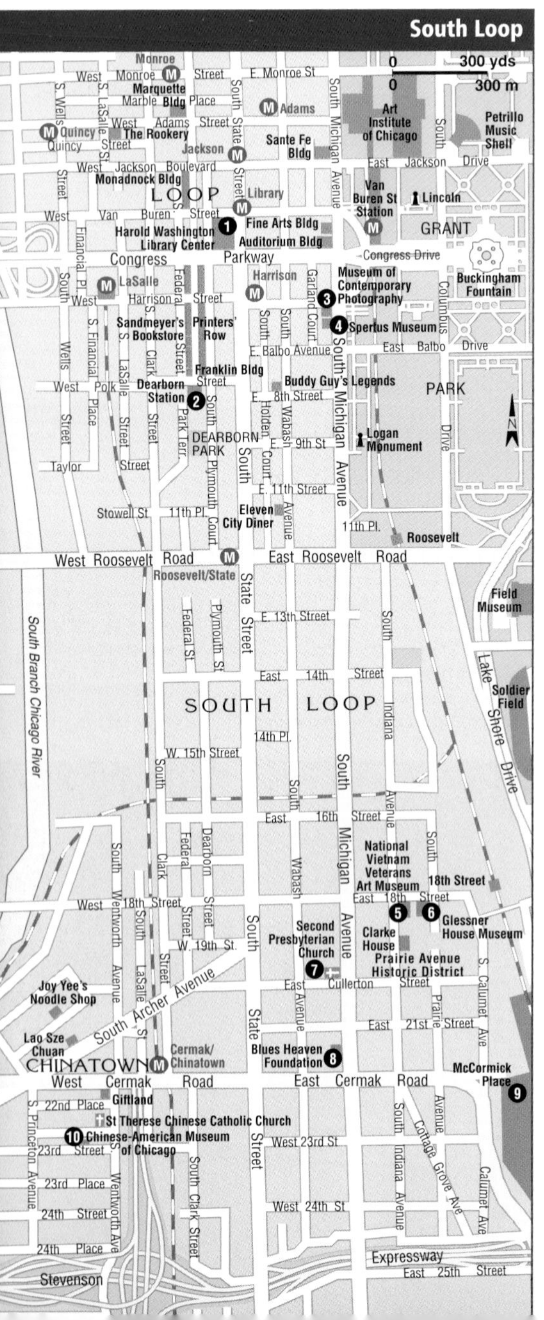


away, chased out by crime in neighboring districts. One such red-light neighborhood, the Levee, flourished between 18th and 22nd streets until a government crackdown brought its high-rolling days to an end in 1912. Around the same time, Chinese immigrants began settling near the South Loop at the intersection of Cermak Road and Wentworth Avenue in the area known to this day as Chinatown.

After World War II, businesses moved from the South Loop to hotter spots elsewhere in the city, leaving historic enclaves like Printers' Row – once the printing center of the Midwest – empty. In the late 1970s, some of the abandoned rail yards were turned into a residential development, but the neighborhood remained quiet until the condo boom began in the late 1990s. Now even Mayor Daley lives here.

## Harold Washington Library Center ❶

✉ 400 South State Street ☎ 312-747-4300, www.chipublib.org
🕒 Mon–Thu 9am–9pm, Fri–Sat 9am–5pm, Sun 1pm–5pm $ free

Start your South Loop tour at the **Harold Washington Library Center**, a red-brick behemoth once listed in the *Guinness Book of World Records* as the world's largest public library building. Free author events take place in the library auditorium, and the glass-roofed Winter Garden on the ninth-floor is a quiet stop.

Walk south on State, then west on Polk to **Printers' Row** (Dearborn Street between Congress Parkway and Polk Street), the 19th-century printing hub of the Midwest. It's anchored now by **Dearborn Station** ❷ (47 West Polk Street), an 1885 train depot turned retail and office space. Pay homage to the area's heritage by stopping at **Sandmeyer's Bookstore** (714 South Dearborn

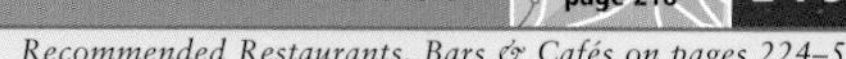

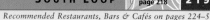

Street; tel: 312-922-2104; Mon–Wed and Fri 11am–6.30pm, Thu 11am–8pm, Sat 11am–5pm, Sun 11am–4pm), a 25-year-old mom-and-pop operation with an excellent selection of Chicago-themed volumes.

## Museum of Contemporary Photography ❸

600 South Michigan Avenue
312-663-5554, http://mocp.org
Mon–Fri 10am–5pm, Thu 10am–8pm, Sat 10am–5pm, Sun noon–5pm free

Backtracking north takes you to Columbia College's free **Museum of Contemporary Photography**. The collection focuses on American photography since 1936, with rotating exhibits that feature work by Robert Heinecken and other masters of the lens. The museum also offers lectures and curator-led tours.

## Spertus Museum ❹

610 South Michigan Avenue
312-322-1700, www.spertus.edu
Mon–Wed, Sun 10am–5pm, Thu 10am–7pm, Fri 10am–3pm charge

Practically next door, the **Spertus Museum** reopened in new digs in late 2007. The museum's exhibits focus on Jewish art and cultural artifacts from around the world.

## National Vietnam Veterans Art Museum ❺

1801 South Indiana Avenue
312-326-0270, www.nvvam.org
Tue–Fri 11am–6pm, Sat 10am–5pm charge

To the south is the **National Vietnam Veterans Art Museum.** The museum displays works of art by not just Vietnam veterans but veterans of all

The retro trappings at the Eleven City Diner (1112 S. Wabash Ave) feel a little calculated, but the food is as solid as it gets. It's hard to go wrong with matzo ball soup, pastrami on rye, and a chocolate egg cream. Breakfast is served all day.

**LEFT:** *Untitled (Wiggles #2)* by Ludwig Schwarz, exhibited at the Spertus Museum. **BELOW:** Harold Washington Library.

**ABOVE:** Dearborn Station (left) and the Franklin Building (right) in the Printers' Row area. **BELOW LEFT:** Minna Everleigh. **BELOW RIGHT:** the Glessner House in the Prairie Avenue Historic District.

wars, including the conflict in Iraq. Look for the *Above and Beyond* memorial, a huge installation composed of thousands of metal dog tags, one for each of the men and women who died in the Vietnam War.

## PRAIRIE AVENUE HISTORIC DISTRICT

A block west lies the **Glessner House Museum** ❻ (1800 South Prairie Avenue; tel: 312-326-1480, www.glessnerhouse.org; tours Wed–Sun 1pm and 3pm; charge), a rare remnant of what was once the city's most fashionable address: Prairie Avenue (now an official historic district). After the Civil War, Marshall Field, George Pullman, and other Chicago tycoons moved here with their families, building elaborate mansions on the blocks between 16th and 22nd streets and 26th and 30th streets. By the 1890s, the millionaires had begun to move out, driven away by a neighboring vice district.

In the 20th century, most of Prairie Avenue's mansions were torn down or neglected, but a few, like the Glessner House, managed to survive. The former home of executive John J. Glessner and his family, the 1886 house features a fortress-like exterior and some 6,000 historical

## The Everleigh Club

When the topic of Chicago's historical crime figures come up, most people think of Al Capone, Bugs Moran, and other nefarious characters. But in the early 1900s, one of the city's most notorious vice dens was run by two genteel sisters named Ada and Minna Everleigh.

The sisters' background is murky, but it's known that they ran a bordello in Omaha, Nebraska, before moving to Chicago in 1899, purchasing a mansion on South Dearborn Street and turning it into the Everleigh Club, the city's most upscale brothel.

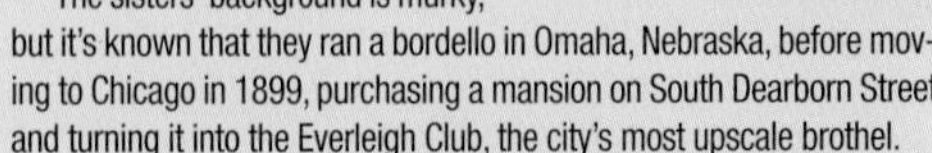

"Working girls" at the Everleigh Club had to eschew alcohol, submit to monthly medical exams, and undergo charm training. Patrons couldn't gain admittance without a letter of reference, and an evening's entertainment cost at least $50 (at a time when a three-course meal could be had for 50¢). Fountains of perfume, chandeliers, statues, and a $15,000 gold piano filled the rooms. The Club closed in 1912.

*Recommended Restaurants, Bars & Cafés on pages 224–5*

artifacts. The museum sometimes offers historical tours of Prairie Avenue for an additional fee.

Down the street, you'll find the even older **Clarke House** (1827 South Indiana Avenue; tel: 312-745-0040; tours Wed–Sun at noon, 1pm, and 2pm; charge). Dating from 1836, the Clarke House may be the oldest existing home in Chicago.

To see some of the most beautiful stained-glass windows in the city, including some by Tiffany, stop at the **Second Presbyterian Church** ❼ (1936 South Michigan Avenue; tel: 312-225-4951; open to visitors most days before 5pm). Built in 1874, the church was largely destroyed by fire in 1900 but was subsequently rebuilt by noted Chicago architect Howard Van Doren Shaw.

## Blues Heaven Foundation ❽

2120 South Michigan Avenue
312-808-1286, www.bluesheaven.com Mon–Fri noon–3pm, Sat noon–2pm charge

Farther south on Michigan Avenue lies the **Blues Heaven Foundation**, notable as the former home of Chess Records. This is where brothers Leonard and Phil Chess recorded such blues and rock legends as Muddy Waters, Howlin' Wolf, Etta James, and the Rolling Stones between 1957 and 1967. It's now an official Chicago landmark.

To the east, **McCormick Place** ❾

*The Checker Record Co. was a subsidiary of classic blues label Chess Records.*

**ABOVE LEFT:** luxury residential development is transforming the neighborhood.
**BELOW:** a local band plays at Buddy Guy's Legends, one of the city's top blues clubs.

*Recommended Restaurants, Bars & Cafés on pages 224–5*

Chinatown gets hip at the Red-I Lounge (2201B S. Wentworth Ave). The karaoke bar-cum-dance hall above the Malaysian restaurant Penang attracts a mixed crowd of young edgy club types looking for the next hot thing.

**ABOVE:** Chinatown grocery store.
**BELOW:** a gate at Wentworth Avenue and Cermak Road marks the entrance to Chinatown.

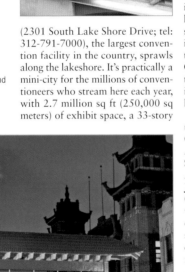

(2301 South Lake Shore Drive; tel: 312-791-7000), the largest convention facility in the country, sprawls along the lakeshore. It's practically a mini-city for the millions of conventioneers who stream here each year, with 2.7 million sq ft (250,000 sq meters) of exhibit space, a 33-story hotel, the 4,239-seat Aerie Crown Theatre, 5,000 parking spaces, and its own Metra stop.

## CHINATOWN

Lively Chinatown radiates from the intersection of Cermak Road and Wentworth Avenue, stretching from 18th Street on the north to 23rd Street on the south, and State Street on the east to the Chicago River on the west. Chicago's Chinese population originally centered in the Loop. The lure of cheaper rents in the early 20th century gradually led its residents to the Cermak-Wentworth area, formerly an Italian enclave. **St Therese Chinese Catholic Church** (218 West Alexander Street; tel: 312-842-6777), once the home of an Italian congregation, displays its mixed heritage with an interior that blends stained-glass windows with Chinese inscriptions. For more history, visit the **Chinese-American Museum of Chicago ⑩** (238 West 23rd Street; tel: 312-949-1000; charge), though it's a good idea to call ahead, as hours are limited.

After stopping for a photo op under the gold-and-red pavilion at Cermak Road and Wentworth Avenue, venture north to **Chinatown Square** (2100 South Wentworth Avenue), an open-air mall that houses **Joy Yee's Noodle Shop** (tel: 312-328-0001; daily 11am–10.30pm). The vast menu includes dishes from all over Asia, including bubble tea (a sweet iced drink containing pearls of chewy tapioca). For fancier fare, nearby **Lao Sze Chuan** (2172 South Archer Avenue; tel: 312-326-5040) offers both traditional and modern cuisine, from "spicy sour squid" to standards like hot-and-sour soup.

Souvenir shops are everywhere, proffering cheongsams (traditional Chinese dresses), tea, fortune cookies, ceramics, and more. One place to start: **Giftland** (2212 South Wentworth Avenue; tel: 312-225-0088).❑

## The Real Blues Brothers

**Two guys with a feel for 'soul' turned their recording studio into a platform for the best in R&B**

Musical history was made when a couple of immigrant boys with "big ears" (as jazzmen like to say) transformed a building on South Michigan Avenue into a sounding board for the "soul" revolution.

The enterprising energies of brothers Leonard and Phil Chess, starting around 1950, helped channel early R&B into the worldwide phenomenon that rock 'n' roll became in the 1960s. Their vehicle was Chess Records, with recording facilities at 2120 South Michigan Avenue.

Leonard, the driving force, was born Lejzor Czyz in 1917 in Motule, Poland. He and younger brother Fiszel (Philip) and family came to Chicago in 1928. By the 1940s, the brothers had bought into several bars on the city's South Side, with its large African-American population. One of their nightclubs, Macomba, frequently featured blues performers with roots in the Mississippi delta region.

Becoming enamored with the music, the Chess brothers joined forces with Charles and Evelyn Aron and their newly formed Aristocrat Records, a label that specialized in blues, jazz, and R&B. Their most promising artist was singer-guitarist McKinley ("Muddy Waters") Morganfield.

Taking over the Aristocrat label, the brothers renamed it Chess Records in 1950. A subsidiary label called Checker, featuring the harmonica player Little Walter, was formed in 1952. Also joining the Chess fold was bluesman Howlin' Wolf and influential songwriter and producer Willie Dixon.

Chess recorded with great success two black vocal groups, the Flamingos and the Moonglows, and by the mid-1950s it came into contact with the soon to be legendary Chuck Berry and Bo Diddley. Chess also set up a jazz subsidiary called Argo Records, featuring such prominent musical figures as Sonny Stitt, Yusef Lateef, Ahmad Jamal, and Ramsey Lewis. Gospel music was recorded, too, among the singers recruited being a minister's daughter named Aretha Franklin.

Skillful as talent spotters, the Chess brothers hired the veteran producer Ralph Bass away from King Records in Cincinnati, and Bass added the services of still another promising producer, Billy Davis. Boosting the careers of such singers as Etta James, Davis gave Chess a distinctive "soul" dimension that made the label preeminent in the blues field.

Chess's fortunes began to decline after 1968, when Davis left the company. Leonard's son, Marshall, took over for a while, but the label was sold soon after his father's death. What was left of the Chess assets was disposed of in 1975 in a deal with All Platinum Records, based in New Jersey. ❑

**ABOVE:** Marshall Chess.

**RIGHT:** Chess Records producer Willie Dixon.

# BEST RESTAURANTS, BARS AND CAFÉS

## Restaurants

Prices for a three-course dinner per person with a half-bottle of house wine:
**$** = under $20
**$$** = $20–$45
**$$$** = $45–$60
**$$$$** = over $60

### Buddy Guy's Legends

754 S. Wabash Ave 312-427-1190 L & D daily **$** [p307, C3]

Buddy Guy's dark, dank honky-tonk, a fixture on the Chicago blues circuit, might seem an odd pick for dinner, but the Cajun-Creole food – including gumbo, jambalaya, fried okra, catfish po' boys, slabs of juicy ribs – is several cuts above your average bar grub and won't put a dent in your wallet.

### Cuatro

2030 S. Wabash Ave 312-842-8856 D daily, Br Sun **$$$** [p309, C1]

This sophisticated nuevo Latino-Caribbean spot occupies an airy space on historic Motor Row. Try the *moqueqa do mar*, an aromatic seafood stew in an addictive tomato-coconut-milk broth laced with saffron and just the right dose of heat. There's live Latin jazz, bossa nova, and house music nightly.

### Custom House

500 S. Dearborn St 312-523-0200 L Mon–Sat, D daily, Br Sun **$$$$** [p306, C3]

With this calmly luxe take on a steakhouse, Shawn McClain, a 2006 James Beard award winner, hits the culinary trifecta. His growing empire also includes the seafood-centric Spring and vegetarian small-plates joint Green Zebra. Be sure to check out some of the infused alcohols at the bar, such as rhubarb-ginger gin or peach- and black-peppercorn-infused vodka.

### Exposure Tapas Supper Club

1315 S. Wabash Ave 312-662-1082 D daily **$$-$$$** [p307, C4]

A recent addition to the booming South Loop nightlife scene, Exposure covers all the critical bases: small plates, late hours, loud crowd ... you get the gist. But the food (mostly contemporary American noshes like bacon-wrapped dates and seared sea scallops) holds its own. There's live music downstairs Friday and Saturday at 10.30pm.

### Gioco

1312 S. Wabash Ave 312-939-3870 L Mon–Fri, D daily **$$$** [p307, C4]

Convenient to Soldier Field and the McCormick Place convention center, Gioco was a pioneer in turning the South Loop into the booming restaurant destination it is today. Occupying two adjacent (and meticulously distressed) buildings, it seats 270; the rustic Italian menu offers lots of slow-cooked meats, handmade pastas, and wood-oven pizza.

### Hi Tea

14 E. 11th St 312-880-0832 B, L & D daily **$** [p307, C3]

This colorfully hip tea shop caters to local Columbia College students and purveys more than 50 loose-leaf teas, all prepared with loving care. There's also a light café menu of soups, salads, and sandwiches, including a few – like chicken salad made from a bird baked with Earl Grey – that manage to incorporate the shop's signature beverage.

### Joy Yee's Noodles

2159 S. China Pl 312-328-0001 L & D daily **$** [p308, B1]

Cheery Joy Yee was one of the first to bring Taiwanese bubble tea to Chicago. The sweet milk teas are flavored with everything from coconut to red bean and loaded

**LEFT AND RIGHT:** diners enjoy a pre-dinner cocktail at Opera, which fuses Chinese and French cuisine.

with pearls of black tapioca; there's also an exhaustive list of fruit freezes and smoothies, and, of course, noodles.

### Kroll's

✉ 1736 S. Michigan Ave ☎ 312-235-1400 ⊙ L & D daily **$** [p309, C1]

This is the first Chicago outpost of the beloved Green Bay, Wisconsin, joint famed for half-pound charcoal-grilled butter burgers. Open at 10am when there's a Bears game – and not just when they play the Packers.

### Manny's Coffee Shop & Deli

✉ 1141 S. Jefferson St ☎ 312-939-2855 ⊙ B & L Mon–Sat **$** [p306, B3]

This is a Chicago institution since 1942, as the walls plastered with clippings attest. Hungry, predominantly male masses of all colors and creeds hit this no-frills Jewish cafeteria and deli for freakishly thick slabs of corned beef on rye, crisp and fluffy latkes, and liver and onions straight from the steam table.

### Opera

✉ 1301 S. Wabash St ☎ 312-461-0161 ⊙ D daily **$$$** [p307, C4]

The dining room at Opera is as colorful and extravagant as a Puccini aria. The food is a freewheeling fusion of traditional Chinese cooking, French technique, and fine-dining presentation. It doesn't pretend to be authentic – for that head to neighboring Chinatown.

### Oysy

✉ 888 S. Michigan Ave ☎ 312-922-1127 ⊙ L Mon–Fri, D daily **$$** [p307, C3]

Enjoy fresh, contemporary sushi in a beautifully minimalist room with floor-to-ceiling windows looking out on Michigan Avenue and Grant Park. The lunch bento box specials are a steal at $12 or so. There's a smaller location at 50 E. Grand in River North.

### Room 21

✉ 2100 S. Wabash Ave ☎ 312-328-1198 ⊙ D daily **$$$** [p309, C1]

Larger-than-life restaurateur Jerry Kleiner (Gioco, Opera) continues his campaign to colonize the South Loop with this 5,000-sq-ft (465-sq-meter) steakhouse on the neighborhood's southern fringe. A warehouse allegedly once used by Al Capone to store his hooch, the place is vintage Kleiner: loud, extravagant, and pricey. Steaks top out at $44, though there is a $10 burger.

### White Palace Grill

✉ 1159 S. Canal ☎ 312-939-7167 ⊙ B, L & D daily **$** [p306, B3]

Open round-the-clock, this vintage diner is a dogged reminder of the area's working-class roots. The food is pretty standard, but the scene is old Chicago and the view is a showstopper.

### Yolk

✉ 1120 S. Michigan Ave ☎ 312-789-9655 ⊙ B & L daily **$** [p307, C3]

This bright, cheery breakfast spot has a great view of the park. In addition to plentiful egg options, there's stuffed French toast, waffles, potato pancakes, oatmeal, and more.

### Zapatista

✉ 1307 S. Wabash Ave ☎ 312-435-1307 ⊙ L & D daily **$$** [p307, C4]

Regional Mexican fare interpreted for the masses, complete with

tableside guacamole and a *"revolucion"* chopped salad. The room is sprawling and noisy thanks to the open kitchen, but with a group it's fun – especially if you sample some of the 100 tequilas.

## Bars

**Kitty O'Shea's**, 720 S. Michigan Ave (tel: 312-294-6860). Authentic Irish pub tucked into the Chicago Hilton and Towers. Staff is straight from the motherland; come here for a properly pulled pint and live music.

**M Lounge**, 1520 S. Wabash Ave (tel: 312-447-0201). Sleek martini lounge with live jazz Tuesday and Wednesday. No cover, but there is a two-drink minimum.

**South Loop Club**, 701 S. State St (tel: 312-427-2787). Thirsty for a beer, a shot, and the Bears? This sports bar can provide them all. The crowd is a casual mix of locals, tourists, and students from nearby Roosevelt and Columbia. Just steer clear of the notoriously cranky management.

**Velvet Lounge**, 67 E. Cermak Rd (tel: 312-791-9050). A founding member of the Association for Advancement of Creative Musicians, Fred Anderson considers jazz Chicago's folk music and he's devoted his life to promoting it. His legendary club moved around the corner from its old location on South Indiana in 2006. While the atmosphere is cleaner than that at the old space – a dark cave smothered in years of smoke – it's still *the* go-to spot in town for live, down-and-dirty jazz that skews toward the experimental. There's live music every night except Monday; the first set starts at 9pm; cover ranges from $5 to $20.

# Field Museum of Natural History

**With a collection of more than 20 million objects, the Field is nothing less than a catalog of the natural world and human cultures**

The Field Museum is one of those places that just screams out "this is what a science museum should look like!" In fact, the building and its celebrated scientific history are so iconic that Hollywood used it as the setting for the 1997 thriller *The Relic* and as the stomping ground of that quintessential archaeologist-on-the-go, Indiana Jones. The Field – originally called the Columbian Museum of Chicago – was founded in 1893 for the World's Columbian Exhibition and set in the Palace of Fine Arts, which today houses the Museum of Science and Industry. It was rechristened in 1905 in honor of chief benefactor Marshall Field, and it came to occupy its present lakeshore setting in 1921. With more than 9 acres (4 hectares) of exhibition space, it is one of world's largest and most highly esteemed science museums.

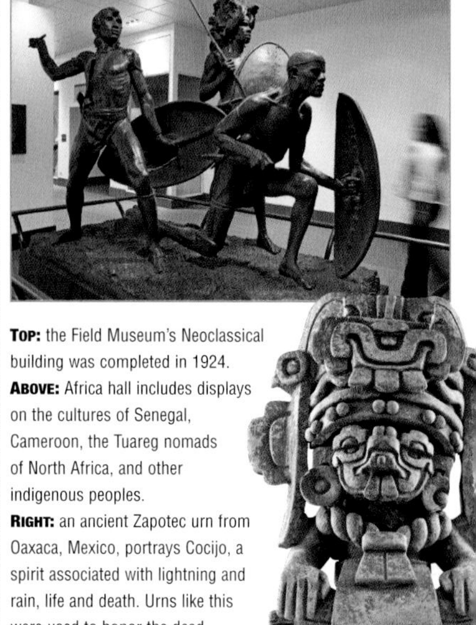

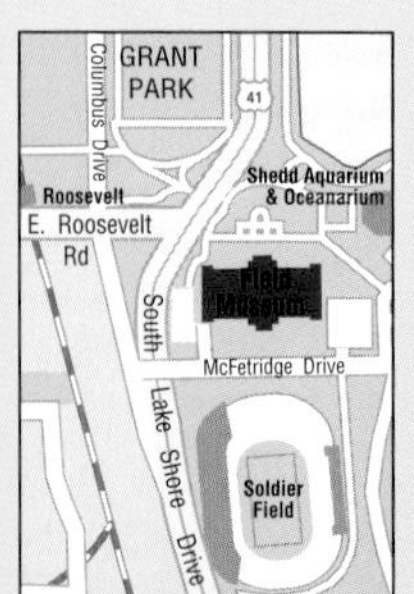


## The Essentials

1400 South Lake Shore Drive
312-922-9410, www.fieldmuseum.org
daily 9am–5pm
charge, free Highlight Tours Mon–Fri 11am and 2pm
CTA bus #146 or #6

**Top:** the Field Museum's Neoclassical building was completed in 1924.
**Above:** Africa hall includes displays on the cultures of Senegal, Cameroon, the Tuareg nomads of North Africa, and other indigenous peoples.
**Right:** an ancient Zapotec urn from Oaxaca, Mexico, portrays Cocijo, a spirit associated with lightning and rain, life and death. Urns like this were used to honor the dead.

**ABOVE:** a life-size model of Beipiaosaurus, a recently discovered carnivorous theropod, illustrates the creature's agile body, lethal front claws, and a light covering of protofeathers.

## SUE'S SAGA

**From Dakota badlands to downtown Chicago, the *Tyrannosaurus rex* named Sue has journeyed farther in the scientific and legal worlds than any other fossil. Sixty-five million years after the dinosaur died, she became the focus of a saga unprecedented in the annals of natural history.**

**Sue's modern story began in August 1990, when an amateur paleontologist spotted her bones protruding from a hillside on an Indian reservation in South Dakota. Susan Hendrickson was prospecting for dinosaur fossils with her boyfriend, Peter Larson, who ran a fossil-selling company. In the hillside she found him the gift of a lifetime – two fragments of vertebrae that led to the most complete *T. rex* ever found.**

**Over the next five years a legal battle ensued pitting Larson against the federal government and the Indian tribe. In the end, Larson's claim was extinguished, and Sue was put up for auction at Sotheby's in New York. The Field Museum, with corporate backing from McDonald's and Disney, bought her for more than $8 million, the highest price ever paid for a fossil. After a contest to rename the dinosaur, the Field stuck with "Sue."**

**TOP:** Sue the *Tyrannosaurus rex*.

**RIGHT:** a small coffin in the blockbuster King Tut exhibit held Tut's mummified organs.

**RIGHT:** "Inside Ancient Egypt" features a diorama detailing the tools and techniques employed by ancient Egyptian embalmers. Two rooms from the tomb of Unis-ankh, son of Fifth Dynasty Pharaoh Unis, are also on display.

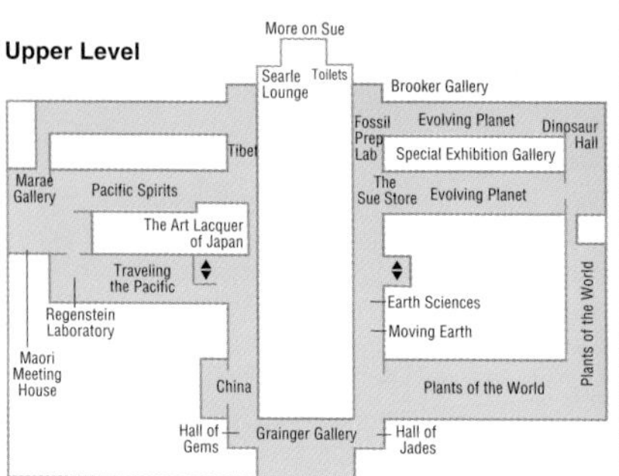


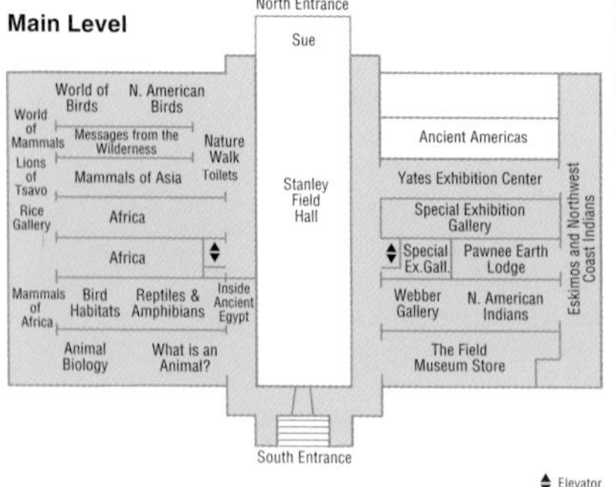


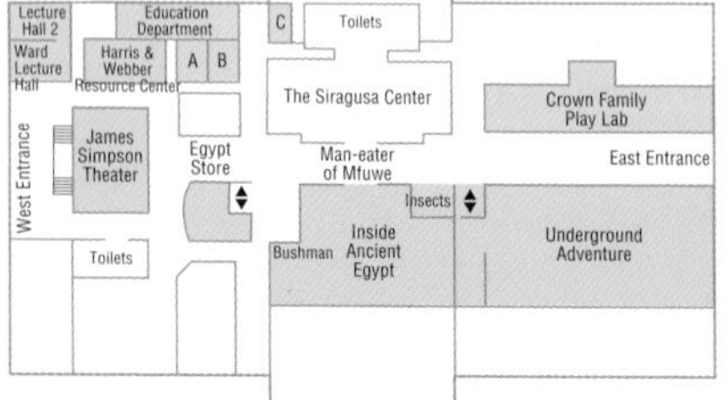

**ABOVE:** visitors take in an exhibit on the life and work of Charles Darwin, whose theory of evolution by natural selection overturned long-held beliefs about the origin of life.
**BELOW:** dioramas illustrate some of the plants and animals Darwin encountered on the Galápagos Islands during his historic five-year sea voyage aboard the *HMS Beagle*.

**RIGHT:** this ceramic mask was created by the people of Teotihuacan in present-day Mexico, one of the largest cities in the world at AD 500, with some 125,000 people.

**ABOVE:** this massive *Majungatholus atopus* skull is one of the best-preserved dinosaur skulls ever discovered. Unearthed in Madagascar, *Majungatholus* lived about 150 million years ago, walked on hind legs, and was a carnivore that occasionally may have eaten its own kind.

**ABOVE:** a model of *Australopithecus afarensis* "Lucy" greets visitors in an exhibit exploring human evolution. Discovered in Ethiopia, Lucy is a bipedal hominid some 3.2 million years old. She is named after the Beatles' song "Lucy in the Sky with Diamonds," which was playing in the paleontologists' camp.

**RIGHT:** a stone figurine made between AD 500 and 1000 by the Wari people of Peru depicts an elaborately dressed leader, distinguished by his headdress and tunic.

**ABOVE:** the "Evolving Planet" exhibit leads museum-goers through 4 billion years of life on earth, including video exhibits that enable visitors to experience the bizarre life-forms that inhabited the earth's ancient oceans.

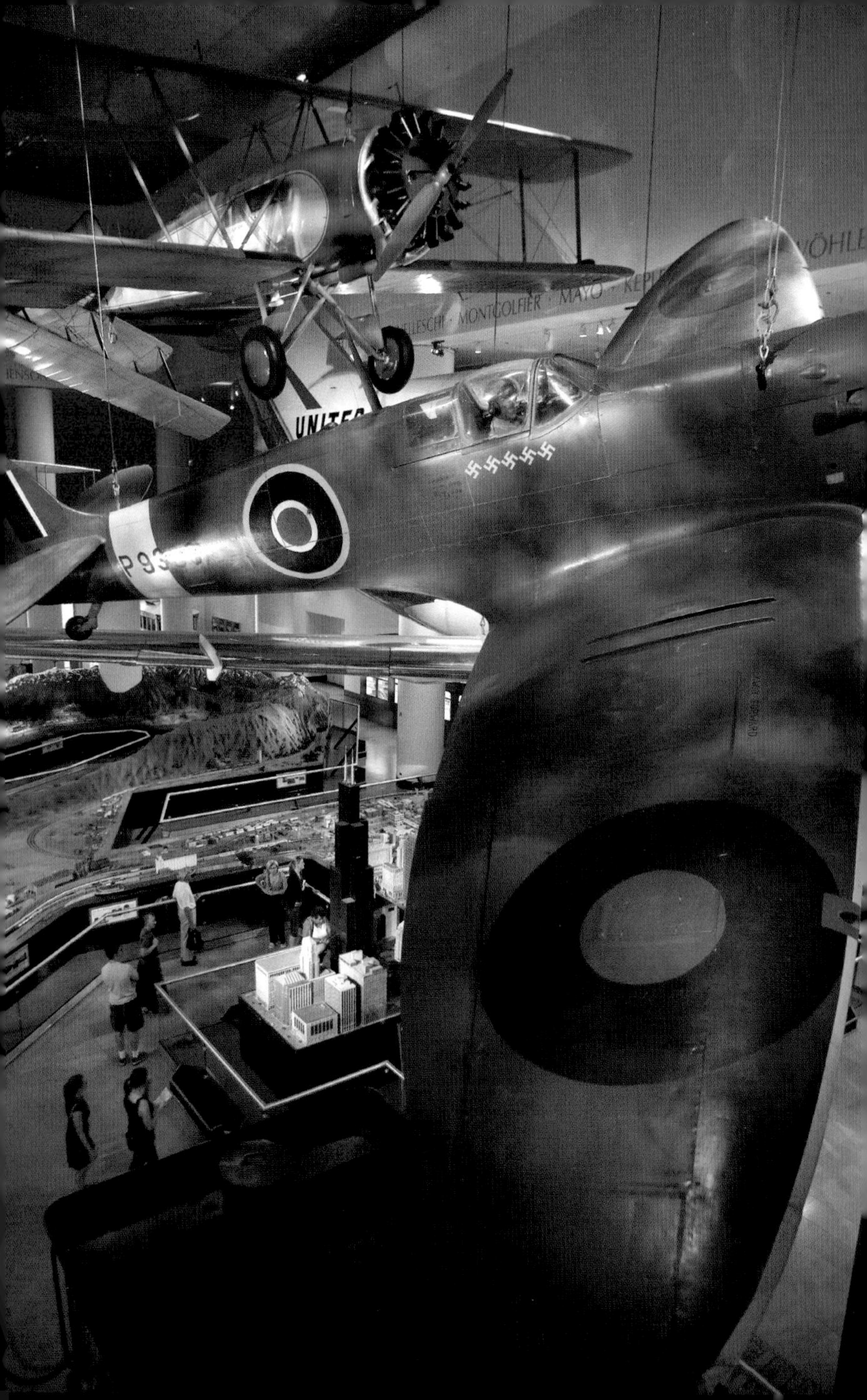
MONTGOLFIER · MAYO

*Recommended Restaurants, Bars & Cafés on pages 240–1*

# SOUTH SIDE AND HYDE PARK

**From Bronzeville to the University of Chicago, the sprawling South Side embodies the city's diversity and contradictions**

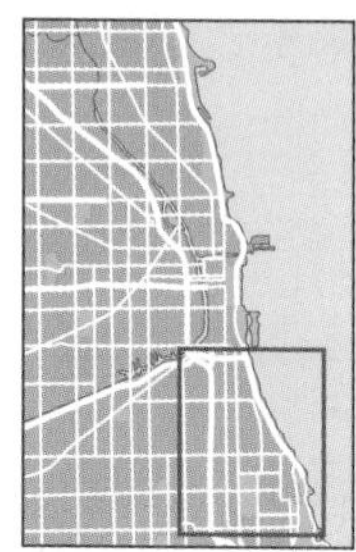

**Main attractions**

- IIT CAMPUS ARCHITECTURE
- HAROLD WASHINGTON CULTURAL CENTER
- WASHINGTON PARK
- DUSABLE MUSEUM OF AFRICAN AMERICAN HISTORY
- UNIVERSITY OF CHICAGO
- SMART MUSEUM OF ART
- ORIENTAL INSTITUTE MUSEUM
- ROCKEFELLER MEMORIAL CHAPEL
- ROBIE HOUSE
- MUSEUM OF SCIENCE AND INDUSTRY
- OSAKA GARDEN
- SOUTH SHORE CULTURAL CENTER

This is famously the part of Chicago where, in the summer of 1922, a young man with a horn arrived from New Orleans en route to making musical history. His name was Louis Daniel Armstrong, still a month short of his 21st birthday, and overwhelmed by the cacophony of the big northern city's sights and sounds.

"I never seen a city that big," he later reflected. He stepped off the Illinois Central train at the 12th Street Station and into a cab that whisked him to the Lincoln Gardens Café and a rendezvous with Joe Oliver, mentor and fellow jazz trumpet virtuoso. Armstrong would soon be basking in the bright lights of South State Street and the bustling strip known familiarly to African-Americans as "The Stroll."

Today, the many jazz and blues clubs that once lined The Stroll have faded, and sadly the South Side itself – the heart of Chicago's African-American community since the days of the Great Migration from the South – has long been diminished by urban deterioration. There are some signs of recovery on the South Side as well as middle-class enclaves such as the Hyde Park neighborhood, which is the home of the University of Chicago, bracketed by Washington Park to the west and lakeside Jackson Park to the east.

## ILLINOIS INSTITUTE OF TECHNOLOGY

Start your tour of the South Side at the **Illinois Institute of Technology** (IIT) ❶. Recognized in 1976 as one of the most significant sites in the country by the American Institute of

**LEFT:** the Museum of Science and Industry occupies a building constructed for the 1893 World's Columbian Exposition.
**RIGHT:** old friends at a Bronzeville diner.

Architects, the IIT campus is predominantly the work of Ludwig Mies van der Rohe.

The German-born Mies came to America in 1938 and took over the directorship of the architecture department at what was then the Armour Institute of Technology, which later merged with another technical school to become IIT. At the time, the university was intent on building a new campus, one of the nation's first federally funded urban-renewal projects. The campus plan, consisting of 22 buildings, was Mies's first American commission, and he is responsible for shaping the style of the modernist campus. The IIT crown jewel, so to speak, is Mies's elegant **S.R. Crown Hall** (3360 South State Street), which houses IIT's College of Architecture.

"I think this is the clearest structure we have done," Mies said of his one-room steel-and-glass structure, "the best to express our philosophy."

**ABOVE:** the Exelon Tube at IIT's McCormick Tribune Campus Center. **BELOW:** breakfast at a South Side restaurant.

## Exelon Tube

After a decades-long lull in building, two exciting new structures were added to the campus in 2003. The CTA Green line train runs through the campus and now passes through the **Exelon Tube**, part of the **McCormick Tribune Campus Center** (3201 South State Street; tel: 312-567-5014, www.iit.edu), the first

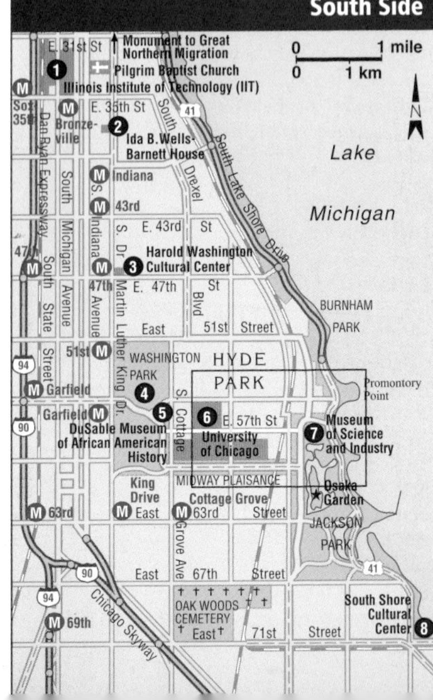

*Recommended Restaurants, Bars & Cafés on pages 240–1*

building designed in the United States by Dutch architect and Pritzker Prize Laureate Rem Koolhaas. Koolhaas's $9 million corrugated steel tube, lined in bright orange, envelopes 350 ft (100 meters) of elevated track above the campus center, dampening the sound of the train and creating a fantastic visual. Adjacent to the student center is Helmut Jahn's **State Street Village**, a space-age, glass-and-steel student dorm.

Architecture students lead tours starting at the McCormick Tribune Campus Center (Tue–Fri 11.30am; free); the tours include a walk through Mies's buildings as well as the two new buildings.

## BRONZEVILLE

IIT is set in the historic Bronzeville neighborhood. Once known as the Black Metropolis or Black Belt, the area became a vibrant center of African-American life and culture in the early 20th century during the Great Migration of southern blacks to Chicago and other northern cities. Alison Saar's **Monument to the Great Northern Migration**, a 15-ft-tall (5-meter) bronze figure of a man waving with one hand and holding a satchel in the other, was installed in 1996 at Martin Luther King, Jr Drive and 26th Street to honor the thousands of African-Americans who came north after the Civil War.

In the heart of the neighborhood is the **Pilgrim Baptist Church** (3300 South Indiana Avenue; tel: 312-842-4417), originally designed as a synagogue by Chicago architects Adler and Sullivan in 1890. In 1922, a Baptist congregation took over the building, and it became

**ABOVE:** South Side artist. **BELOW:** barbershops are community hubs.

**ABOVE:** postgame celebration in Washington Park.

one of the city's largest African-American congregations and a seminal force in the development of gospel music. Unfortunately, a fire ravaged the building in 2006, destroying valuable archival documents and sparing only three exterior walls. Services are being held across the street while the original church is rebuilt. Visitors are welcome to join the congregation Sunday at 10:45am for a rousing gospel service.

## Civil rights landmark

Farther south, on Martin Luther King, Jr Drive near 37th Street, is the **Ida B. Wells-Barnett House** ❷ (3624 South Martin Luther King, Jr Drive), a 19th-century stone structure where the civil rights activist lived from 1919 to 1929. In her career as a journalist and organizer, Wells was instrumental in resisting racial violence and segregation and was a founding member of the National Association for the Advancement of Colored People.

At Martin Luther King, Jr Drive and 47th Street is the **Harold Washington Cultural Center** ❸ (4701 South Martin Luther King, Jr Drive; tel: 773-924-5156, www.haroldwashingtonculturalcenter.com), a community center in the former Blues District on a lot once occupied by the Regal Theater, which presented such celebrated musicians as Duke Ellington and Cab Calloway. The Center stages concerts, films, and other special events at a 1,000-seat theater.

**Hyde Park and the University of Chicago**

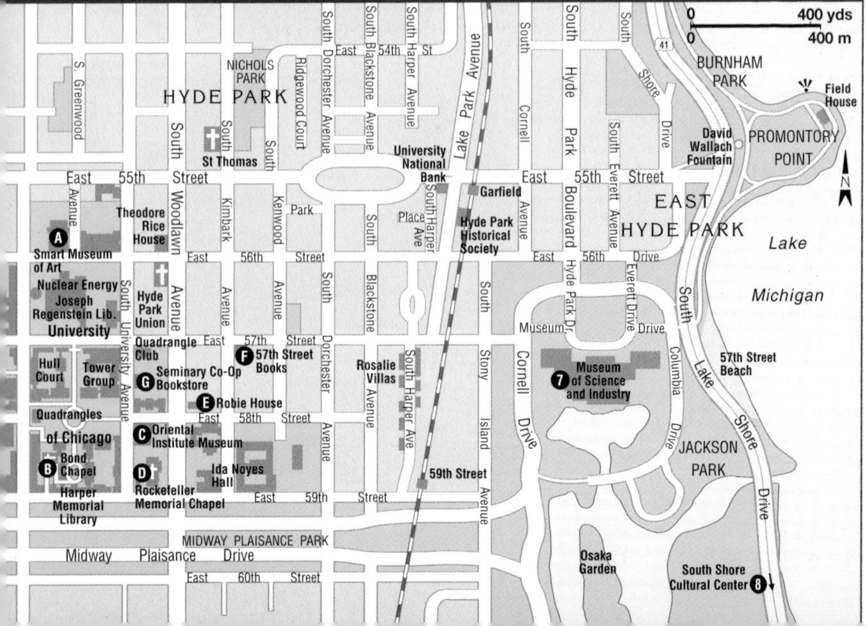

Recommended Restaurants, Bars & Cafés on pages 240–1

## WASHINGTON PARK

Farther south is **Washington Park ❹**. Planned in 1870 by landscape architect Frederick Law Olmsted (best known for designing Central Park in New York City), the park is connected by the green strip of the **Midway Plaisance** to **Jackson Park** to the east. Contained within its 372 acres (150 hectares) are numerous ball fields and playgrounds, natural areas, and sculptures such as Lorado Taft's ***Fountain of Time***, composed of a hundred human figures under the gaze of Father Time. Amble through the lush green fields, attend one of the festivals that are periodically held here, and try to envision an Olympic stadium, as proposed in Chicago's bid to host the 2016 Olympic Games.

## DuSable Museum of African American History ❺

740 East 56th Place 773-947-0600, www.dusablemuseum.org Jun–Dec Tue–Sat 10am–5pm Sun noon–5pm, Jan–May Mon–Sat 10am–5pm Sun noon–5pm charge

Along the eastern edge of the park is the DuSable Museum of African American History, designed in 1910 as the park administration building by Daniel Burnham's architectural firm. Named after Jean Baptiste Pointe DuSable, the Haitian fur trader who first settled in Chicago, the museum chronicles African and African-American history and culture.

Not to be missed is Robert Ames' carved wood mural depicting black history from the African diaspora of the 1600s to the civil rights movement of the 1960s. A small collection of traditional African art includes masks and other ritual objects as well as practical items such as chairs, combs, and assorted tools. A permanent exhibit on aviation underscores the achievements of the first African-American pilot, Bessie Coleman, and the Tuskegee Airmen, a squad of

black fighter pilots who served in World Word II. In the building's basement, a collection of African-American art includes the jazzy, colorful paintings of Chicagoan and Harlem Renaissance artist Archibald Motley.

## HYDE PARK

From the DuSable Museum, head east on 57th Street toward the center of the **University of Chicago ❻** campus, with Washington Park at your back. The campus sits in the middle of the Hyde Park neighborhood, considered to be one of Chicago's first suburbs; it was annexed to the city in 1889. Its founder, Paul Cornell, named the area after a London park of the same name, hoping to create a pros-

**TIP**

If you happen to be strolling through Washington Park on Sunday afternoon, you may see a most unexpected sight: a cricket match. Fans of the game can take in a game or two at the city's only public cricket fields, host to a league of local players spring through fall.

**ABOVE:** DuSable Museum.
**BELOW:** the African Festival of the Arts is held in Washington Park during the Labor Day weekend.

**ABOVE:** *Homer* by Émile-René Ménard (left) and *The Sleeping Congregation* by William Hogarth (right) at the Smart Museum. **BELOW:** a quiet spot in the University's Quadrangles.

perous bedroom community for the city's well-to-do professionals.

The University of Chicago was established in 1890 with funds provided largely by industrialist John D. Rockefeller; its first classes were held in 1892. Regarded as one of the country's finest universities, its alumni include such notable figures as Saul Bellow, Carl Sagan, Susan Sontag, and Kurt Vonnegut, Jr. Numbered among its faculty and research associates are some 80 Nobel Prize laureates.

## Smart Museum of Art Ⓐ

✉ 5550 South Greenwood Avenue ☎ 773-702-0200, www.smartmuseum.uchicago.edu ⓒ Jun–Sep Tue–Fri 10am–4pm Sat–Sun 11am–5pm, Oct–May Tue, Wed, Fri 10am–4pm Thu to 8pm Sat–Sun 11am–5pm ⓢ free

From 57th Street, take a left on Ellis Avenue toward the northern edge of campus and the **Smart Museum of Art**. Set in a pleasant courtyard where university profs and students often gather for lunch, this modest but eclectic museum has changing exhibits curated by faculty members as well as a permanent collection of some 10,000 objects ranging over 5,000 years. Twentieth-century art is well represented, and there's an interesting collection of furniture designed by Frank Lloyd Wright. You will also find a creditable selection of Old Masters as well as ancient Asian art.

Head back to 57th Street, continue toward the library, and pass under the arch on your right straight into the **Quadrangles**. Follow the circle counterclockwise for half a turn and just steps away you'll find **Bond Chapel** Ⓑ (1050 East 59th Street), an intimate and ornately decorated chapel cloaked in ivy. The chapel is an exquisite example of Gothic design and a favorite of students and alumni for weddings.

## Oriental Institute Museum Ⓒ

✉ 1155 East 58th Street ☎ 773-702-9514, www-oi.uchicago.edu
Ⓒ Mon–Thu, Sat 10am–4pm, Wed 10am–8.30pm, Sun noon–4pm Ⓢ free

Retrace your steps to the circle drive, continue counter-clockwise and straight out on 58th Street to the **Oriental Institute Museum.** Founded in 1919 by James Henry Breasted, the nation's first professor of ancient Egyptian studies, the Institute is dedicated to the study of the ancient Near East. Among its most impressive artifacts is the massive Assyrian Bull, discovered in 1929 in Iraq by Institute archaeologists. The 40-ton sculpture was given to the Institute in more than a dozen pieces and now stands, reassembled, in the Institute's Mesopotamian gallery. Down a few hallways and around the corner stands the tallest ancient Egyptian statue in the Western Hemisphere: a 17-ft-tall (6-meter) representation of King Tut unearthed at temple ruins in Western Thebes. A matching statue is housed in the Egyptian Museum in Cairo.

Directly behind the Oriental Institute is the **Rockefeller Memorial Chapel** Ⓓ (5850 South Woodlawn Avenue; tel: 773-702-2100, http://rockefeller.uchicago.edu; daily 8am–4pm; tours of the carillon tower Mon–Fri 11.30am and 5.30pm; free), which has the tallest tower on campus. The Gothic structure was built between 1925 and 1928 and was named for university benefactor John D. Rockefeller, who donated the 72-bell tower in 1932 in his mother's honor. It is the second-largest carillon in the world, surpassed only by Riverside Church in New York City, another Rockefeller project.

*Physicist Enrico Fermi created the world's first controlled nuclear reaction at the University of Chicago on December 2, 1942. A sculpture by Henry Moore marks the spot, now a National Historic Landmark.*

**LEFT:** furniture designed by Frank Lloyd Wright at the Smart Museum.
**BELOW:** much of the campus was built in English Gothic style.

Jutting into Lake Michigan east of Lake Shore Drive between 54th and 56th streets is Promontory Point. With its photo-perfect skyline view, this grassy lakefront picnic area may be one of Chicago's most pleasing spots, where nature and the city come together to beautiful effect.

**ABOVE:** the Robie House.
**BELOW LEFT:** the original Ferris wheel at the World's Columbian Exposition.
**BELOW RIGHT:** a traditional Greek caryatid adorns the facade of the Museum of Science and Industry.

## Robie House Ⓔ

✉ 5757 South Woodlawn Avenue
☎ 773-834-1847, http://wrightplus.org
🕒 tours daily Ⓢ charge

A short block north of the Rockefeller Chapel is Frank Lloyd Wright's **Robie House.** Completed in 1910, Wright designed the residence for bicycle and motorcycle manufacturer Frederick C. Robie. The house is a fine example of the Prairie School style championed by Wright, who emphasized the use of natural materials, open interiors, and low-lying horizontal planes.

When Robie's business went belly up in 1925, the house was turned into a dormitory for the neighboring Chicago Theological Seminary, which nearly tore it down in favor of high-rise dorms. The house was eventually rescued, restored, and given to the University of Chicago, which used it for office space. Wear and tear, along with ill-advised attempts at conservation, led to further deterioration. In 1997, the Frank Lloyd Wright Preservation Trust stepped in and initiated a restoration program. Work continues, but the house, closed for many years, is now open for tours.

### Books and more books

Exit the Robie House and head for 57th Street toward **57th Street Books** Ⓕ (1301 East 57th Street; tel: 773-684-1300), a cozy bookshop with a maze of rooms tightly packed with shelves. Although the stock here is quite extensive, 57th Street Books is merely an offshoot of the **Seminary Co-Op Bookstore** Ⓖ (5757 South University Avenue, tel: 773-752-4381) around the block on University Avenue. The Co-Op was founded in 1961 by 17 book lovers who each contributed $10 to create a bookstore in the basement of the Chicago Theo-

## A World of Firsts

Chicago played host to a grand world's fair in 1893, and a rip-roaring success it surely was. Major architects and designers were involved, such as Frederick Law Olmsted, Daniel Burnham, and Richard Morris Hunt, and all manner of novelties were introduced: the zipper, Middle Eastern belly dancing, Juicy Fruit chewing gum, the electric iron, Thomas Edison's first moving pictures, and a new beer that would forever after be called Pabst Blue Ribbon.

Most thrilling, and terrifying, was a Pittsburgh bridge builder's innovation: the Ferris wheel. Erected at the center of the Midway Plaisance between Washington and Jackson Parks, it stood 264 ft (80 meters) high and had 36 swaying cars carrying over 2,000 riders. It was the sensation of the "White City" exposition, once a long delay over safety fears was overcome and it was allowed to operate. By the time the fair was over, more than 1,450,000 people paid to ride it.

*Recommended Restaurants, Bars & Cafés on pages 240–1*

logical Seminary; the store claims to have the country's most extensive inventory of academic volumes.

## Museum of Science and Industry ❼

57th Street and South Lake Shore Drive 773-684-1414, www.msichicago.org Mon–Sat 9.30am–4pm Sun 11am–4pm charge

Following 57th Street toward Lake Michigan leads you directly to Jackson Park and the **Museum of Science and Industry**, a favorite among kids and adults alike, with highlights like the Coal Mine, an authentic ride into the depths of a mine; the Pioneer Zephyr, a diesel railroad train with regular tours; and U-505, a German submarine captured during World War II. (See pages 242-243.)

The museum occupies the former Palace of Fine Arts, the only survivor of the 200 white plaster buildings that were constructed for the 1893 World's Columbian Exposition – a complex that became known as the White City. Designed by Frederick Law Olmsted and Daniel Burnham, the fairgrounds were visited by some 27 million people, more than a third of the US population at the time.

### Osaka Garden and the lakefront

Japan was the first foreign government to support the Exposition. In addition to a gift of $500,000, the government built a replica of Phoenix Hall in Uji, Japan, on Jackson Park's Wooded Island. The pavilion was developed into the Japanese Garden for the 1934 World's Fair. The building was destroyed by fire in 1944, but the garden remains. Renovated in 1981 and later renamed **Osaka Garden** in honor of Chicago's "sister city," it may be one of the city's prettiest and most underappreciated settings.

On the southern end of Jackson Park, the historic lakeside South

Shore Country Club now serves as the **South Shore Cultural Center** ❽ (7059 South Shore Drive; tel: 773-256-0149; Mon–Fri 9am–6pm, Sat 9am–5pm), thanks to the Chicago Park District, which purchased the property in 1974. Marshall and Fox (of the Drake Hotel) designed the striking 1916 Mediterranean Revival-style clubhouse, now a community facility offering yoga and dance classes. The grand interiors and ballroom are worth a visit. ❑

*The squawking you hear in treetops around the Hyde Park neighborhood may be monk parakeets, a bright green subtropical species that flew the coop in the 1970s and managed to establish a feral population despite Chicago's bitter winters. The federal government tried to eliminate the birds, but eventually gave up the effort due in part to the protests of local residents.*

**ABOVE:** Museum of Science and Industry, formerly the Palace of Fine Arts.
**BELOW:** the museum's "Take Flight" exhibit explores the technology of air travel.

# BEST RESTAURANTS, BARS AND CAFÉS

## Restaurants

Prices for a three-course dinner per person with a half-bottle of house wine:
**$** = under $20
**$$** = $20–$45
**$$$** = $45–$60
**$$$$** = over $60

### Army & Lou's

422 E. 75th St 773-483-3100 B, L & D Sun–Mon, Wed–Sat **$**
The late Mayor Harold Washington famously held court over Army & Lou's ribs. Open since 1945, this beloved southern and soul food restaurant is still a favorite of Chicago politicos, including the current mayor and both generations of Jesse Jacksons. It's hard to single out one dish for praise, but it's probably a toss-up between fried chicken and the heavenly peach cobbler.

### Barbara Ann's BBQ

7617 S. Cottage Grove Ave 773-651-5300 L & D Tue–Sat **$**
A standout in the South Side barbecue sweepstakes, Barbara Ann's is also famed for exceptional hot links, made of coarse-ground pork amply speckled with fat and laced with sage. It's takeout only and open till 3am Friday and Saturday.

### Calumet Fisheries

3259 E. 95th St 773-933-9855 B, L & D daily **$**
A bit of living history, this tiny shrimp shack on the banks of the Calumet River dishes up fresh-fried, cornmeal-breaded shrimp, smelt, and catfish along with glorious views of the South Side's abandoned industrial past. Chubs and trout are smoked on-site and dangerously addictive. Takeout only.

### Dixie Kitchen & Bait Shop

5225 S. Harper Ct 773-363-4943 L & D daily **$** [p311, D1]
A Hyde Park mainstay, this cajun and creole kitchen is the original location for what's now a small local chain. The down-home roadhouse decor and bouncy zydeco music make a lively setting for authentic crawfish étouffée and oyster po' boys – not to mention baskets of free, melt-in-your-mouth Johnny cakes.

### Ed's Potsticker House

3139 S. Halsted St 312-326-6898 L & D daily **$$** [p308, A4]
Ask for the menu with English translations at this northern Chinese spot on Chinatown's western fringe, a favorite of local food cognoscenti. The offerings can be overwhelming, but good bets include piping hot soup dumplings, scallion pancakes with smoked pork, spicy lamb with cumin and chilies, and the namesake potstickers – plump, crispy dumplings stuffed with succulent pork.

### Helen's

1732 E. 79th St 773-933-9871 B, L & D **$**
Breakfast at this soul food institution has a particularly avid following thanks to the signature Legs 'n' Eggs special – an oversize smoked turkey leg with a side of eggs.

### La Petite Folie

1504 E. 55th St 773-493-1394 L Tue–Fri, D Tue–Sun **$$** [p311, D2]
One of Hyde Park's few upscale dining options, this quaint, unpretentious French restaurant is run by two former University of Chicago students, one of whom went on to become a Cordon Bleu chef. A three-course prix fixe meal is offered daily from 5pm to 6.30pm.

### Lem's Bar-B-Q

311 E. 75th St 773-927-7807 L & D Sun–Mon, Wed–Sat **$**
In any Chicago barbecue debate, Lem's comes

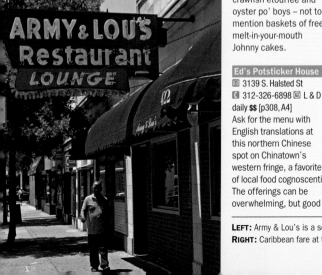

**LEFT:** Army & Lou's is a soul food favorite.
**RIGHT:** Caribbean fare at the African Festival of the Arts.

out at or near the top of the list. Ribs and tips are smoked till crisp on the outside but succulent and moist at the core, then doused with a rich, spicy sauce and served over white bread and fries. Takeout only; open to 2am on weeknights, 4am Friday and Saturday.

**Medici**
✉ 1327 E. 57th St ☎ 773-667-7394 Ⓒ L & D daily **$**
[p311, C3]
A beloved University of Chicago hangout, complete with battered wooden booths and erratic service, "the Med" serves reliably satisfying café fare: soups, salads, pizza, hummus. And the apple pie is something to write home about.

**The Parrot Cage**
✉ 7059 S. South Shore Dr
☎ 773-602-5333 Ⓒ D Wed–Sat **$$**
This casually elegant teaching restaurant inside the landmark South Shore Cultural Center is staffed by students from Washburne Culinary Institute, but you'd never know it. The contemporary American menu is as pro as it gets, and the view of the lake is unparalleled.

**Soul Queen**
✉ 9031 S. Stony Island
☎ 773-731-3366 Ⓒ L & D **$**
As the photos on the walls attest, Helen Maybell Anglin's soul food buffet has been attracting celebs from Bill Cosby to Bill Clinton for more than 30 years. The quality of the food – an all-you-can-eat steam table loaded with fried chicken, barbecued ribs, ham hocks, succotash, black-eyed peas, and meat loaf – can be spotty, but the staff is always warm and welcoming.

**Soul Vegetarian East**
✉ 205 E. 75th St ☎ 773-224-0104 Ⓒ B, L & D daily **$**
Vegetarian barbecue may seem the ultimate oxymoron, but this no-frills spot founded by the African Hebrew Israelites of Jerusalem serves amazingly flavorful renditions of the standards, including savory barbecue "ribs" of wheat gluten and rich, creamy vegan mac and cheese made with soy cheese whipped to an ethereal fluff. Note that while it's all vegetarian, it's not necessarily heart-healthy.

**Szalas**
✉ 5214 S. Archer Ave
☎ 773-582-0300 Ⓒ L & D daily **$$**
Near Midway Airport, this Polish restaurant is a fantasy of a highlands hunting lodge, an A-frame chalet decked out with twinkling lights, sleighs, and a working waterwheel. There are plenty of familiar plates (borscht, pierogi, potato pancakes, sauerkraut soup), but the adventurous can also dig into regional specialties like baked partridge and tripe soup.

**Top Notch Beefburger**
✉ 2116 W. 95th St ☎ 773-445-7218 Ⓒ B, L & D Mon–Sat **$**
A Beverly landmark purveying what may be the best burgers in the city. Fresh ground beef is seasoned with just a pinch of salt and grilled to order. Paired with hand-cut fries and a chocolate malt, they can't be beat.

**Yassa African Caribbean Restaurant**
✉ 716 E. 79th St ☎ 773-488-5599 Ⓒ L & D daily **$**
Chicago's only Senegalese restaurant was on the verge of going under until it got rave reviews from a local TV show. Now there's a healthy audience for its stewed fish, millet couscous with lamb, spicy marinated chicken, and grilled marinated chicken in a mustard-palm oil sauce.

## Bars

**The Cove**, 1750 E. 55th St (tel: 773-684-1013). Nautically themed dive near the University of Chicago that caters to both neighborhood regulars and students, with cheap shots and $6 pitchers of Bud.

**New Checkerboard Lounge for Blues 'n' Jazz**, 5201 S. Harper Ave (tel: 773-684-1472). Owner L.C. Thurman relocated his venerable blues club – once home to Junior Wells and Muddy Waters – from Bronzeville to this Hyde Park shopping mall in 2005. The digs are spiffier, and the expanded programming includes jazz acts.

**Schaller's Pump**, 3714 S. Halsted St (tel: 773-376-6332). The oldest bar in Chicago, Schaller's has been owned and operated by one family since 1881. White Sox fans and 11th Ward politicos crowd the warehouse-like space for cold brews and plates of corned-beef hash. Don't even think about showing up in a Cubs jersey.

**Woodlawn Tap**, 1152 E. 55th St (tel: 773-643-5516). Want to toss one back where Bellow once bellied up to the bar? Known to one and all as "Jimmy's" – after long-time owner James Wilson, who died in 1999 – the Tap is dark, scuffed, encrusted with decades of cigarette smoke, and beloved by generations of University of Chicago students and faculty.

# Museum of Science and Industry

## Multimedia shows and high-tech exhibits give museum-goers an engaging lesson in how things work

A monumental homage to technological advancement, the Museum is housed in a grand Beaux Arts temple designed by Daniel Burnham for the Columbian Exposition of 1893. More than 2,000 exhibits occupying four floors are enjoyed by kids and adults in equal measure. Highlights of the permanent exhibit include a journey 50 ft (15 meters) underground into a replica of a coal mine on a rickety trolley. In the genetics exhibit is a chick hatchery where fluffy, loose-limbed chicks peck their way into the world. The human biology exhibits include a walk-through, 70-ft (21-meter) model of a human heart and preserved slices of human cadavers (dissected with a band saw in the 1930s). Transportation is one of the museum's central themes, and there are excellent collections of vintage planes, trains, and automobiles.

**Top:** vintage toys reflect the space craze of the 1960s, during the early days of the US space program.
**Left:** a collection of aircraft ranging from prop planes to Mercury and Apollo space modules illustrates the development of aviation and space technology.

**Left:** scale-model Chicago skyscrapers are part of the "Great Train Story," an elaborate model train layout depicting a railroad journey between the Windy City and Seattle.
**Below:** Tylosaurus, the 40-ft (12-meter) super predator often called the "T-Rex of the ocean," blasts through the surface of an ancient sea in a computer-generated Omnimax film.

**ABOVE:** the 999 Empire State Express steam locomotive is exhibited in the "Transportation Zone." Other vehicles on display include a 1914 Ford Model T and the *Spirit of America* jet car. **BELOW:** "Earth Revealed" uses digital multimedia technology to give viewers a global perspective on climate change, land-use patterns, ocean currents, population growth, and habitat loss.

## THE RETURN OF U-505

Captured in 1944, the German submarine U-505 was a menacing presence off the coast of West Africa, having already dispatched eight Allied ships. The USS *Chatelain* altered the course of the war when it blasted the U-505 with depth charges, disabling the vessel and capturing secret documents and an Enigma decoding machine. It took a herculean effort and more than $35 million to relocate the 252-ft (77-meter) long, 700-ton vessel to Chicago, where it serves as a memorial to the 55,000 American sailors who perished during World War I and II. A tour of the vessel's kitchen, engine room, captain's quarters, and torpedo room illustrates the vessel's operation and the cramped conditions in which the crew of 59 submariners worked, and relates the ship's turbulent history during the height of World War II naval combat.

**ABOVE:** U-505 is an authentically restored German submarine captured during World War II. The vessel is exhibited in a subterranean vault built especially to hold it. A 15-minute, on-board tour reqires a separate ticket.

Map on page 246
*Recommended Restaurants, Bars & Cafés on pages 250–1*

# OAK PARK

**You'll find some of Chicago's most fascinating history – architectural and otherwise – in an unassuming suburban enclave**

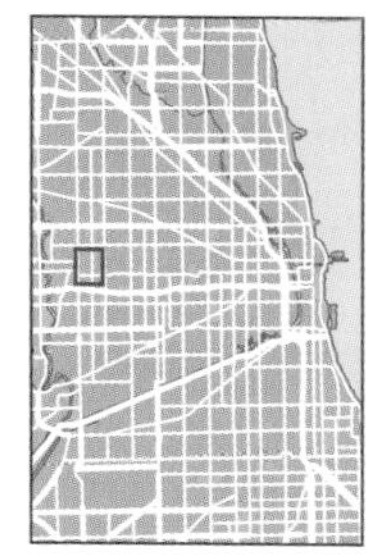

Ernest Hemingway famously dismissed his boyhood home as "a place of wide lawns and narrow minds." Yet, this trim suburb about 10 miles (16 km) west of the Loop nurtured quite a few big imaginations, including those of *Tarzan* author Edgar Rice Burroughs, hamburger magnate Ray Kroc, and Papa Hemingway himself. The man who left the most indelible mark on the place, however, was Frank Lloyd Wright, who moved to Oak Park in 1887 and soon launched an architectural practice that would redefine American design.

## Coming to town

The most convenient way to reach Oak Park from Chicago is via the CTA Green line or Metra commuter line. The Green line station is at Oak Park Avenue, the Metra station at Harlem Avenue. Either way, it's a short walk from the station to the **Oak Park Visitor's Center** (158 Forest Avenue; tel: 888-625-7275, www.visitoakpark.com; daily 10am–5pm) ❶, where you'll find free maps, helpful clerks, and tickets for a selection of area attractions. An informative, self-guided audio tour is also available, with the option for discounted tickets to Unity Temple, the Hemingway Home and Museum, and Pleasant Home.

Opposite the Visitor's Center, **Austin Gardens** is furnished with benches and lots of shade trees, which are a godsend in the heat of summer. A cluster of shops and restaurants on nearby Lake Street is convenient for coffee, ice cream, or an entire meal before or after your tour.

**Main attractions**

- OAK PARK VISITOR'S CENTER
- FRANK LLOYD WRIGHT HOME AND STUDIO
- BOOTLEG HOUSES
- NATHAN MOORE HOUSE
- ARTHUR HEURTLEY HOUSE
- UNITY TEMPLE
- MRS. THOMAS GALE HOUSE
- PETER A. BEACHY HOUSE
- FRANK W. THOMAS HOUSE
- UNITY TEMPLE
- HEMINGWAY MUSEUM
- HEMINGWAY BIRTHPLACE HOME
- HISTORIC PLEASANT HOME

**LEFT AND RIGHT:** the Frank Lloyd Wright Home and Studio in Oak Park served not only as a family residence but as a workshop and laboratory for the architect's ever-evolving ideas.

*With the exception of the Wright Home and Studio, all the Wright houses on this tour are private residences. Please respect the occupants' privacy. View the houses only from the street or sidewalk.*

## Frank Lloyd Wright Home and Studio ❷

✉ 951 Chicago Avenue ☎ 708-848-1976, www.wrightplus.org ⓒ tours Mon–Fri 11am, 1pm, 3pm, Sat–Sun every 20 minutes 11am–3.30pm Ⓢ charge

From the Visitor's Center, walk about four blocks north on Forest Avenue to the **Frank Lloyd Wright Home and Studio**, where the architect lived and worked from 1889 to 1909. An hour-long tour guides visitors through the workshop where Wright and his colleagues designed more than 120 buildings, including such seminal works as the Robie House in Chicago and the Unity Temple. Although the house was built early in Wright's career, elements of what would later be termed Prairie style are evident in the structure's simple geometry, open interiors, natural materials, and earth-toned palette. The house also served as a sort of laboratory, where Wright tried out new ideas over the course of numerous renovations.

A short walk west on Chicago Avenue leads past three of Wright's **Bootleg houses** (1019, 1027, and 1031 Chicago Avenue), so named because he designed them for extra cash while still working at the firm of Adler & Sullivan, a practice that cost him his job. An interpretation of Queen Anne style built in 1892 and 1893, the houses suggest the simplification of form that Wright's work was evolving toward.

## FOREST AVENUE

Double back on Forest Avenue for a look at another example of Wright's early work. At 333 Forest Avenue is the **Nathan Moore House** ❸, Wright's first commission in Oak Park after he left the offices of Adler & Sullivan. The young architect was approached by friend and neighbor Nathan Moore to design a house in English Tudor style. Wright had no

**BELOW:** Wright left his mark on buildings throughout Oak Park and, in a larger sense, on the whole of American architecture.

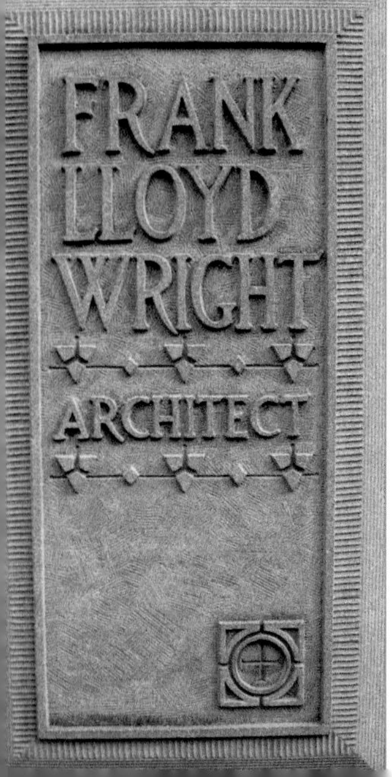

*Recommended Restaurants, Bars & Cafés on pages 250–1*

affinity for the period, but, newly unemployed, he agreed to take the job. Completed in 1895, the result is a house with uncharacteristically ornate touches, including steep gable roofs, half-timbering in the upper story, medieval chimneys, and diamond-pane windows. After a fire destroyed much of the house in 1922, Wright was asked to redesign and rebuild it, which he did rather conservatively, retaining much of the work's period elements.

On the opposite side of the street, at 318 Forest Avenue, is the **Arthur Heurtley House** ❹, one of Wright's more mature Prairie style residences, built in 1902. Particularly noteworthy is the flattened hip roof, the band of casement windows on the upper floor, and the horizontal bands of textured brick – all of which give the house a low-slung, horizontal orientation that would become a trademark of Prairie style. The house received a lukewarm response from the public, but it drew considerable praise from fellow architects and was one of Wright's personal favorites. He later modeled the much-lauded Robie House in Chicago on this work.

A quick detour down curvy Elizabeth Court leads to the **Mrs Thomas Gale House** (6 Elizabeth Court) ❺, built in 1909. Wright's use of large geometric masses gives the house a blocky, rectilinear feeling that inspired the European modernists of the 1920s and 30s. A prominent second-story balcony juts from the house, presaging the "floating horizontal planes" that reached full expression in such later works as the celebrated Fallingwater in Pennsylvania.

Farther along Forest Avenue, the **Peter A. Beachy House** ❻ (238 Forest Avenue) of 1906 was one of Wright's remodeling jobs. Though it's not typical of Prairie style, Wright clearly put his signature on what originally was a Gothic cottage. Just beyond, the **Frank W. Thomas House** (210 Forest Avenue), built in 1901, is considered Wright's first Prairie style house in Oak Park. Similar in some respects to the Heurtley House, the Thomas residence has flattened roofs, an arched entrance, and a raised first floor with a band of leaded windows. The use of stucco gives the house a clean but organic finish that emphasizes its mass.

## Unity Temple ❼

875 Lake Street 708-383-8873, www.unitytemple-utrf.org Mon–Fri 10.30am–4.30pm, Sat–Sun 1pm–4pm charge

About two and a half blocks away, at Lake Street and Kenilworth Avenue, is Wright's greatest work in Oak

**ABOVE:** the Nathan Moore House was one of Wright's earliest and least characteristic Oak Park commissions. **BELOW:** the Heurtley House reflects Wright's emerging Prairie style.

*Recommended Restaurants, Bars & Cafés on pages 250–1*

*The Hemingway Museum traces the author's life, career, and legacy.*

Park, **Unity Temple**. Completed in 1909 after three years of construction, the Temple's cubist design shattered traditional notions of church architecture, doing away entirely with steeples, Gothic windows, and a conventional sanctuary with rows of pews. Even the front entrance is obscured. Budgetary constraints dictated, in part, the use of poured concrete, which accentuates the building's mass and the clean intersection of vertical and horizontal planes.

Leaded skylights and windows bathe the interior in natural light. The sanctuary's muted colors, hanging lamps of Wright's own design, and geometric wood trim move the eye rhythmically over an array of balconies, ledges, and alcoves that put flesh (or, in this case, stucco) on Wright's lofty notion that "space is the breath of art."

## Hemingway Museum 8

200 North Oak Park Avenue 708-848-2222, www.ehfop.org Sun–Fri 1pm–5pm, Sat 10am–5pm charge

For a glimpse into the life of Oak Park's other favorite son, stop at the **Hemingway Museum**, a former church that now houses displays of rare photos, personal papers, manuscripts, and videos that chronicle the author's upbringing and his later adventures in Italy, France, Cuba, Africa, and the American West. Though Hemingway often dismissed his hometown's parochial attitudes, his Oak Park boyhood clearly had a formative influence on his later work and life. "Papa," as he later called himself, published his first work here at age 14, learned to fish and hunt with his father, and studied cello at the insistence of his musician mother. In 1917, after graduating from high school, he became a reporter for the *Kansas City Star* and by 1918 was driving an ambulance on the Italian front in World War I.

The nearby **Hemingway Birthplace Home** (339 North Oak Park Avenue; Sun–Fri 1pm–5pm, Sat 10am–5pm; charge) is a more intimate experience. The house where Hemingway was born and lived the first six years of his life has been restored in period style and, though short on biographical details, it offers a glimpse into the author's home life at an early age.

**BELOW:** Unity Temple.

## PLEASANT HOME

Before leaving Oak Park, consider one last stop at the **Historic Pleasant Home** (217 Home Avenue; tel: 708-383-2654, www.oprf.com/phf; tours Thu–Sun 12.30pm, 1.30pm, 2.30pm; charge), another fine example of Prairie style architecture, although this one was designed not by Wright but by George Washington Maher, in 1897. Knowledgeable docents lead tours of the 30-room mansion, which also houses a modest collection of vintage photographs and artifacts maintained by the Historical Society of Oak Park and River Forest.

The house is situated on the south side of the railroad tracks within walking distance of the Metra and Green line stations. ❑

## Frank Lloyd Wright

**America's most famous architect cut his teeth here, setting new standards for designs in living and influencing generations to come**

It was in Chicago that Frank Lloyd Wright began his storied career as America's pre-eminent master builder. Raised on a Wisconsin farm, he arrived in the Windy City on a spring evening in 1887, just turning 21 and seeking fame and fortune by hitching his wagon to the building boom that was transforming Chicago seemingly overnight.

Wright found work as a draftsman, eventually gravitating to the firm co-founded by Louis Sullivan that was on the cutting edge of architectural design in that metropolis. Later, as the young architect's reputation grew through the bold unconventionality of his creative outpourings at the drawing board, Wright was offered a munificent all-expenses-paid opportunity at studying the classic design of the "old masters" in Europe. The invitation was made by that other leading light of the Chicago architectural scene, Daniel Burnham – and it was rejected. Wright, proud and egotistical, would not have his style cramped by the visions of other times, other places.

The budding architect made his presence felt most forcefully in Oak Park, the tree-lined suburban village where he and his equally strong-willed mother, Anna, made their home. He would put Oak Park on the map through his design of some two dozen structures as he began to implant his ideal of "organic architecture" on the public consciousness.

Unconventional, too, was Wright's knack for flaunting social norms. A flashy dresser, he was given to driving clients around Oak Park in equally flashy automobiles, and he was quite the ladies' man. He became especially enamored of the wife of one of his clients, Mamah Borthwick Cheney, to such a point that they decamped together to Europe, abandoning their respective spouses and children. The scandal boosted newspaper circulation.

Wright eventually reconciled with his wife, at least formally. But more notoriety followed, this time on an atrociously deadly scale. On an August day in 1914 Wright received the awful news that his ex-paramour Mamah Cheney and her two children, in addition to four other people, were savagely hacked to death by a deranged servant who at the same time had set fire to Wright's now famous Taleisin estate in Wisconsin.

An accidental fire in 1925 again destroyed the living quarters at Taliesin, causing Wright to rebuild for a second time. It was another turbulent event in the often tempestuous saga of this genius of design whose life stretched nearly from the American Civil War to the Space Age – he was born in 1867 and died in 1959. ❑

**ABOVE:** Wright's signature geometric stained-glass panels. **RIGHT:** the architect in 1954.

# BEST RESTAURANTS, BARS AND CAFÉS

## Restaurants

Prices for a three-course dinner per person with a half-bottle of house wine:
**$** = under $20
**$$** = $20–$45
**$$$** = $45–$60
**$$$$** = over $60

### Buzz Café

905 S. Lombard Ave 708-524-2899 B & L daily, D Mon–Sat **$**
Popular with students and families, this café next to the CTA Blue Line station is a good stop for a tofu-veggie wrap or juicy organic burger. Home-style specials include meat loaf with gravy, shepherd's pie and roast chicken with colcannon. With events ranging from stitch-and-bitch sessions to tarot readings, there's no reason to be bored.

### Café le Coq

734 Lake St 708-848-2233 D Tue–Sun **$$$**
A standout in a small field, Café le Coq is one of Oak Park's most polished fine dining options, a cozy bistro complete with a tiled floor and tin ceiling. Despite a rotating cast of chefs, owner Jim August keeps the focus firmly on expertly prepared French classics.

### Caribou Coffee

423 N. Harlem Ave 708-358-1212 B, L & D daily **$**
Order a cup of java and check your e-mail at this café chain, which has rich coffee, fruit smoothies, and wi-fi.

### Fuego Loco

722 Lake St 708-763-0000 L Fri–Sun, D daily **$**
It's owned by the Taco Fresco chain, but Fuego Loco's a surprisingly good bet for fresh, inexpensive enchiladas, tamales, and burritos, as well as more substantial platters of chicken in mole sauce and grilled meats.

### Gene and Jude's Red Hots

2720 River Road, River Grove 708-452-7634 L & D daily **$**
Pilgrims in search of the ultimate Chicago dog make the trek to River Grove in droves. This hot dog stand sells just that: a boiled Vienna sausage stuffed, sans blinding green relish, into a steamed bun and topped with a mound of piping hot fresh-cut fries.

### Hemmingway's Bistro

211 N. Oak Park Ave 708-524-0806 B daily, L Mon–Sat, D daily, Br Sun **$$-$$$**
Elegant French standards prepared with an eye toward local, seasonal ingredients. At $21.95, the Sunday brunch is a steal. The spread includes salads, cold cuts, cheese, and sweets in addition to eggs, chocolate French toast, and a glass of bubbly.

### Jerusalem Café

1030 Lake St 708-848-7734 L & D daily **$**
If you don't mind counter service and fast-food-style decor, Jerusalem Café is a great bet for tasty and affordable falafel, shawirma, and kababs. Nothing is priced over $10, and there's a juice bar to boot.

### Khyber Pass

1031 Lake St 708-445-9032 L & D daily **$$**
Kababs and tandoor-cooked meats are reliable bets at this Indian restaurant, but the specialty of the house is *dumbuc khana* – meats, sauces, and spices steam cooked in a clay pot. Vegetarian options are plentiful; the buffet lunch draws a regular crowd.

### La Piazza

410 Circle Ave, Forest Park 708-366-4010 D Mon–Sat **$$$**
A frescoed treasure in the western suburbs, La Piazza is a casual place

**LEFT:** Buzz Café has a vegetarian-friendly menu.
**RIGHT:** Petersen's Ice Cream is an Oak Park tradition.

to dig into seriously good regional Italian cuisine. Sicilian chef Gaetano Di Benedetto produces lush *involtini di melanzane* and a decadent gnocchi tossed with veal confit and a mushroom ragu; wine is available by the bottle, glass, or quartino.

**Marion Street Grille**
189 N. Marion St 708-383-1551 D Tue–Sun **$$$**
This welcoming American bistro is considered one of the best fine dining options west of the city. Steaks and seafood are given a creative twist with discerning use of French, Creole, and Cajun flavors. The understated, candlelit space is conducive to a romantic tête-a-tête.

**New Pot Rice & Noodles**
27 Lake St 708-383-1625 L & D Mon–Sat, D Sun **$$**
Contemporary, casual noodle shop that gets high marks for excellent preparations of Thai classics like Panang curry, *pad sie euw*, coconut soup, and papaya salad. It's a favorite of locals for takeout, and delivery is usually fast.

**Nola's Cup**
800 S. Oak Park Ave 708-524-1520 B & L daily, D Mon–Sat **$**
Festooned with Mardi Gras beads and folk art, Nola's brings the Big Easy north. Homemade soups and gumbo are a standout, or stop in for a breakfast of sugary beignets and chicory-laced coffee.

**Petersen's Ice Cream**
1100 Chicago Ave 708-386-6131 B, L & D daily **$**
After 85 years churning sugar and cream into their signature butterfat-rich confection, the folks at Petersen's know what they're doing. Their award-winning ice cream is distributed to restaurants and sweet shops around metropolitan Chicago. Flavors range from old-time favorites like peppermint stick and rocky road to thoroughly modern concoctions like Oreo cookies and cream.

**La Quebrada**
4859 W. Roosevelt Rd, Cicero Tel: 708-780-8110 B, L & D daily **$**
Tiny and in a dingy industrial neighborhood, La Quebrada doesn't look like much, but those adventurous enough to cross the border into Cicero will be rewarded. Specializing in the food of Guerrero, on the Pacific coast of Mexico, La Quebrada has grown into a small local chain. Sop up goat *barbacoa* or chicken in *molcajete* sauce with thick, soft, handmade tortillas. Wash it all down with a hibiscus aqua fresca.

**Robinson's #1 Ribs**
940 W. Madison St 708-383-8452 L daily, D Mon–Sat **$**
Barbecue master Charlie Robinson opened this, his first rib shack, in 1982, after trouncing the competition at Mike Royko's inaugural Ribfest. He's now king of a mini-empire of rib trucks, restaurants, and retail sauces. Quality control at this flagship is sometimes an issue, but on a good day he still hickory-smokes a fine piece of meat.

**Trattoria 225**
225 Harrison St 708-358-8555 L Sat–Sun, D daily **$$**
Come to this trattoria for rustic Italian cooking with an emphasis on local, seasonal ingredients and clean, authentic flavors. Wood-oven pizzas come charred around the edges and topped with every-

thing from wild mushrooms to fennel sausage.

**Wishbone**
6611 Roosevelt Rd, Berwyn 708-749-1295 L Tue–Fri, D Tue–Sun, Br Sat–Sun **$**
This Berwyn outpost of Chicago's popular Southern-food empire is attached to Fitzgerald's, a destination for alt-country and roots fans from the city and suburbs. Food from the restaurant can be brought into the adjacent club, tavern, and beer garden.

## Bars

**Avenue Ale House**, 825 S. Oak Park Ave (tel: 708-848-2801). The big draw at this sprawling bar and grill is the hoppin' rooftop deck, a great place to kick back on a summer afternoon with one of more than 70 beers. Inside, televised sports are hard to avoid.

**Oak Park Abbey**, 728 Lake St (tel: 708-358-8840). The community's first wine bar offers a broad selection of vino by the glass, bottle, or flight. A smattering of premium beers are available as well. Selected bottles are half-price on Tuesday.

**Poor Phil's**, 139 S. Marion St (tel: 708-848-0871). Actor John Mahoney (aka "Frasier's dad") has been known to raise a pint at this bar next to Philander's, in the Carleton Hotel. There's an excellent list of craft and imported beers, and ample outdoor seating in the summer.

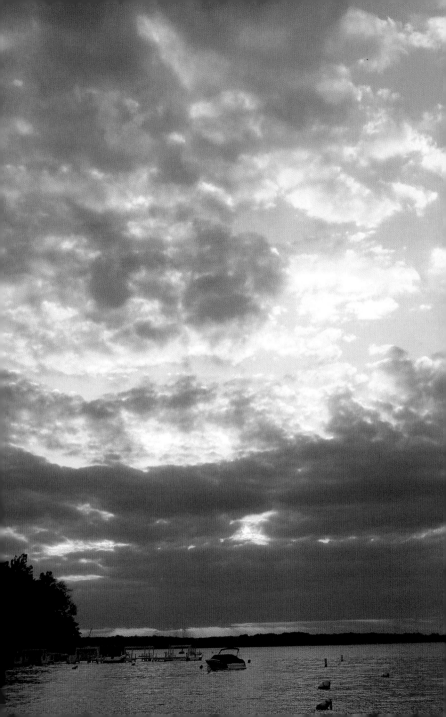

# DAY TRIPS

**Venture beyond the city limits and you'll find fine art, natural beauty, and a roller coaster for every taste**

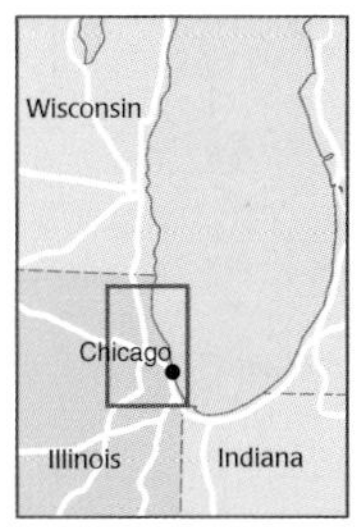


The first town north of Chicago's city limits is **Evanston** ❶, home of **Northwestern University** (633 Clark Street, Evanston; tel: 847-491-3741, www.northwestern.edu) and the city's most cosmopolitan suburb. Northwestern was founded by Chicago Methodists in 1855 and has grown into one of the finest universities in the Midwest, with a student body of about 16,000 and a 240-acre (100-hectare) lakeshore campus.

## College town

Stop for a stroll around the grounds or pop into the **Mary & Leigh Block Museum of Art** (40 Arts Circle Drive, Evanston; tel: 847-491-4000; Tue 10am–5pm, Wed–Fri 10am–8pm, Sat–Sun noon–5pm; free), which mounts several exhibitions a year covering a wide range of themes and periods, including several in recent years featuring pieces from the museum's strong collection of prints and photographs. A sculpture garden contains more than 20 pieces, including work by such notable modern sculptors as Joan Miró, Jacques Lipchitz, Barbara Hepworth, and Henry Moore. Free tours of the sculpture garden can be arranged by calling 847-491-4852.

Beyond the university, you'll find a compact downtown area of shops, cafés, and restaurants around the Davis CTA (Purple line) and Metra stations. Two organizations – the **Evanston Art Center** (2603 Sheridan Road, Evanston; tel: 847-475-5300) and the **Noyes Cultural Arts Center** (927 Noyes Street, Evanston; tel: 847-448-8260) – showcase the work of regional artists, and the **Mitchell**

**Main attractions**

- NORTHWESTERN UNIVERSITY
- BAHA'I TEMPLE
- CHICAGO BOTANIC GARDEN
- RAVINIA PARK
- SIX FLAGS GREAT AMERICA
- MILWAUKEE ART MUSEUM
- DISCOVERY WORLD AT PIER WISCONSIN
- MILWAUKEE PUBLIC MUSEUM
- MITCHELL PARK HORTICULTURAL CONSERVATORY
- PULLMAN
- BROOKFIELD ZOO
- MORTON ARBORETUM
- LAKE GENEVA

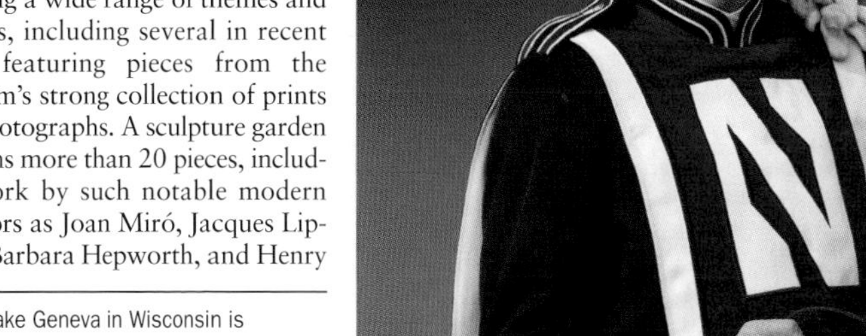

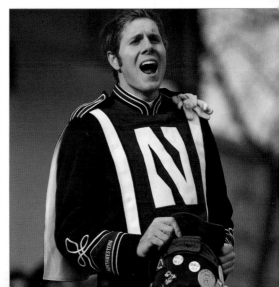

**LEFT:** Lake Geneva in Wisconsin is a popular weekend getaway.
**RIGHT:** cheering on the Northwestern University team at the school's Ryan Field.

Day Trips
0
5 miles
0
5 km
N
Lake Michigan
Round Lake Beach
Fourth Lake
Milwaukee, Lake Geneva
Six Flags Great America
5
Gurnee
Waukegan
Green Bay Road
Round Lake Park
Belvedere Road
Grayslake
Des Plaines
North Chicago
Libertyville
Lake Bluff
Wauconda
Lake Geneva
Mundelein
94
Town Line Road
Lake Forest
Vernon Hills
Hawthorn Woods
Rand Road
Tower Lakes
Tri-State Tollway
Skokie Highway
Lake Zurich
Long Grove
Lincolnshire
Highwood
Highland Park
Deer Park
Lake County
Buffalo Grove
Lake Cook Road
Deerfield
Edens Expressway
4 Ravinia Park
3 Chicago Botanic Garden
Barrington
Dundee Road
Glencoe
Wheeling
294
Inverness
Palatine Road
Northbrook
Winnetka
Palatine
South Barrington
Arlington Heights
Prospect Heights
Rolling Meadows
Glenview
Wilmette
2 Baha'i Temple
Mitchell Mus. of the American Indian
Northwestern University
90
Northwest Tollway
Rockford
Mount Prospect
Morton Grove
Woodfield Shopping Mall
Evanston
C. Gates Dawes House
1
Schaumburg
Busse Woods Res.
Des Plaines
Niles
Skokie
Hanover Park
290
Elk Grove Village
Park Ridge
N. Shore Channel
Elgin O'Hare Expressway
Roselle
Wood Dale
O'Hare
100
Lincolnwood
Bloomingdale
Bensenville
Schiller Park
Norridge
Harwood Heights
John F. Kennedy Expressway
Lake Shore Drive
Wrigley Field
355
St Charles
Carol Stream
Franklin Park
River Grove
Addison
Melrose Park
Elmwood Park
North Avenue
Glendale Heights
Northlake
Garfield Park Conservatory
Wicker Park
Villa Park
Elmhurst
Berkeley
River Forest
Oak Park
Sears Tower
Navy Pier
Geneva
Glen Ellyn
Lombard
York Center
Hillside
Maywood
D. Eisenhower Expwy
Chicago
Field Museum
88
Broadview
22nd Street
Westchester
Cicero
Wheaton
Du Page County
North Riverside
Berwyn
55
Morton Arboretum
8
Tollway
La Grange Park
Oak Brook
7 Brookfield Zoo
Stickney
Adlai E. Stevenson Expwy
East-West
Western Springs
Brookfield
Aurora
Lisle
Downers Grove
Clarendon Hills
La Grange
Countryside
Chicago Midway
Museum of Science and Industry
North-South Tollway
Westmont
Burr Ridge
Indian Head Park
Summit
Naperville
Willowbrook
Bridgeview
79th Street
Cicero Avenue
Chicago Skyway
Woodridge
Darien
Adlai E. Stevenson Expressway
Hickory Hills
Burbank
Evergreen Park
95th Street
Calumet Expressway
Oak Lawn
57
Pullman Historic District
6
W.W. Powers Conservation Area
Bolingbrook
Des Plaines
Palos Hills
Harlem Avenue
Chicago Ridge
Merrionette Park
Cook County
Worth
Whiting
Lake Calumet
Wolf Lake
Alsip
Lemont
Calumet
Romeoville
Palos Heights
Bloomington
Palos Park
Blue Island
Riverdale
Gary

Cyclists can follow the Green Bay Trail through the North Shore. It runs about 18 miles (29 km) from Wilmette to Lake Bluff right past the entrance of Ravinia Park. The trail is part of the longer Robert McClory Bike Path, which runs all the way to the Wisconsin state line.

**Museum of the American Indian** (2600 Central Park Avenue, Evanston; tel: 847-475-1030; Tues–Sat 10am–5pm, Thu to 8pm, Sun noon–4pm; charge) has a modest but worthy collection of Native American art and artifacts.

South of downtown is the **Charles Gates Dawes House** (225 Greenwood St, Evanston; tel: 847-475-3410; Fri–Sun 1pm–5pm; charge), a grand 1895 chateaux overlooking Lake Michigan. A prominent banker and politician, Dawes served a troubled term as US vice president under Calvin Coolidge and was awarded a Nobel Peace Prize in 1925 for his work on the issue of German reparations after World War I. Guided tours of the house are available.

## NORTH SHORE

To the north of Evanston, **Sheridan Road** winds along the lakeshore past the grand homes and landscaped gardens of **Wilmette** on the exclusive, suburban North Shore. Just over the Evanston town line, at Sheridan Road and Linden Avenue, is the **Baha'i Temple** ❷ (100 Linden Ave, Wilmette; tel: 847-853-2300; auditorium open daily 7am–10pm, prayer services at 9.15am, 12.30pm, 5.15pm daily; free), a domed, white, mosque-like structure with lacy ornamentation. The Baha'i faith emphasizes "the oneness of God, the oneness of humanity and the oneness of religion." One of only seven Baha'i temples in the world, the building is surrounded with gardens and fountains and is open to people of all faiths for prayer and meditation.

## Chicago Botanic Garden ❸

1000 Lake Cook Road, Glencoe
847-835-5440, www.chicagobotanic.org 8am–sunset free

Farther north, in **Glencoe**, is the **Chicago Botanic Garden**. Spread out over 385 acres (156 hectares) are 23 formal gardens, from a proper **English Walled Garden** and a **Rose Garden** with more than 5,000 rosebushes to a serene **Japanese Garden** on three small islands. Gardeners with mobility difficulties will be interested in the **Enabling Garden**. Those curious about native flora will find a 15-acre

**ABOVE:** Chicago Botanic Garden.
**BELOW:** the Baha'i Temple in Wilmette welcomes people of all faiths for prayer and meditation.

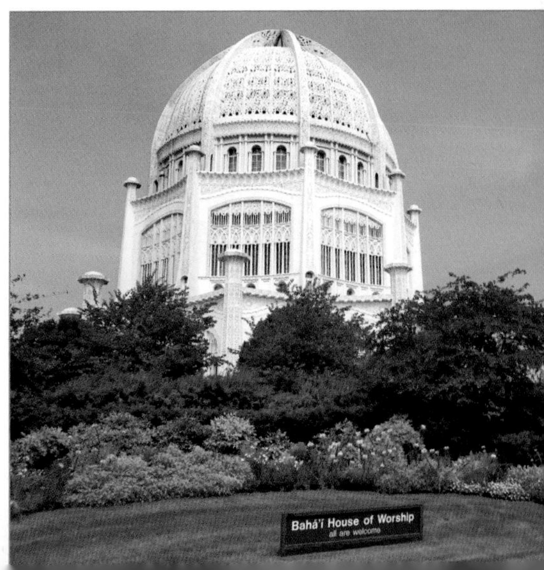

**ABOVE LEFT:** a drawing by American artist George Bellows on display at the Milwaukee Art Museum.
**ABOVE RIGHT AND BELOW:** museum pavilion designed by Spanish architect Santiago Calatrava.

(6-hectare) **Prairie** exhibiting six individual ecosystems and a **Native Plant Garden** with wildflowers, shade trees, and specially designed habitats for birds and butterflies.

### Ravinia

Nearby is **Ravinia Park** ❹ (Green Bay and Lake Cook roads, Highland Park; tel: 847-266-5100, www.ravinia.org), summer home of the Chicago Symphony Orchestra and a lovely spot to enjoy a concert under the stars. Tickets run $10-$15 for the lawn, where music lovers spread out elaborate picnics, and $25-$50 for the 3,200-seat pavilion. The summer season runs from June to September and includes jazz, folk, and pop acts as well as symphonic music.

### Six Flags Great America ❺

542 Route 21, Gurnee 847-249-4636, www.sixflags.com May–Oct charge

Farther north, about halfway between Chicago and Milwaukee, is this amusement park. If you're a fan of thrill rides, this place is the next best thing to heaven, with no less than 10 state-of-the-art roller coasters, including two cyclone-style wooden coasters. A sprawling water park, a "Wiggles World" mini-park for young children, parades, stunt shows, concerts, and other entertainment round out the attractions.

## MILWAUKEE

It's another city in another state, but it's worth traveling a couple of hours to poke around this metropolis of some 600,000 residents known for its breweries, factories, and hardworking immigrant population. Plan to devote much of your time to the **Milwaukee Art Museum** (700 North Art

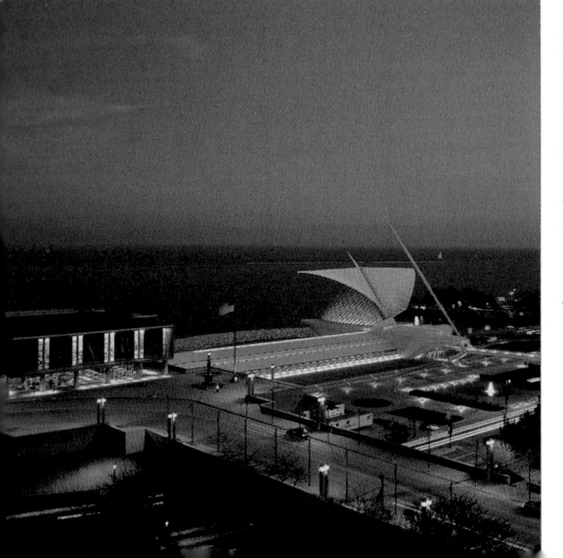

Museum Drive; tel: 414-224-3200, http://mam.org; daily 10am–5pm, Thu to 8pm; charge), whose intriguing new pavilion – the first American design by Spanish architect Santiago Calatrava – has a retractable sunscreen that rises like outstretched wings over the lakefront facility. The wide-ranging collection contains more than 20,000 artworks and artifacts from classical Greek, Egyptian, and Roman civilizations to the work of such modern masters as Pablo Picasso, Wassily Kandinsky, Georgia O'Keeffe, and Andy Warhol.

Nearby is the **Discovery World at Pier Wisconsin** (500 North Harbor Drive; tel: 414-765-9966, www.discoveryworld.org; Tue–Sun 9am–5pm; charge), a combination aquarium, nautical museum, and science center. Also on the lakefront is the annual **Summerfest** (www.summerfest.com), a series of big-name rock and pop bands in late June and early July, plus numerous other festivals celebrating the city's various ethnic communities.

Downtown, the **Milwaukee Public Museum** (800 West Wells Street; tel: 888-700-9069, www.mpm.edu; Mon–Sat 9am–5pm, Sun noon–5pm; charge) is a natural history museum with dinosaur exhibits, a tropical butterfly habitat, ethnological collections, a planetarium, and an IMAX theater.

Farther afield, the **Mitchell Park Horticultural Conservatory** (524 South Layton Boulevard; tel: 414-649-9800; daily 9am–5pm; charge), also known as "The Domes," has three seven-story glass domes filled with desert, tropical, and seasonal vegetation. The **Milwaukee County Zoo** (10001 West Blue Mound Road; tel: 414-256-5412; daily 9am–4.30pm, extended summer hours; charge) isn't as big or elaborate as the Brookfield Zoo (see next page), but has the expected exhibits of bears, gorillas, elephants, big cats, and other exotic wildlife.

### Beer and bikes

Beer drinkers should make a point of taking a free tour of the **Miller Brewing Company** (4251 West State Street; tel: 414-931-2337; Mon–Sat 10am–5.30pm; free). The one-hour tour of the production and shipping departments ends with a sample of up to three brews in the outdoor beer garden or inn. On the outskirts of Milwaukee is the **Harley-Davidson Tour Center** (11700 West Capitol Drive, Wauwatosa; tel: 877-883-1450; Mon–Fri 9.30am–1pm; free), where visitors on the factory tour can watch engines being built and sit astride new and vintage "hogs."

*The Miller Brewing Company offers free factory tours.*

## PULLMAN ❻

On the south end of Chicago, about 14 miles (23 km) from the Loop, is the neighborhood of **Pullman**. Established as an independent town in the 1880s and later annexed by the city of Chicago, Pullman was built as a model industrial town by railroad-car manufacturer George M. Pullman, who wanted to ensure a stable workforce for his factory by offering good wages and providing decent living

**BELOW:** Pullman was a planned community built for the company's workers.

*Wisconsin dairy is a $20 billion industry, a larger segment of the state's economy than both manufacturing and tourism.*

conditions. He also wanted to make a profit. The Pullman company retained ownership of all the buildings and reserved the right to determine rents and set prices at the local stores. Alcohol, trade unions, an independent press, and anything else the boss frowned upon were strictly forbidden.

## Labor unrest

Initially, Pullman was regarded as a model community. Residents enjoyed such modern conveniences as sanitary sewers and indoor plumbing, and children were provided with a free education up to the eighth grade. During the recession of 1893, however, one-third of Pullman's employees were laid off, and the remainder had their wages cut by 30 to 40 percent. When the workers demanded a corresponding rent reduction, Pullman refused. A strike followed and after violent clashes between workers and police, federal troops were called in to restore order. The strike collapsed, but only after 30 workers were shot and killed.

Pullman's victory was short-lived. In 1898, the Illinois Supreme Court ordered the company to sell its houses and other non-industrial property. The community of Pullman was never the same.

The best place to start a tour of the area is at the **Pullman Visitor Center** (11141 South Cottage Grove Avenue; tel: 773-785-8901; Tue–Sun 11am–3pm, closed Jan 1–Feb14; charge), where you can view a video and exhibits about the man, the company, and the town. Free brochures with a self-guided walking tour are also available. Included in the tour is the once grand **Hotel Florence**, named after Pullman's favorite daughter and now undergoing a long process of restoration; the handsome **Greenstone Church**; and various blocks of housing intended for workers at different levels of the company hierarchy.

## Brookfield Zoo ❼

3300 Golf Road, Brookfield 708-688-8000, www.brookfieldzoo.org
daily 10am–5pm, extended summer hours charge

About 16 miles (28 km) west of the Loop is the **Brookfield Zoo**. Much

**BELOW RIGHT:** bikers pay a visit to the Harley-Davidson Tour Center near Milwaukee.

### Lake Geneva

Northwest of Chicago, on the Illinois–Wisconsin state line, is Lake Geneva, a rustic resort area where for more than a century city dwellers have been escaping the pressures of urban life. The area is a hiker's dream come true. A gorgeous 26-mile (42-km) footpath encircles the glistening lake. Many hikers prefer the sweet-smelling springtime to follow the old trail, originally tramped out by the region's Native American inhabitants. Others opt for winter, when the trail is used by those equipped with cross-country skis or snowshoes. The trail occasionally cuts through private property, though the courts have ruled that common law over generations has made the path a public right of way. Legally, however, access to the trail must be through public property. Experienced hikers in the area suggest using Big Foot Beach Park, Lake Geneva Library Park, Williams Bay Beach, or Fontana Beach, all of which make good entry points.

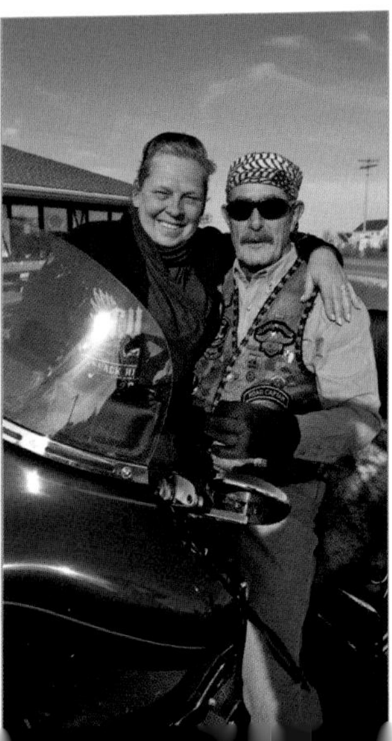

Recommended Restaurants, Bars & Cafés on pages 260–1

larger than the Lincoln Park Zoo, Brookfield encompasses more than 200 acres (80 hectares) of naturalistic habitats for lions, polar bears, hippos, rhinos, penguins, kangaroos, orangutans, gorillas, and many other animals. **Habitat Africa** is a 30-acre (12-hectare) re-creation of savannah and forest environments, where okapi and river hogs graze in the leafy understory, giraffes roam the open spaces, and a pack of African wild dogs laze in the shade. In the **Fragile Kingdom**, visitors explore several threatened habitats and the highly specialized animals that inhabit them, including otters, clouded leopards, and tigers from Asian rain forests, and a colony of meerkats from southern Africa.

The **Dolphin Arena** is a perennial favorite; the dolphin show sometimes sells out, so buy tickets early in the day. Two areas are set aside for small children: the **Hamill Family Play Zoo**, which has interactive exhibits as well as roaming musicians, actors, and other "play partners" who lead kids in a variety of special activities, and the **Children's Zoo**, where kids can pet and feed cows, goats, sheep, and other farm animals and have close encounters with a select few "wild" animals, including eagles, reindeer, and a bobcat.

## Morton Arboretum 8

4100 Illinois Route 53, Lisle
630-719-2400, www.mortonarb.org
daily 7am–7pm or sunset, whichever is earlier charge

You'll have a more serene encounter with nature at the **Morton Arboretum**, 1,700 acres (690 hectares) of woodland, gardens, and prairie laced with 14 miles (23 km) of hiking trails and 9 miles (15 km) of paved biking paths. Pick up a map and chat with staff members at the **Visitor Center**, where you can also buy tickets for a tram ride (daily Apr–Oct, weekends Nov–Mar) or join a free, one-hour walking tour (Sat, Sun, and Wed). In addition to thousands of trees from around the world are a number of formal gardens, including a one-acre **Maze** and an elaborate **Children's Garden** designed for play and exploration.

Hikers can roam more than 500 acres (200 hectares) of woodlands and restored prairies, stroll along the **East DuPage River**, or visit one of the lakes and ponds. Live chamber music, theatrical performances, lectures, nature walks, and other special events are held throughout the year. ❑

**ABOVE:** the Maze at Morton Arboretum.
**BELOW:** crooner Myles Hayes belts out a tune at a Lake Geneva bar.

# Best Restaurants, Bars and Cafés

## Restaurants

Prices for a three-course dinner per person with a half-bottle of house wine:

**$** = under $20
**$$** = $20–$45
**$$$** = $45–$60
**$$$$** = over $60

### Burt's Place

8541 N. Ferris Ave, Morton Grove 847-965-7997 L Mon–Fri, D daily **$**

Pan pizza doesn't have to be the dairy bomb purveyed by the big-name chains. Discriminating pizza junkies make the trek to Morton Grove (about 5 miles/8 km west of downtown Evanston) for one of Burt Katz's perfectly balanced pies. The dense, flaky crust is given a light bath of chunky tomato sauce, topped with meats or veggies, and finished with just the right dose of fresh mozzarella.

### Chef Paul's Bavarian Lodge

1800 Ogden Ave, Lisle 630-241-4701 L Sun, D Wed–Sun **$$**

You'll find German home cooking minutes from the Morton Arboretum, with a menu that runs from bratwurst to all manner of schnitzel. The outstanding beer list – which includes a staggering number of German and Belgian ales, lagers, bocks, lambics, and seasonal craft brews – is one of the best in the region.

### Chef's Station

915 Davis St, Evanston 847-570-9821 D daily **$$$**

Silverware comes tucked into the pocket of an old pair of jeans at this quirky bistro on the ground floor of the Davis Street Metra station. The ever-changing menu showcases creative Franco-American dishes like pan-roasted chicken breast stuffed with wild mushrooms and Taleggio, but many diners opt for the six-course tasting menu ($55, $75 with wine pairing).

### Café Central

455 Central Ave, Highland Park 847-266-7878 L Tue–Sat, D Tue–Sun **$$$**

Café Central's storefront setting is home to classic French bistro dishes prepared with all the attention to detail found at the restaurant's elegant, four-star sibling, Carlos. Between the two, owners Carlos and Debbie Nieto have cornered the market on fine dining in Highland Park.

### Elegant Farmer

1545 Main St, Mukwonago, WI 262-363-6770 daily **$**

Don't dare leave this deli, bakery, and farmers' market in the countryside around Lake Geneva without sampling its trademark "apple pie baked in a paper bag," declared one of "America's top ten pies" by *Gourmet* magazine.

### Francesco's Hole in the Wall

254 Skokie Blvd, Northbrook 847-272-0155 L Mon, Wed–Fri D Wed–Mon **$$**

Everyone is family at this cozy Italian restaurant convenient to the Botanic Garden. The menu is small, but the *osso bucco* is as authentic as you'll find anywhere on Taylor Street.

### Homer's Restaurant & Ice Cream Parlor

1237 Green Bay Rd, Wilmette 847-251-0477 L & D daily **$**

In the Poulos family for more than 60 years, Homer's is a regular on both local and national best-of lists. The rich, dense, high-butterfat ice cream, available in dozens of flavors, is made by hand with fresh ingredients, including seasonal specials like peach and pumpkin pie.

### Johnnie's Italian Beef

7500 W. North Ave, Elmwood Park 708-452-6000 L & D daily **$**

Some connoisseurs

**LEFT:** Elegant Farmer's award-winning apple pie.

consider Johnnie's the Holy Grail of Italian beef sandwiches: moist, tender meat; rich, flavorful "gravy"; tangy *giardinera*. Inside, the facilities are bare-bones, but in summer the outdoor picnic tables and benches provide ample room for crowds of beef pilgrims.

**Katy's Dumpling House**
665 N. Cass Ave, Westmont 630-323-9393 L & D Sun–Tue, Thu–Sat **$**
Championed by the local food site LTH Forum, one of the best Chinese restaurants in the region lies in a suburban strip mall near the Morton Arboretum. Inside it's tiny and spare, but the food – in particular any of the numerous noodle dishes – is wonderfully flavorful and fresh. Cash only.

**Lovell's of Lake Forest**
915 S. Waukegan Rd, Lake Forest 847-234-8013 L & D daily, Br Sun **$$-$$$**
Apollo 13 commander Captain James Lovell bankrolled this country club-like steak house, a showcase for his collection of space memorabilia and his son James III's cooking. The vintage mural behind the bar, *Steeds of Apollo*, was donated to the restaurant by a big fan, Tom Hanks.

**Michael**
4 Green Bay Rd, Winnetka 847-441-3100 L Fri, D Tue–Sun **$$$$**
Chef Michael Lachowicz bounced around some of the region's top French restaurants before launching his own idiosyncratic spot. The food is as posh as any Escoffier classic, but the gregarious Lachowicz puts an informal spin on things, making Michael uniquely unstuffy for the North Shore.

**Oceanique**
505 Main St, Evanston 847-864-3435 D Mon–Sat **$$$$**
Expect elegant, eclectic French-influenced fine dining with an emphasis on (surprise) seafood. Chef-owner Mark Grosz trained with Chicago's grandmaster of French cuisine, Jean Banchet, and his wine list is a perennial award-winner. A six-course tasting menu is available for $75; add another $49 for wine.

**Pita Inn**
3910 Dempster St, Skokie 847-677-0211 L & D daily **$**
Falafel-crazed fans make the trek to Skokie (just west of Evanston) for fast, affordable deals like the $3.95 lunch special, a combo of shawirma, kifta kabob, shish kabob, and falafel, with sides of pilaf, salad, and homemade pita bread. Check out the adjacent Pita Inn Market and Bakery for Mediterranean groceries and fresh bread to go.

**Prairie Grass Café**
601 Skokie Blvd, Northbrook 847-205-4433 L Tue–Fri, D Tue–Sun **$$$**
Award-winning chefs Sarah Stegner and George Bumbaris left longtime positions at the Ritz-Carlton to open this contemporary American restaurant in a nondescript corporate plaza. Inside, the Prairie School-inspired room is a graceful setting for dishes showcasing local, seasonal ingredients. Stegner is also a founder of the Green City Market.

**Trattoria D.O.C.**
706 Main St, Evanston 847-475-1111 L & D daily **$$**
Wood-oven pizza is the star at this casual Italian spot, thought by many fans to be superior to its urban sibling, Chicago's Pizza D.O.C. In addition to pizza, there's a range of reasonably priced pastas and salads, though *secondi* like veal saltimbocca pass the $20 mark.

**Vie**
4471 Lawn Ave, Western Springs 708-246-2082 708-246-2082 D Mon–Sat **$$$$**
A 30-minute trip from downtown Chicago, Vie stole the spotlight when Chef Paul Virant was named one of *Food and Wine's* Best New Chefs of 2007. A vet of Everest and Blackbird, Virant is a preacher of the gospel of local, seasonal eating, and Vie is a casually elegant showcase for creative, contemporary dishes featuring his own pickles and preserves.

## *Bars*

**Charlie Beinlich's** (290 Skokie Blvd, Northbrook; tel: 847-714-9375). Wood paneled bar and grill with excellent burgers and fries. Convenient to the Chicago Botanic Garden, it's a little bit of the North Woods on the North Shore.

**Flossmoor Station Brewery** (1035 Sterling Ave, Flossmoor; tel: 708-957-2739). This award-winning craft brewery and brewpub was named "Best Small Brewpub Brewer in America" at the 2006 Great American Beer Festival. Set in the south suburb of Flossmoor, about 25 minutes from downtown and right next to the Metra stop, it's well worth the trip for any beer fan.

**Tommy Nevin's Pub** (1450-1458 Sherman Ave, Evanston; tel: 847-869-0450). Irish pub packed with Evanston families drawn by the authentic Irish grub during the day and Northwestern students drawn to pints of Guinness after dark.

INSIGHT GUIDES

# CHICAGO

## Travel Tips

# TRANSPORTATION

## GETTING THERE AND GETTING AROUND

As big cities go, getting around Chicago is a snap. With few exceptions, the city is laid out in an orderly grid, with block numbers radiating out from the intersection of State and Madison streets in the Loop. If you need to get anywhere beyond walking distance, hop on the El (elevated trains and subways), which circles the Loop and has color-coded branches into the surrounding neighborhoods. Buses are equally convenient and, in the downtown core, taxis are rarely far away.

### GETTING THERE

#### By Air

Chicago's O'Hare International Airport is the world's second busiest airport and is served by most domestic and international carriers. It is located 18 miles (29 km) northwest of downtown, a 30- to 45-minute drive, depending on traffic. For flight departure and arrival information, go to www.flychicago.com, or call 773-686-2200 or 800-832-6352.

Alternatively, Midway International Airport lies 10 miles ( km) southwest of downtown, a 20- to 30-minute drive, outside of rush hour. Midway is one of the fastest growing airports in the Americas, serving primarily domestic but a growing number of international airlines. For flight departure and arrival information, go to www.flychicago.com/midway/MidwayHomepage.shtm, or call 800-832-6352.

#### *Ground Transportation*

For both O'Hare and Midway airports, ground transportation directly from the airport terminal to downtown is convenient, efficient, and inexpensive.

**Taxis, limousines, and shuttles**: From O'Hare, expect to spend approximately $35 (including tip) for a taxi to downtown Chicago. For wheelchair accessible vehicles (at either airport), call **United Dispatch** at 800-281-4466. Limousines are also available for Chicago and the suburbs. W-limo (tel: 800-966-0602; www.w-limo.com) charges $69–99 (depending on the number of passengers) from O'Hare to downtown, or reference the directory of pre-arranged limousine services posted near the airport information booths on the lower-level of each terminal. Shuttles such as the **Continental Airport Express** run approximately every 5 to 10 minutes outside the baggage-claim areas between 6am and 11.30pm, with fees of around $25 into the city.

From Midway, expect to spend approximately $25–28 for a taxi to downtown Chicago. Pre-arranged limousine services are provided at the Ground Transportation Information Booth located on the bag claim level near Door 3 LL. Continental Airport Express departures are about every 15 minutes. The fare to the city is approximately $19.

**Trains and Buses**: The **Chicago Transit Authority** (CTA), www.transitchicago.com, or the "El," is an inexpensive and convenient method of transportation into and around the city. From O'Hare, the Blue Line runs directly in and out of the airport terminal, traveling through the northwest side until reaching downtown within 45 minutes. Two Pace bus routes also run through O'Hare airport, although they require more time and do not run directly into the downtown area. **The Metra** commuter rail (www.metrarail.com) is another alternative for traveling in and around the Chicagoland area, servicing O'Hare and extending to the suburbs and counties outside of the city.

From Midway, the CTA Orange Line runs through Chicago's southwest side to downtown in about 30 minutes. Five Pace bus routes also offer a variety of routes throughout the city. For more specific itineraries and city destinations, contact the RTA Travel Information Center at www.rtachicago.com.

### *Transportation between O'Hare and Midway*

**Coach USA Wisconsin** offers hourly service between O'Hare International Airport and Midway Airport from 6.30am–10.30pm costing $14 one way. The CTA Blue and Orange lines can be used but are extremely time consuming – around two hours including a downtown El transfer.

### *Car Rental*

Visitors planning on spending most of their time in the downtown area should avoid using a car. Almost all tourist areas are accessible via public transportation and walking. Taxis are plentiful and public transportation maps are easy to come by. If you decide to drive, reservations through one of the following rental agencies are recommended:

| | |
|---|---|
| Alamo | 800-327-9633 |
| Avis | 800-331-1212 |
| Budget | 800-527-0700 |
| Dollar | 800-800-4000 |
| Enterprise | 800-867-4595 |
| Hertz | 800-654-3131 |
| National | 800-227-7368 |

## By Rail

Amtrak, the national railway system, services Chicago's Union Station and Northwestern Station. **Amtrak fare and schedule information**, call 800-872-7245 or go to www.amtrak.com.

## By Bus

Two Chicago Greyhound Bus Terminals allow visitors to arrive by bus from cities and towns throughout the US. Both the downtown station and the South Side station connect travelers to CTA railway and bus routes throughout the city. **Greyhound Bus Lines fare and schedule information**: call 800-231-2222 or go to www.greyhound.com.

## By Car

**From the north**: The Kennedy Expressway (I-90) runs from O'Hare Airport east and then south to downtown Chicago, interchanging with the Edens Expressway (I-94) on Chicago's North Side at Montrose Avenue and with the Dan Ryan (I-90/94) and Eisenhower Expressways (I-290), which runs east into Chicago from the western suburbs.

**From the east**: I-80 and I-90 skirt northern Illinois. I-90 forks to form the Chicago Skyway near 66th Street.

**From the west**: From Seattle, I-90 enters Chicago from Wisconsin.

**From the south**: From Tennessee, the Stevenson Express-

**AIRLINES**

| | |
|---|---|
| Air Lingus | 888-474-7424 |
| Air Canada | 888-247-2262 |
| Air Canada Jazz | 888-247-2262 |
| Air France | 800-237-2747 |
| Air India | 800-621-8231 |
| Air Jamaica | 800-523-5585 |
| Air Midwest | 800-MESA-AIR |
| Air Tran | 800-825-8538 |
| Alaska Airlines | 800-252-7522 |
| Alitalia | 800-223-5730 |
| All Nippon | 800-235-9262 |
| American Airlines | 800-443-7300 |
| American Eagle | 800-433-7300 |
| America West | 800-428-4322 |
| Asiana Airlines | 800-227-4262 |
| ATA | 800-225-2995 |
| Austrian Airlines | 800-843-0002 |
| British Airways | 800-247-9297 |
| BMI British Midland | 800-788-0555 |
| Cayman Airways | 800-422-9626 |
| ComAir | 800-927-0927 |
| Continental Airlines | 800-525-0280 |
| Delta Air Lines | 800-221-1212 |
| El Al | 800-223-6700 |
| Frontier Airlines | 800-432-1359 |
| Iberia Airlines | 800-772-4642 |
| Japan Airlines (JAL) | 800-525-3663 |
| Jet Blue | 800-JET-BLUE |
| KLM Royal Dutch | 800-225-2525 |
| Korean Air | 800-438-5000 |
| LOT Polish Airlines | 212-789-0970 |
| Lufthansa | 800-645-3880 |
| Mexicana | 800-531-7921 |
| Northwest Airlines | 800-225-2525 |
| Pakistan International | 800-221-6024 |
| Royal Jordanian | 800-223-0470 |
| Scandinavian Airlines (SAS) | 800-221-2350 |
| Southwest Airlines | 800-435-9792 |
| Spirit Airlines | 800-772-7117 |
| SWISS | 877-359-7947 |
| TACA Airlines | 800-400-TACA |
| Ted | 800-225-5833 |
| Turkish Airlines | 800-874-8875 |
| United Airlines | 800-241-6522 |
| United Express | 800-241-6522 |
| US Airways | 800-428-4322 |
| USA 3000 | 877-872-3000 |
| Virgin Atlantic | 800-821-5438 |

way (I-55) heads north to Chicago. I-57 runs from Florida as far as southern Illinois.

### Parking

Parking in Chicago varies from sidewalk meters to expensive public lots for daily use. While most of Chicago's neighborhoods have allocated metered parking interspersed with residential permit parking, trying to find a parking spot in the downtown area can be a stressful and expensive experience. Take note of all signs denoting parking regulations. Illegal parking will most likely result in hefty fines and the possibility of getting towed. If you find that your car has been towed, call the **Chicago Police Department** at 312-746-6000.

If you are planning a long day in the city, it is advised to take public transportation or find a public garage. Parking garages downtown tend to be very expensive; taking a taxi is often cheaper and more relaxing. Main attractions such as the Sears Tower or Navy Pier offer convenient but pricy parking on or near the premises. Some recommended public lots and garages around the downtown area include:

**Park One Incorporated**, 525 South Wabash Avenue
**Park One Incorporated**, 201 East Ohio Street
**Lake & Wells Self Park**, 171 North Wells Street
**Wabash & Randolph Self Park**, 20 East Randolph Street
**Grant Park North Garage**, Michigan Avenue and Washington Street

## GETTING AROUND

Chicago's public transportation network is the most efficient and inexpensive method of getting around. The CTA El operates seven train lines throughout downtown Chicago and the surrounding neighborhoods that first-time visitors will find simple to navigate. Bus and El fare cards cost $1.75 per trip, an extra 25¢ allows for two additional bus and El transfers within two hours of ticket purchase. Fare cards can be used but not purchased on buses; make sure you have correct change. A 24-hour Visitor Pass ($5) permits unlimited rides on the El and CTA buses. For further information on route and station information, contact the CTA (tel: 312-836-7000) or see the website (www.transitchicago.com), which provides detailed schedules and maps.

### DRIVING DISTANCES

| | Miles | KM |
|---|---|---|
| Albuquerque,NM | 1310 | 2108 |
| Atlanta, GA | 715 | 1150 |
| Denver, CO | 1085 | 1746 |
| Houston, TX | 805 | 1295 |
| Kansas City, MO | 526 | 846 |
| New York, NY | 787 | 1266 |
| Los Angeles, CA | 2077 | 3343 |
| San Diego, CA | 2090 | 3364 |
| San Francisco, CA | 2170 | 3492 |
| Seattle, WA | 2050 | 3299 |
| Washington, D.C. | 710 | 1143 |

### Handicapped Travelers

The CTA's website has detailed information on accessible bus and train routes and stations throughout the city. Go to www.transitchicago.com/maps/accessible.html, or contact the RTA Travel Information Center at 312-913-3110.

### Taxis

Cabs are available at most tourist attractions and hotels and are easy to flag down on the street. Taxis are metered, with fares beginning at $2.25 and increasing per mile and/or extended period of waiting. A 10 to 15 percent tip is customary. If ordering ahead of time, leave at least 30 minutes waiting time.

**Yellow Cab**, tel: 312-829-4222
**Checker Taxi**, tel: 312-243-2537
**Flash Cab**, tel: 773-561-1444

### Carriages

Though less practical than other modes of transportation, horse and carriage rides are a charming and unforgettable way to experience views of the city. Most carriages congregate at Michigan Avenue, across from the historic Water Tower, though they can also be arranged ahead of time. Behind the reins is your very own tour guide, ready to recommend a variety of routes from which to choose.

**Chicago Horse and Carriage Ltd.**, Michigan Avenue and Pearson Street, tel: 773-395-3950
**Antique Coach and Carriage**, Michigan Avenue and Huron Street, tel: 773-735-9400.

**RIGHT:** the CTA Blue Line stops at Damen and North avenues.

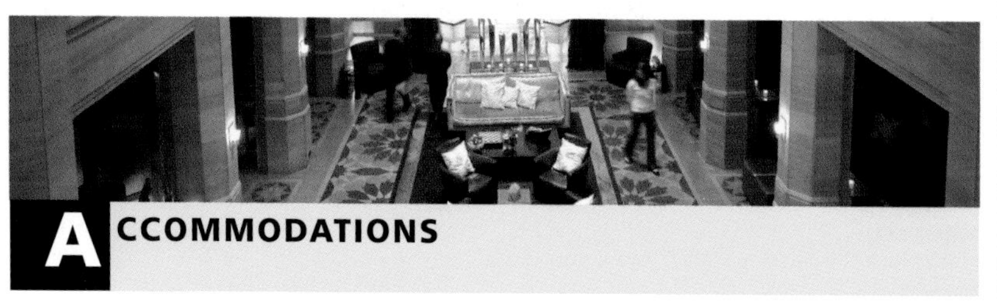

# ACCOMMODATIONS

## SOME THINGS TO CONSIDER BEFORE YOU BOOK THE ROOM

One of the nice things about Chicago's landmark architecture – and make no mistake, this is a city that is justifiably proud of its buildings – is that, if you pick the right hotel, you can actually live in it – at least for a few days. In the following list, you will find some the city's grand old buildings as well as its little-known gems. Prices range widely depending on location and amenities. Don't be shy about asking for weekend or corporate rates or package deals, and don't forget to make reservations well in advance of your arrival.

### Choosing a Hotel

There are hundreds of hotels to choose from in Chicago, ranging from glass and steel monoliths to quirky boutique hotels, Victorian B&Bs, and landmark buildings designed by Chicago's visionary 19th-century architects. The constant development of new hotels and the growth of Chicago's convention industry ensure strong competition among upscale hotels.

The downtown hotels are, for the most part, resolutely aimed at the business traveler with prosaic, neutral decor and high-tech amenities. Prices in Chicago are high and on the rise – though not on a par with New York just yet – and there is a paucity of good budget hotels; those that do exist are snapped up months in advance. Spending up does not necessarily guarantee the luxury, service, and creature comforts that you might expect; it's not unusual to find hotels in the $200-plus category with dingy rooms and faded decor. Historic hotels may have sumptuous public areas dripping with marble and a classic Chicago aura, but that's where it stops. Many landmark hotels rest on their laurels, and guest rooms are often in need of upgrading. Decide what is important to you before you book: location, atmosphere, personal services, or a bathroom that can fit two people at one time.

Location is certainly what you pay for, and during the peak summer months rooms book up fast in the River North, Gold Coast, Loop, and Michigan Avenue vicinities. Always check the online travel sites for the lowest rates.

The cheapest deals are to be found in outlying neighborhoods, which are just a short hop on the El or in a taxi from the Loop. Here you will find Victorian mansions and stone houses crammed with antiques tastefully converted into good value bed and breakfast lodgings (for further information contact the Chicago Bed and Breakfast Association: www.chicago-bed-breakfast.com).

Chicago's booming convention industry means that prices tend to be cheaper on weekends, and hotels will often be block booked for days and weeks at a time. It's worth checking with the Convention Center (tel: 312-567-8500) to see what events are scheduled during your trip. Not surprisingly, January through March is the low season and often a steal as far as hotel prices are concerned.

Its a good idea to book by credit card to secure a guaranteed late arrival, just in case your flight is stacked up over the runway or your cab gets stuck in traffic on the way into town from the airport.

ACCOMMODATIONS LISTINGS

## THE LOOP

### Expensive

**Hotel Allegro**
171 West Randolph Street
Tel: 312-236-0123 [p306, C1]
www.allegrochicago.com
In keeping with its position in the heart of the Theatre District, the flamboyant Allegro has a carnival atmosphere and plush Art Deco furnishings throughout the public areas. Rooms are a riot of color, and whimsical touches distract from the cozy dimensions. (Premier rooms are more spacious.) All guest rooms have a flat screen TV and complimentary Wi-Fi, and the Aveda bath products are a nice touch. The adjacent Encore bar invites indulgence with lavish red velvet booths and an extensive list of potent cocktails. The hotel is pet-friendly.

**Hotel Burnham**
1 West Washington Avenue
Tel: 312-782-1111 [p307, C2]
www.burnhamhotel.com
The Hotel Burnham (originally the Reliance Building) was built in 1895 by visionary architect Daniel Burnham and is a predecessor of the modern glass-and-steel skyscraper. Now a landmark hotel, the Burnham exudes history and good taste with original period features and modern amenities fused with aplomb in a bustling downtown location close to Millennium Park and State Street theaters and shops. After an extensive refurbishment, classically decorated rooms are warm and comfortable, but it is the exquisite lobby and the Atwood Café, which ooze 1920s glamour, that are essential viewing for anyone with even a passing interest in Chicago architecture and history.

**Hotel Monaco**
225 North Wabash Avenue
Tel: 312-960-8500 [p307, C1]
www.monaco-chicago.com
With playful French decor, warm service, and an intimate boutique ambience, this is one of the most interesting downtown hotels. Relaxation is the hotel's ethos. The in-room yoga programs and window seating "meditation stations" with feather pillows encourage a mellow mood. The Monaco's vivacious peppermint green and cream rooms are larger than those of most other downtown hotels, and the spacious bathrooms stocked with L'Occitane bath products add to the hotel's soothing allure. There is a small fitness center, and the adjacent South Water Kitchen restaurant is a popular spot serving modern American comfort food. There is a complimentary wine hour each evening in the lobby. A good value.

**Palmer House Hilton**
17 East Monroe Street
Tel: 312-726-7500
[p307, C2]
www.hilton.com
There is nothing understated about the Palmer House, named after Chicago businessman Potter Palmer who was

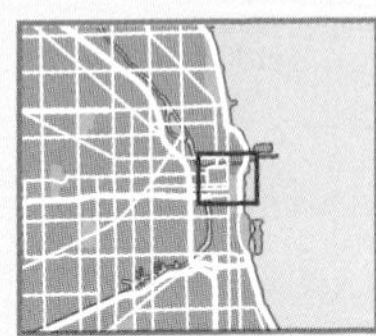

responsible for much of State Street's development. Palmer built the hotel's first incarnation (this is the third) for his wife Bertha. Sadly, the building burned down in the Chicago Fire just 13 days after it was completed on October 9, 1871. The hotel has become a Chicago landmark due to the unbridled opulence of its lobby and other public areas; the gilded mural is rather too extravagant for some tastes. At the time of this writing, the hotel is undergoing extensive renovations to update the faded guest rooms. Amenities include a fitness center, several restaurants, a steam room, sauna, and an indoor lap pool.

## NEAR NORTH

### Luxury

**Conrad Hotel**
521 North Rush Street
Tel: 312-645-1500 [p304, C4]
www.conradhotels.com/chicago
One of Chicago's top-tier hotels, within easy walking distance of all the downtown sights, this swanky Hilton boasts hi-tech amenities on a grand scale with 42-inch plasma TVs, iPod alarm clocks, and Bose stereo systems. The spacious rooms are comfortable and have sharper decor than most other properties in the Hilton chain. There is a fitness center and Wi-Fi access throughout the hotel. The latest addition – a rooftop terrace – is an enticing early evening spot to unwind with cocktails and tapas. Frequent seasonal offers make this an especially appealing choice.

**Drake Hotel**
140 East Walton Place
Tel: 312-787-2200
Toll free: 800-332-3442
[p305, C3]
www.thedrakehotel.com

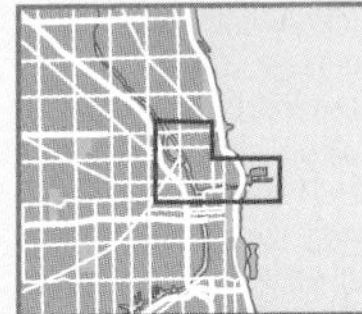

Steps from Chicago's Magnificent Mile and Oak Street Beach, this lavish hotel is more than a sight for sore eyes. Home to four restaurants, including the Cape Cod Room, which affords exquisite views of the city, the Drake also boasts The Palm Court, a magnificent Baroque setting for high afternoon tea accompanied by classical music. Guest rooms are equipped with comfy beds, executive desks, high-speed internet access, 24-hour room service, and oversized closets. It's worth splurging for the antique-furnished deluxe rooms, which provide skyline views, marble bathrooms, fluffy robes, and daily chocolates.

**Four Seasons Hotel**
120 East Delaware Place
Tel: 312-280-8800 [p304, C3]
www.fourseasons.com/chicagofs
Just a short walk to the distinguished stores of Michigan Avenue, this tasteful hotel offers a variety of rooms with stylish and comfortable furniture, deep-soaking marble bathtubs, and a choice of skyline or lake views. The hotel's spa features an extensive range of treatments, including body massages and eucalyptus steams, and offers access to a full fitness center and 50-ft (15-meter) indoor swimming pool. The hotel's beautifully appointed Seasons Restaurant is worth the multisensory indulgence.

**James Hotel**
55 East Ontario Street
Tel: 312-337-1000 [p304, C3]
www.jameshotels.com/chicago
One of the most hyped hotels in the city, and justifiably so, the James is the paradigm of urban chic. Stylish studios and lofts, warmly decorated in earthy tones, are provided with cocktail bars, iPod docking stations, marble and slate bathrooms and twice-daily maid service. There is a gigantic fitness room and modern art gallery. The acclaimed James Burke Steakhouse has an on-site salt cave for dry-aging its beef.

**Omni Hotel**
676 North Michigan Avenue
Tel: 312-944-6664 [p305, C3]
www.omnihotels.com
One of the most thoughtfully conceived hotels in the city, the Omni's spacious rooms have a separate parlor area, two TVs, wet bar, and coffee maker. If you sign up for their Select Guest Program (which is free), you'll receive all manner of additional perks and goodies ranging from free Wi-Fi to morning newspapers, express checkout, and an evening turndown service. There is a fitness room and the fancy 676 Restaurant & Bar. The hotel also has a children's program with an array of amenities and activities.

**Peninsula Chicago**
108 East Superior Street
Tel: 312-337-2888
Toll Free: 866-288-8889
[p304, C3]
http://chicago.peninsula.com/
State-of-the-art facilities, classic decor, and superlative service make this the most luxurious – and most expensive – hotel in the city. Rooms and junior suites, which are surprisingly on the small side, cater to every whim, with flat screen TVs, Wi-Fi, and bedside panels that allow you to control lighting and temperature and even open and close the drapes without getting out of bed. Spacious bathrooms drip with marble and feature separate tubs and power showers. There is a much hyped spa, four restaurants, and an enticing Art Nouveau bar.

**Ritz-Carlton Chicago**
160 East Pearson Street
Tel: 312-266-1000 [p305, C3]
www.fourseasons.com/chicagorc
Perched atop Chicago's Water Tower Place, this plush hotel features cherry wood and richly upholstered furniture, a choice between city and lake views, and an aura of distinguished grandeur that permeates every nook, from the guest rooms to the award-winning restaurant, The Café. The Ritz accommodates families with unique accommodations and special offers for children and parents seeking babysitters.

## Expensive

**Chicago Hilton and Towers**
720 South Michigan Avenue
Tel: 312-922-4400
Toll free: 800-445-8667
[p307, C3]
www.hilton.com
Perfectly centered between the Magnificent Mile, Museum Campus, Millennium Park, and the Loop's business and shopping district, as well as being the closest luxury hotel to the city's convention center, this imposing site provides more than 1,500 classically designed and meticulously maintained guest rooms aimed at the upscale business traveler – and his pooch. The pet-friendly Hilton also provides a free Michigan Avenue Shopping Shuttle, sight-seeing tours, and a full business center.

**Embassy Suites**
600 North State Street

### PRICE CATEGORIES

Price categories are for a double room without breakfast:
**Luxury** over $300
**Expensive** $175–$300
**Moderate** $125–$175
**Inexpensive** under $125

**BELOW:** Hotel InterContinental on Michigan Avenue.

Tel: 312-943-3800 [p304, C4]
www.embassysuiteschicago.com
Set in the heart of downtown, just minutes away from both the Magnificent Mile and the Financial District, this classic but vibrantly designed hotel puts you right in the center of the action. Indulge yourself at the on-site Osteria Via Stato & Enoteca, an elegant Italian restaurant and wine bar. Revel in the complimentary full breakfast service every morning of your stay, or enjoy complimentary cocktails at the daily manager's reception.

**Fairmont Chicago**
200 North Columbus Drive
Tel: 312-565-8000
Toll free: 800-257-7544
[p305, C4]
www.fairmont.com
Perfect for business or pleasure, the Fairmont is an elegant choice for travelers who want to combine a day of sightseeing with a workout at the health club or a massage at the European-style spa. The Fairmont's big selling point is its unbeatable packages for excursions to nearby museums, shows, galleries, and festivals. The award-winning Aria Restaurant offers twists on classic American comfort food. The more casual Aria Bar has a communal dining style influenced by traditional Japanese noodle houses.

**Hotel 71**
71 East Wacker Drive
Tel: 312-346-7100
Toll free: 800-621-4005
[p304, C4]
www.hotel71.com
This is a contemporary hotel with colorful decor that provides a relief from the bland guest rooms of older hotels. In a prime riverside location at the pinnacle of the Magnificent Mile, the hotel offers fitness facilities and a business center. All guest rooms are spacious enough to include sitting areas, complete with either a leopard-print chaise or oversized chairs, plus nice touches such as designer bath products.

**Hotel InterContinental**
505 North Michigan Avenue
Tel: 312-944-4100 [p305, C4]
www.icchicagohotel.com
With panoramic views of the city and Lake Michigan, the InterContinental, built in 1929, successfully fuses urban sophistication and old-world grandeur in the restored public areas. The rooms are a different story, lacking in style and facilities. Unusual in this price category, the hotel charges for water and internet access, and bathrooms are very small. Website deals (notably Priceline) and the unrivaled location, however, make it a practical choice. It is also popular for its Olympic-size swimming pool, on-site restaurant, and 1920s-style bar complete with a master sommelier offering wine, chocolates, and cheeses from around the world.

**BELOW:** the W hotel is aimed at hip, upscale travelers.

**Park Hyatt**
800 North Michigan Avenue
Tel: 312-335-1234 [p304, C3]
www.parkchicago.hyatt.com
A modern hotel with a Zen aura in an unbeatable location right off Michigan Avenue, the Hyatt pitches itself to the stylish business traveler, with hi-tech amenities, a fitness center with swimming pool and spa, and artfully designed public spaces. The neutral rooms may lack warmth but are slickly appointed and airy and have lake and city views. On the upper level, Nomi is one of the city's most highly rated restaurants; its rooftop cocktail bar is an enticing spot to take in the cityscape.

**Sofitel**
20 East Chestnut Street
Tel: 312-324-4000 [p304, C3]
www.sofitel.com
With the understated elegance that characterizes Sofitel hotels, this architecturally striking hotel three blocks from Michigan Avenue has sharp rooms complete with dark woods and frosted glass. Abstaining from frill and fluff, the attention to detail is exceptional, with comfortable beds draped in fine linens and sparkling bathrooms with separate shower-tubs. The light filled lobby and slick cocktail bar are popular meeting spots for local businessmen.

**The W Chicago Lakeshore**
644 North Lakeshore Drive
Tel: 312-943-9200 [p305, D3]
www.starwoodhotels.com
Resolutely aimed at the hip, urban traveler, this signature W hotel overlooking Lake Michigan has minimalist Asian-inspired rooms and sultry public spaces where moody staff members strut to an ambient soundtrack. All rooms provide high-speed internet access and have flat screen TVs, DVDs, desks, chaises, and robes. The rooftop Whiskey Sky bar has more than a whiff of pretention; the Wave bar and restaurant serves cocktails and is a solid choice for Mediterranean inspired small plates.

## Moderate

**Allerton Hotel**
701 North Michigan Avenue
Tel: 312-440-1300 [p305, C3]
www.theallertonhotel.com
This landmark hotel (proudly declaring its status as one of the first skyscrapers) is worthy of consideration for its convenient location, right off the Magnificent Mile, and low rates. The rooms are, for the most part, in need of upgrading, and bizarrely configured. Standard rooms are very small but clean and well equipped with internet access, cable TV, and marble baths.

**Comfort Inn**
15 East Ohio Street
Tel: 888-775-9223 [p304, C4]
www.chicagocomfortinn.com
This no-frills choice has clean, spacious, motel-style rooms. The rates, for this area, are hard to beat, and it has a friendly, down-to-earth ambience and a surprising range of amenities, including a small pool, free breakfast, and Wi-Fi.

**Homewood Suites**
40 East Grand Avenue
Tel: 312-744-2222 [p304, C4]
www.homewoodsuites.com
A good, economical choice for families, these two-bedroom suites are fully equipped with kitchen and dining facilities and small sitting areas. Renovated in 1999, the generic rooms fail to inspire but are roomy and practical, with Wi-Fi access. The location is ideal for walking to nearby Millennium Park, the State Street Theatre District, Michigan Avenue shops, and River North restaurants. There is also a rooftop pool.

## Inexpensive

**Cass Hotel**
640 North Wabash Avenue
Tel: 312-787-4031 [p304, C3]
www.casshotel.com
Following extensive renovations, the scruffy Cass Hotel has been given a facelift worthy of its River North location. Smart, cozy rooms have modern amenities such as Wi-Fi and flat screen TVs. A complimentary breakfast is served in the restaurant. Check the website for special offers.

**Hampton Inn and Suites**
33 West Illinois Street
Tel: 312-832-0330 [p304, C4]
www.hamptonsuiteschicago.com
This crisp modern hotel is a solid budget choice for families. Less than 10 years old, the generic studios with kitchenettes are spotless and spry. It's a comfortable walk to all key downtown attractions. There is a small indoor pool, pleasant lounge area in the lobby, free breakfast, friendly staff, and parking.

# GOLD COAST

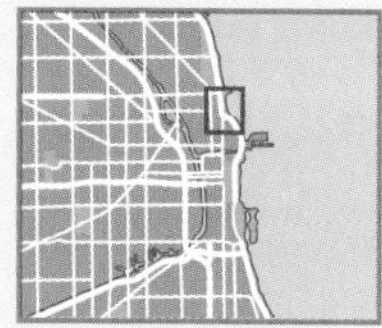

## Expensive

**Ambassador East Hotel**
1301 North State Parkway
Tel: 312-787-7200 [p304, C2]
www.theambassadoreasthotel.com
Quietly tucked away in a 1926 landmark building, the Ambassador exudes an air of faded grandeur. Back in the day, Sinatra stayed here, and more recently Richard Gere and Vince Vaughn have chosen the Ambassador for its discrete accommodations. Rooms are for the most part unexceptional, but they are spacious, spotless, and well appointed. Rooms do vary, so it's worth asking to see a few. The Pump Room is one of the city's most acclaimed hotel restaurants.

**Hotel Indigo**
1244 North Dearborn Parkway
Tel: 312-787-4980 [p304, C2]
www.hotelindigo.com
If you prefer to stay in a low-key residential area within walking distance of the Magnificent Mile, and you don't require the facilities of a larger hotel, this nautically inspired boutique hotel has a prime Gold Coast location surrounded by the mansions of Astor Street. Refurbished in 2005, rooms are crisp and fresh, with hardwood floors, white wood furnishings, and marine inspired artworks. Room sizes vary, but space is creatively employed throughout, with streamlined bathrooms featuring glass shower stalls (no bathtubs). There is Wi-Fi in the public areas, a fitness room, and a breezy restaurant lounge serving light meals.

**Talbott Hotel**
20 East Delaware Place
Tel: 312-239-8016 [p304, C3]
www.talbotthotel.com
This smart, gentlemanly hotel is close to Newberry Park and the nightlife nexus of Rush and Division Streets. European in style and sensibility, it has plenty of charm and old-world flavor but lacks the modern amenities of its luxury peers. The large rooms were totally refurbished in 2005, although the decor may still be rather fusty for some tastes. Guests receive free passes to a nearby gym. Basil's sidewalk café is a civilized breakfast and lunch spot.

**Whitehall Hotel**
105 East Delaware Place
Tel: 312-944-6300 [p304, C3]
www.thewhitehallhotel.com
This intimate boutique hotel frequently makes it onto the "Best of" lists for its stately European aura and impeccable rooms, which are luxuriously appointed with mahogany furniture and equipped with Wi-Fi (additional charge). The limited facilities include a small fitness center, valet parking, and laundry service.

## Moderate

**Flemish House of Chicago**
68 East Cedar Street
Tel: 312-664-9981 [p304, C2]
wwww.chicagobandb.com
This turn-of-the-19th-century stone town house in the heart of the Gold Coast has been graciously converted into a B&B attracting a gay and straight crowd. Six English Arts and Crafts style guest rooms are fully equipped with kitchens, private bathrooms, cable TV, DVDs, air conditioning, Wi-Fi, and telephones. Continental buffet breakfast is included. The house is smoke-free; there is a two-night minimum stay.

**PRICE CATEGORIES**

Price categories are for a double room without breakfast:
**Luxury** over $300
**Expensive** $175–$300
**Moderate** $125–$175
**Inexpensive** under $125

## LINCOLN PARK

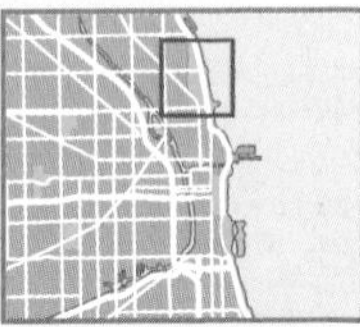

### Expensive

**Belden Stratford Hotel**
2300 North Lincoln Park West
Tel: 773-281-2900
www.beldenstratfordhotel.com

This Jazz Age hotel overlooking Lincoln Park has a sumptuous gilded lobby. Some of the rooms are rough around the edges but are redeemed by ornate original features and soaring ceilings. There are rooftop views of the city and lakefront, and the charming bistro Mon Ami Gabi serves solid French cuisine.

### Moderate

**Days Inn Lincoln Park**
644 West Diversey Parkway
Tel: 773-525-7010
wwww.lpdaysinn.com

This good value hotel is close to the bars, shops, and restaurants of Lincoln Park and a short walk from the most animated stretches of the lakefront. There is nothing special about the decor, but the amenities are hard to beat for this price range. There is free wireless, cable TV, American and continental breakfast, and access to a nearby fitness center.

**Windy City Inn**
607 West Deming Avenue
Tel: 773-248-7091
www.windycityinn.com

This relaxed inn is housed in a brownstone close to Lincoln Park and the neighborhood's lively bars and restaurants. Loaded with Chicago memorabilia, rooms in the main house are named after the city's legendary denizens. Rooms are heavy on chintz but snug and well equipped. All have fireplaces; most have private bathrooms.

## LAKEVIEW

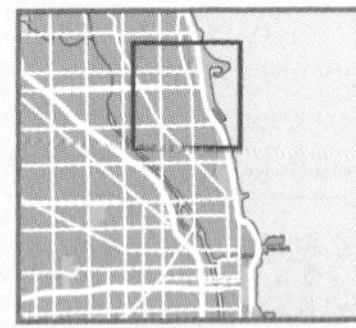

### Moderate

**City Suites Hotel**
933 West Belmont Avenue
Tel: 773-404-3400
wwww.cityinns.com

The Art Deco features of this boutique hotel distract from the otherwise bland guest rooms and noisy location near the El. Its friendly inclusiveness draws a lively clientele of gay men, designers, and performance artists. Continental breakfast is included.

**Villa Toscana**
3447 North Halsted Street
Tel: 773-404-2643
wwww.thevillatoscana.com

This 1890 Victorian frame house in the center of Boys Town has been converted into a smoke-free, gay-friendly B&B. The six rooms are on the small side and fussily decorated. Only three of the rooms have private bathrooms. The communal living room has a fireplace, and there is a private sundeck. A breakfast buffet is served each morning.

## WICKER PARK AND BUCKTOWN

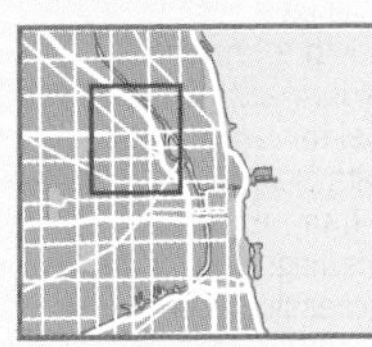

### Moderate

**House of Two Urns**
1239 North Greenview Avenue
Tel: 773-235-1408
www.twourns.com

This historic brownstone B&B in artsy Wicker Park is an ideal base for a second visit to the city, or if you want to get under the skin of Chicago's eclectic West Side. A range of cheerful rooms and apartments are available with amenities ranging from satellite TV and DVDs to Jacuzzi tubs and fireplaces. On the downside, most rooms have shared bathrooms. Parking is available on request.

**Ray's Bucktown B&B**
2144 North Leavitt Street
Tel: 773-384-3245

Photographer and writer Ray Reiss runs this thoughtfully conceived B&B, which has five tasteful bedrooms, each with satellite TV, Wi-Fi, and private bath. A gregarious vibe prevails with communal living spaces, a sauna, and a high-density TV room. A full breakfast is cooked to order, and Ray provides a wealth of information on the arts scene.

**Wicker Park Inn**
1329 North Wicker Park Avenue
Tel: 773-486-2743
www.wickerparkinn.com

This smart B&B is in a prime location two blocks from leafy Wicker Park and a short walk from the hip attractions around Damen and North avenues. There are five bedrooms and two apartments, each with private bathrooms. Spacious rooms have a contemporary feel, with exposed brick, hardwood floors, and pleasant furnishings as well as satellite TV and Wi-Fi. Continental breakfast is served. A three-night stay is required.

# SHOPPING

## BEST BUYS

Chicago shoppers are spoiled for choices. If you're into glitz and glamour, head for the Magnificent Mile on Michigan Avenue or Oak Street in the Gold Coast. If secondhand chic is more your style, there's the Maxwell Street Market. Hip and quirky? Try the boutiques on Armitage Avenue and Halsted Street in Lincoln Park or Milwaukee and Damen avenues in Wicker Park. And don't dare leave town without popping into Macy's – formerly Marshall Field's – the glorious grandaddy of Chicago department stores.

### WHERE TO SHOP

The glitzy stores and mesmerizing architecture of the Magnificent Mile is Chicago's primary retail destination. This shopper's dreamscape starts at Oak Street at the northern end of North Michigan Avenue and funnels south to the Chicago River. Here, Bloomingdale's, Nordstrom, and Neiman Marcus rub shoulders with Burberry, Ralph Lauren, Tiffany, and Cartier flanked by the flagship stores of more accessible retailers such as Crate & Barrel, Pottery Barn, and Gap. Continuing south of the river and a couple of blocks west, State Street's Theatre District is punctuated with big name retailers; Macy's, Old Navy, H&M, Borders, and Sears. Oak Street is home to the Gold Coast's exclusive boutiques and galleries, while more youthful, idiosyncratic fashion and accessories tend to be found in the neighborhoods to the north and west; popular areas include the Armitage and Halsted intersection in Lincoln Park and the Southport Corridor in Lakeview. For a more punky, alternative vibe, check out the consignment stores, funky boutiques, and independent music and bookstores in Lakeview (Belmont Avenue between Southport Avenue and Clark Street) and Wicker Park (Damen Avenue and North Avenue intersection). The River North district is where the majority of the downtown furniture stores and antique emporiums are located, anchored by the gargantuan Merchandise Mart design center (primarily trade only). Chicago's mega malls are situated in the suburbs.

#### Malls and Marketplaces

**900 Shops**, 900 North Michigan Avenue, tel: 312-915-3916. Bloomingdale's flagship store is the linchpin for this easy to navigate upscale mall close to Oak Street Beach. Some 80 shops, including J. Crew, Coach, MaxMara, and Williams-Sonoma, draw throngs of female shoppers.

**Water Tower Place**, 835 North Michigan Avenue, tel: 312-440-3166. At the northern flank of the Magnificent Mile, the Water Tower's fashion and interior design stores have a European slant: French Connection, Mango, Custo-Barcelona, Lacoste, Crabtree and Evelyn, Lush, Abercrombie and Fitch, The Limited, and Godiva.

**Westfield North Bridge**, 520 North Michigan Avenue, tel: 312-327-2300. Close to the river, Nordstrom is this mall's major draw, with just 50 specialty shops, including Bose, Tommy Bahama, and Hugo Boss.

**Westfield Old Orchard**, 66 Old Orchard Road, tel: 847-673-6800. Upscale mall with an agreeable outdoor setting and 180 shops, including Armani, Apple, Bloomingdale's, Restoration Hardware, Lulu Guinness, BCBG, and Banana Republic.
**Woodfield Mall**, 5 Woodfield Shopping, Golf Road, Route 53, Schaumburg, tel: 847-330-1537. If you love shopping enough to leave Chicago and head to the suburbs, Woodfield is the largest mall in Illinois with more annual visitors than any other attraction. There are some 300 stores, including all the major department stores and the predictable panoply of chain eateries.

## Antiques

Summer "antiquing" is a popular endeavor in Chicago; look out for the Randolph Street antique market held the last weekend of every month in summer.
**Antique Resources**, 1741 West Belmont Avenue, tel: 773-871-4242. For the serious collector, this Lakeview antique store specializes in European antiques. The magnificent collection includes rosewood English breakfast tables, French Empire consoles, Walnut Beidermier consoles, satinwood work tables, and 17th-century, ivory inlaid Portuguese cabinets.
**Architectural Artifacts**, 4325 North Ravenswood Avenue, tel: 773-348-0622. Located beside the Metra rail tracks on the North Side, this wonderful loft space houses a jaw-dropping array of one-of-a-kind artifacts, furniture, and decorative pieces salvaged from wealthy estates in North and South America. Stained glass, crystal chandeliers, marble fountains, church doors, antique clocks, chaises, and marble pillars are just a few of the treasures to be found here.
**Asian House of Chicago**, 159 West Kinzie Street, tel: 312-527-4848. In the River North furniture district, this multilevel space is crammed with antique Chinese art and furniture as well as some French colonial pieces; the prices are much more reasonable than its neighborhood peers.
**Chen & Chen Oriental Furniture**, 501 North Wells Street, tel: 312-245-3000. Small, select pieces of primarily Chinese antiques, including altar pieces, screens, vases, sculptures, art, and decorative objects, are well priced and in excellent condition.
**Christa's LTD**, 217 West Illinois Street, tel: 312-222-2520. Every inch of this antique emporium is packed with century-old artifacts from around the world, including Venetian mirrors, French armchairs and chaises, English buffets, and Austrian clocks, many in desperate need of restoration. A hunting ground for discerning antique specialists, pieces here are considerably more expensive than in other antique stores.
**Daniel's Antiques**, 3711 Ashland Avenue, tel: 773-868-9355. An eclectic collection of European antiques and decorative objects with a French bias. At the time of this writing, the store was in the process of moving to new premises, call ahead for location information.
**Evanstonia**, 120 West Kinzie Street, tel: 773-907-0101. A fine collection of 19th- and early 20th-century European and North American antiques restored by Polish owner Ziggy Osak. There is a larger store at 4555 North Ravenswood on Chicago's North Side, close to Lincoln Square.
**Jan's Antiques**, 225 North Racine Avenue, tel: 312-563-0275. Some 18,000 sq ft (1,700 sq meters) of architectural artifacts, including hardware, mirrors, furniture, mantles, iron gates, and vintage stained glass salvaged from homes and commercial buildings from 1800 to 1950.
**Old Plank Antiques**, 3 East Huron Street, Third Floor, tel: 312-981-7000. A small but interesting collection of antiques gathered from Europe and the Americas. French and Argentinean artifacts predominate with Louis XV- and XVI-style commodes, accent tables, and gilt settees. This is one of the most welcoming and accessible of the River North antique stores.
**Pagoda Red**, 1714 North Damen Avenue, tel: 773-235-1188. Artsy Wicker Park space with beautifully restored 19th-century Chinese antiques, including apothecary coffers, engraved burl cabinets, calligraphy brushes, and lanterns. The staff is knowledgeable, passionate, and keen to inform.
**Portals LTD**, 742 North Wells Street, tel: 312-642-1066. This beautiful River North town house has been converted into a gallery and antique store that focuses primarily on the English Aesthetic movement, including 19th-century Realist paintings. There is also a pristine collection of French and Italian antiques.

## Art Galleries

River North, namely the streets that surround the intersection of Superior and Franklin, is officially Chicago's gallery district. However, more recently, galleries have begun to spring up in the slowly gentrifying West Loop district. In River North, most galleries are open weekdays and Saturdays 10am–5pm. Some galleries close on Mondays. Friday night is reserved for opening new exhibits. Listings of current exhibitions are available in the *Chicago Reader* (www.chicagoreader.com) and the *Chicago Gallery News* (www.chicagogallerynews.com), which you can pick up in most galleries around River North.
**Aldo Castillo**, 675 North Franklin Street, tel: 312-337-2536, www.artaldo.com. Former Nicaraguan activist Aldo Castillo founded this vibrant gallery space in 1993 with the aim to promote emerging Latin American artists and increase awareness of established artists. Renowned Cuban artist

Wilfredo Lam and contemporary Mexican muralist Alejandro Romero, now a Chicago resident, are represented.

**Anne Nathan**, 218 West Superior Street, tel: 312-664-6622, www.annenathangallery.com. A strong focus on contemporary realism with paintings, sculptures, and mixed media by emerging and established artists, in addition to a small collection of African artworks and furniture.

**Andrew Bae Gallery**, 300 West Superior Street, tel: 312-335-8601, www.andrewbaegallery.com. Established collector Andrew Bae represents a small group of emerging Japanese and Korean artists and sculptors whose strong visual narratives fuse Eastern and Western aesthetics and philosophical ideals.

**Belloc Lowndes Fine Art**, 226 West Superior Street, tel: 312-266-2222, www.belloclowndes.com. The collection is mostly dedicated to contemporary landscape and still life paintings as well as etchings and portraits by emerging and established British and American artists.

**Bucket Rider**, 119 North Peoria Street, tel: 312-421-6993, www.bucketridergallery.com. Focusing on experimental mixed media by local and international artists, this contemporary West Loop space is exemplified by the work of resident photographer Greg Stimac, whose images of melting snowmen, elderly men mowing Midwestern lawns, and bottles of urine tossed by a Texas roadside represent an irreverent vision of American iconography.

**Jean Albano**, 215 West Superior Street, tel: 312-440-0770, www.jeanalbanogallery.com. Labyrinthine galleries display contemporary paintings, sculpture and mixed media from emerging and established local and international artists, including Argentinean Luciana Abait, Texan Valerie Beller, and Chicagoan Gladys Nilsson.

**Judy Saslow**, 300 West Superior Street, tel: 312-943-0530, www.jsaslowgallery.com. The gallery specializes in outsider and intuitive artworks in addition to a small collection of tribal art, jewelry, and ethnographic artifacts.

**Monique Meloche**, 118 North Peoria Street, tel: 312-455-0299, www.moniquemeloche.com. An active participant on the national and international art fair scene, Meloche selects provocative artists whose vision touches on themes such as race, class, gender, and politics to fill this avant-garde space.

**Primitive Art Works**, 130 West Jefferson, tel: 312-575-9600, www.primitiveartworks.com. A great way to spend an afternoon, this 31,000-sq-ft (3,000-sq-meter) store houses a truly unique collection of furniture, artworks, textiles, costumes, and jewelry from China, Myanmar, Ethiopia, Mongolia, Japan, India, and other destinations. Every piece has a story, and the passionate, well-traveled staff members are only too keen to divulge their origins.

**Zg Gallery**, 300 West Superior Street, tel: 312-654-9900, www.zggallery.com. This relative newcomer to the River North art scene focuses on emerging contemporary artists, with an unusually high number of installations.

**Zygman Voss**, 222 West Superior, tel: 312-787-3300, www.zygmanvoss.com. Unlike its River North peers, this traditional gallery focuses on the masters of the last three centuries, including Renoir, Whistler, Picasso, Toulouse-Lautrec, Dalí, and Miró.

## Bookstores

**57th Street Bookstore**, 1301 East 57th Street, tel: 773-684-1300. Seminary Co-op's *(see below)* nonacademic sibling with mainstream fiction and nonfiction titles that have an alternative flavor.

**Barbara's Bookstores**, 1218 South Halsted Street, tel: 312-413-2665. An intelligent aura pervades this intimate store, which has a well-conceived collection of quality and alternative fiction and stages excellent author nights; Margaret Atwood and David Sedaris have chosen Barbara's as the place to meet and mingle with their readers. There's another small Barbara's in Macy's on State Street *(see below)* and also in Sears Tower.

**Barnes & Noble**, 1130 North State Street, tel: 312-280-8155, www.barnesandnoble.com. There's plenty of space to browse at this two-level Gold Coast flagship store, which also has a Starbucks. Farther north in Lincoln Park there's another branch at 659 West Diversey Avenue (tel: 773-871-9004) and one in Lakeview at 1441 West Webster Avenue (tel: 773-871-3610).

**Borders**, 150 North State Street, tel: 312-606-0750; 4718 North Broadway Avenue, tel: 773-334-7338; 830 North Michigan Avenue, tel: 312-573-0564; 2817 North Clark Street; tel: 773-935-3909; 755 West North Avenue; tel: 312-266-8060. The State Street flagship store has four floors stocked with over 180,000 books, CDs, DVDs, reference material, stationery supplies, and a coffee shop that hosts frequent readings and musical performances.

**Myopic Books**, 1564 North Milwaukee Avenue, tel: 773-862-4882. Wicker Park denizens flock here to peruse an epic collection of used books, ranging from classic and contemporary fiction to history, psychology, art, travel, and social sciences. With a coffee shop, readings, chess nights, and a Sunday poetry series, it has become a Wicker Park cultural institution.

**The Book Cellar**, 4736 North Lincoln Avenue, tel: 773-293-2665. A North Side neighborhood bookstore with a strong emphasis on first-time and local authors. Coffee and wine are served. Check the schedule for book clubs, readings, and special events.

**Unabridged Books**, 3251 North Broadway, tel: 773-883-9119. Independent Lakeview bookstore with a focus on gay and lesbian titles and a thoughtful selection of general-interest titles.
**Seminary Co-op**, 5757 South University Avenue, tel: 773-752-4381. Frequently lauded as one of the best academic bookstores in the country, indeed the world, featuring over 100,000 titles across the humanities and social sciences.

## Department Stores

**Bloomingdale's**, 900 North Michigan Avenue, tel: 312-440-4460; 600 North Wabash Avenue, tel: 312-324-7500. There are six levels of fashion, cosmetics, and accessories at the Michigan Avenue flagship store. Bloomingdale's upscale home furnishings store on North Wabash is housed in the former Medinah Temple, an Islamic Revival-style landmark.
**Lord & Taylor**, 835 North Michigan Avenue, tel: 312-787-7400. You will find affordable and stylish fashions for men, women, and children at this department store in the Water Tower Place shopping mall.
**Macy's**, 111 State Street, tel: 312-781-1000; 836 North Michigan Avenue, tel: 312-335-7700. Formerly Marshall Field's – a bastion of Midwest consumer traditionalism – Macy's on State is the second-largest department store in the country, with men's and women's designer boutiques, three floors of furniture including a French "flea market," every cosmetics brand imaginable, gourmet eateries, and more.
**Neiman Marcus**, 737 North Michigan Avenue, tel: 312-642-5900. Tony designer merchandise reigns at this high-end retailer.
**Nordstrom**, 55 East Grand Avenue, tel: 312-464-1515. A prime fashion retailer with upscale apparel, shoes, and accessories for men, women, and children.
**Saks Fifth Avenue**, 700 North Michigan Avenue, tel: 312-944-6500. The store has high-end designer labels as well as a more affordable collection of wearable men's and women's fashions. The store is known for its cosmetics department.

## Food and Drink

**Garrett Popcorn Shop**, 670 North Michigan Avenue, tel: 312-944-2630. Long lines and gruff service are the sacrifice you make for what is reputed to be the best popcorn in the city. Butter, caramel, and cheese varieties are served in standard bags and large holiday tins that can be shipped.
**Giselle's**, 1967 North Halsted Street, tel: 312-266-7880. Family-run, French-style deli with a hearty selection of prepared meats dressed in unusual sauces as well as vegetarian sandwich and salad offerings, including zingy Asian slaw. Save room for the fudge swirl chocolate tart.
**Fox and Obel Food Market**, 401 East Illinois Street, tel: 312-410-7301. This upscale deli, café, and market encompasses a prime butcher shop that ages its beef, a fish market, a specialty cheese shop with exotic cheeses, and an artisan bakery. You can sample pizza, rotisserie chicken, ciabatta sandwiches, and soups at the adjoining café.
**Southport Grocery and Café**, 3552 North Southport Avenue, tel: 773-665-0101. This smart Lakeview café serves indulgent, modern American comfort food. An adjoining deli stocks Mediterranean and ethnic delicacies, including cheese, bread, olives, tapenade, chocolate, cakes, pasta, and a small but considered selection of wine.
**The Fudge Pot**, 1532 North Wells Street, tel: 312-943-1777. An Old Town institution since 1963, the shop serves a mouth-watering array of chocolate-coated strawberries, slabs of fudge, taffy apples, and chocolate-molded Ferraris and baseball players. Try the signature Toodle: chocolate, caramel, and pecans.
**The Spice House**, 1512 North Wells Street, tel: 312-274-0378. This overwhelmingly aromatic shop has every conceivable spice and attractive gift packages.
**Trotters to Go**, 1337 West Fullerton Avenue, tel: 773-868-6510. Managed by one of Chicago's best restaurants, this gourmet deli has picnic food, gifts, wine, and tasty lunch items such as Israeli couscous with dried cherries and Darjeeling-cured salmon sandwiches.
**Whole Foods Market**, 30 West Huron Street, tel: 312-932-9600. The world's leading organic food retailer has stores all over Chicago stocking a bewildering array of exotic fruits, vegetables, breads, cheeses, ethnic foods, healthy deli meals, a salad and fruit bar, herbs, cereals, juices, hormone-free fish and meat, and wine. Table seating in each store allows you to buy and dine on the premises.

## Women's Clothing

**Active Endeavours**, 838 West Armitage Avenue, tel: 773.281-2002. This shop on the Halsted/Armitage boutique corridor has stylish and wearable fashions from big-name designers such as Paul & Joe and Ana Sui as well as more affordable, idiosyncratic apparel from up-and-coming designers.
**Anthropology**, 1120 North State Street, tel: 312-255-1848. Expect youthfully feminine attire from a range of designers at this shop, which has racks of fashion-conscious prints, lace, puffs, and frills plus sporty casual wear, lingerie, and accessories.
**Charlotte Russe**, 10 South State Street, tel: 312-726-4205. This new flagship store – the first downtown outlet for this suburban fixture – has flirtatiously skimpy fashions with plenty of bold prints, baby doll swings, and tight denim.

**Daffodil Hill**, 1659 North Damen Avenue, tel: 773-489-0101. The fresh seasonal lines from an eclectic mix of high-fashion brands include Michael Stars, Sweet Pea, and Saint Grace, all with a vintage chic emphasis.

**Eliana Lily**, 1628 North Wells Street, tel: 312-337-0999. This innovative boutique stocks a selection of contemporary and classic apparel. In the Re-Style department, Eliana will take your passé old clothes and revamp them into a one-of-a-kind piece.

**Krista K**, 3458 North Southport Avenue, tel: 773-248-1967. This Lakeview boutique features sophisticated clothing from Marc Jacobs and Robert Rodriguez, jewelry by Lana, and purses by Gustto and Botkier. Krista K is also known for its picks of cutting-edge denim designers such as Aristocrat and William Rast.

**Jake**, 3740 North Southport Avenue, tel: 773-929-5253. This luxury boutique on the booming Southport corridor has perfectly tailored suits and cocktail dresses plus exclusive denim lines for the style-oriented North Sider with lots of disposable income.

**The Denim Lounge**, 2004 West Roscoe Street, tel: 773-935-2820. Serfontaine, True Religion, Hudson, and Rock & Republic are just some of the hyped jean brands represented at this friendly Roscoe Village jean store.

**True Religion**, 2202 North Halsted Street, tel: 773-281-9590. Come here for the classic rock-and-roll, must-have jean brand designed by LA's husband and wife fashion team Jeffrey and Kym Lubell, plus a selection of classic Americana T-shirts, sweaters, and jackets.

## Men's Clothing

**Cole Haan**, 673 North Michigan Avenue, tel: 312-642-8995. The store is known for its stylish shoe collection, owing to its recent acquisition by Nike. There is also a small but discriminating collection of classic cut attire.

**Ermenegildo Zegna**, 645 North Michigan Avenue, tel: 312-587-9660. The finest cashmere, lamb's wool, and mohair, woven in the Zegna textile mill in Italy, are used in this collection of fine sweaters and immaculately tailored suits. Zegna Sport is the more casual sports line.

**Paul Stuart**, 875 North Michigan Avenue, tel: 312-640-2650. Situated in the John Hancock Building, this exclusive store has a preppy but debonair line of luxury suits and slick sportswear and offers exceptional customer service.

**Lacoste**, 835 North Michigan Avenue, tel: 312-951-1300. The polo shirt is the backbone of this classically preppy line of cashmere knits, vintage blazers, and comfortable footwear.

**Mark Shale**, 900 North Michigan Avenue, tel: 312-440-0720. This slick store is primarily known for a conservative line of professional apparel but also has laid-back sportswear from a plethora of established designers. A large collection of ready-made suits are available from Tommy Bahama, Ermenegildo Zegna, and Joseph Abboud.

**Shirts on Sheffied**, 2807 North Sheffield Avenue, tel: 773-868-1600. This Lakeview men's boutique has high-quality original-design shirts (only six of each style are available) at reasonable prices. This is one of the only Chicago retailers of Lee Allison's sometimes eccentric but always original neckties.

**Syd Jerome**, 2 North LaSalle Street, tel: 312-346-0333. Syd Jerome suits up the financial district's big players in luxurious custom designs. Italian suits, cashmere sweaters, and ties are also available from elite designers Armani, Zegna, and Canali.

## Music

**Coconuts Music & Movies**, 959 West Diversey Parkway, tel: 773-477-1014. A knowledgeable staff and relaxed atmosphere make this competitively priced store one of the most appealing of the national chains.

**Dusty Groove America**, 1120 North Ashland Avenue, tel: 773-342-5800. Classic and contemporary jazz, funk, and soul are available on CDs and vinyl. The in-store computer lets you search the extensive database. Also on sale are vintage comic books and used DVDs and novels.

**Groove Distribution**, 1164 North Milwaukee Avenue, tel: 773-435-0250. There's an insider feel to this warehouse stacked with CDs and vinyl. The store is usually packed with local DJs. Listening stations allow you to sample before you commit.

**Jazz Record Mart**, 27 East Illinois Street, tel: 312-222-1467. A 1960s time warp, the Mart stocks an unparalleled inventory of jazz and blues on CD and vinyl. There are occasional live performances by local artists.

**Laurie's Planet of Sound**, 4639 North Lincoln Avenue, tel: 773-271-3569. Tucked away in Lincoln Square is this musical Holy Grail, with an eclectic collection of inexpensive, rare CDs, vinyl, videos, and books as well as memorabilia and souvenirs.

**Reckless Records**, 3161 North Broadway Street, tel: 773-404-5080. Fighting iTunes domination, Reckless guides its patrons to commendable choices with sample booths and descriptions of the "if you like this, then you'll like that" variety. Specializing in indie and alternative, the store cultivates a relaxed aura that is conducive to browsing and appreciating.

**Vintage Vinyl Records**, 925 Davis Street, Evanston, tel: 847-328-2899. It's worth a trip north to Evanston to this shrine of musical obscurity, where rare recordings and original albums from legendary artists such as the Beatles, Janis Joplin, Johnny Cash, and Pink Floyd are stacked against a discriminating modern collection, including The Coral and White Stripes.

# ACTIVITIES

## THE ARTS, NIGHTLIFE, EVENTS, TOURS AND SPORTS

When it comes to nightlife, Chicago has some serious mojo. And we're not just talking about the city's legendary blues clubs, though you should definitely drop by for a guitar lick or two. Jazz or rock? Classical or country? Brewpub, wine bar, or cocktail lounge? Whatever your taste in music (or liquor), the Windy City has a venue to suit your needs. And much the same can be said about theater and sports. Looking for a party? The Chicago Blues Festival and Taste of Chicago are two of the biggest in the country.

### THE ARTS

#### Theater

**Briar Street Theater**, 3133 North Halsted Street, tel: 773-348-4000, www.blueman.com. The multisensory theatrical experience featuring three bald, blue men continues its long run at Lakeview's Briar Theater.

**Cadillac Palace Theatre**, 151 West Randolph Street, tel: 312-902-1400, www.cadillac-palace.com. This opulent theater steeped in Chicago history was restored to its former vaudeville glory in 1999, following stints as a rock venue and a movie theater. Broadway shows range from *The Color Purple* to *Dirty Dancing*.

**Chicago Theatre**, 175 North State Street, tel: 312-462-6300, www.chicagotheatre.com. The iconic, six-story, vertical C-H-I-C-A-G-O sign has become synonymous with the city's Theatre District. Restored in 1886, dripping with gold and marble (the majestic lobby was modeled after Versailles), the theater now operates as a concert and performance venue, having recently played host to Oasis, Beck, the Buena Vista Social Club, and David Letterman.

**Chopin Theater**, 1543 West Division Street, tel: 773-278-1500, www.chopintheater.com. The antithesis of commercial art, this irreverent Wicker Park theater surprises, shocks, challenges, and inspires with visionary productions that push the boundaries of contemporary theater.

**Ford Center for the Performing Arts/Oriental Theater**, 24 West Randolph Street, tel: 312-977-1700. Part of the Broadway in Chicago theater group (www.broadwayinchicago.com), the Oriental Theater has been exquisitely restored. Its soaring domed ceiling and marble pillars exude 1920s glamour. Blockbuster, family-oriented shows, such as *Wicked*, dominate the season.

**Goodman Theatre**, 170 North Dearborn Street, tel: 312-443-3800, www.goodmantheatre.org. This nonprofit theater produces a dynamic, diverse program that ranges from Shakespeare to Arthur Miller and David Mamet. The theater also hosts the Latin American Theater Festival.

**LiveBait Theater**, 3914 North Clark Street, tel: 773-871-1212, http://livebaittheater.org. This innovative and visually stimulating theater ensemble is composed of up-and-coming actors that focus on irreverent, emotionally engaging themes.

**Navy Pier**, 600 East Grand Avenue, tel: 312-595-5022, www.navypier.com. The Pier's Skyline stage focuses on performance art. Previous performances have included the Cirque Shanghai acrobat troupe, while the Chicago Shakespeare Theatre (www.chicagoshakes.com) provides more cerebral fare with classic and modern Bard renditions that have included an acclaimed Second City collaborative staging of *Romeo and Juliet*.

**Red Orchid Theatre**, 1531 North Wells Street, tel: 773-310-7794, www.aredorchidtheatre.org. Set in Old Town, this tiny venue ripples with an uncompromising repertoire of offbeat works.

**Royal George Theatre**, 1641 North Halsted Avenue, tel: 312-988-9000, www.theroyalgeorgetheatre.com. With a prime Lincoln Park location, this is one of the most popular midsized venues, with a crowd-pleasing lineup of enjoyable, if rather safe, shows.

**Steppenwolf Theatre Company**, 1650 North Halsted Avenue, tel: 312-335-1650, www.steppenwolf.org. This theater company of international renown produces edgier works than its midsized peers, in an intimate and engaging setting. The outstanding ensemble includes John Malkovich and Joan Allen. If you call at 11am, day-of-performance tickets are available for $20.

**Theatre Building Chicago**, 1225 West Belmont Avenue, tel: 773-327-5252, www.theatrebuildingchicago.org. A neighborhood institution that aims to cultivate grassroots talent. Musicals are the primary genre, but it's also an upbeat venue for seasonal classics, comedies, and sketch shows.

**TimeLine Theatre Company**, 615 West Wellington, tel: 773-281-8463, www.timelinetheatre.com. This small, highly talented North Side theater company stages engaging classic American plays with socially aware themes.

**Victory Gardens**, 2257 North Lincoln Avenue, tel: 773-871-3000, www.victorygardens.org. With an emphasis on nurturing Chicago writers and actors, this innovative Tony-Award-winning theater focuses primarily on world premieres.

## Comedy and Stand-up

Chicago is renowned for its improvisational comedy, and on any given night there are scores of original and engaging improv and sketch performances. Routines are often absurd and frequently peppered with culturally specific humor that may elude many foreign visitors.

**Comedy Sportz**, Chicago Center for the Performing Arts, 777 North Green Street, tel: 312-733-6000, www.comedysportzchicago.com. Dynamic game-based improv that may not have the consistent comic agility of Second City but is hugely entertaining thanks to an infectious energy and lighthearted atmosphere appealing to families and older crowds. Weekend shows only at 6pm and 10pm.

**Second City,** 1616 North Wells Street, tel: 312-337-3992, www.secondcity.com. This is the hallowed stage that launched the careers of Bill Murray, Mike Myers, and John Belushi and spawned the seminal *Saturday Night Live* show. The company still specializes in sharp sketch comedy aimed at the political establishment and pop culture.

**Playground Theater**, 3209 North Halsted Street, tel: 773-871-3793, www.the-playground.com. A 14-member ensemble cast forms this nonprofit improv and stand-up theater in Lakeview.

**Annoyance Theatre**, 4830 North Broadway, tel: 773-561-4655, www.annoyanceproductions.com. A relaxed Uptown bar/lounge that runs the gamut of late-night burlesque, comedy, cabaret, and improv.

## Film

Every Tuesday night in July and August, Grant Park hosts the Movies in the Park series, where Chicagoans pack a picnic and sit on blankets under the stars for movie classics. From June through September, the Chicago Park District also shows more than 150 new releases and classics in neighborhood parks throughout the city. For more information, visit www.chicagoparkdistrict.com.

**600 North Michigan**, 600 North Michigan Avenue, tel: 312-255-9340. Old school, somewhat threadbare theater showing mainstream movies.

**Davis Theater**, 4614 N Lincoln Avenue, tel: 773-784-0893, www.davistheater.com. Charming old theater in Lincoln Square featuring first-run movies with occasional forays into classics, foreign, and art house flicks.

**Gene Siskel Film Center**, 164 North State Street, tel: 312-846-2800. Named after the late film critic, the Art Institute's Film Center presents a dynamic lineup of independent, classic, and foreign features.

**Landmark's Century Cinema**, 2828 North Clark Street, tel: 773-509-4949. State-of-the-art projection technology is employed to showcase world-class foreign and independent movies at this Lakeview venue.

**Music Box Theatre**, 3733 North Southport Avenue, tel: 773-871-6604. A beloved city institution that first opened its doors in the North Side neighborhood of Lakeview in 1929, this large vintage theater features foreign, classic, and independent movies and an organist that plays before each performance.

**Pipers Alley**, 1608 North Wells Street, tel: 312-642-7500. Choice picks of mainstream and indie productions at this small but high-tech Old Town theater.

**River East 21**, 322 East Illinois Street, tel: 312-596-0333. River North behemoth with 21 screens showcasing Hollywood blockbusters; comfortable seating and superlative sound and projection.

**Webster Place**, 1471 West Webster Street, tel: 800-326-3264. Blockbusters and occasional independent and foreign movies form the lineup at this Lincoln Park multiplex.

## Classical Music and Opera

**Chicago Opera Theater**, 205 East Randolph Drive, tel: 312-334-7777, www.harristheaterchicago.org. With a focus on engendering mass appeal and nurturing new talent from across the US, this talented repertory performs 17th-, 18th-, 19-, and 20th-century opera classics such as Mozart's *Don Giovanni* and Handel's *Orlando*. The company places an emphasis on American composers and has presented performances in English. Chicago's opera buffs delight in the opera season's unusual longevity; the Opera Theater's season follows the Lyric Opera of Chicago's spring finale.

**Chicago Symphony Orchestra**, Orchestra Hall, 220 South Michigan Avenue, tel: 312-294-3000, www.cso.org. Founded in 1891, this is one of the world's leading and oldest orchestras. The season runs from September through May, with many performances selling out weeks in advance. The dazzling Orchestra Hall, part of Symphony Center, was designed by Daniel H. Burnham and completed in 1904.

**Grant Park Symphony Orchestra**, Jay Pritzker Pavilion, Millennium Park, tel: 312-742-1168, www.millenniumpark.org. Frank Gehry designed this state-of-the-art music pavilion with an open-air acoustical canopy for the resident Grant Park Symphony Orchestra, which gives free concerts throughout summer.

**Lyric Opera of Chicago**, 20 North Wacker Drive, tel: 312-332-2244, www.lyricopera.org. Contemporary works such as *The Great Gatsby* and *Doctor Atomic* complement the customary operatic repertoire, including recent performances of *Julius Caesar, La Bohème, La Traviata,* and *The Barber of Seville*. The Opera House's stunning Art Nouveaux interior was magnificently restored in 1996.

## Blues

**Blue Chicago**, 736 North Clark Street, tel: 312-642-6261, www.bluechicago.com. This is one of the more tourist-oriented venues, with exposed brick walls, booth seating, and a 1920s ambience. Regulars, including Willie Kent, Big Time Sarah, and Shirley Johnson, perform to an upbeat, dancing crowd. The club's sibling, Blue Chicago on Clark (536 North Clark Street, tel: 312-661-0100), showcases female jazz artists. The $8 weekday/$10 weekend cover is good for entry to both clubs.

**B.L.U.E.S.**, 2519 North Halsted Street, tel: 773-528-1012, www.chicagobluesbar.com. Arrive early at this ebullient blues club where the informed crowd revels in high-caliber performances by the likes of Jimmy Burns, J.W. Williams, and Nellie "Tiger" Travis.

**Buddy Guy's Legends**, 754 South Wabash Avenue, tel: 312-427-0333, www.buddyguys.com. Despite persistent rumors of relocation (call ahead), this Chicago institution festooned with memorabilia – Buddy Guy's Grammys, Eric Clapton's guitar, and wall-to-wall photographs – packs in blues devotees from across the country with a myriad of artists. Considered one of the best blues venues in the nation, Van Morrison, Bo Diddley, and John Mayer have all performed here, and Buddy Guy himself plays to sold-out crowds every January.

**House of Blues**, 329 North Dearborn Avenue, tel: 312-923-2000, www.hob.com. House of Blues is somewhat of a misnomer for this pricey and flamboyant concert venue on the river beneath Marina City, which plays host to legendary jazz, rap, alternative, funk, and blues artists from Al Green to Crowded House as well as emerging bands and local talent. The Sunday gospel brunch is popular.

**Kingston Mines**, 2548 North Halsted Street, tel: 773-477-4646, www.kingstonmines.com. Celebrating its 40th anniversary in 2008, this is one of the largest and most popular blues clubs in the city, with established artists playing two stages simultaneously. The long communal tables and smoky eats, courtesy of Doc's Ribs Joint, add to the festive vibe. Book tickets in advance or arrive early. Weekday cover is $12, weekend cover $15.

**Smoke Daddy**, 1804 West Division Street, tel: 773-772-6656, www.thesmokedaddy.com. Famed hickory-, cherry-, and apple-smoked ribs and pulled meat are devoured by locals and tourists in this earthy bar with a sultry soundtrack of nightly blues performed on a tiny stage.

**Underground Wonder Bar**, 10 East Walton Street, tel: 312-266-7761, www.undergroundwonderbar.com. This intimate Gold Coast venue was opened by musician Lonie Walker in the late 1980s and is host to electric blues and jazz artists playing nightly from 8pm. There are occasional forays into acoustic rock, pop, funk, and reggae, with artists such as Steve Winwood performing to a 30-something, laid-back audience.

## Jazz

**Andy's**, 11 East Hubbard Street, tel: 312-642-6805, www.andysjazzclub.com. One of the most active jazz haunts in the city, with lunchtime, late afternoon, and nightly live performances that run the gamut of mainstream, traditional, modern, and bebop. Previous performers include legends Marcus Belgrave and Lonnie Smith.

**Backroom**, 1007 North Rush Street, tel: 312-751-2433. Since it opened in the 1960s, this upscale jazz bar with intimate seating at candlelit tables has taken its music seriously, with a varied lineup of traditional and contemporary jazz as well as blues, R&B, and soul.

**Checkerboard Lounge**, 5201 South Harper, tel: 773-684-1471. Despite its relocation to Hyde Park from the South Side, this earthy bar continues to deliver an authentic jazz and blues experience with up-and-coming and legendary musicians performing to a mix of University of Chicago students, locals, and die-hard jazz aficionados.

**Cornelia's**, 750 West Cornelia Avenue, tel: 773-248-8333. Expect sultry dinner jazz every night at 8pm from regulars Paul Marinaro (Mondays), Buddy

Charles (Wednesdays) and Ginger Tam (Fridays) at this inviting Mediterranean/French restaurant in Lakeview. The vodka infusions are potent.

**Cuatro**, 2030 South Wabash Avenue, tel: 312-842-8856, www.cuatro-chicago.com. Run by four siblings, this flashy Latin restaurant and bar features live traditional jazz on Tuesdays and live Latin jazz on Fridays. There is a bossa nova brunch on Sunday.

**Empty Bottle**, 1035 North Western Avenue, tel: 773-276-3600, www.emptybottle.com. The Wednesday night jazz series featuring vanguard and emerging performers of traditional, improvised, and free jazz draws a devout crowd. In spring the club hosts the highly acclaimed Empty Bottle Festival of Jazz.

**Green Dolphin Street**, 2200 North Ashland, tel: 773-395-0066, www.jazzitup.com. This sophisticated wood-paneled, velvet-draped restaurant and jazz club has high-quality live music ranging from bebop to Latin jazz every night except Monday.

**Green Mill**, 4802 North Broadway, tel: 773-878-5552. The legendary former haunt of Al Capone still bristles with a speakeasy vibe. The Green Mill's history and ambience alone make it worth the trek to Uptown. The lineup features Dixieland, progressive, and bebop.

**M Lounge**, 1520 South Wabash Avenue, tel: 312-447-0201, www.mloungechicago.com. An upscale, South Loop martini bar with live jazz on Tuesday and Wednesday nights. No cover, two drink minimum.

## Rock

**Aragon Ballroom**, 1106 West Lawrence Avenue, tel: 773-561-9500, www.aragon.com. Built in 1926 to mimic the whimsical style of a Spanish ballroom, this venue presents big-name rock, indie, and alternative bands, including acts such as Interpol, the Pixies, White Stripes, Flaming Lips, and Cold War Kids.

**Auditorium Theatre**, 50 East Congress Parkway, tel: 312-922-2110, www.auditoriumtheatre.org. Described by Frank Lloyd Wright as "The greatest room for music and opera in the world – bar none," this 1889 landmark theater with 24-karat gold leaf ceiling arches was designed by Louis Sullivan. Tori Amos, White Stripes, and Ani DiFranco have all performed here.

**Elbo Room**, 2871 North Lincoln Avenue, tel: 773-549-5549, www.elboroomchicago.com. This Lakeview spot is popular with a young weekend crowd that dances to a repertoire of reggae, house, alternative, and rock. The upstairs bar has a mellow social scene. Low-priced tickets ensure a diverse party atmosphere.

**Hideout**, 1354 West Wabansia Avenue, tel: 773-227-4433, www.hideoutchicago.com. The best dive bar in town, where everyone is an aspiring artist. The big-name lineup of primarily rock and indie bands packs in capacity crowds (100 people).

**Hothouse**, 31 East Balbo Avenue, tel: 312-362-9707, www.hothouse.net. This vibrant nonprofit cultural center showcases an eclectic program of world music in a plush, artsy setting with a welcoming ambience. At the time of this writing, the Hot House was preparing to move from its South Loop location. Check the website for further details.

**Metro**, 3730 North Clark Street, tel: 773-549-0203, www.metrochicago.com. This former movie theater is the best place in the city to see alternative bands. Iconic figures such as Nirvana, Prince, Bob Dylan, James Brown, and REM have all played this small, intimate venue, which has a raucous mosh pit, depending on whose playing. The after-hours scene continues downstairs in the Smart Bar, where DJs spin house and dance music for an appreciative crowd.

**Old Town School of Folk Music**, 4544 North Lincoln Avenue, tel: 773-728-6000, www.oldtownschool.org. Situated in a former Lincoln Square library, this renowned music school and concert hall is the neighborhood's cultural hub. A variety of world music styles, from Afrofolk to flamenco, predominates with Brazilian artist Ceú and the Ivory Coast's Dobet Gnahoré having performed in the footsteps of legends such as Joni Mitchell.

**Park West**, 322 West Armitage Avenue, tel: 773-929-1322, www.jamusa.com/parkwest. Built as a movie theater in the 1920s, Park West still has a classic aura, with glittering disco balls and intimate candlelit tables grouped in a semicircle around the main stage. Jamie Cullum, The Eels, Zero 7, and Bebel Gilberto are among the performers who have benefited from the superlative acoustics.

**Riviera**, 4746 North Racine Avenue, tel: 773-275-6800. With an air of faded glory, the 2,500-seat Riviera attracts less commercial bands than its small and midsized counterparts, Metro and Vic.

**Schubas**, 3159 North Southport Avenue, tel: 773-525-2508, www.schubas.com. This bar-restaurant-nightclub on the Southport strip is recognized for its discriminating lineup of local and international breakthrough bands. The relaxed bar scene and friendly, diverse crowd make for a great night's entertainment regardless of who is playing. The adjoining Harmony Grill serves decent regional American dishes.

**Vic Theatre**, 3145 North Sheffield Avenue, tel: 773-472-0449, www.victheatre.com. Up-and-coming rock, indie, and alternative bands play Lakeview's Vic, which has a balcony for more relaxed viewing away from the sticky floor and raw, smoky atmosphere.

## Dance

**Athenaeum Theatre**, 2936 North Southport Avenue, tel: 312-902-1500, www.athenaeumtheatre.com. The annual dance slam, in which the audience votes for the best performance out of 20 up-and-coming

Chicagoland dance troupes, is the Athenaeum's season highlight.

**Auditorium Theatre**, 50 East Congress Parkway, tel: 312-922-2110, www.auditoriumtheatre.org. Founded in 1952, the sublime Joffrey Ballet is one of the world's leading repertory companies. The May to October season is staged here with classics such as *Giselle* and *The Nutcracker* (December) in addition to contemporary choreography.

**Columbia College Dance Center**, 1306 South Michigan Avenue, tel: 312-344-8300, www2.colum.edu. Columbia Dance School presents bold and innovative performances by emerging Chicago-based contemporary dance companies as well as playing host to international dance festivals.

**Harris Theatre**, 205 East Randolph Drive, tel: 312-334-7777, www.harristheatrechicago.org. Chicago's Hubbard Street Dance is renowned as one of the most original and dynamic contemporary dance groups in the world. The group usually performs twice a year at this sleek, modern theater in Millennium Park. Highly recommended.

**Millennium Park**, Pritzker Pavilion, 205 East Randolph Street, tel: 312-742-7638, www.grantparkmusicfestival.com. All summer long, Grant Park hosts a free performance series featuring classical and contemporary dance. It's a great opportunity to see class acts such as the Joffrey Ballet and Hubbard Street Dance in a stirring setting, without the wallet-hemorrhaging prices.

**Ravinia**, 418 Sheridan Road, Highland Park, tel: 847-266-5100, www.ravinia.org. This is a quintessential Chicago experience. Pack a picnic, take the Metra north, and pitch a blanket on the hallowed lawn of Ravinia. This four-month festival (May–September) has a legacy of scintillating dance performances. Each season brings a myriad of emerging and established choreography from the Luna Negra Dance Theater, Hubbard Street Dance, and the Chicago Tap Theater. Each year Ravinia showcases the Ruth Page Festival of Dance.

## NIGHTLIFE

### Nightclubs

**Berlin**, 954 West Belmont Avenue, tel: 773-348-4975, www.berlinchicago.com. An inclusive vibe reigns at this dark 1980s-style space with two bars and a spatially challenging dance floor. The gender bending lineup of theme nights – Prince Night, Madonna Madness, Women's Obsession Party – feature everything from drag queens to tropical dancers. Music runs the gamut of pop, alternative, and disco.

**Club 720**, 720 North Wells Street, tel: 312-397-0600, www.720chicago.com. This stylish mega-club showcases big-name and local DJs who play different musical genres in five separate areas: salsa, pop, jazz, rock, alternative, dance, and Latin house. The Cityscape Show Lounge has dazzling skyline views, while the Catacombs is a hardcore dance space.

**Crobar**, 1543 North Kingsbury Street, tel: 312-266-1900, www.crobar.com. This gigantic warehouse is on every serious clubber's agenda. The impressive sound and spectacular light displays draw a much-hyped lineup of international DJs.

**Hydrate**, 3458 North Halsted Street, tel: 773-975-9244, www.hydratechicago.com. This is an upbeat club that doesn't take itself too seriously. Expect a young, mixed crowd in early evening and a largely gay crowd after midnight. The special drink nights are extremely popular, as are the Wednesday night drag shows. Nightly DJs spin retro, dance, and Latin house. There is a $5 cover before midnight.

**Liar's Club**, 1665 West Fullerton Avenue, tel: 773-665-1110. A boho vibe prevails at this long-standing North Side haunt, where underground music and cheap liquor keep the 30-something regulars swaying on the dance floor. Pool tables and sofas on the second floor provide a comfortable retreat. $5 cover.

**Nacional 27**, 325 West Huron Street, tel: 312-664-2727, www.nacional27.net. After the kitchen closes, this slick Miami-style restaurant and nightclub is transformed into a pulsating Latin dance club, where dancers take to the floor for seductive meringue and salsa. The cover is a steep $15 unless you dine in the restaurant before 10pm (reservations essential).

**Neo**, 2350 North Clark Street, tel: 773-528-2622, www.neo-chicago.com. A welcome aberration in the yuppie enclave of Lincoln Park, this dark and moody gothic nightclub at the end of an alley is one of Chicago's oldest clubs. The music changes from industrial to punk to new wave, but the perpetually black-clad crowd stays the same. Reasonable drink prices and covers.

**Smart Bar**, 3730 North Clark Street, tel: 773-549-0203, www.metrochicago.com. Metro's *(see above)* late night subterranean bar features local DJs and international imports spinning funk, alternative, dance, and industrial. The club opens at 10pm.

**Sound-Bar**, 226 West Ontario Street, tel: 312-787-4480, www.sound-bar.com. This pricey downtown club may have lost its edge but still seduces hardcore dancers with an impressive roster of DJs spinning techno and trance.

**Spy Bar**, 646 North Franklin Street, tel: 312-587-8779, www.spybarchicago.com. Smaller than its peers, this industrial-style River North club beneath the El tracks has exposed brick, velvet lounge seating, and a small dance floor that stays packed until early morning with primo DJs playing techno, house, and hip-hop.

## Gay Scene

The Lakeview enclave known as Boys Town is the epicenter of Chicago's gay community. It encompasses the area east of Halsted Street to the lakefront and north of Belmont Avenue to Grace Street. Most of the gay bars, clubs, and restaurants are to be found at the intersection of Halsted and Roscoe streets. In recent years, the scene has spread north to the former Swedish neighborhood of Andersonville, which begins at the nexus of North Clark Street and Foster Avenue and funnels north to Bryn Mauer Avenue.

As the largest metropolis in the Midwest, it's not surprising that Chicago has long been the region's gay capital, passing antidiscrimination legislation in the spirit of inclusiveness. Never one to miss out on a PR opportunity, Mayor Daley has actively sought gay-friendly credentials. He welcomed the 2006 Gay Games to Chicago with a speech at Soldier Field declaring that gay people "have made what Chicago is all about." In 2004, Daley stated that he had "no problem" issuing marriage licenses to same-sex couples and reiterated his support of gay marriage equality.

The city's flamboyant gay festivals, most notably the Pride Festival (last weekend in June) and Northalsted Market Days (second weekend in August) are staged on a grand scale.

### *Resources*

The following free press weeklies (available in coffee shops and bars) and websites provide listings and information on Chicago's gay and lesbian scene, including festivals, parties, concerts, clubs, and restaurants.
*Chicago Free Press* (wwww.chicagofreepress.com)
*Boi Chicago* (www.boimagazine.com)
*Windy City Times* (wwww.outlineschicaco.com)
www.boystownchicago.com
www.chicagopride.com
www.outinchicago.com

### *Gay and Lesbian Bars and Nightclubs*

**Big Chicks**, 5024 North Sheridan Road, tel: 773-728-5511, www.bigchicks.com. Owner Michelle Fire gives out free drinks and food (Sunday 4.30pm) and brings in a mixed crowd, despite the ostensible gay bar status, for an assortment of theme nights. With a snug lounge area, free Wi-Fi, a dance floor on weekends, pool table, darts, and a beer garden, it's a great place to hang out and meet people.
**Charlie's**, 3726 North Broadway, tel: 773-871-8887, www.charlieschicago.com. A cowboy theme permeates this country bar, which packs in the leather-clad masses cheek by jowl. There is line-dancing on Mondays and Wednesdays at 7.30pm.
**Crew Bar**, 4804 North Broadway, tel: 773-784-2739, www.worldsgreatestbar.com. This gay sports bar has sleek steel and granite decor, sports memorabilia, and 16 plasma TVs showing college and professional games. Music plays later in the evening. More than 40 beers are served.
**Kit Kat Lounge and Supper Club**, 3700 North Halsted Street, tel: 773-525-1111, www.kitkatchicago.com. There's a hip, exotic atmosphere at this supper club, with exposed brick, white leather booths, and a smattering of leopard skin. The entertainment features drag artists who camp it up with impersonations of gay icons of the 1940s and 50s.
**Lucky Horseshoe Lounge**, 3169 North Halsted Street, tel: 773-404-3169. In a prime location on the Halsted strip, this closet-sized bar is always lively – night and day. There are male dancers nightly until the early hours.
**Roscoe's**, 3356 North Halsted Street, tel: 773-281-3355, www.roscoes.com. This Boys Town gay bar has a youthful, welcoming vibe and a prime people-watching patio in summer. Labyrinthine rooms provide changes of scene and ambience, with a pool table, video screens, a fireplace, and a large, tear-it-up dance floor. Cover on Saturdays.
**Sofo**, 4923 North Clark Street, tel: 773-784-7636, www.sofobar.com. Sofo, or South-of-Foster Avenue, denotes this newcomer's location south of Andersonville and north of Uptown. A friendly, down-to-earth gay bar, it's as welcoming to dogs as it is to people and is characteristic of this area's changing face. The warmly decorated bar features paintings by local artists, and the TVs, pool tables, and reams of gay magazines and newspapers encourage socializing.

# EVENTS

Listings and advertisements for upcoming events can be found in *The Chicago Reader, New City, Time Out Chicago Magazine, Chicago Tribune's Metromix* or *Chicago Magazine*.

## January

**Chicago Polar Bear Plunge.** If you're feeling adventurous, join the freezing fun as Chicagoans take an early swim on the first day of the New Year.
**Chicago Winter Delights**. From creative and stimulating activities celebrating history to the best venues for sketch-comedy or live blues, this winter festival offers a plethora of ways to keep the festive spirit alive with (mostly) free entertainment. Tel: 877-CHICAGO; www.winterdelights.com.
**Light Nights on the Magnificent Mile.** On Saturday evenings through January, fireworks extravaganzas illuminate the Chicago River and skyline. Check for daily offers such as complimentary cocoa or live ice-carving shows through March. Tel: 312-642-3570; www.themagnificentmile.com.

## February

**Black History Month**. Experience and celebrate a monthlong series

of festivals, exhibitions, performances, markets, and learning opportunities across the city, plus special events through the Dusable Museum of African American History and the Harold Washington Library. Tel: 773-947-0600; www.dusablemuseum.org.
**Chicago Auto Show.** The largest auto exhibition in the country boasts bold and creative displays in Chicago's McCormick Place. Tel: 630-495-2282; www.chicagoautoshow.com.
**Chinese New Year Parade and Festivities.** March along a 100-ft-tall (33-meter) dancing Mystical Dragon, then indulge in authentic Chinese cuisine to celebrate the Lunar New Year and Chicago's Chinese community. Tel: 312-326-5320; www.chicagochinatown.org.
**University of Chicago Folk Festival.** The best bluegrass, country blues, old-time fiddle, and klezmer music in addition to a range of free workshops led by performers. Tel: 773-702-9793; www.uofcfolk.org.

## March

**Around the Coyote Spring Festival.** A weekend-long series of art exhibits, lectures, and performances in Wicker Park and Bucktown galleries, schools, and nonprofit organizations, with the aim to promote accessible art in the community. Dates vary. A second Around the Coyote Festival is held in October. Tel: 773-342-6777; www.aroundthecoyote.org.
**Chicago Flower and Garden Show.** A spectacular floral display with hands-on workshops and lectures led by expert gardeners, florists and growers plus activities such as creative flower-arranging demonstrations and competitions. Tel: 773-435-1250; www.chicagoflower.com.
**ComedySportz March Madness.** The bawdiest battle in town, this contest features four teams of improv performers who vie for the ultimate in cut-throat, comedic championships at the Chicago Center for the Performing Arts. Tel: 312-733-6000; www.comedysportzchicago.com.
**South Side Irish Parade.** The weekend before St Patty's Day holds even more boisterous revelry than one day alone can hold. March at 103rd and Western Avenue. www.saintpatricksdayparade.com/chicago.
**St Patrick's Day Parade and Festivities.** Celebrate with Chicago's Irish community and take part in the famous parade along Columbus Drive or the lucky-green, river-dyeing activities. www.chicagostpatsparade.com.

## April

**Chicago Improv Festival.** A week packed with some of the most talented improvisational and sketch acts from around the world. Tel: 773-935-9810; www.chicagoimprovfestival.org.
**International Antiques and Fine Art Fair.** More than 100 antiques and fine art dealers from around the world gather in the heart of downtown's Merchandise Mart, offering collections and pieces from a variety of periods and places. Tel: 312-527-4141; www.mmart.com/chicagoantiques.
**Spring and Easter Flower Shows.** Both Garfield Park and Lincoln Park Conservatories host a variety of garden tours and activities celebrating the blooming season. Tel: 312-746-5195 (Garfield Park) or 312-742-7736 (Lincoln Park); www.chicagoparkdistrict.com.

## May

**Chicago Gospel Music Festival.** A gospel extravaganza featuring more than 50 local and national performances on three stages in Millennium Park. Tel: 312-744-3315; http://chicagogospelfestival.com.
**Cinco de Mayo Festival and Parade.** Ebullient annual celebration at Douglas Park, with live music, food vendors, and carnival rides, that reaches its zenith with a Sunday parade. Tel: 773-847-9889 or 312-744-3315.
**Great Chicago Places and Spaces.** A festival in celebration of the exemplary architecture and design heritage of Chicago, with engaging tours of the city's renowned historical sites and neighborhoods as well as art tours and kid-friendly activities. Tel: 312-744-3315; http://egov.cityofchicago.org.

## June

**57th Street Art Fair.** A historic and much-loved art fair held in the University of Chicago's Hyde Park neighborhood, which displays an abundance of media, unique styles, and opportunities to learn techniques. There are designated play areas for children and a handful of booths serving local foods. Tel: 773-493-3247; www.57thstreetartfair.org.
**Chicago Blues Festival.** Celebrating its 25th anniversary in 2007, this festival draws more than 750,000 blues lovers a year. Held in Grant Park, six stages offer an unmatched lineup of both established and upcoming blues musicians over four days. Tel: 312-744-3315; www.chicagobluesfestival.us.
**Chicago Country Music Festival.** Concurrent with the Taste of Chicago, this free festival brings a raw, western flavor to the Taste Stage with a two-day lineup of honky-tonk headliners. Between acts, there are free line dancing lessons. Tel: 312-744-3315; www.chicagocountrymusicfestival.us.
**Gay and Lesbian Pride Parade.** This raucous parade celebrating individuality, community, culture, and expression takes place on the last Sunday of June at the intersection of Halsted Street and Belmont Avenue and is accompanied by a variety of events and specials deals at shops and bars in the surrounding area. www.prideparadechicago.com.
**Old Town Art Fair.** Set in Chicago's historic Old Town neighborhood, this outdoor fair features hundreds of artists presenting works across a wide range of media. Historic tours, garden walks, chil-

dren's shows, and food from local eateries are also available. Tel: 312-337-1938; www.oldtowntriangle.com/artfair.html.

**Ravinia.** Ravinia opens its summer season in June, presenting everything from symphonic orchestras to Motown favorites in an outdoor pavilion surrounded by the expansive Ravinia lawn, where locals congregate around picnics and enjoy stirring performances beneath the stars. Lawn tickets, $15. Tel: 847-266-5100; www.ravinia.org.

**Taste of Chicago.** One of the best attended events in the city, held during the last week of June and the first week of July, Chicago's chefs and restaurateurs present over 70 iconic and innovative dishes for sampling, including hot dogs, sushi, Chicago-style deep dish pizza, barbecued turkey, and steak. The last weekend features concerts and climaxes with Fourth of July fireworks and events. Tel: 312-744-3315; www.tasteofchicago.us.

## July

**Chicago Outdoor Film Festival.** The Movies in the Park series runs through July and August, with classic movies presented in Grant Park every Tuesday. Tel: 312-744-3315; www.chicagooutdoorfilmfestival.us.

**Chinatown Summer Fair.** Chinatown's annual fair features live music, Chinese dancers, martial arts demonstrations, public contests, craft tables, and Chinese and American food. The major crowd pleaser is the traditional Lion Dance. www.chicagochinatown.com.

**Fourth of July.** This spectacular fireworks display (the main show is actually July 3rd) over the lakefront at Grant Park packs in crowds from across Illinois. The show kicks off at sunset.

**Taste of Lincoln Avenue.** This former fund-raising event has blossomed into a full-blown festival featuring many of the flavors of the much larger Taste of Chicago but in an intimate, neighborhood setting. Music and theatrical performances take place on five small stages and feature high-profile bands. There is also a kids' carnival area. www.wrightwoodneighbors.org/taste.htm.

**Venetian Night Boat Parade and Fireworks.** This formal maritime pageant is one of Chicago's longest-running events, with 35 decorated and twinkling boats and gondolas sailing across the lake. The parade, which adopts a different theme each year, culminates in a spectacular fireworks display synchronized to music. Tel: 312-744-3370.

## August

**Air and Water Show**. This exhilarating lakefront display from Fullerton Street to Oak Street Beach is one of the largest of its kind in the US and features performances by Air Force Thunderbirds, Navy Blue Angels, and the Army Parachute Team Golden Knights. Tel: 312-744-3315.

## September

**Celtic Fest.** A spirited two-day festival of music and dance celebrating the Celtic heritage of Ireland, Scotland, Wales, Isle of Man, Cornwall, Galicia, and Brittany. Tel: 312-744-3315.

**Mexican Independence Day Parade**. Chicago's Mexican community celebrates during this colorful street festival of floats, mariachis, and pulsating dance music along 26th Street from Albany to Kostner. Tel: 773-868-3010.

**Oktoberfest Chicago**. Expect German oompah music, *lederhosen, schnitzel, spaten, stiegl* and *bitburgerand* at this annual event held in the wood-paneled beer houses of the North Side German enclave of Lincoln Square. www.lincolnsquare.org.

**World Music Festival**. Weeklong festival held at multiple venues across the city to showcase traditional, classical, and contemporary music from around the world. The final performances are held at Millennium Park. Tel: 312-742-1938; http://egov.cityofchicago.org/worldmusic.

## October

**Chicago International Film Festival**. One of the most respected and established film festivals in the world, with more than 300 screenings (feature films, documentaries, and shorts) from 35 countries. Films are often introduced by directors and actors; past attendees include Geoffrey Rush, Liv Ullmann, Spike Lee, and Billy Bob Thornton. Tel: 312-683-0121; www.chicagofilmfestival.org.

**Chicago Marathon**. More than a million Chicagoans line the sidewalks as runners pace the city's fast, flat streets from the starting line in Grant Park through 12 Chicago neighborhoods.

**Halloween Pumpkin Plaza**. During one of the city's most entertaining children's events, Daley Plaza is transformed into a Haunted Village where kids can carve and decorate pumpkins, watch magicians and jugglers, visit the Midnight Circus, and hear ghost stories. www.cityofchicago.org/specialevents.

## November

**Christkindlmarket**. This open-air Christmas market in the German tradition transforms Daley Plaza into a kitsch wonderland with a Santa house and nativity scenes as well as twinkling stalls selling beer steins, hand-made Christmas ornaments, sauerkraut, roasted nuts, and warm, spicy *glühein*. www.christkindlmarket.com.

**Sofa**. This annual international exposition of Sculpture Objects & Functional Art (SOFA), held at Navy Pier, features more than 100 galleries and dealers presenting works by emerging and established artists and designers. www.sofaexpo.com.

**State Street Thanksgiving**

**Parade**. Whimsically decorated floats led by marching bands and TV personalities parade north along State Street from Congress Parkway during this beloved Thanksgiving tradition. www.chicagofestivals.org.

### December

**The Nutcracker**. Millennium Park's Harris Theater is the venue for this annual holiday ballet performed by the sublime Joffrey Ballet. Tel: 312-334-777; www.harristheaterchicago.org.

**Winter Wonderfest**. Santa's Holiday Village sets up on Navy Pier for the Christmas season, with hundreds of decorated trees, lights, frolicking elves, and an ice-skating rink. Magical for kids. www.navypier.com.

## TOURS

### Guided Tours

**ArchiCenter Shop and Tour Center**, Santa Fe Building, 224 South Michigan Avenue, tel: 312-922-3432, www.architecture.org. The Chicago Architectural Foundation runs highly informative walking and bus tours. The Historic Skyscraper Walking Tour is recommended.

**Bike Chicago**, 600 East Grand Avenue, tel: 312-595-9600, www.bikechicago.com. Hire a bike ($30 per day if you book online) or take one of the informative guided tours that cover the Lakefront, North Side, South Side, or public sculptures. Tours range in price ($30–40), distance (8–16km), and duration (2–3 hours).

**Chicago History Museum**, 1601 North Clark Street, tel: 312-642-4600. This fascinating museum runs such theme tours as a history pub crawl through the Swedish enclave of Andersonville; the "Murder and Mystery in Chicago" tour; and the "Devil in the White City" tour, which visits places mentioned in Erik Larson's best-selling book.

**Chicago Hop-On, Hop-Off Trolley**, 615 West 41st Street, tel: 773-648-5000, www.coachusa.com/chicagotrolley. Fully narrated, two-hour tours of downtown Chicago with pick-up/drop-off stops every 10 to 15 minutes. The route includes Sears Tower, Millennium Park, the Theatre District, the Art Institute, Navy Pier, and the John Hancock Center. Check the website for route information.

**Chicago Segway Tours**, 400 East Randolph Street, tel: 877-734-8687, www.citysegwaytours.com. Experience the highlights of the city on a two-wheeled Segway. Daily tours are offered April to September at 10am, 2pm, and 6pm and include a 30-minute orientation. Daytime tours are three hours; evening tours are two hours.

**Food Tasting Walking Tour**, tel: 800-979-3370, www.chicagofood-planet.com. A leisurely, three-hour walking tour samples the iconic and ethnic flavors of Lincoln Park, Old Town, and the Gold Coast.

**Ghost Tours**, PO Box 557544, tel: 708-499-0300, www.ghosttours.com. TV psychic Richard T. Crowe uncovers the city's sinister and gruesome underbelly in his tour of Chicago's paranormal hot spots. Nightly four-hour bus tours include a visit to John Dillinger's death site and Al Capone's grave. Supernatural dinner cruises are available in summer.

**Untouchables Tour**, 600 North Clark Street, tel: 773-881-1195, www.gangstertour.com. Daily two-hour bus tours delve into Chicago's Prohibition-era gangster lore. Stops include the site of the St Valentine's Day massacre.

### Cruises

**Mystic Blue Cruises**, Navy Pier, tel: 888-957-2324, www.mysticbluecruises.com. Enjoy views of the skyline while being served a better than expected brunch, lunch, or dinner. There's live jazz during the day and an up-tempo DJ soundtrack in the evening.

***Odyssey***, Navy Pier, tel: 888-957-2324, www.odyssey.com. This upscale cruise ship offers champagne brunch cruises and dinner dances with fireworks and music.

**Shoreline Architecture Cruise**, Navy Pier, tel: 312-222-9328, www.shorelinesightseeing.com. Departing from Navy Pier, one-hour river cruises feature 40 landmark buildings designed by legendary architects, including Mies van der Rohe and Helmut Jahn. April to November only.

***Spirit of Chicago***, tel: 866-273-2469, www.spiritofchicago.com. Pleasant, slick, if rather dated, theme cruises with dancing, DJs, gift bags, and fair food. Advance reservations are recommended for celebration cruises, including the October fireworks displays, monumental Thanksgiving buffet, and gospel brunches.

**Wendella Sightseeing Boats**, Wrigley Building, 400 North Michigan Avenue, tel: 312-337-1446, www.wendellaboats.com. This family-run company offers one- and two-hour cruises on the Chicago River, including wine-tasting and architecture tours and a sunset tour that climaxes with the Buckingham Fountain water show. Wendella also operates a convenient water taxi service from Madison Avenue to Michigan Avenue. Check the website for schedules.

## SPORTS

### Spectator Sports

#### *Baseball*

**Cubs**, Wrigley Field, 1060 West Addison Street, tel: 312-831-2827, www.chicago.cubs.mlb.com. The North Side's beloved Cubs play in the National League from April to October. The "Cubbies" play at the iconic, ivy-draped Wrigley Field, a bastion of baseball traditionalism with an ambience and history that draws legions of loyal fans despite the team's less-than-stellar record. The second-oldest ballpark in Major League Baseball, Wrigley acquired lighting for night games only in 1988, much to the chagrin of traditionalists. Tickets sell out fast, but you can usually find tickets for sale outside the park on the day of the game.

**White Sox**, 333 West 35th Street, tel: 866-SOX-GAME, www.chicago.whitesox.mlb.com. The South Side's White Sox play in the American League at the prosaic US Cellular Field. While they may lack the history and glamour of their North Side counterparts, the Sox's blue-collar soul remains true to Chicago's roots. In 2005, they showed their substance when they swept the American League Championship Series to play in the World Series. Tickets are usually easy to come by.

### *Basketball*

**Bulls**, United Center, 1901 West Madison Street, tel: 312-455-4000, www.nba.com/bulls. Six-time NBA champions, the Chicago Bulls have struggled to recapture the victorious record that characterized the Michael Jordan era of the 1980s. Epic losing streaks have become the norm, but that makes tickets ($14–80) easy to find. Regardless of whether you are a basketball fan, the spectacle and pizzazz that accompanies every game makes for a compelling night of sports entertainment.

### *Football*

**Bears**, Soldier Field, 12th Street, tel: 847-615-2327, www.chicagobears.com. The Bears reached the Super Bowl in 2006, capping a solid record of eight NFL Championships. The Bears also hold the record for the most team members (26) enshrined in the Pro Football Hall of Fame. Despite the brutal Siberian winds that whip up off the lake, tickets sell out fast.

### *Soccer*

**Fire**, Toyota Park, 71st Street and Harlem Avenue, tel: 888-MLS-FIRE, www.chicago.fire.mlsnet.com. In their first Major League Soccer season in 1998, the Chicago Fire established a stellar record, winning the MLS Cup and the US Open Cup. The team won the US Open Cup again in 2006, much to the pleasure of loyal fans who make the trip to its 20,000-seat stadium in suburban Bridgeview. The season runs from late May through October; tickets are affordable and usually easy to come by.

## Participant Sports

### *Bicycling*

Chicago is an extremely bicycle-friendly city, with 18 miles (29 km) of lakefront cycle paths. For a moderately strenuous, wonderfully scenic ride, head north along the lakefront from Navy Pier to Montrose Beach. Take care and keep right; the paths can be congested in summer with rollerbladers, joggers, and walkers. Always pass on the left, announcing "on your left" to those around you.

**Bike Chicago** (www.bikechicago.com), see tours above, rents mountain bikes, children's bikes, and quad bikes from $8 per hour (book online for discount rates); helmets and locks are included.

### *Golf*

Chicago has numerous golf facilities, and there's an even greater number in the suburbs (information is available at www.cdga.org).

**Diversey Driving Range**, 141 West Diversey Pkwy, tel: 312-742-7929. Located within leafy, laid-back Lincoln Park, this friendly and economical range is popular with golfers of all skill levels.

**The Green at Grant Park**, Monroe Street, tel: 312-642-7888, www.thegreenonline.com. A family-oriented, inexpensive 18-hole course east of Millennium Park.

**Sydney Marovitz Course**, 3600 North Lake Shore Drive, tel: 312-245-0909, www.cpdgolf.com. This popular 9-hole course with a glorious lakefront setting is one of nine courses run by the Chicago Park District. Reservations are required.

### *Ice Skating*

**McCormick-Tribune Ice Rink at Millennium Park**, 55 North Michigan Avenue, tel: 312-742-5222. This rink has views of Frank Gehry's Pritzker Pavilion and Anish Kapoor's "Bean" sculpture. A family-friendly, festive experience, open from November to March, 9am to 9pm. Skates are available to rent.

### *Sailing*

**Chicago Sailing Club**, Belmont Harbor, tel: 773-871-SAIL, www.chicagosailingclub.com. Sailboats are available for rent or charter in summer. Rates are significantly cheaper during the week. An orientation is required if you want to skipper the boat yourself. Reservations highly recommended.

### *Swimming*

If you can bear the chill, swimming in Lake Michigan (Memorial Day through Labor Day only) from Ohio Street Beach (alongside Lakepoint Tower, just north of Navy Pier) is the most exhilarating workout in the city. Keep to the areas that are monitored by lifeguards. Less atmospheric are some 33 indoor pools maintained by the Chicago Park District (tel: 312-742-PLAY).

### *Tennis*

There is no shortage of public outdoor tennis courts maintained by the Chicago Park District (for a full list, visit www.chicagoparkdistrict.com). The most accessible venues include:

**Grant Park**, 337 East Randolph Street, tel: 312-742-7648.

**Garfield Park**, 100 North Central Park Avenue, tel: 312-746-5092.

**Oz Park**, 2021 North Burling Street, tel: 312-742-7898.

### *Volleyball*

North Avenue Beach is the closest beach to downtown that provides volleyball facilities and an outdoor gym. Foster Beach, a few miles farther north, also has several volleyball courts.

# A–Z

## AN ALPHABETICAL SUMMARY OF PRACTICAL INFORMATION


A Accidents 288
B Budgeting for a Visit 288
Business Hours 288
C Car Rentals 288
Climate and Clothing 288
Consulates 289
D Discounts 289
E Electricity 289
Emergency Numbers 289
Entry Regulations 289
G Government 289
H Handicapped Access 289
Health & Medical Care 290
L Liquor Laws 290
M Maps 290
Media 290
P Parking 291
Postal Services 291
R Religious Services 291
S Security and Crime 292
T Taxes 292
Telephone Codes 292
Time Zones 292
Tipping 292
Tourist Information 292
W Websites 292
Weights and Measures 292


### Accidents

In case of an emergency or accident, dial 911. Do not leave the scene of an auto accident until the police arrive.

### Budgeting for a Visit

While Chicago is not as expensive as, say, New York or San Francisco, downtown hotels, restaurants, and taxis can soon send your budget into orbit. However, with some careful planning there are many ways to keep costs down that also provide the opportunity to get under the skin of the city. Travel websites offering hotel discounts include; www.expedia.com, www.sidestep.com, www.orbitz.com, www.hotwire.com, www.travelocity.com. Staying in a bed and breakfast can also be less costly than a hotel, especially for groups and families: www.bedandbreakfast.com/chicago-illinois.html.

With epic Chicago portion sizes, there is no need to go hungry; fill up on brunch, then try an early pre-theater, prix-fixe meal, a great way to sample upscale restaurants at more affordable prices. Chinatown's authentic storefronts and the string of Indian restaurants on Devon Avenue, just west of Clark Street, are culturally and gastronomically intriguing and inexpensive. Selecting a BYOB restaurant will also dramatically reduce your bill. Popular with Chicagoans, there are more than 400 BYOBs, primarily in the city's North Side neighborhoods.

### Business Hours

Businesses and government offices in Chicago are generally open from 9am to 5pm Monday to Friday. Banking hours are generally 8.30am to 5pm, with many branches open on Saturdays and several open on Sundays.

### Car Rentals

Driving in the downtown area is not necessary or advised. Should you wish to explore farther afield, however, car rental agencies are located throughout the city and at the airports. Drivers must be at least 21 and have a driver's license and a valid credit card.

### Climate and Clothing

Spring is often rainy and gray but is relieved by perfect 75°F (24°C) days. Summer can be stiflingly hot and humid with temperatures

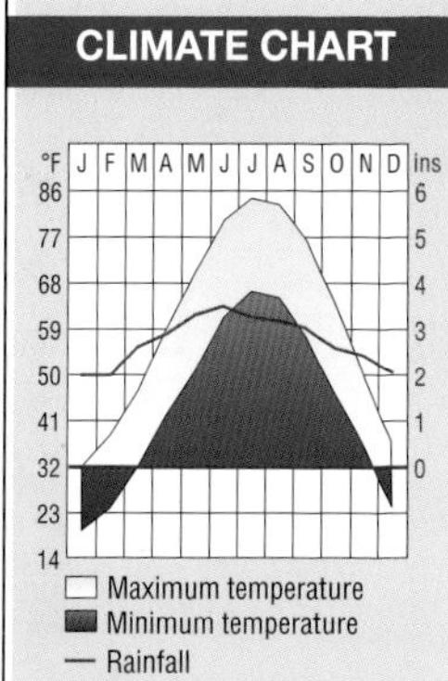


exceeding 90°F (32°C); nighttime temperatures seldom drop below 70°F (21°C). Autumn is pleasant, with crisp sunny days, moderate temperatures, and colorful fall foliage. Winter, especially January and February, is brutally cold, with below-freezing temperatures, biting winds, and desolate streets. For updated information, visit www.weatherpages.com/chicago.

Chicago weather is extreme and unpredictable, with four clearly defined seasons. Dressing in layers is highly recommended. Frequent and extreme temperature changes, often within just a few hours, can leave you shivering or sweltering unexpectedly. Powerful air conditioning and heating in stores and restaurants can be extremely uncomfortable. Dress codes in Chicago are relaxed, for the most part; sneakers and shorts are not uncommon in upscale restaurants. There are exceptions: sophisticated establishments often have a dress code, usually a suit jacket and tie for men and dress slacks, skirt, or dress for women.

## Consulates

**Australia:** 123 North Wacker Drive, Suite 1330, tel: 312-419-1480.
**Canada:** Two Prudential Plaza, 180 North Stetson Avenue, Suite 2400, tel: 312-616-1860.
**France:** 737 North Michigan Avenue, tel: 312-787-5359.
**Ireland:** 400 North Michigan, Suite 911, tel: 312-337-1868.
**Israel:** 111 East Wacker Drive, tel: 312-565-3300.
**Italy:** 500 North Michigan Avenue, tel: 312-467-1550.
**Japan:** 737 North Michigan Avenue, tel: 312-280-0400.
**New Zealand:** 8600 West Bryn Mawr Avenue, Suite 500N, tel: 773-714-9461.
**UK:** Wrigley Building, 13th floor, 400 North Michigan Avenue, Suite 1300, tel: 312-970-3800.

## Customs

Information on regulations and restrictions when entering the US is available at www.customs.ustreas.gov. Only people 21 years old and over may bring alcohol and tobacco into the US. Meat and dairy products, seeds, plants, fruits, and Cuban cigars are not permitted into the US.

## Discounts

**City Pass**, tel: 888-330-5008, www.citypass.com. Valid for nine days, City Pass permits entry to six attractions. It costs $49.50 for adults and $39 for children (ages 3–11). You can purchase the pass online, by phone, or at any of the participating attractions: Adler Planetarium, Museum of Science and Industry, Field Museum, Art Institute, Shedd Aquarium, and Hancock Observatory.
**Chicago Plays**, tel: 312-554-9800, www.chicagoplays.com. The League of Chicago Theatres, which has almost 200 members ranging from small companies to the major "Broadway in Chicago" venues, offers the HotTix discount ticket program.
**Go Chicago Card**, tel: 312-282-4555, www.gochicagocard.com. This flexibility card is available in one-, two-, three-, five-, or seven-day increments and includes more than 25 attractions. Purchasing and presenting a Go Chicago Card entitles the holder to discounts of up to 20%. It costs $49–139 for adults and $29–99 for children (3–12).

## Electricity

Standard American electric current is 110 volts with standard two-pin plugs. Adapters will be required for foreign visitors. Standard European is 220-240 volts.

## Emergency Numbers

Police, Ambulance, Fire: 911
Credit cards lost or stolen: AmEx: 800-528-2121
Diners Club/Carte Blanche: 800-307-7309
Mastercard: 800-307-7309
Visa: 800-336-8472

## Entry and Regulations

For a breakdown of up-to-date US entry regulations, visit http://travel.state.gov/visa/index/html. Visa inquiries, tel: 202-663-1225, usvisa@state.gov.

## Government

The mayor is the city's chief executive officer. He directs city departments and appoints department heads, with the consent of the city council. The mayor is elected for a four-year term in the year preceding each presidential election year. Mayor Richard M. Daley was first elected April 4, 1989.

Since the late 1990s, the Illinois Democratic Party has been immensely successful in statewide elections. In both the Illinois Senate and Illinois House of Representatives, the Democratic Party holds a strong majority. Democrat Rod Blagojevich was re-elected governor of Illinois in 2006, and Barack Obama, the young, charismatic Illinois Democratic Senator, entered the race for US president in 2007.

## Handicapped Access

For further information on handicapped facilities in Chicago, check www.accessiblechicago.org, which provides a rating system of disabled-friendly facilities and activities in the city. General information and tips on mobility-impaired travel throughout Illinois can be found at www.vacationsmadeeasy.com/chicago and www.globalaccessnews.com. A list of hotels in Chicago detailing handicapped-accessible facilities can be found at www.access-able.com.

There are many Chicago tour organizations that specifically cater to disabled travelers. For neighborhood tours, Walk Chicago Tours (www.walkchicagotours.com) will custom design itineraries for disabled visitors. For boat trips, Lucky Dog Charters (www.luckydogcharters.com) can accommodate three wheelchair users per excursion.

The CTA has information on stations and services that are wheelchair accessible: www.transitchicago.com/maps/accessible.html.

## Health and Medical Care

There is a limited public health care system in the US. Should you require medical assistance, you will need to present your insurance information or pay for treatment at the time of your visit, which for foreign visitors accustomed to subsidized health care is likely to cause extreme sticker shock. Always attempt to contact your insurance company before you receive treatment; many companies require immediate notification and may require that you receive treatment at designated hospitals. For immediate attention, dial 911 or go directly to a hospital emergency room. There are 24-hour emergency centers at the following hospitals:

Cook County Hospital, 1835 West Harrison Street, tel: 312-633-6000.

Northwestern Memorial Hospital, 251 East Huron Street, tel: 312-926-2000, www.nmh.org.

Rush-Presbyterian, 1650 West Harrison Street, tel: 312-942-5000, www.rush.edu.

University of Chicago Hospital, 901 East 58th Street, Hyde Park, tel: 773-702-6250.

## Internet Access

You will find that most hotels in the moderate to luxury categories provide internet access, usually in-room Wi-Fi. Large business hotels will also provide business centers with computers, printers, and office equipment for rent. **Fedex Kinko's** provide internet and other computer/fax/copy/mailing services for a fee. For a list of offices and hours, go to www.fedex.com/us/officeprint/main. Centrally located branches include:

225 North Michigan Avenue, tel: 312-819-0940.

444 North Wells Street, tel: 312-670-4460.

Every Starbucks is a T-mobile hot spot charging $9.99 per day for unlimited access. A much better option is to seek out one of more than 200 free Wi-Fi spots in cafés and other establishments around the city.

The Chicago Public Library system also provides free internet facilities:

**Downtown:** The Harold Washington Library, 400 South State Street, tel: 312-747-4999.

**Lincoln Park:** 1150 West Fullerton Street, tel: 312-744-1926.

**Bucktown:** 2056 Damen Avenue, tel-312-744-6022.

## Liquor Laws

The legal drinking age is 21 and is strictly enforced. Many bar and restaurant proprietors will card people who appear 35 years and younger. Always carry identification.

## Maps

The Insight Guide Chicago Flexi-Map is laminated for durability and easy folding and contains listings and travel information.

## Media

### Print

***Chicago Tribune*** (www.chicagotribune.com) The "Trib" is Chicago's principal daily newspaper and one of the nation's largest dailies. With a history of an unequivocal Republican ethos, the paper supported President Bush for re-election in 2004, yet has endorsed Democrats, including Barack Obama for

**LEFT:** traffic on State Street.

the Senate. The paper's fiscally conservative stance and centrist editorial policy, despite its electoral endorsements, often results in the *Tribune* being endowed with a Libertarian label.

***Chicago Sun-Times*** (www.suntimes.com) The *Sun-Times* is Chicago's answer to the *New York Post*, a tabloid with a sensationalist bent. The paper's editorial policy shifted to the right in 1984 when it was acquired by Rupert Murdoch's News Corp. Dramatic changes occurred in 2007, when new editor Cheryl Reed declared that the paper was returning to its "liberal, working-class roots."

***Chicago Reader*** (www.chicagoreader.com) Free cultural and entertainment weekly with local social, cultural, and political features and reams of reviews. A great source for concert, movie, theater, gallery, and stand-up comedy listings, as well as restaurant reviews and a weekly lineup of the best events in and around the city. Free copies are available in street boxes and at bars, coffee shops, delis, and bookstores throughout the city.

***New City*** (www.newcitychicago.com) A popular commuter's read with quick-flick commentary, profiles, reviews, and news features often with an irreverent tone.

### Television

KYW Channel 3 (CBS)
WPV1 Channel 6 (ABC)
WCAU Channel 10 (NBC)
WHYY Channel 12 (PBS)
WPHL Channel 17 (WB)
WPSG Channel 57 (UPN)
WTXF Channel 29 (Fox)

### Radio Stations

**News**

| | |
|---|---|
| WBBM 780 AM | NewsRadio |
| WLS 890 AM | News Talk |
| WSCR 670 AM | Sports Radio |
| WVON 1450 AM | News Talk |
| WGN 720 AM | New Talk |
| WBEZ 91.5 FM | Chicago Public Radio |

**Music**

| | |
|---|---|
| 93 XRT 93.1 FM | Rock |
| WKQX 101.1 FM | Alternative |
| WTMX 101.9 FM | Contemporary |
| WNUA 95.5 FM | Smooth Jazz |
| WDRV 97.1 FM | Classic Rock |
| WUSN 99.5 FM | Country |

## Parking

Parking meters accept coins and are generally limited to a two-hour maximum. Permit restrictions apply in most neighborhoods; always check the red-and-white signs that designate parking restrictions and tow zones, and look out for temporary signs that indicate street cleaning. Traffic police are omnipresent and efficient, so it's best not to take chances. Driving downtown should be avoided; despite the grid system, which makes orientation relatively straightforward, the many one-way streets can be confounding. On balance, parking garages are as expensive as taxis: average one to four hours $19, up to 24 hours, $20–28.

## Parking Garages

General Parking, 215 East Chicago Avenue
General Parking, 111 East Wacker Drive
Central Parking, 115 West Illinois Street
Standard Parking, 911 North Rush Street
Standard Parking, 1250 North Dearborn Street
System Parking, 113 East Randolph Street
InterPark, 747 North Wacker Drive
Interpark, 20 East Randolph Street

## Postal Services

Most post offices are open 8.30am–5pm Monday–Friday and 8.30am–1pm Saturday. The post office at 540 North Dearborn is also open Sunday 9am–2pm.

### US Post Offices

845 North Michigan Avenue, 60611
540 North Dearborn Street, 60610
358 West Harrison Street, 60607
433 West Van Buren Street, 60607
3635 North Lincoln Avenue, 60657
3024 North Ashland Avenue, 60657
1343 West Irving Park Road, 60613
2405 North Sheffield Avenue, 60614

## Religious Services

### Christian Churches

Assumption Church Servite Fathers, 323 West Illinois Street, tel: 312-664-0036.
Cathedral Church of St James, 65 East Huron Street, tel: 312-787-7360.
Central Church of Chicago, 18 South Michigan Avenue, tel: 312-332-4840.
Chicago Temple, 77 West Washington Street, tel: 312-236-4548.
Holy Name Cathedral, 735 North State Street, tel: 312-787-8040.
Grace Episcopal Church, 637 North Dearborn Street, tel: 312-922-1426.
St Luke Church of God in Christ, 914 North Orleans Street, tel: 312-266-7258.

### Synagogues

Central Synagogue of the South Side Hebrew Congregation, 150 East Huron Street, tel: 312-787-0450.
Chicago Loop Synagogues, 16 South Clark Street, tel 312-346-7370.
Lubavitch Chabad of the Loop, 401 South LaSalle Street, Suite 9-770, tel: 312-337-6811.
Temple Sholom of Chicago, 3480 North Lakeshore Drive, tel: 773-525-4707.
Temple Menorah, 2800 West Sherwin Avenue, tel: 773-761-5700.
Congregation Tiseres Yisoroel, 6336 North Lincoln Avenue, tel: 773-478-1515.

### Mosques

Downtown Islamic Center, 218 South Wabash Avenue, Suite

500, tel: 312-939-9095.
Ephraim Cultural Center, 2525 West 71st Street, tel: 773-476-8825.
Islamic Center of Chicago, 5933 North Lincoln Avenue, tel: 773-989-9330.
Islamic Circle Center (Masjid Al Latif), 5033 North Clark Street, tel: 773-792-6825.
Masjid Al-Muhajreen, 3777 West Columbus Avenue, tel: 773-581-1083.

## Reservations

It is highly recommended that you book hotels well in advance, especially during the peak summer season (May through September) and holidays (Thanksgiving and Christmas). Good restaurants book up quickly on weekends, so always try to book at least a couple of weeks ahead of time. If you have a strong desire to dine at a particular restaurant but can't get a reservation, it's often worth arriving early, putting your name down, and having a few drinks at the bar; most restaurants keep a couple of tables open, and dining in the bar is often a good fallback. Architectural River Cruises are also extremely popular and sell out fast, as do tickets for Second City, Hubbard Street Dance, and the Joffrey Ballet.

## Security and Crime

Like most modern cities, Chicago has its no-go areas that should be avoided at night and pockets of petty crime where common sense should prevail at all times. Within a couple of blocks, you can easily find wealthy enclaves of yuppie condos and Victorian mansions giving way to bleak high-rises and public housing. Chicago crime has fallen dramatically in the past five years due partly to the demolition of notorious tower blocks like Cabrini Green, where shootings were not uncommon. The South and West Sides are still blighted by drug and gang related crime. It is advisable to avoid Cottage Grove Avenue to the west, 51st Street south and the southern boundary of the Midway Plaisance.

## Taxes

Hotel tax is 14.9%; sales tax is 9%, restaurant tax is 10.25%.

## Telephone Codes

312 and 773 are the area codes for the metropolitan area. Other useful codes: 630 western suburbs; 708 southern and western suburbs; 847 northern suburbs.

## Time Zones

Chicago is in the central time zone (-6 GMT). Daylight saving begins the first Sunday in April and ends the last Sunday in October. Flights from Australia and New Zealand cross the international date line; you will arrive in Chicago before you left home.

## Tipping

Service personnel depend to a large extent on tips. Gratuities are expected at all full-service restaurants unless a 15 percent service charge has been added to your bill, often the case with large parties.
**Waiters:** Standard 15 percent, for exceptional service 20–25 percent
**Doormen, bell boys, porters:** $1–$2 per bag
**Taxi Drivers:** 10–15 percent
**Hairdressers, manicurists, and masseurs:** 10–15 percent
**Valets:** $2 per car
**Chamber staff:** discretionary according to standard of service and length of stay

## Tourist Information

Chicago Cultural Center, 78 East Washington Street, tel: 312-744-6630, www.cityofchicago.org/tourism
Chicago Office of Tourism, 163 East Pearson Street, tel: 312-744-2400
Illinois Bureau of Commerce, James R. Thompson Center, 100 West Randolph, tel: 312-814-7179, www.enjoyillinois.com

## Websites

The following sites contain a wealth of information on Chicago's cultural sites, history, politics, literature, sports, and entertainment as well as trivia, facts, and anecdotes.

www.centerstage.net
www.chicagoarchitecture.info
http://chicagonews.net
www.chicagopublicradio.org/
www.chireader.com
www.chicago.citysearch.com
www.choosechicago.com
www.cityofchicago.org/exploringchicago
www.cityofchicago.org/Landmarks/index
www.corsinet.com/chicago/
www.cubune.com/
www.metromix.com
www.onlinetouristguide.net/chicago
www.ticketweb.com

### *Blogs*

www.chicagoist.com
www.chicagofoodies.com/
www.chicagoreader.com/features/stories/hottype/070907/
www.gapersblock.com/

## Weights and Measures

The US uses the imperial system.
1 inch = 2.54 centimeters
1 foot = 30.48 centimeters
1 yard = 0.9144 meter
1 mile = 1.609 kilometers
1 pint = 0.473 liter
1 quart = 0.946 liter
1 ounce = 28.4 grams
1 pound = 0.453 kilogram
1 acre = 0.405 hectare
1 square mile = 259 hectares
1 centimeter = 0.394 inch
1 meter = 39.37 inches
1 kilometer = 0.621 mile
1 liter = 1.057 quarts
1 gram = 0.035 ounces
1 kilogram = 2.205 pounds
1 hectare = 2.471 acres
1 square kilometer = 0.386 square mile

# FURTHER READING

## Fiction set in Chicago

***The Adventures of Augie March*** by Saul Bellow (Viking, 1953).
***City on the Make*** by Nelson Algren (University of Chicago Press, 1951).
***The Coast of Chicago*** by Stewart Dybek (Picador, 2004).
***Native Son*** by Richard Wright (Harper Perennial, 1940).
***The Jungle*** by Upton Sinclair (Doubleday, Page and Company, 1906).
***The House on Mango Street*** by Sandra Cisneros (Vintage, 1984).
***Man with the Golden Arm*** by Nelson Algren (Doubleday, 1949).
***The Razor's Edge*** by Somerset Maugham (Doubleday, 1944).
***Sister Carrie*** by Theodore Dreiser (Doubleday, 1900).
***Studs Lonigan*** by James T. Farrell (Library of America, 2004).
***There are no Children Here*** by Alex Kotlowitz (Doubleday, 1991).

## Nonfiction

***American Apocalypse: The Great Fire and the Myth of Chicago*** by Ross Miller (University of Chicago Press, 1990).
***Chicago: Then and Now*** by Elizabeth McNulty (Thunder Bay Press, 2000).
***Chicago's Famous Buildings***,ed. Ira J. Bach (University of Chicago Press, 1980).
***City of the Century: The Epic of Chicago and the Making of America*** by Donald L. Miller (Simon and Schuster, 1997).
***Devil in the White City*** by Erik Larson (Random House, 2003).
***Lost Chicago*** by David Garrard Lowe (Watson Guptill, 2000).
***The Plan of Chicago: Daniel Burnham and the Remaking of the American City*** by Carl Smith (University of Chicago Press, 2007).
***Murder City: The Bloody History of Chicago in the Twenties*** by Michael Lesy (W.W. Norton, 2007).
***Never a City So Real: A Walk in Chicago*** by Alex Kotlowitz (Crown, 2004).
***Sin in the Second City: Madams, Ministers, Playboys and the Battle for America's Soul*** by Karen Abbott (Random House, 2007).
***The St. Valentine's Day Massacre: The Untold Story of the Gangland Bloodbath That Brought Down Al Capone*** by William J. Helmer & Arthur J. Bilek (Cumberland House, 2006).
***Twenty Years at Hull-House*** by Jane Addams, Ruth Sidel, Nora Hamilton (Penguin, 1998).
***Urban Disorder and the Shape of Belief: The Great Chicago Fire, the Haymarket Bomb, and the Model Town of Pullman*** by Carl Smith (University of Chicago Press, 1996).
***The Wicked City: Chicago from Kenna to Capone*** by Curt Johnson and Craig Sautter (DaCapo, 1998).

## Other Insight Guides

More than 50 Insight Guides, in various formats, provide comprehensive coverage to destinations in the United States.

**Insight Guides** cover major areas of the country, from Alaska to Florida, from New England to California. One title, *USA On the Road*, suggests itineraries designed to explore every part of the country. Individual city guides (companions to the present volume) cover Boston, Las Vegas, Los Angeles, Miami, New York City, Orlando, Philadelphia, San Francisco, Seattle, and Washington DC.

**Insight FlexiMaps** cover 35 destinations, from Atlanta to Indianapolis. They are laminated for ease of use and durability.

## FEEDBACK

We do our best to ensure the information in our books is as accurate and up-to-date as possible. The books are updated on a regular basis, using local contacts, who painstakingly add, amend and correct as required. However, some mistakes and omissions are inevitable and we are ultimately reliant on our readers to put us in the picture.

We would welcome your feedback on any details related to your experiences using the book "on the road". Maybe we recommended a hotel that you liked (or another that you didn't), as well as interesting new attractions, or facts and figures you have found out about the place itself. The more details you can give us (particularly with regard to addresses, e-mails and telephone numbers), the better.

We will acknowledge all contributions, and we'll offer an Insight Guide to the best letters received.

Please write to us at:

Insight Guides
PO Box 7910
London SE1 1WE
United Kingdom
Or send e-mail to:
insight@apaguide.co.uk

# Art & Photo Credits

**All photography by Dávid Dunai except the following:**

**Arcaid/Corbis** 232T

**The Art Institute of Chicago** 10T, 11BL

**Chuck Berman** 23TC

**Bettmann/Corbis** 21, 33B, 38, 39, 41TL, 41TC, 43, 114B, 118BL, 163T

**Richard Bryant/Arcaid/Corbis** 238T

**Matthew Cavanaugh/epa/Corbis** 48L

**Chicago Historical Society** 23TL, 23, 32B, 40, 42L, 42R, 46L, 49L, 50TL, 51C, 52TL, 52C

**Chicago Sun-Times** 36TR, 41BL, 44, 46R, 52B, 59R, 66L, 67R, 213, 223T, 223B

**Field Museum** 11C

**Firestone/Sipa-Press/Rex Features** 48R

**Glyn Genin** 257B

**Myles Hayes** 250, 251

**Kelly-Mooney Photography/Corbis** 56

**Library of Congress** 20, 22L, 22R, 23T, 23BL, 24L, 24BR, 25, 26, 27 (all), 28 (all), 29, 30, 31 (all), 32, 32-33T, 34 (all), 35 (all), 36L, 37L, 45, 47R, 50B, 50-51C, 51T, 51B, 57, 58L, 59L, 62T, 89T, 89B, 97, 238BL, 249B

**Milwaukee Art Museum** 256 (all)

**Morton Arboretum** 259T

**Museum of Contemporary Art** 149TR, 149TC, 150TC

**Scott Olson/Getty/AFP** 161B

**Chris Pizzello/Reuters/Corbis** 199B

**James Quinn** 67L

**Reuters/Corbis** 199T

**Sten M. Rosenlund** 58R

**Smart Museum of Art** 236TR, 236TL

**Spertus Institute** 94R, 219T

**Topham** 47L

**John Zich/zrImages/Corbis** 197BR

## Picture Spreads

**Pages 62/63**
**Library of Congress** 62TL; **Rex Features** 62BL; **David James AFP/Getty** 62-63; **Bettmann/Corbis** 62CR; **Courtesy of the Academy of Motion Pictures Arts & Sciences** 62BC, 63LC

**Pages 98/99**
**All pictures by Dávid Dunai**

**Pages 130/131 and 132/133**
**All pictures courtesy of the Art Institute of Chicago except: Dávid Dunai** 130TL

**Pages 140/141**
**All pictures by Dávid Dunai except: Glyn Genin** 140BC

**Pages 188/189**
**All pictures by Dávid Dunai**

**Pages 226/227 and 228/229**
**All pictures courtesy of the Field Museum except: Dávid Dunai** 226TL; 226RC; 227T, 228TL, 229LC, 229RB

**Pages 242/243**
**All pictures courtesy of the Museum of Science and Industry except: Dávid Dunai** 242LC, 242LB, 242-243T

**Map Production** Phoenix Mapping
Original map data supplied by American Map.

# CHICAGO STREET ATLAS

**The key map shows the area of Chicago covered by the atlas section. An index of street names and places of interest shown on the maps can be found on the following pages. For each entry there is a page number and grid reference**

A
B
1
2
3
4
LINCOLN PARK
OLD TOWN
GOLD
COAST
CABRINI
GREEN
STANTON PARK
SEWARD
PARK
NEAR NORTH
WASHINGTON
SQUARE
CONNORS
PARK
RIVER
NORTH
Steppenwolf
Theatre
Company
North-Clybourn
St Michael's
Second
City
Sedgwick
Noble Horse Theatre
Chicago
History
Museum
Archbishop's
Residence
Madlener House
Patterson-
McCormick
Mansion
Charnley-Pers
House
Former
Playboy
Mansion
Three
Arts Club
Ambassador
East Hotel
LaSalle
Towers
Fisher Studi
Houses
Clark/Division
Newberry Library
Chicago
Holy Name
Cathedral
St James
Cathedral
Cable House
Former
Medinah Temple
Grand
Trump
Tower
Marina
City
Merchandise
Mart
Apparel Mart
& Expocenter
Sun-Times
Bldg
Fulton Street Market
Clinton
Clark
Chicago Theatre
North Branch
Chicago
Kennedy Expwy
Hubbard's Tunnel
90
94
Clybourn Avenue
Ogden Avenue
Milwaukee Ave
Kingsbury Street
Clark Street
LaSalle Drive
North Boulevard
North Avenue
Division Street
Chicago Avenue
Grand Avenue
Ohio Street
Ontario Street
Wacker Drive
Halsted Street
Wells Street
State Street
Dearborn Street
Sedgwick Street
Orleans Street
Larrabee Street
Canal Street

298

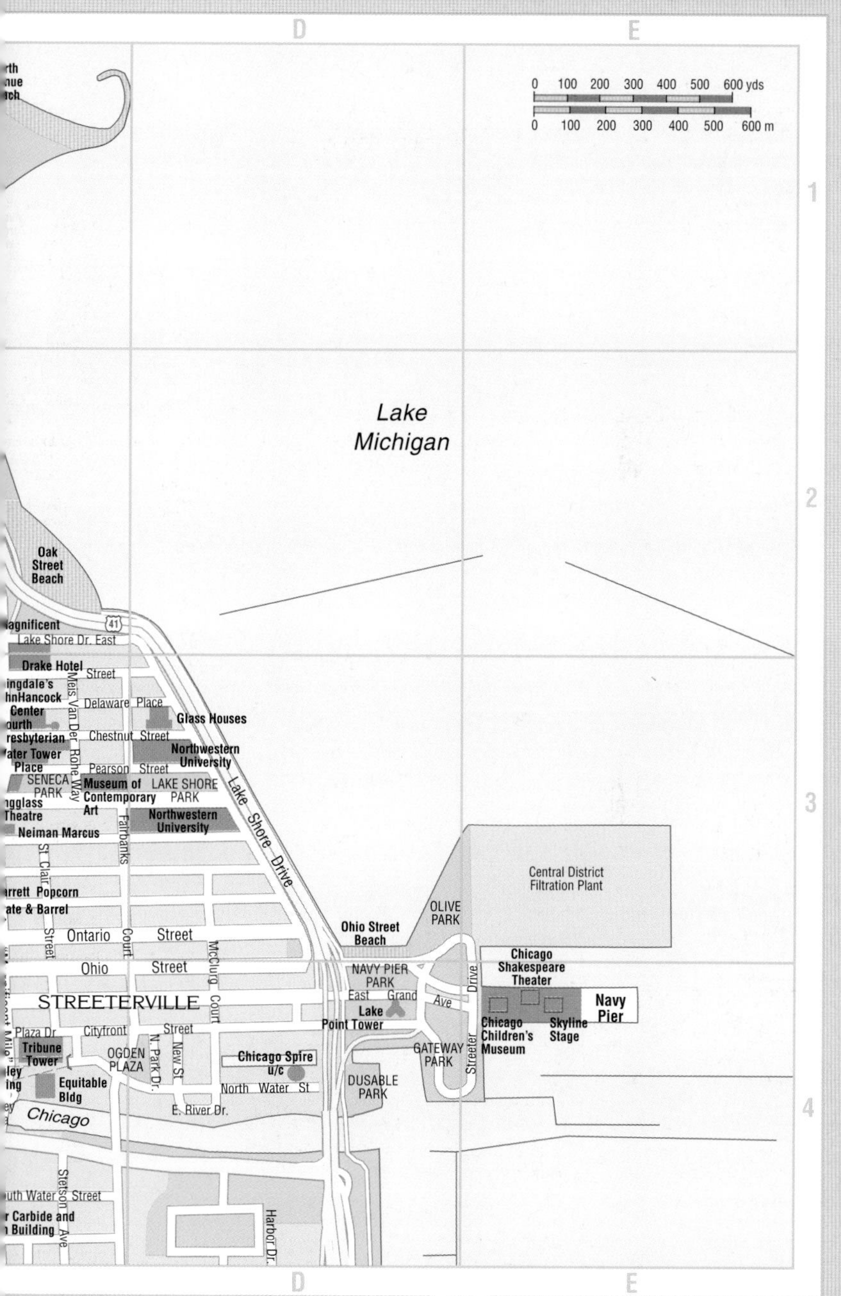

0 100 200 300 400 500 600 yds
0 100 200 300 400 500 600 m
Lake Michigan
Oak Street Beach
41
Lake Shore Dr. East
Drake Hotel
Street
Meis Van Der Rohe Way
Delaware Place
Glass Houses
Chestnut Street
Northwestern University
Pearson Street
SENECA PARK
Museum of Contemporary Art
LAKE SHORE PARK
Lake Shore Drive
Northwestern University
Neiman Marcus
Fairbanks
St Clair
Central District Filtration Plant
OLIVE PARK
Ohio Street Beach
Ontario Street
Court
Street
McClurg Court
Ohio Street
Chicago Shakespeare Theater
NAVY PIER PARK
East Grand Ave
Drive
Navy Pier
STREETERVILLE
Lake Point Tower
Plaza Dr
Cityfront
Street
Chicago Children's Museum
Skyline Stage
Tribune Tower
OGDEN PLAZA
N. Park Dr.
New St
Chicago Spire u/c
GATEWAY PARK
Streeter
Equitable Bldg
North Water St
DUSABLE PARK
E. River Dr.
Chicago
Stetson Ave
Street
Harbor Dr.


299

296
300
GREEKTOWN
LITTLE ITALY
UNIVERSITY VILLAGE
PILSEN
LOOP
Merchandise Mart
Apparel Mart & Expocenter
Sun-Times Bldg
Fulton Street Market
Harpo Studios
Clinton
Ogilvie Transportation Center (Northwestern Station)
Cadillac Palace Theater
City Hall
Daley Center & Plaza
James R. Thompson Center
Civic Opera House
Chicago Temple
Hellenic Museum and Cultural Center
Union Station
Sears Tower
The Rookery
Chicago Board of Trade
Main Post Office
Old Colony Building
Jane Addams Hull-House Museum
Daley Library
University of Illinois at Chicago
Chicago Circle Center
Site of Chicago Fire (1871)
Maxwell Street Market
UIC ATHLETIC FIELDS
Eisenhower Expressway
Dan Ryan Expressway
South Branch Chicago

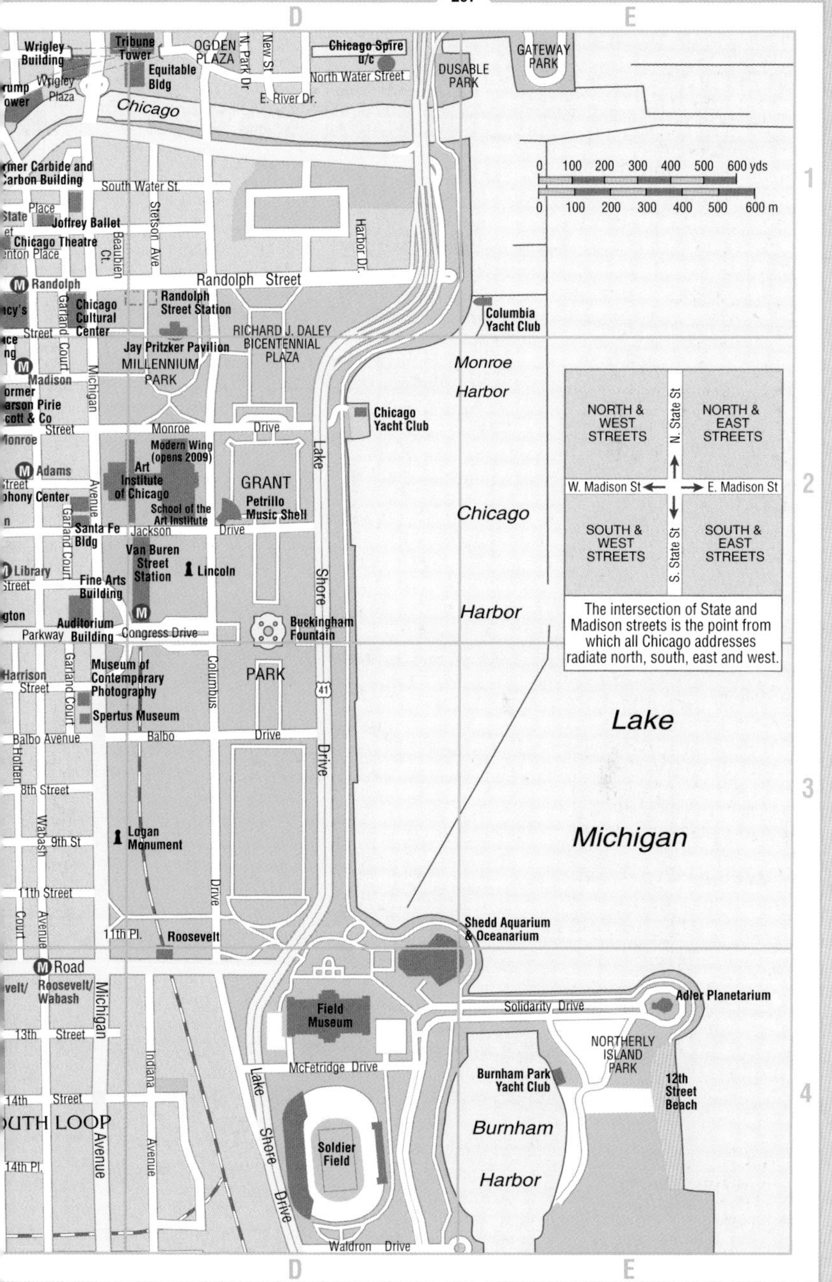
297
D
E
Wrigley Building
Tribune Tower
OGDEN PLAZA
N. Park Dr
New St
Chicago Spire u/c
North Water Street
DUSABLE PARK
GATEWAY PARK
Equitable Bldg
Wrigley Plaza
E. River Dr.
Chicago
South Water St.
Joffrey Ballet
Chicago Theatre
Beaubien Ct.
Stetson Ave
Harbor Dr.
Randolph
Randolph Street
Randolph Street Station
Chicago Cultural Center
Garland Court
Columbia Yacht Club
RICHARD J. DALEY BICENTENNIAL PLAZA
Jay Pritzker Pavilion
MILLENNIUM PARK
Madison
Michigan
Monroe Harbor
Chicago Yacht Club
Monroe
Drive
Modern Wing (opens 2009)
Art Institute of Chicago
School of the Art Institute
Adams
Avenue
GRANT
Petrillo Music Shell
Lake
Chicago
Santa Fe Bldg
Jackson
Drive
Van Buren Street Station
Lincoln
Library
Fine Arts Building
Shore
Harbor
Auditorium Building
Parkway
Congress Drive
Buckingham Fountain
Harrison Street
Museum of Contemporary Photography
Columbus
PARK
41
Spertus Museum
Balbo Avenue
Balbo
Drive
Lake
Holden
Drive
8th Street
Wabash
9th St
Logan Monument
Michigan
11th Street
Drive
Court
Avenue
11th Pl.
Roosevelt
Shedd Aquarium & Oceanarium
Road
Roosevelt/ Wabash
Michigan
Field Museum
Solidarity Drive
Adler Planetarium
13th Street
NORTHERLY ISLAND PARK
McFetridge Drive
Indiana
Lake
Burnham Park Yacht Club
12th Street Beach
14th Street
Shore
Burnham
Soldier Field
Avenue
Avenue
14th Pl.
Drive
Harbor
Waldron Drive
0 100 200 300 400 500 600 yds
0 100 200 300 400 500 600 m
NORTH & WEST STREETS
N. State St
NORTH & EAST STREETS
W. Madison St
E. Madison St
SOUTH & WEST STREETS
S. State St
SOUTH & EAST STREETS
The intersection of State and Madison streets is the point from which all Chicago addresses radiate north, south, east and west.
1
2
3
4
D
E
301

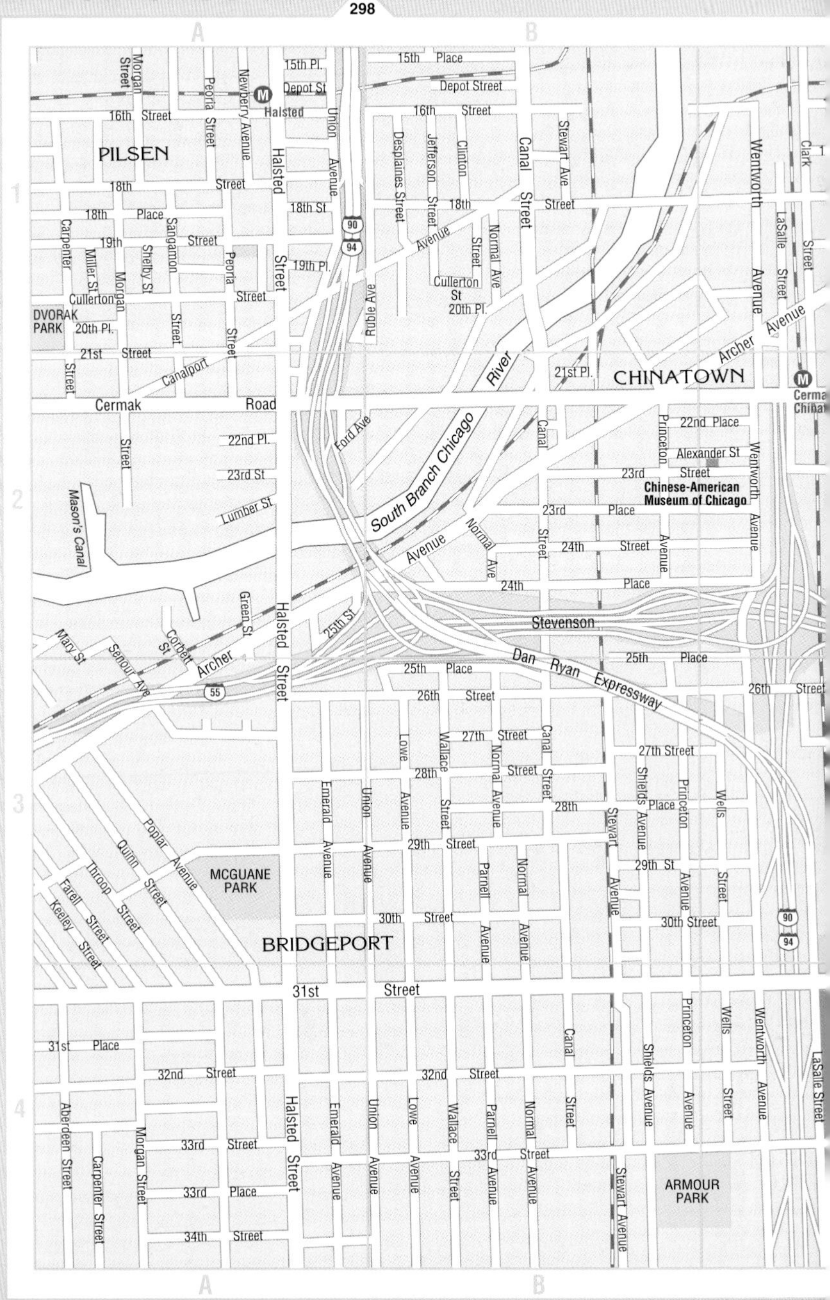
298
PILSEN
CHINATOWN
BRIDGEPORT
DVORAK PARK
MCGUANE PARK
ARMOUR PARK
Chinese-American Museum of Chicago
Halsted
Cermak Road
South Branch Chicago River
Stevenson
Dan Ryan Expressway
Archer Avenue
Mason's Canal
31st Street
Halsted Street
Canal Street
Wentworth Avenue

299
D
E
SOUTH LOOP
Waldron Drive
0 100 200 300 400 500 600 yds
0 100 200 300 400 500 600 m
Lake Shore Drive
National Vietnam Veterans Art Museum
18th Street
18th St
Glessner House Museum
Second Presbyterian Church
Clarke House
Burnham
Harbor
Cullerton St
Prairie Avenue Historic Distric
21st St
McCormick Place North
Blues Heaven Foundation
Road
McCormick Place Lakeside Center
23rd Street
Cottage Grove Ave
McCormick Place
Calumet Ave
Lake
McCormick Place South
BURNHAM PARK
24th Street
24th Place
Michigan
Expressway
25th Street
Dr. M.L. King Drive
26th Street
26th St
27th Street
Wabash Avenue
Indiana Avenue
Prairie Avenue
Calumet Avenue
Ellis Avenue
28th Street
28th Pl.
Vernon Avenue
Moe Drive
Fort Dearborn Drive
29th Street
29th Pl.
DUNBAR PARK
PRAIRIE SHORES
Lake Park Avenue
30th St
State
31st Street
LAKE MEADOWS PARK
Rhodes Avenue
Institute of Technology
32nd Street
Giles Avenue
McCormick Tribune Campus Center
State Street Village
33rd Street
33rd St
33rd Place
34th Street
1
2
3
4

A
B
1
2
3
4
KENWOOD
48th Street
49th Street
50th Street
50th Place
51st Street
51st Street
Vincennes Avenue
Forestville Avenue
St Lawrence Avenue
Champlain Avenue
Langley Avenue
HOUSTON PARK
Drexel Boulevard
Ellis Avenue
University Avenue
Michigan Avenue
Indiana Avenue
Prairie Avenue
Calumet Avenue
Dr Martin Luther King Drive
Cottage Grove Avenue
Drexel Avenue
Ingleside Avenue
Greenwood Avenue
Ellis Avenue
53rd Street
54th Street
54th Place
STOUT PARK
Garfield/Green
Garfield Boulevard
WASHINGTON
PARK
55th Place
Smart Museum of Art
Morgan Drive
56th Street
Joseph Regenstein Library
University
DuSable Museum of African-American History
Wabash Avenue
57th Street
Hull Court
Lagoon
Ellis Avenue
Quadrangle
of Chicago
58th Street
University of Chicago Medical Center
Bond Chapel
Harper Memorial Library
59th Street
59th Street
Midway Plais
Best Drive
Midway Plais
60th Street
60th Street
61st Street
Vernon Avenue
Eberhart Avenue
Rhodes Avenue
St Lawrence Avenue
Champlain Avenue
Langley Avenue
Evans Avenue
Cottage Grove Avenue
Drexel Avenue
Ingleside Avenue
Ellis Avenue
Greenwood Avenue
62nd St
King Drive
63rd Street
East 63rd/Cottage Grove

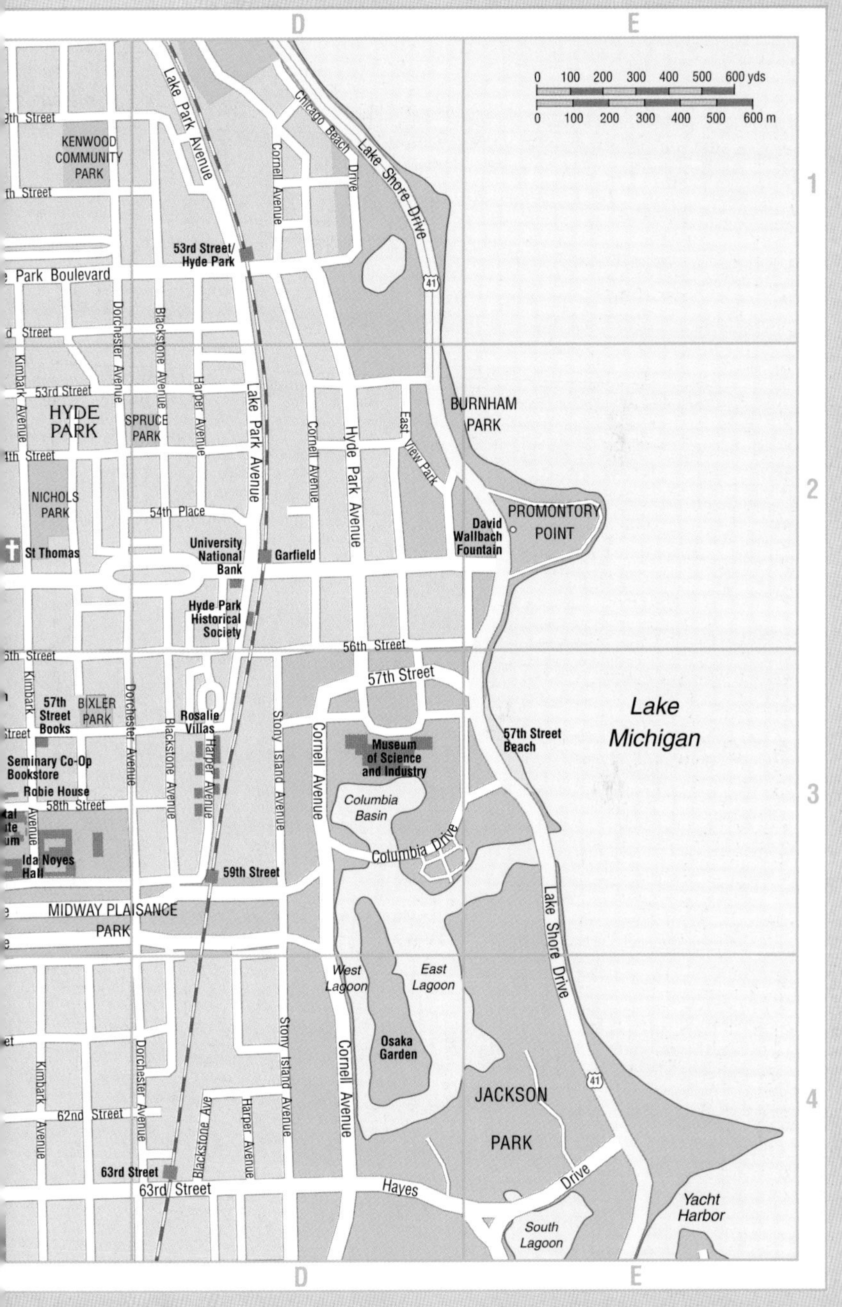
D
E
0 100 200 300 400 500 600 yds
0 100 200 300 400 500 600 m
1
2
3
4
KENWOOD COMMUNITY PARK
Lake Park Avenue
Chicago Beach Drive
Lake Shore Drive
Cornell Avenue
53rd Street/ Hyde Park
Park Boulevard
Dorchester Avenue
Blackstone Avenue
Harper Avenue
Kimbark Avenue
53rd Street
HYDE PARK
SPRUCE PARK
East View Park
Hyde Park Avenue
BURNHAM PARK
NICHOLS PARK
54th Place
PROMONTORY POINT
David Wallbach Fountain
St Thomas
University National Bank
Garfield
Hyde Park Historical Society
56th Street
57th Street
Lake Michigan
57th Street Books
BIXLER PARK
Rosalie Villas
Stony Island Avenue
Museum of Science and Industry
57th Street Beach
Seminary Co-Op Bookstore
Robie House
58th Street
Columbia Basin
Columbia Drive
Ida Noyes Hall
59th Street
MIDWAY PLAISANCE PARK
West Lagoon
East Lagoon
Osaka Garden
JACKSON PARK
62nd Street
Blackstone Ave
63rd Street
Hayes Drive
South Lagoon
Yacht Harbor
41

A
B
1
2
3
4
OLD TOWN
LINCOLN PARK
GOLD
COAST
CABRINI
GREEN
STANTON PARK
SEWARD
PARK
NEAR NORTH
RIVER
NORTH
WASHINGTON
SQUARE
Boka
Alinea
Steppenwolf
Theatre
Company
North-Clybourn
St Michael's
Sedgwick
Noble Horse Theatre
Adobo
Grill
Second
City
Chicago
History
Museum
Archbishop's
Residence
Madlener House
Patterson-
McCormick
Mansion
Charnley-Persky
House
Kamehachi
Old Jerusalem
Former
Playboy
Mansion
Three Arts Club
Third Coast
Salpicon
Hotel
Indigo
LaSalle
Towers
Clark/Division
Table Fifty-Two
Tsunami
Bistro
Zinc
Ashkenaz
Deli
Il Mulino
Merlo on Maple
Original
Pancake
House
Gibson's
Le Colonial
Four Seasons
Talbott
Hotel
Cru Café
CONNORS
PARK
Sofitel
Newberry Library
Ambassador
East Hotel
The Pump Room
Fisher Studio
Houses
Chicago
Café Iberico
Holy Name
Cathedral
St James
Cathedral
Cable House
Quartino
Former
Medinah
Temple
Osteria Via Stato
Embassy Suites
Sushi Naniwa
Pizzeria Uno
Comfort Inn
Home
Suites
Cyrano's
Grand
Gene and
Georgetti
Frontera Grill
Hampton
Inn
Shaw's Crab House
Algre Doux
Merchandise
Mart
Marina
City
Bin 36
Apparel Mart
& Expocenter
Sun-Times
Bldg
Fulton Street Market
Clinton
Clark
Chicago Theatre
Dayton
Halsted
Burling
Orchard
Howe St
Larabee
Cleveland
Ave.
Sedgwick
Street
Menomonee
Willow
St Paul Ave
Eugenie St
Eugenie Street
Concord Pl
Concord Place
Mohawk
Meyer Ave
St Michaels Ct
Fern Ct
Vine
Clark Street
LaSalle Drive
North Avenue
North Boulevard
Weed Street
Blackhawk Avenue
Blackhawk Ave
Clybourn Avenue
Hudson
Orleans
Northpark Avenue
Wieland
Wells
LaSalle
Burton St
Burton Place
State P'way
Astor
Dearborn
Eastman St
Ogden Avenue
Evergreen Ave
Evergreen Avenue
Schiller St
Goethe
Scott Street
Scott St
E. Scott Street
Division Street
Elm St
Cambridge St
Felton Ct
Crosby
Kingsbury
Hobbie Street
Hill Street
Wendell Street
Cedar
Maple Street
Oak Street
Walton Street
Delaware Pl.
Washington Pl.
Rush
Locust Street
Franklin
Chestnut Street
Chestnut St
Institute Place
Chicago Avenue
Lessing St
Superior St
Huron St
Peoria St
Ancona St
Erie Street
Green St
North Branch
Ontario Street
Ohio Street
Campbell Pl.
Grand Avenue
Kennedy Expwy
Milwaukee Ave
Hubbard Street
Hubbard's Tunnel
Illinois
Kinzie Street
Carroll Ave
Wayman Street
Walnut St
Lake Street
Kingsbury Street
Chicago
Canal Street
Merchandise Mart Dr.
Wacker Drive
Haddock Place
Garvey St
Wabash
90
94
306

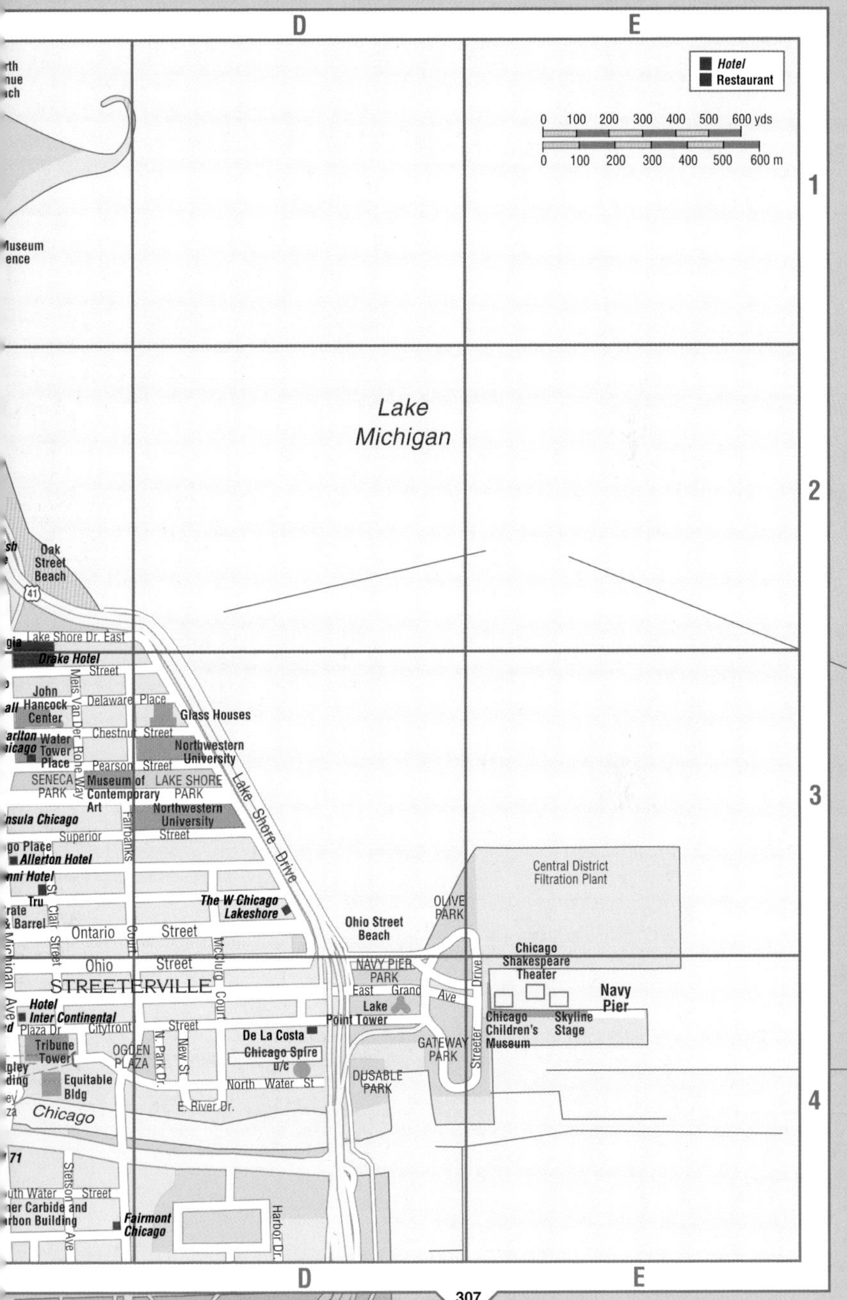
D
E
Hotel
Restaurant
0 100 200 300 400 500 600 yds
0 100 200 300 400 500 600 m
1
2
3
4
Lake Michigan
Oak Street Beach
41
Lake Shore Dr. East
Drake Hotel
Street
John Hancock Center
Delaware Place
Glass Houses
Chestnut Street
Water Tower Place
Northwestern University
Pearson Street
Mies Van Der Rohe Way
SENECA PARK
Museum of Contemporary Art
LAKE SHORE PARK
Lake Shore Drive
Insula Chicago
Northwestern University
Superior Street
Fairbanks
Allerton Hotel
St. Clair Street
The W Chicago Lakeshore
Ontario Street
Court
Ohio Street Beach
Central District Filtration Plant
OLIVE PARK
Ohio Street
McClurg Court
STREETERVILLE
NAVY PIER PARK
East Grand Ave
Chicago Shakespeare Theater
Navy Pier
Hotel Inter Continental
Lake Point Tower
Plaza Dr
Cityfront
Street
Chicago Children's Museum
Skyline Stage
Tribune Tower
OGDEN PLAZA
N. Park Dr.
New St
De La Costa
Chicago Spire u/c
GATEWAY PARK
Streeter Drive
Equitable Bldg
North Water St
DUSABLE PARK
E. River Dr.
Chicago
Stetson Ave
Street
Fairmont Chicago
Harbor Dr.
D
E

307

304
308
A
B
1
2
3
4
Hubbard Street
Kinzie Street
Carroll Avenue
Wayman Street
Fulton Street Market
Moto
Lake Street
Sushi Wabi
Randolph Street
Harpo Studios
Wishbone
Marché
Le Sardine
Washington Street
Madison Street
GREEKTOWN
Arcade Pl.
Monroe Street
Hellenic Museum and Cultural Center
Adams Street
Greek Islands
Quincy St
Jackson Boulevard
Artopolis
Van Buren Street
Eisenhower Expressway
Congress Parkway
Harrison Street
Vernon Park Place
Jane Addams Hull-House Museum
Daley Library
University of Illinois at Chicago
Chicago Circle Center
LITTLE ITALY
Polk St
Taylor
Roosevelt Road
UNIVERSITY VILLAGE
UIC ATHLETIC FIELDS
Maxwell St
14th Pl.
Water Market Pl.
15th St.
PILSEN
Milwaukee
Hubbard's Tunnel
Halsted
Walnut St
Couch Pl.
Court Pl.
Blackbird
Avec
Warren Ave
Desplaines Street
Jefferson
Ryan Expressway
Dan
Site of Chicago Fire (1871)
Maxwell Street Market
Manny's Coffee Shop & Deli
12th Place
O'Brien St
13th St
Hashbrowns
Liberty St
14th St
Barber St
Depot St
Union Avenue
Ruble Avenue
Apparel Mart & Expocenter
Kingsbury St
Sun-Times Bldg
Merchandise Mart
Merchandise Mart Dr.
Clinton
Canal Street
Ogilvie Transportation Center (Northwestern Station)
Civic Opera House
Wacker Drive
Giordano's
Union Station
Lou Mitchell's
Main Post Office
Tilden Street
Cabrini
Lexington Street
DeKoven St
Grenshaw St
White Palace Grill
South Branch Chicago
Roosevelt
15th St
15th Place
Depot Street
Cadillac Palace Theater
Franklin
Hannah's Bretzel
Calhoun
Sears Tower
Quincy
LOOP
Chicago Board of Trade
Old Colony Building
Everest
Custom House
Lasalle
Financial Place
Wells Street
LaSalle
Clark
Franklin Bldg
Dearborn Station
Taylor
Stowell St
James R. Thompson Center
The Allegro
City Hall
Bombon Café
Daley Center Plaza
Chicago Temple
Chase Tower
Italian Village
Shikago
The Rookery
Marquette Building
Haddock
Post

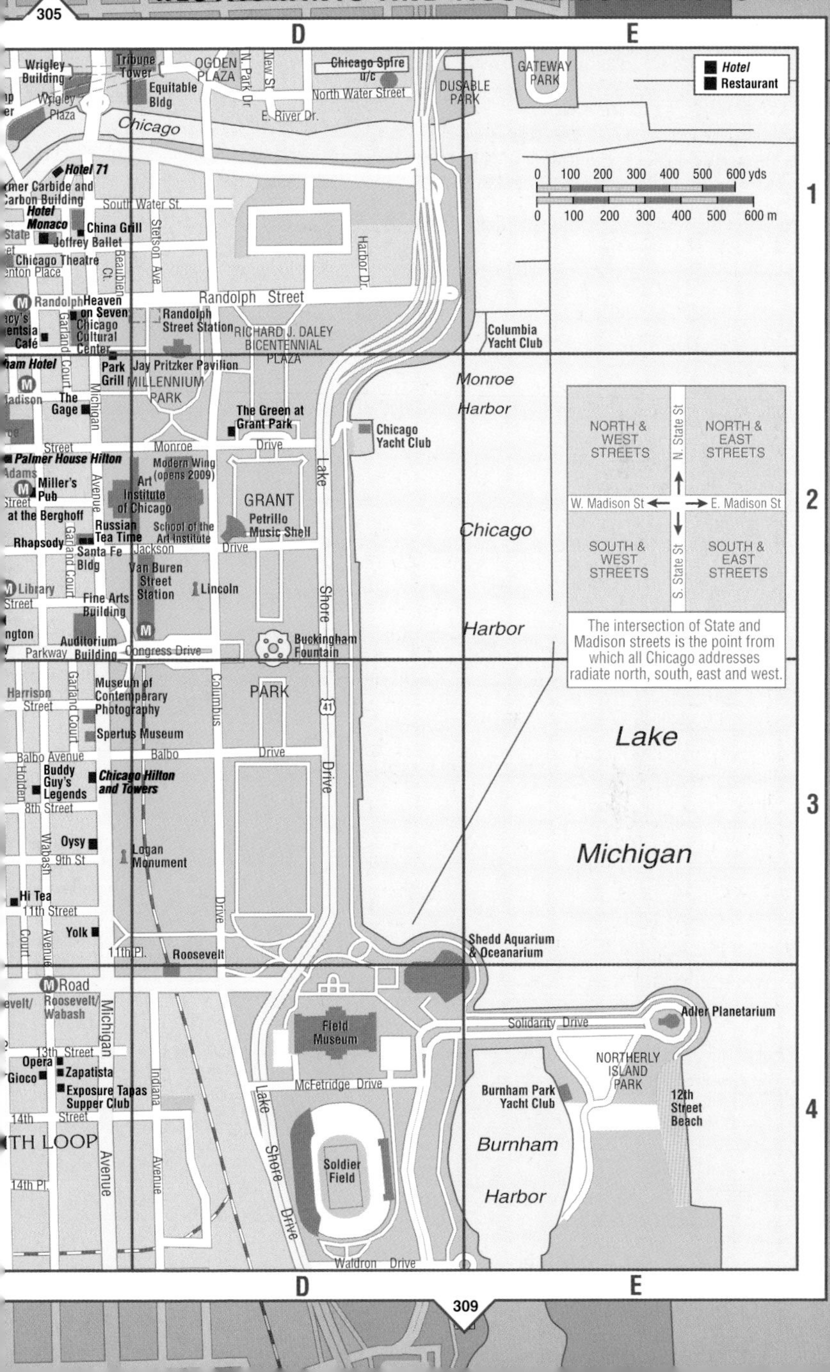

305

D E

■ *Hotel*
■ Restaurant

0 100 200 300 400 500 600 yds
0 100 200 300 400 500 600 m

1 2 3 4

Wrigley Building
Tribune Tower
OGDEN PLAZA
Equitable Bldg
Wrigley Plaza
N. Park Dr
New St
Chicago Spire u/c
North Water Street
E. River Dr.
DUSABLE PARK
GATEWAY PARK
Chicago
*Hotel 71*
Carbide and Carbon Building
*Hotel Monaco*
South Water St.
China Grill
Joffrey Ballet
Chicago Theatre
Stetson Ave
Beaubien Ct.
Harbor Dr.
Randolph Street
Randolph
Heaven on Seven
Chicago Cultural Center
Randolph Street Station
RICHARD J. DALEY BICENTENNIAL PLAZA
Columbia Yacht Club
Garland Court
Park Grill
Jay Pritzker Pavilion
MILLENNIUM PARK
Monroe Harbor
The Gage
Michigan
The Green at Grant Park
Chicago Yacht Club
Monroe Street
Drive
*Palmer House Hilton*
Modern Wing (opens 2009)
Art Institute of Chicago
Miller's Pub
Avenue
GRANT
Lake
Petrillo Music Shell
at the Berghoff
Russian Tea Time
School of the Art Institute
Rhapsody
Santa Fe Bldg
Jackson
Drive
Chicago Harbor
Library
Van Buren Street Station
Lincoln
Shore
Fine Arts Building
Auditorium Building
Buckingham Fountain
Parkway
Congress Drive
Harrison Street
Museum of Contemporary Photography
Columbus
PARK
41
Spertus Museum
Balbo Avenue
Balbo
Drive
Holden
Buddy Guy's Legends
*Chicago Hilton and Towers*
8th Street
Oysy
Wabash
9th St
Logan Monument
Hi Tea
11th Street
Yolk
Court
Avenue
11th Pl.
Roosevelt
Shedd Aquarium & Oceanarium
Road
Roosevelt/Wabash
Solidarity Drive
Adler Planetarium
Field Museum
13th Street
Opera
Gioco
Zapatista
Exposure Tapas Supper Club
Indiana
McFetridge Drive
NORTHERLY ISLAND PARK
Burnham Park Yacht Club
12th Street Beach
14th Street
TH LOOP
Lake Shore Drive
Soldier Field
Burnham Harbor
Avenue
14th Pl.
Waldron Drive

Lake Michigan

NORTH & WEST STREETS
NORTH & EAST STREETS
N. State St
W. Madison St
E. Madison St
SOUTH & WEST STREETS
SOUTH & EAST STREETS
S. State St

The intersection of State and Madison streets is the point from which all Chicago addresses radiate north, south, east and west.

309

306
A
B
1
2
3
4
PILSEN
DVORAK PARK
CHINATOWN
Joy Yee's Noodles
Cermak/Chinatown
Chinese-American Museum of Chicago
Mason's Canal
South Branch Chicago River
Stevenson
Dan Ryan Expressway
MCGUANE PARK
BRIDGEPORT
Ed's Potsticker House
ARMOUR PARK
Halsted
Cermak Road
Archer Avenue

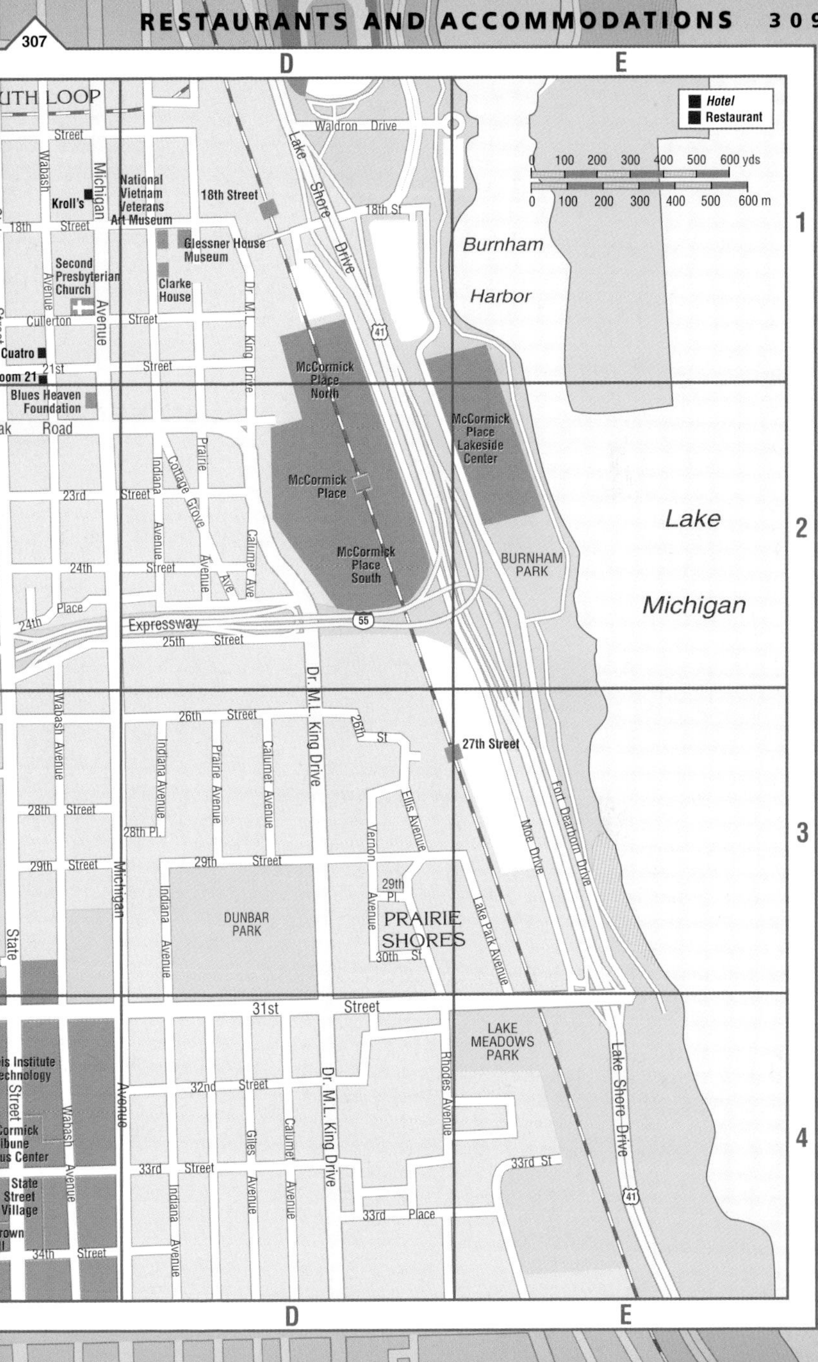
307
D
E
Hotel
Restaurant
0 100 200 300 400 500 600 yds
0 100 200 300 400 500 600 m
1
2
3
4
Burnham
Harbor
Lake
Michigan
McCormick Place North
McCormick Place
McCormick Place South
McCormick Place Lakeside Center
BURNHAM PARK
DUNBAR PARK
PRAIRIE SHORES
LAKE MEADOWS PARK
National Vietnam Veterans Art Museum
Glessner House Museum
Clarke House
Second Presbyterian Church
Kroll's
Cuatro
Blues Heaven Foundation
18th Street
27th Street
Waldron Drive
Lake Shore Drive
18th St
Dr. M.L. King Drive
Michigan Avenue
Wabash Avenue
Cullerton Street
21st Street
23rd Street
24th Street
24th Place
Expressway
25th Street
26th Street
26th St
28th Street
28th Pl.
29th Street
29th Pl.
30th St
31st Street
32nd Street
33rd Street
33rd St
33rd Place
34th Street
Indiana Avenue
Prairie Avenue
Calumet Avenue
Cottage Grove Ave
Ellis Avenue
Vernon Avenue
Lake Park Avenue
Moe Drive
Fort Dearborn Drive
Rhodes Avenue
Giles Avenue
State Street
State Street Village
41
55
D
E

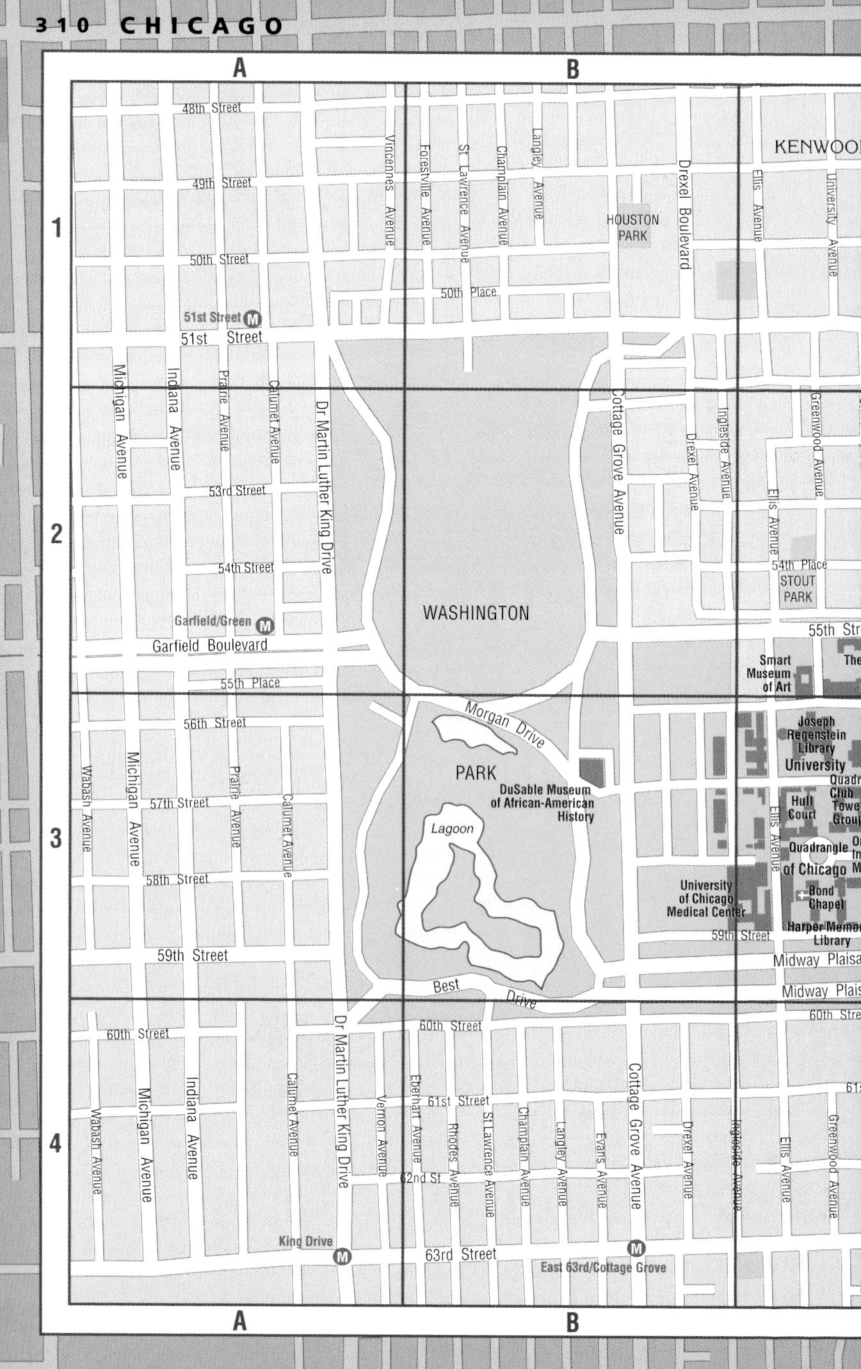
A
B
1
2
3
4
48th Street
49th Street
50th Street
50th Place
51st Street
51st Street
KENWOOD
HOUSTON PARK
Vincennes Avenue
Forestville Avenue
St Lawrence Avenue
Champlain Avenue
Langley Avenue
Drexel Boulevard
Ellis Avenue
University Avenue
Michigan Avenue
Indiana Avenue
Prairie Avenue
Calumet Avenue
Dr Martin Luther King Drive
Cottage Grove Avenue
Drexel Avenue
Ingleside Avenue
Greenwood Avenue
53rd Street
54th Street
54th Place
STOUT PARK
Garfield/Green
Garfield Boulevard
55th Place
WASHINGTON
PARK
55th Street
Smart Museum of Art
Morgan Drive
56th Street
57th Street
58th Street
59th Street
Wabash Avenue
Joseph Regenstein Library
University of Chicago
DuSable Museum of African-American History
Lagoon
Hull Court
Quadrangle
Bond Chapel
Harper Memorial Library
University of Chicago Medical Center
59th Street
Midway Plaisance
Best Drive
60th Street
61st Street
62nd St
Vernon Avenue
Eberhart Avenue
Rhodes Avenue
St Lawrence Avenue
Champlain Avenue
Langley Avenue
Evans Avenue
King Drive
63rd Street
East 63rd/Cottage Grove

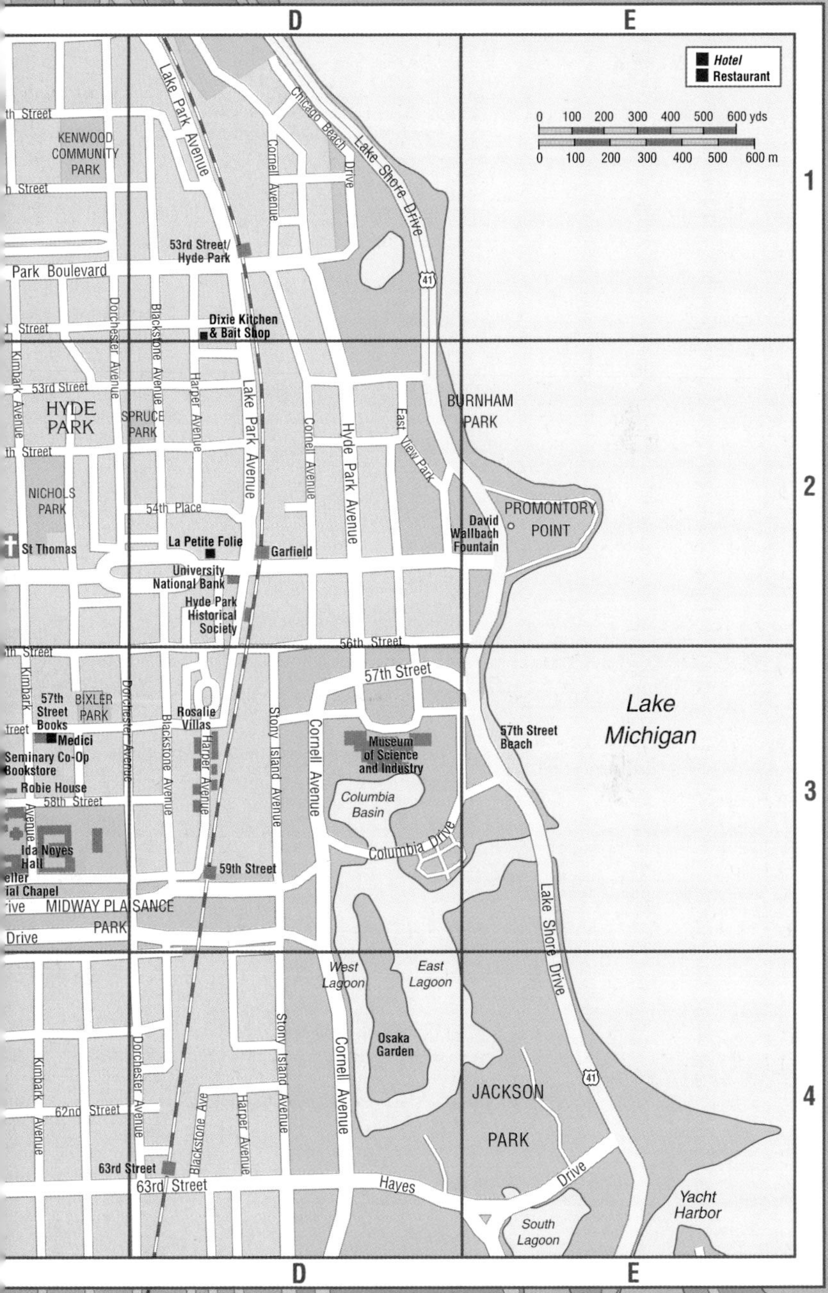

D E

Hotel
Restaurant

0 100 200 300 400 500 600 yds
0 100 200 300 400 500 600 m

KENWOOD COMMUNITY PARK
Lake Park Avenue
Chicago Beach Drive
Lake Shore Drive
Cornell Avenue
53rd Street/ Hyde Park
Park Boulevard
Dixie Kitchen & Bait Shop
Dorchester Avenue
Blackstone Avenue
Harper Avenue
Kimbark Avenue
53rd Street
HYDE PARK
SPRUCE PARK
Hyde Park Avenue
East View Park
BURNHAM PARK
NICHOLS PARK
54th Place
PROMONTORY POINT
David Wallbach Fountain
St Thomas
La Petite Folie
Garfield
University National Bank
Hyde Park Historical Society
56th Street
57th Street
57th Street Books
BIXLER PARK
Medici
Seminary Co-Op Bookstore
Robie House
58th Street
Rosalie Villas
Stony Island Avenue
Museum of Science and Industry
Columbia Basin
Columbia Drive
57th Street Beach
Lake Michigan
Ida Noyes Hall
59th Street
MIDWAY PLAISANCE PARK
West Lagoon
East Lagoon
Osaka Garden
JACKSON PARK
62nd Street
63rd Street
Hayes Drive
South Lagoon
Yacht Harbor

1 2 3 4

D E

# STREET INDEX

8th Street **299** C3, **303** C3
9th Street **299** C3
11th Place **299** C3–D3
11th Street **299** C3
12th Place **298** A4–B4
12th Street Beach **299** E4
13th Street **298** A4
14th Place **298** A4–B4, **299** C4
14th Street **298** A4–C4, **299** C4
15th Street **298** A4–C4, **299** C4–D4
15th Place **298** A4–B4, **299** C4
16th Street **300** A1–C1
17th Street **300** C1, **301** C1–D1
18th Place **300** A1, **301** D1
18th Street **300** A1–C1
19th Place **300** A1, **301** C1–D1
19th Street **300** A1, C1
20th Place **300** A1, B1, **301** D1
21st Place **300** B2
21st Street **300** A1
22nd Place **300** A2–C2, **301** C1–D1
23rd Place **300** B2–C2
23rd Street **300** A2–C2
24th Place **300** A2–C2, **301** C2–D2
24th Street **300** B2–C2, **301** C2–D2
25th Place **300** B3–C3, **301** C2–D2
25th Street **300** A2
26th Street **300** A3–C3, **301** C2–D2
27th Street **300** B3–C3, **301** C3–D3
28th Place **300** B3–C3
28th Street **300** A3–B3, **301** D3
29th Place **301** C3–D3
29th Street **300** A3–C3
30th Street **300** A3–C3, **301** C3–D3
31st Place **300** A4, **301** D3
31st Street **300** A4–C4
32nd Street **300** A4–C4, **301** C4–E4
33rd Place **300** A4
33rd Street **300** A4–C4, **301** D4
34th Street **300** A4–C4, **301** C4, E4
48th Street **301** C4–D4, **302** A1–C1
49th Street **302** A1–C1, **303** C1
50th Place **302** A1–B1, **303** C1–D1
50th Street **302** A1–C1
51st Street **302** A1–B1, **303** C1–D1
52nd Street **302** B1–C1
53rd Street **302** A2, C2 **303** C1–D1
54th Place **302** B2–C2, **303** C2–D2
54th Street **302** A2–C2, **303** C2–D2
55th Place **302** A2, **303** C2–D2
55th Street **302** B2–C2
56th Street **302** A3–C3, **303** C2–E2
57th Street **302** A3–C3, **303** C3–D3
57th Street Beach **303** C3–E3
57th Street Books **303** C3
58th Street **302** A3–C3
59th Street **302** A3–C3, **303** C3–D3
60th Street **302** A4–C4, **303** C3–D3
61st Street **302** A4–C4, **303** C4–D4
62nd Street **302** A4–C4, **303** C4–D4
63rd Street **302** A4–C4, **303** C4–D4
64th Street **302** C3, **303** C4–D4

### A

Aberdeen Street **300** A4
Adams Street **298** A2–C2
Adler Planetarium **299** C2, E4
Alexander Street **300** B2–C2
Ancona Street **296** A3
Apparel Mart & Expocenter **296** B4
Arcade Place **298** A2
Archbishop's Residence **296** C1
Archer Avenue **300** A3–C1
Armour Park **300** B4–C4, **301** C1
Art Institute of Chicago **299** C2–D2
Astor Street **296** C1–C2
Auditorium Building **299** C2

### B

Balbo Avenue **299** C3
Balbo Drive **299** C3–D3
Banks Street **296** C2
Barber Street **298** A4
Beaubien Court **299** C1
Bellevue Place **296** C2, **297** C2
Benton Place **299** C1
Best Drive **302** A3–B3
Bixler Park **303** C3
Blackhawk Avenue **296** A1–B1
Blackstone Avenue **303** D1–D4
Bloomingdales **297** C3
Blues Heaven Foundation **301** C2
Bond Chapel **302** C3
Buckingham Fountain **299** D3
Burling Street **296** A1–A2
Burnham Park **301** D1–E4
Burnham Park Yacht Club **299** E4, **303** D1–E2
Burton Place **296** B1–C1
Burton Street **296** B1

### C

Cable House **296** C3
Cabrini Street **298** B3
Cadillac Palace Theater **298** C1
Calhoun Place **298** B2–C2
Calumet Avenue **301** D2–D4
Cambridge Street **296** A2, **302** A1–A4
Campbell Place **296** B4
Canal Street **296** A4
Canalport Avenue **298** B1–B4, **300** A2–B4
Carbide and Carbon Building, Former **297** C4
Carpenter Street **298** A1–A3
Carroll Avenue **296** A4, **300** A1–A4
Carson Pirie Scott & Co. **299** C2
Cedar Street **296** C2
Cermak Road **300** A2–C2
Champlain Avenue **301** C2–D2, **302** B1–B4
Charnley-Persky House **296** C2
Chase Tower **298** C2
Chestnut Street **296** A3–C3
Chicago Avenue **296** A3–C3, **297** C3–D3
Chicago Beach Drive **297** C3–D3, **303** D1
Chicago Board of Trade **298** C2
Chicago Children's Museum **297** E4
Chicago Circle Center **298** A3
Chicago Cultural Center **299** C1
Chicago Historic Museum **296** B1
Chicago Place **297** C3
Chicago Shakespeare Theater **297** E4
Chicago Spire **297** D4
Chicago Temple **298** C2
Chicago Theatre **299** C1
Chicago Yacht Club **299** D3
Chinese-American Museum of Chicago **300** C2
City Hall **298** C1
Cityfront Street **297** C4–D4
Civic Opera House **298** B2
Clark Street **296** B1–B4
Clarke House **301** D1
Cleveland Avenue **296** A1–A3, **298** C1–C2, **300** C1–C3
Clinton Street **298** B1–B4
Clybourn Avenue **296** A1–B2, **300** B1
Columbia Drive **303** D3
Columbia Yacht Club **299** E1
Columbus Drive **299** D1–D4
Concord Place **296** A1
Congress Drive **299** C2–D2
Congress Parkway **298** A3–C2
Connors Park **296** C3, **299** C2
Corbett Street **300** A2–A3
Cornell Avenue **303** D1–D4
Cottage Grove Avenue **301** D2
Couch Place **298** A1–C1, **302** B1–B4
Court Place **298** A1–C1
Crate & Barrel **297** C3
Crosby Street **296** A2–A3
Cullerton Street **300** A1–C1

### D

Daley Center & Plaza **298** C1, **301** C1–D1
Daley Library **298** A3
Dan Ryan Expressway **298** A3–A4
David Wallbach Fountain **300** A1–C4, **303** E4
Dayton Street **296** A1–A2
Dearborn Park **298** C3
Dearborn Street **296** C1–C4
Dearborn Station **298** C3
DeKoven Street **297** C1–C2, **298** B3, **299** C1–C3
Delaware Place **296** B3–C3
Depot Street **297** C3–D3, **298** A4–B4
Desplaines Street **298** A2, **300** B1
Division Street **296** A2–C2
Dorchester Avenue **303** C1–D4
Dr. Martin Luther King Drive **301** D1–D4
Drake Hotel **297** C3, **302** A1–A4
Drexel Avenue **302** B1–B2
Drexel Boulevard **302** B1
Dunbar Park **301** D3
DuSable Museum of African-American History **302** B3
DuSable Park **297** D4
Dvorak Park **300** A1

### E

East River Drive **297** D4
East Grand Avenue **297** D4
Eastman Street **296** A2
Eats View Park **303** D2
Eberhart Avenue **302** B4
Eisenhower Expressway **298** A3
Ellis Avenue **301** D3, **302** C1–C4
Elm Street **296** A2–C2
Emerald Avenue **300** A3–A4
Equitable Bldg **297** C4
Erie Street **296** A3–C3
Ernst Court **296** C3, **297** C3–D3
Eugenie Street **296** A1–B1
Evans Avenue **302** B4
Evergreen Avenue **296** A2–B2

### F

Fairbanks Court **297** C3–C4
Farell Street **300** A3–A4
Federal Avenue **300** C3
Federal Center & Plaza **298** C2
Federal Street **298** C2–C4
Felton Court **296** B2, **300** C1
Fern Court **296** B1
Field Museum **299** D4
Financial Place **298** C2–C3
Fine Arts Building **299** C2
Fisher Building **298** C2
Fisher Studio Houses **296** C2
Ford Avenue **300** A2–B2
Ford Center for the Performing Arts **298** C1
Forestville Avenue **302** B1
Fort Dearborn Drive **301** D1–E3
Fourth Presbyterian Church **297** C3
Franklin Street **296** B2–B4
Fulton Market Street **296** A4–B4, **298** B1–B3
Fulton Street Market **296** A4

### G

Garfield Boulevard **302** A2
Garland Court **299** C1–C3
Garrett Popcorn **297** C3
Garvey Street **296** C4
Gateway Park **297** D4
Giles Avenue **301** D4
Glass Houses **297** D3
Glessner House Museum **301** D1
Goethe Street **296** B2–C2
Grand Avenue **296** A4–C4
Grant Park **297** C4–D4, **299** D1–D4
Green Street **296** A3–A4
Greenwood Avenue **298** A1–A2, **300** A2, **302** C1–C4
Grenshaw Street **298** B3

### H

Haddock Place **296** B4–C4
Halsted Street **296** A1–A4
Harbor Drive **297** D4
Harold Washington Library Center **299** C2–D1
Harper Avenue **303** D1–D4
Harpo Studios **298** A1
Harrison Street **298** A3–C3
Hayes Drive **299** C3, **303** D4–E4
Hellenic Museum & Cultural Center **298** A2
Hill Street **296** B2
Hobbie Street **296** A2
Holy Name Cathedral **296** C3
Houston Park **302** B1
Howe Street **296** A1–A2
Hubbard Street **296** A4–C4
Hudson Avenue **296** B1–B3
Huron Street **296** A3–C3
Hyde Park Avenue **297** C3–D3, **303** D1–D3
Hyde Park Boulevard **302** B1–C1
Hyde Park Historical Society **303** C1–D2

### I

Illinois Street **296** B4–C4
Illinois Institute of Technology **301** C4
Indiana Avenue **299** D4
Ingleside Avenue **301** D1–D4, **302** A1–A4, B1–C4
Inland Steel Bldg **298** C2
Institute Place **296** B3
International Museum of Surgical Science **296** C1

## J

Jackson Boulevard **298** A2–C2
Jackson Drive **299** C2–D2
Jackson Park **303** D3–E4
Jay Pritzker Parilion **299** D1
James R. Thompson Center **298** C1
Jane Addams Hull-House Museum **298** A3
Jeferson Street **298** B1–B4
Jeffrey Ballet **299** C1
John Hancock Center **297** C3, **300** B1

## K

Keeley Street **300** A3–A4
Kennedy Expressway **296** A4
Kenwood Community Park **298** A1–A2, **303** C3
Kimbark Avenue **303** C1–C4
Kingsbury Street **296** A2–B4
Kinzie Street **296** A4–C4, **298** B2

## L

Lake Meadows Park **301** E4
Lake Park Avenue **301** E3, **303** D1–D2
Lake Point Tower **297** D4
Lake Shore Drive **296** C1–C2
Lake Shore Park **297** C2–D4, **301** D1–E4, **303** D1–E4
Lake Street **296** A4–C4
Langley Avenue **297** C4, **302** B1, B4
Larabee Street **296** A1–A3
LaSalle Drive **296** B1–C1
LaSalle Street **296** B2–B4, **298** C1–C3, **300** C1–C4
LaSalle Towers **296** B2
Lessing Street **296** A3
Lexington Street **298** B3
Liberty Street **298** A4
Lincoln Monument **296** B1
Lincoln Park **296** B1–C1
Lincoln Statue **299** D3
Locust Street **296** B3
Logan Monument **299** C3
Lookingglass Theatre **297** C3
Lowe Avenue **300** B3–B4
Lumber Street **300** A2

## M

Macy's **299** C1
Madison Street **298** A2–C2
Madlener House **296** C1, **299** C2
Main Post Office **298** B2
Manhattan Bldg **298** C2
Maple Street **296** B2–C2
Marina City **296** C4
Marquette Building **298** C2
Mary Street **300** A2–A3
Maxwell Street **298** A4–B4
Maxwell Street Market **298** B3
McClurg Court **297** D3–D4
McCormick Place Lakeside Center **301** E2
McCormick Place North **301** D1
McCormick Place South **301** D2
McCormick Tribune Campus Center **301** C4
McFetridge Drive **299** D4
McGuane Park **300** A3
Medinah Temple, Former **296** C3
Meis van der Rohe Way **297** C3
Menomonee Street **296** A1–B2
Merchandise Mart **296** B4
Merchandise Mart Drive **296** B4
Meyer Avenue **296** A1
Michigan Avenue **297** C3–C4
Midway Plaisance Drive **299** C1–C4, **301** C1–C4, **302** A1–C3
Midway Plaisance Park **302** B3–C4, **303** C3–D3
Millenium Park **299** C1–C2, D1–D2, **303** C3–D3
Miller Street **298** A3, **300** A1
Milwaukee Avenue **296** A3–A4
Moe Drive **301** D1–E3
Mohawk Street **296** A1–A3
Monadnock Building **298** C2
Monroe Drive **299** C2–D2
Monroe Street **298** A2–C2
Morgan Drive **299** C2, **302** A2–B3
Morgan Street **298** A1–A4
Museum of Contemporary Art **297** C3
Museum of Contemporary Photography **299** C3
Museum of Science and Industry **303** D3

## N

North Park Drive **297** D4
National Vietnam Veterans Art Museum **301** D1
Navy Pier **297** E4
Navy Pier Park **297** D4
Neiman Marcus **297** C3
New Street **297** D4
Newberry Avenue **298** A4
Newberry Library **296** B/C3
Nichols Park **300** A1, **303** C2
Noble Horse Theatre **296** B1
Normal Avenue **300** B2–B4
North Avenue **296** A1–B1
North Avenue Beach **296** C1
North Boulevard **296** B1–C1
North Water Street **297** D4
Northerly Island Park **299** E4
Northpark Avenue **296** B1–B2
Northwestern University **297** D3

## O

O'Brien Street **298** A4
Oak Street **296** A3–C2
Oak Street Beach **297** C2
Ogden Avenue **296** A2
Ogden Plaza **297** D4
Ogilvie Transportation Center (Northwestern Station) **298** B1
Ohio Street **296** A4–C4
Ohio Street Beach **297** C4–D4
Old Colony Building **298** C2
Olive Park **297** D3
One Magnificent Mile **297** C3
Ontario Street **296** A3–C3
Orchard Street **296** A1, **297** C3–D3
Oriental Institute Museum **302** C3
Orleans Street **296** B1–B4
Osaka Garden **298** B1, **303** D3

## P

Park Terrace **298** C3
Parnell Avenue **300** B3–B4
Patterson-McCormick Mansion **296** C1
Pearson Street **297** C3–D3
Peoria Street **296** A3–A4
Petrillo Music Shell **299** D2
Playboy Mansion, Former **296** C2
Plaza Drive **297** C4, **298** A1–A4, **300** A1–A2
Plymouth Court **298** C3–C4
Polk Street **298** A3–C3
Poplar Avenue **299** C3, **300** A3–A4
Prairie Avenue **301** D2–D4
Prairie Avenue Historic District **301** D1
Princeton Avenue **300** B2–B4, **302** A1–A4
Promontory Point **303** E4

## Q

Quincy Street **298** A2–C2
Quinn Street **300** A3–A4

## R

Randolph Street **298** A1–C3
Reliance Building **299** C1–D1
Rhodes Avenue **301** D4, **302** B4
Richard J. Daley Bicentennial Plaza **299** D1–D2
Ritchie Court **296** C2
Robie House **303** C3
Rockefeller Memorial Chapel **302** C3
Rookery, The **298** C2
Roosevelt Road **298** A4–C4
Ruble Avenue **298** A4, **299** C4, **300** B1
Rush Street **296** C2–C4

## S

Sangamon Street **297** C4, **298** A4
Santa Fe Bldg **299** C2
Schiller Street **296** B2–C2, **300** A1–A2
Scott Street **296** A2, B2–C2
Second City **296** B1
Second Presbyterian Church **301** C1
Sedgwick Street **296** B1–B3
Seminary Co-Op Bookstore **303** C3
Seneca Park **297** C3
Senour Avenue **300** A2–A3
Seward Park **296** B2
Shedd Aquarium & Oceanarium **299** D4
Shelby Street **300** A1
Shields Avenue **300** B3–B4
Siskel Film Center **298** C1
Site of Chicago Fire-1871 **298** A3
Skyline Stage **297** E4
Smart Museum of Art **302** C2
Soldier Field **299** D4
Solidarity Drive **299** E4
South Water Street **296** C4
Spertus Museum **297** C4, **299** C3
Spruce Park **303** D2
St Clair Street **297** C3–C4
St Lawrence Avenue **302** B1, B4
St James Cathedral **296** C3
St Michaels **296** A/B1
St Michaels Court **296** B1
St Paul Avenue **296** B1
Stanton Park **296** A2
State Parkway **296** C1
State Street **296** C1–C4
State Street Village **301** C4
Steppenwolf Theater Company **296** A1
Stetson Avenue **297** C4
Stevenson Expressway **299** D1, **300** A3–C2
Stewart Avenue **300** B1, B3–B4, **301** C2–D2
Stone Street **296** C2
Stony Island Avenue **303** D3–D4
Stout Park **302** C2
Stowell Street **298** C3
Streeter Drive **297** E4
Sun-Times Bldg **296** B4
Superior Street **296** A3–C3
Symphony Center **299** C2

## T

Taylor Street **297** C3–D3, **298** A3–C3
Theodore Rice House **303** C2
Three Arts Club **296** C2
Throop Street **300** A3–A4
Tilden Street **298** B2
Tribune Tower **297** C4
Trump Tower **296** C4

## U

UIC Athletic Fields **298** A4
Union Avenue **298** A4
Union Station **298** B2, **300** A1–A4
University Avenue **302** C1–C4
University of Chicago **302** C3
University of Chicago Medical Center **302** B3
University of Illinois **298** A3

## V

Van Buren Street **298** A2–C2
Van Buren Street Station **299** C2–D3
Vernon Avenue **301** D3, **302** A4
Vernon Park Place **298** A3–B3
Vincennes Avenue **302** A1
Vine Street **296** A1

## W

Wabash Avenue **296** C2–C4
Wacker Drive **296** B4–C4, **299** C1–C4, **301** C1–C4, **302** A1–A4
Waldron Drive **297** C4–D4, **298** B1–B2, **299** D4
Wallace Street **300** B3–B4
Walnut Street **296** A4
Walton Street **296** B3–C3
Warren Avenue **297** C3–D3, **298** A2
Washington Boulevard **298** A2–C2
Washington Park **299** C2, **302** A1–B4
Washington Place **296** B3–C3
Washington Square **296** B3–C3
Water Market Pl. **298** A4
Water Tower **297** C3
Water Tower Place **297** C3
Wayman Street **296** A4
Weed Street **296** A1
Weiland Street **296** B1–B2
Wells Street **296** B1–B4, **298** B1–C4, **300** C3–C4
Wendell Street **296** B2
Wentworth Avenue **300** C1–C4
Willow Street **296** A1–B2
Woodlawn Drive **302** C1
Wrigley Building **297** C4, **303** C2–C4
Wrigley Plaza **297** C4

# General Index


## A

**accommodations** 13, 123, 267–72
**Addams, Jane** 30, 31, 163, 194
**Adler, Dankmar** 92, 125, 233
**Adler Planetarium** 138–9
**African-Americans** 32, 35–7, 47, 59, 66–7, 71, 233–4, 235
**Albany Park** 82
**Algren, Nelson** 47, 58, 60, 209, 210, 213
**Alinsky, Saul** 31
**Ambassador East Hotel** 163
**American Girl Place** 99
**Ames, Robert** 235
**amusement parks** 12, 149, 150, 151, 256
**Andersonville** 184–5
**Andy's Jazz Club** 11, 102–3
**antiques** 185, 192, 195, 274, 284
**Aqua** 95
**aquariums** 138, 257
**Aragon Ballroom** 183
**Arboretum** 12, 259
**Archbishop's Residence** 160, 161
**Archicenter** 126
**ArchiTech** 73
**architecture** 8, 9, 10, 12, 27–8, 29, 91–7
  *see also* **Chicago Architecture Foundation; skyscrapers**
**Argyle Street** 82, 184
**Aristocrat Records** 66, 223
**Armitage Avenue** 173
**Armour, Philip** 91
**Armstrong, Louis** 32, 33, 65, 231
**art and culture** 11, 71–5, 140–41, 278–82
  *see also* **festivals and events**
**Art Dealers Association of Chicago tours** 155
**Art Deco** 94, 123–4, 152
**art galleries** 73, 126, 131, 152–3, 155, 197, 205, 207–8, 209, 274–5
**art museums** 9, 11
  Art Institute of Chicago 9, 11, 28, 72, 110, 112–13, 114, 130–33
  Block Museum of Art 253
  Blues Heaven Foundation 69, 221
  Center for Book & Paper Arts 73
  Milwaukee Art Museum 256–7
  Museum of Contemporary Art 72, 74, 98, 149–50
  Museum of Contemporary Photography 73, 219
  Museum of Holography-Chicago 193
  National Museum of Mexican Art 73, 197–8
  National Vietnam Veterans Art Museum 219–20
  Smart Museum of Art 73, 236
  Spertus Institute & Museum 94, 96, 219
  Ukrainian Institute of Modern Art 74, 210, 211
**Arthur Heurtley House** 247
**Ashland Avenue** 192
**Astor Street District** 159–63
**Atwood, Charles** 29, 97, 116, 117
**Auditorium Building** 28, 73, 92, 124, 125
**Austin Gardens** 245

## B

**Back of the Yards** 31–2, 58
**Bacon, Francis** 149
**Baha'i Temple (Wilmette)** 255
**ballet** 75, 114, 125
**barbecue** 12, 81, 82
**bars** 78, 83, 164–5, 172–3, 181, 197, 209, 212, 282–3
  *see also end of each section*
**baseball** 9, 86–7, 179, 180, 196, 286–7
**basketball** 88, 198, 287
**Bayless, Rick** 78
**beaches** 11, 158, 163, 164, 172, 175
**Beachy, Peter A. (House)** 247
**Bean (Cloud Gate) sculpture** 10, 72, 136, 140–41
**Bears** 85–6, 139, 287
**beer** 83, 209–210, 212, 238, 257
**Bellow, Saul** 58, 60–61, 236
**Bennett, Edward H.** 93, 141
**bicycling** 19, 88, 89, 255, 287
**Bilandic, Michael A.** 48
**Billy Goat Tavern** 86, 145
**Biograph Theater** 39, 40, 172
**Black Sox scandal** 87, 89
**Blackhawks ice hockey team** 88, 198
**Bloomingdale's** 149, 276
**B.L.U.E.S.** 11, 172
**blues** 65–9, 74, 194–5, 221, 223
  clubs 9, 11, 68, 74, 172, 223, 231, 280
  *see also* **Chicago Blues Festival**
***Blues Brothers*** 62, 63, 118
**Blues Heaven Foundation** 69, 221
**Board of Trade Building** 94
**bookstores** 181, 185, 206, 207, 218–19, 238–9, 275–6
**Boone, Levi** 45
**Bootleg Houses** 246
**bootleggers** 32–4, 41, 83
**Boring Store** 206
**boxing** 88, 139, 195
**Boys Town** 179, 180–81
**BP Bridge** 53, 137
**Brennan, Edward P.** 105
**Bridgeview** 88
**Brogger, Mary** 30
**Bronzeville** 233–4
**Brookfield Zoo** 258–9
**Brooks, Gwendolyn** 59
**Brooks, Lonnie** 74
**Brooks, Wayne Baker** 69
**Brown Elephant stores** 185, 208
**Buckingham Fountain** 136, 141
**Bucktown** 78, 212, 213
**Buddy Guy's Legends** 9, 11, 69, 74, 221
**Bulls** 88, 198, 287
**Burnham, Daniel H.** 92–3, 97, 122, 123, 124, 151, 185, 249
  *Plan of Chicago* 29, 51, 92, 93, 112, 126, 135–6, 143
  Reliance Building 10, 97, 117
  White City (Columbian Exposition) 28, 29, 51, 93, 97, 238
**Burnham Hotel** 10, 97, 117
**Burroughs, Edgar Rice** 245
**Busse, Fred A.** 33, 46
**Byrne, Jane** 37, 48, 118

## C

**Cable House** 153
**Café Brauer** 171
**cafés** *see also end of each section*
**Caillebotte, Gustave** 72, 131

**Calatrava, Santiago** 95, 115, 256, 257
**Calder, Alexander** 93, 122, 149
**Camp Douglas** 169
**canals** 24, 127
**Capone, Al** 32–4, 38–42, 46, 183
*see also* **Untouchables**
**Carl Sandburg Village** 165
**Carson Pirie Scott Building** 28, 117–18
**Carter, Jimmy** 37, 45
**Casa Aztlan** 196–7
**Cathedral District** 153–4
**cathedrals**
Holy Name 42, 153–4
Holy Trinity Russian Orthodox 212
St James 154
St Nicholas Ukrainian Catholic 204, 210, 211, 212
**cemeteries** 169, 179, 185
**Centennial Fountain** 127
**Center for Book & Paper Arts** 73
**Cermak, Anton** 34, 47
**Cézanne, Paul** 114, 130
**Chagall, Marc** 10
*America Windows* 113, 132
*The Four Seasons* 10, 118–19, 141
**chapels** *see under* **churches**
**Charles Gates Dawes House** 255
**Charnley-Persky House** 162–3
**Chase Tower & Plaza** 10, 118–19, 141
**Checker Record Co.** 221, 223
**Chess Records** 68, 74, 221
**Chicago 7** 36
**Chicago Architecture Foundation** 12, 91, 126, 185
**Chicago Blues Artists Coalition** 69
**Chicago Blues Festival** 9, 13, 64, 65, 74, 114, 135, 188, 284
**Chicago Board of Trade** 122, 123–4, 128, 165
**Chicago Botanic Garden** 255–6
**Chicago Cultural Center** 11, 73, 115–16
**Chicago Place** 98
**Chicago River** 16–17, 24, 105, 126, 127, 154
**Chicago School (architecture)** 10, 93, 117, 122, 124, 125, 165
**Chicago Spire** 95, 115
**Chicago Symphony Orchestra** 28, 74, 114, 188, 256
**Chicago Temple Building** 120, 141
**Chicago Visitor Center** 115
**children and families** 12, 138, 146, 173, 182, 198, 242–3, 257, 259
**Chinatown** 218, 222, 285
**chronology** 50–53
**churches**
Baha'i Temple (Wilmette) 255
Bond Chapel 236–7
Chicago Temple Building 120, 141
Church of the Epiphany 192
Fourth Presbyterian 154
Greenstone Church (Pullman) 258
Old St Patrick's 190
Pilgrim Baptist 233–4
Rockefeller Memorial Chapel 237
St Mary of the Angels 205
St Therese Chinese Catholic 222
Second Presbyterian, 221
Sky Chapel 120
Sts Volodymyr and Olha Ukrainian Catholic 211
Unity Temple 246, 247–8
**cinema** 62–3, 75, 113, 114, 118, 182, 183, 238
**Cisneros, Sandra** 61
**City Gallery** 147
**City Hall** 120–21
**Citypass** 13
**Civic Opera House** 114
**Clark Street** 179, 184–5
**Clarke House** 91, 221
**Close, Del** 72
**Cloud Gate sculpture ("The Bean")** 10, 72, 136, 140–41
**clubs** 11, 163, 165, 206, 210, 220, 282–3
*see also* **blues**; **comedy**; **jazz**
**Coleman, Deborah** 69
**Columbia College** 73, 219
**Columbian Exposition (1893)** 28, 29, 51, 93, 97, 238, 239
**comedy** 13, 63, 74, 173–4, 279
**Comisky Park** 87
**conservatories, horticultural** 171, 191, 198, 257
**Cook County Hospital** 197
**Couch Mausoleum** 171
**cricket** 235
**crime** 32–4, 39–43, 194
**Criminal Courts Building** 40
**The Crotch** 206
**Crown Fountain** 12, 71–2, 136–7, 141
**Crown Hall** 93, 232
**cruises** 12, 126, 127, 285
**Cubs** 9, 13, 31, 50–51, 86–7, 179, 180, 181, 286–7

## D

**Daley, Richard J.** 36–7, 39, 44–8, 57, 71, 132
**Daley, Richard M.** 34, 37, 45, 49, 53, 71, 73, 112, 120, 218
**Daley Center & Plaza** 92, 118, 119–20, 141
**Damen Avenue** 206, 210–211, 212
**dance** 75, 135, 149, 281–2
**Darrow, Clarence** 30, 154
**Darwin, Charles** 228–9
**Dawes, Charles Gates, House** 255
**De Beauvoir, Simone** 213
**Dearborn Station** 218, 220
**Dearborn Street** 93, 113
**Delilah's** 172
**Democratic Convention (1968)** 36, 74
**DePaul University** 172
**Depression** 34, 39, 80
**Devon Avenue** 82
**Dillinger, John** 39, 40, 172
**dinosaurs** 11, 138, 227, 229, 257
**discounts and passes** 13
**Discovery World at Pier Wisconsin** 257
**Disney, Walt** 131
**Division Street** 208, 209–210
Russian and Turkish Baths, 207
**Dixon, Willie** 65, 68, 69, 223
**Dobmeyer, Douglas** 31
**Dooley, Martin J**, 58
**Drake Hotel** 148, 239
**Driehaus, Richard H.** 153
**Dubuffet, Jean** 121, 141
**Dunne, Finley Peter** 58
**DuSable, Jean Baptiste Point** 22, 23, 145, 235
**DuSable Museum of African American History** 235

## E

**Earwax Café** 205, 214
**eating out** 12, 13, 77–82
*see also end of each section*
**Eisenhower Expressway** 29, 193
**The El** 13, 185, 217
**Englewood** 43
**equestrian theater** 174
**Essanay Studios** 183
**ethnic cuisine** 82, 184, 193, 195
**ethnicity** 35–7
**Evanston** 253–5
**Evanston Art Center** 253
**events**
listings 13, 283
*see also* **festivals and events**

**Everleigh Club** 220
**Exelon Tube** 232–3

## F

**FAB Gallery** 126
**Facets Multimedia** 75
**family activities** *see* **children and families**
**Farr, Deitra** 69
**Farrell, James T.** 60
**Federal Center & Plaza** 10, 93, 122
  market, 98, 111, 125
**Fermi, Enrico** 35, 140, 237
**Ferris wheel** 28, 238, 239
**festivals and events** 113–14, 135, 147, 188–9, 283–6
  African Festival of the Arts 235
  Around the Coyote Arts Festival 206, 207
  Chicago Blues Festival 9, 13, 64, 65, 74, 114, 135, 188, 284
  Chicago International Film Festival 75, 285
  Chicago Jazz Festival 74
  Chicago Underground Film Festival 75
  Gay & Lesbian Pride 180, 182, 189, 284
  Greek Independence Day Parade 194
  Holiday Flower Show 198
  Jazz Fair 74
  Mexican Independence Day Parade 189
  Old Town Art Fair 174, 284–5
  Ravinia 13, 74–5, 256, 282, 284–5
  Sculpture, Objects & Functional Art (SOFA) Show 99, 150
  Summerdance 135
  Summerfest (Milwaukee) 257
  Taste of Chicago 12, 135, 188, 189
  Taste of Greece 193, 194
  Viva Aztlan Festival 196–7
  World Music Festival 114, 188, 285
**Field, Marshall** 27, 116, 152, 185, 220, 226
**Field Building** 94
**film** 62–3, 75, 113, 114, 118, 182, 183, 238, 279
**Financial District** 123–4
**Fine Arts Building** 126
**Fire (1871)** 20, 26, 27, 111, 115, 174
**Fisher Building** 92, 124
**Fisher Studio Houses** 163
**500 Clown Company** 74
**Flat Iron Arts Building** 206
**Florence Hotel (Pullman)** 258
**Flossmoor** 83
**food and drink** 12, 13, 77–82, 135, 146
**football** 84, 85–6, 139, 287
**Forest Avenue** 246–7
**Fort Dearborn** 24, 111
  Massacre, 217
**Fountain of Time sculpture** 235
**Four Seasons sculpture** 10, 118–19, 141
**Frank Lloyd Wright Home & Studio** 244, 246
**Frank Lloyd Wright Preservation Trust** 238
**Frank W. Thomas House** 247
**Franklin, Jonathan** 140
**Franklin Building** 220
**Fremont Street** 172
**Frontera Farmer Foundation** 78
**Frost, Charles Summer** 151
**Fullerton Avenue Beach** 172
**Fulton Street Market** 191–2

## G

**Gale, Mrs Thomas (House)** 247
**Gallery District** 73, 152–3, 155, 274–5
  *see also* **art galleries**
**Gandil, Arnold "Chick"**, 89
**gangsters** 12, 32, 39–43, 62–3
**gardens**
  Austin 245
  Chicago Botanic Garden 255–6
  Lurie 137
  Osaka 239
  Rick Bayless Organic Garden 78
  *see also* **conservatories; parks**
**Garfield Park & Conservatory** 191, 198
**Garrett Popcorn Shop** 146, 276
**Gary Comer Youth Center** 95–6
**gay scene** 180–81, 185, 189, 283
**Gehry, Frank** 72, 96
**Gene Siskel Film Center** 75, 113, 114
**German immigrants** 169, 179, 196
**Glass Houses** 150
**Glencoe** 255
**Glessner House** 91, 93, 220–21
**Gold Coast** 159–65
**Goldberg, Bertrand** 10, 94, 152
**golf** 287
**Goose Island Beer Company** 83
**Gorey, Edward** 131
**Graceland Cemetery** 179, 185
**Grand Crossing** 95–6
**Grant Park** 29, 74, 114, 135–6, 141, 188, 189
**Great Chicago Fire (1871)** 20, 26, 27, 111, 115, 174
**Great Northern Migration** 32, 67, 231, 233
**Greektown** 193–4
**Green Bay Trail**, 255
**Green City Market** 12, 80, 81, 98, 168, 175
**Green Mill** 11, 74, 75, 179, 182, 183–4
**Guerin, Jules** 152
**Guilfoile, Kevin** 60
**Guy, Buddy** 11, 65, 69, 74

## H

**Haas, Richard** 165
**Halstead Street** 193
**Hancock Center & Observatory** 9, 10, 13, 94, 142, 147–8
**Harley-Davidson Tour Center** 257, 258
**Harold Washington Cultural Center** 234
**Harold Washington Library Center** 60, 218, 219
**Harpo Studios** 192–3, 199
**Harrison, Carter H.** 34
**Haymarket Square Riot (1886)** 29, 30, 50, 204
**Hecht, Ben** 59, 63
**Hellenic Museum & Cultural Center** 193–4
**Hemingway, Ernest** 60, 245
  Birthplace Home 249
  Museum 248
**Hepworth, Barbara** 253
**Heurtley, Arthur (House)** 247
**Highland Park (Ravinia)** 13, 74–5, 256
**hiking** 258
**Hillside** 42
**hip-hop** 74, 152, 206
**Historic Pleasant Home** 248
**hockey** 88, 198
**Holabird, William** 92, 123, 124, 163
**Holmes, Dr. H.H.** 43
**holograms** 193
**Home Insurance Building** 92
**Hooker, John Lee** 65, 67
**Hopper, Edward** 11, 130, 132
**hot dogs** 12, 82, 193
**House of Blues** 68, 94, 143, 152, 153
**Howlin' Wolf** 67, 68, 74, 221
**Hull-House** 30, 194
**Humboldt Park** 210
**Hyde Park** 73, 231, 235–9

## I

**I Space** 73
**ice hockey** 88, 198
**ice rinks** 8, 137, 139, 287
**Ida B. Wells-Barnett House** 234
**Illinois Institute of Technology** 93, 231–3
**IMAX** 151, 257
**immigrants** 30–32, 35, 47, 169, 179–80, 184, 193–8, 203–212
**Indian cuisine** 82
**Inland Steel Building** 118
**Irish community** 33, 48, 58, 127, 188, 196, 284
**Italian beef** 12, 80
**Italian community** 195–6

## J

**Jackson, Fruteland** 69
**Jackson, Jesse** 47
**Jackson, "Shoeless" Joe** 87, 89
**Jackson Boulevard Historic District** 192
**Jackson Park** 29, 43, 138, 239
**Jahn, Helmut** 28, 94, 112, 121, 233
**James, Etta** 65, 221, 223
**James R. Thompson Center** 94, 121, 141
**Jay Pritzker Pavilion** 11, 14–15, 74, 96, 134, 137
**jazz** 33, 65, 150, 188, 231
  clubs 11, 32, 74, 75, 179, 182, 183–4, 280–81
**Jenney, William LeBaron** 92, 124
**Jewish community** 61, 94, 96, 219
**Joffrey Ballet** 75, 114, 125, 282
**John Hancock Center & Observatory** 9, 10, 13, 94, 142, 147–8
**Jolliet, Louis** 21–2
**Jordan, Michael** 198, 199

## K

**Kahan, Paul** 79
**Kandinsky, Wassily** 257
**Kapoor, Anish** 10, 72, 136, 140–41
**Kelly, Edward** 48
**Kenelly, Martin** 48
**Kenna, "Hinky Dink",** 27
**King, Dr Martin Luther, Jr** 35–6, 47
**Kingston Mines** 9, 11, 172
**Kleiner, Jerry** 78–9
**Koolhaas, Rem** 95, 233
**Koreatown** 82

## L

**labor movement** 29–30
**Lake Geneva** 258, 259
**Lake Point Tower** 150
**Lake Shore Drive** 150, 180
**Lakefront** 11, 164
**Lakeview** 179–80
**Lardner, Ring** 58, 59
**LaSalle Street** 94, 123, 153
**LaSalle Towers** 165
**Lewis, Sinclair** 58
**libraries** 60, 115, 154, 218, 219
**Lincoln, Abraham** 46, 59, 140
**Lincoln Park** 11, 13, 73, 80–81, 98, 169–72
  Conservatory, 171
  Zoo, 12, 170–71
  *see also* **Green City Market**
**Lincoln Square, market** 98
**Lipchitz, Jacques** 253
**Little Egypt** 28
**Little Italy** 191, 195–6
**Little Village** 61, 82
**Logan Square** 80
**Lonigan, Studs** 60
**Loop** 72–3, 90, 91–4, 98, 111–29
**LTH Forum** 81
**Lucy (*Australopithecus afarensis*)** 229
**Lurie Garden** 137
**Lyric Opera of Chicago** 74, 114, 134, 188

## M

**MacArthur, Charles** 63
**McCormick, Cyrus Hall, II** 161
**McCormick Place** 221–2
**McCormick Row House District** 172
**McCormick Tribune Campus Center** 95, 232–3
**McCormick Tribune Freedom Museum** 146
**McCormick Tribune Plaza & Ice Rink** 137, 139
**McGurn, Jack "Machine Gun"** 42, 183
**McKim, Charles F.** 29, 97
**Mackinac Island race** 88
**Macy's (formerly Marshall Field's)** 9, 98, 99, 114, 116–17, 146, 276
**Madlener House** 161
**Magness, Janiva** 68
**Magnificent Mile** 9, 72, 98–9, 143–7, 273
**Maher, George Washington** 248
**Manhattan Building** 92, 124–5
**Marathon** 85, 88, 285
**Marina City** 10, 94, 95, 152
**markets** 12, 80, 81, 98, 111
  Chicago Antique Market 192
  farmers' 12, 98, 111, 119, 125, 149, 209
  Fulton Street 191–2
  Green City Market 12, 80, 81, 98, 168, 175
  Maxwell Street 98, 99, 194–5, 198
**Marquette, Jacques** 21–2, 50, 122
**Marquette Building** 10, 121–2
**Marshall Field's** *see* **Macy's**
**Matisse, Henri** 130
**Mausoleum of Ira Couch** 171
**Maxwell Street Market** 98, 99, 194–5, 198
**mayors** 45–9
**maze** 12, 259
**Medill, Joseph** 46, 160
**Medinah Temple** 149
**Melman, Richard** 78
**Merchandise Mart** 152
**Mexican community** 82, 195, 196–8, 285
**Mexican cuisine** 12, 82, 195, 197
**Michigan Avenue** 98, 111–13, 125–6
**Michigan Avenue Bridge** 143–5, 146
**Midway Plaisance** 235
**Mies van der Rohe, Ludwig** 28, 93–4, 112, 117, 119, 122, 150, 185, 232
**Millennium Park** 8, 11, 37, 53, 71–2, 114, 136–7, 282
**Miller Brewing Company** 257
**Milwaukee** 256–7
**Milwaukee Avenue** 207–8
**Milwaukee County Zoo** 257
**Miró, Joan** 141, 253
**Mitchell Museum of the American Indian** 253–5
**Mitchell Park Horticultural Conservatory (Milwaukee)** 257
**Monadnock Building** 10, 92–3, 124
**Monet, Claude** 72, 114, 132
**Monroe, Harriet** 59
**Monument with Standing Beast** 121, 141
**Monument to the Great Northern Migration** 233
**Moore, Henry** 140, 237, 253
**Moore, Nathan, House** 246
**Morton Arboretum** 12, 259
**Motley, Archibald** 235
**Mount Carmel Cemetery** 42
**Mrs Thomas Gale House** 247
**Muddy Waters** 65, 66, 67, 68, 69, 74, 221, 223

**Mudgett, Herman Webster** 43
**murals** 152, 165, 196, 198, 211
**Museum Campus** 137–9
**museums** 11
Blues Heaven Foundation 69, 221
Chicago Children's Museum 12, 151
Chicago History Museum 11, 171, 174–5
Chinese-American Museum of Chicago 222
DuSable Museum of African American History 235
Field Museum of Natural History 11, 28, 137–8, 226–9
Glessner House Museum 91, 93, 220–21
Hellenic Museum & Cultural Center 193–4
International Museum of Surgical Science 161–2
Jane Addams Hull-House Museum 30, 194
McCormick Tribune Freedom Museum 146
Milwaukee Public Museum 257
Mitchell Museum of the American Indian 253–5
Museum of Contemporary Photography 73, 219
Museum of Holography-Chicago 193
Notebaert Nature Museum 12, 171–2, 175
Oriental Institute 73, 237
Polish Museum of America 204
Science & Industry 11, 97, 226, 230, 239, 242–3
Spertus Institute & Museum 94, 96, 219
Swedish American Museum Center 184
Ukrainian National Museum 211
*see also* **art museums**
**music** 28, 74–5, 149, 256, 279–81
stores 99, 207, 209, 277
*see also* **blues**; **hip-hop**; **jazz**; **rock**

## N

**Nathan Moore House** 246–7
**National Italian American Sports Hall of Fame** 195–6
**National Museum of Mexican Art** 73, 197–8
**National Vietnam Veterans Art Museum** 219–20
**Native Americans** 21, 23–4, 25, 127, 138, 255, 258
**Navy Pier** 8, 12, 99, 143, 150, 151, 189, 278–9
**Nelson Algren Fountain** 209
**Ness, Eliot** 33, 40
**Newberry Library** 154
**nightlife** 164–5, 206, 282–3
*see also* **bars**; **clubs**
**North Avenue** 206
Baths 206
Beach 11, 175
**North Lake Shore Drive** 159, 161, 164, 175
**North Michigan Avenue** 143–5
**North Pond (Lincoln Park)** 13, 81
**North Shore** 255–6
**North Side** 71, 82, 179–85
**Northwestern University** 84, 252, 253
**Notebaert Nature Museum** 12, 171–2, 175
**Noyes Cultural Art Center** 253

## O

**Oak Park** 96, 245–9
Frank Lloyd Wright Home & Studio 244, 246
Visitor's Center 245
**Oak Street**, 98, 164
Beach, 158, 163, 164
**Obama, Barack** 49
**O'Banion, Dion** 41–2
**Observatory** 13, 147–8
**Oceanarium** 138
**Ogden, William B.** 25, 45
**O'Keeffe, Georgia** 112, 130, 131, 257
**Old Colony Building** 92, 124
**Old Town** 98, 169, 173–5
**Oldenburg, Claes** 131
**Oliver, Joe "King"** 32, 33, 65
**Olmsted, Frederick Law** 235, 238
**Olympic Games bid** 235
**opera**, 74, 114, 134, 188, 279–81
***Oprah Winfrey Show*** 192–3, 199
**Oriental Institute Museum** 73, 237
**Osaka Garden** 239
**Oz Park** 173

## P

**Pakistani cuisine** 82
**Palace of Fine Arts** 97, 138, 226, 239
**Palmer, Bertha Honoré** 114, 130
**Palmer, Potter** 27, 111, 114, 159
**Palmer House Hotel** 111
**parakeets** 239
**Paretsky, Sara** 60, 61
**parks** 8, 12, 29
Garfield 191, 198
Grant 13, 29, 74, 114, 135–6, 141, 188, 189
Highland Park (Ravinia) 13, 74–5, 256
Jackson 29, 43, 138, 239
Lincoln 11, 13, 73, 80–81, 98, 169–72
Millennium 8, 11, 37, 53, 71–2, 114, 136–7
Oz 173
Washington 29, 235
Washington Square 154
Wicker 208–9
*see also* **conservatories**; **gardens**
**Parsons, Lucy** 154
**Patterson-McCormick Mansion** 160–61
**Peggy Notebaert Nature Museum** 12, 171–2, 175
**Peter A. Beachy House** 247
**Piano, Renzo** 113
**Piazza DiMaggio** 196
**Picasso, Pablo** 11, 130, 257
"the Picasso" sculpture 10, 71, 92, 119–20, 141
**Pier Park** 12, 151
**Pier Wisconsin** 257
**Pilsen** 61, 71, 73, 82, 189, 196–8
**Pioneer Square** 145
**pioneers** 22–4
**pizza** 12, 81, 82, 83, 154, 184, 191
**planetariums** 138–9, 257
**Playboy Mansion** 163
**Pleasant Home** 248
**Plensa, Jaume** 72, 141
**poetry** 59, 184, 213
**Polish community** 193, 204, 205, 208, 209
**Polish cuisine** 82, 209
**politics** 32–4, 45–9
**popcorn** 146, 182, 276
**Prairie Avenue Historic District** 91, 93, 220–21
**Prairie School (architecture)** 96, 162, 171, 238, 246–9
**Preston Bradley Hall** 116
**Printers' Row** 60, 218, 220
**Prohibition** 32, 83, 183
**Promontory Point** 13, 238
**pubs** *see* **bars**

**uerto Rican community** 210
**ullman, George M.** 91, 185, 220, 257–8
**ullman (neighborhood)** 257–8
**ump Room** 163

## R

**ace issues**, 35–7
**adio** 75, 118, 145, 183
**ailroads** 25, 26, 36, 242
**ainbo Club** 210
**and, Sally** 34–5
**andolph Street** 113
**avinia** 13, 74–5, 256
**eliance Building** 10, 97, 117
**enoir, Pierre Auguste** 114, 130
**estaurants** 12, 13, 77–82 *see also end of each section*
**ichardson, Henry Hobson** 91, 93
**ots** 29–30, 35, 36, 50, 204
**iver North** 73, 143, 152–5, 274–5
**obie House** 95, 238, 246, 247
**ck music** 74, 152, 206, 223, 281
**ockefeller, John D.** 236, 237
**olling Stones** 68, 221
**ookery Building** 122, 123, 124
**oosevelt University** 125
**oot, John Wellborn** 28, 92, 97, 117, 122, 123, 124
**osa's Lounge** 74
**ostenkowski, Dan** 49
**oyko, Mike** 57, 58
**ush Street** 164–5
**ussian community** 206, 207, 212

## S

**ar, Alison** 233
**gan, Carl** 236
**Valentine's Day Massacre (1929)** 12, 32, 39, 42, 52, 175, 286
**ks Ukrainian Village** 211
**Sandburg, Carl** 58, 59, 91
**Santa Fe Building**, 97
**School of the Art Institute of Chicago (SAIC)** 131
**Schuba's Tavern** 75, 178, 182, 183
**Sculpture, Objects & Functional Art (SOFA) Show** 99, 150
**sculpture, public** 10, 71, 92, 93, 94, 118–20, 122, 140–41, 173
**Sears Tower** 8, 10, 18, 48, 93, 94, 114–15
**Second City** 13, 63, 74, 118, 173
**Seurat, Georges** 72, 130–31
**Shaw, Howard Van Doren** 161, 221
**Shedd Aquarium** 138
**Sheerin, Mike** 79
**shopping** 98–9, 146, 164, 173, 183, 185, 206, 208, 212, 273–7
**Siebel Institute of Technology** 83
**Sikora, Joseph** 70
**Sinclair, Upton** 30, 31, 58
**Singh, Alpana** 81
**Six Flags Great America** 256
**Sky Chapel** 120
**skyscrapers** 8, 9, 10, 12, 27–8, 92–5, 97
**Smart Museum of Art** 73, 236
**soccer** 88, 287
**softball** 88, 209
**Soldier Field** 85–6, 88, 139
**South Loop** 217–23
**South Pond (Lincoln Park)** 171
**South Shore Cultural Center** 239
**South Side** 12, 32, 71, 73, 82, 169, 188, 231–9
**Southport Corridor** 181–2
**Sox Park** 87
**Spertus Institute & Museum** 94, 96, 219
**Spire** 95, 115
**sports** 85–9, 127, 165, 195–6, 209, 235, 285, 286–7
**S.R. Crown Hall** 93, 232
**State of Illinois Center** 28
**State Street** 188–9
**State Street Village** 233
**stockyards** 31–2, 58, 71, 80
**Storrs, John** 94
**Streeterville** 143, 149
**The Stroll** 32, 231
**Sue (*T. rex*)** 11, 138, 227
**Sullivan, Louis** 28, 96, 97, 162–3, 165, 185, 212, 233, 249
  Auditorium Building 92, 125
  Carson Pirie Scott Building 27, 117–18
**Sultan's Market** 207
**Swedish community** 179, 184
**Symphony Center**, 114

## T

**Taft, Lorado** 235
**Taylor, Koko** 68, 69, 74
**tennis** 287
**Terkel, Studs** 56, 60, 75, 175, 213
**Thai cuisine** 207
**Theatre District** 113–14
**theaters** 13, 73–4, 113–14, 149, 278–9
  Auditorium 28, 73, 92, 124, 125
  Biograph 39, 40, 172
  Cadillac Palace 73, 113, 278
  Chicago 113, 278
  Chopin 209, 278
  Congo Square 73
  Goodman 73, 113, 278
  House 74
  Lookingglass 74, 147
  Music Box 75, 182
  Neo-Futurarium 185
  Noble Horse 174
  Redmoon 74
  Regal 234
  Steppenwolf 13, 63, 73, 174, 279
  Storefront 113
  Theater on the Lake 172
  Trap Door 212
  Vic 54–5
  Victory Gardens 73, 172, 279
**Thomas, Frank W. (House)** 247
**Thomas, Irma** 152
**Thomas, Theodore** 28
**Thompson, William ("Big Bill") Hale** 33–4, 37, 46, 47
**Thompson Center** 94, 121, 141
**Three Arts Club** 163
**Three First National Plaza** 140
**333 West Wacker** 95, 96
**Tiffany glass** 73, 116, 117, 122, 221
**Toulouse-Lautrec, Henri de** 133
**tours** 12, 91, 126, 127, 155, 185, 257, 285
**Toyota Park** 88
**transportation** 264–6
**Travis, Nellie Tiger** 68
**Tree Studios** 149
**Tribune Tower** 145
**Trotter, Charlie** 77, 79, 173
**Trump International Hotel & Tower** 95
**Tuckwell, Liz** 70
**Turow, Scott** 60, 61

## U

**Ukrainian community** 74, 206, 210–212
**Uncle Fun** 182
**Union Station** 112
**United Center** 198
**Unity Temple** 246, 247–8
**University of Chicago** 28, 35, 73, 88, 95, 235–6
**University of Illinois** 73
**Untouchables** 33, 40
  tour, 12, 286
**Uptown** 179, 183
**Urbana-Champaign** 73
**US Cellular Field** 87

## V

**Van Gogh, Vincent** 72, 130
**Van Osdel, John M.** 112
**Velvet Lounge** 74

**Vietnamese cuisine**, 82, 184
**Visitor Center** 115
**volleyball** 88, 165, 287
**Vonnegut, Kurt, Jr.** 236

## W

**Wacker Drive** 111, 112
**Ward, Aaron Montgomery** 28–9, 135, 152
**Warhol, Andy** 149, 257
**Warrenville** 83
**Washington, Harold** 34, 37, 47, 48–9
**Washington Park** 29, 235
**Washington Square Park** 154
**Water Tower & Pumping Station** 72, 74, 143, 147
**Water Tower Place** 98–9, 147, 273
**watersports** 88, 127, 287
**Weiss, Earl** 41–2
**Wellington, Valerie** 69
**Wells, Ida B.** 234
**Wells, Junior** 67, 69
**Wentworth "Long John"**, 24, 25–6
**West Side** 81, 82, 98, 191–9
**White, Stanford** 160
**White City** *see* **Columbian Exposition**
**White Sox** 85, 87, 89, 189, 287
**Wicker Park** 208–9
**Wicker Park (neighborhood)** 9, 80, 83, 203–210
**Wilmette** 255
**Winfrey, Oprah** 192, 199
**Wisniewski, Steve** 41–2
**Wood, Grant** 11, 72, 112, 133
**Woolworth, Frank W.** 152
**World's Fair (1893)** *see* **Columbian Exposition**
**World's Fair (1933–4)** 34, 239
**World's Fair Hotel** 43
**Wright, Frank Lloyd** 28, 92, 96, 123, 125, 162, 236, 237, 245–9
Home & Studio 244, 246
Robie House 95, 238, 246, 247
**Wright, Richard** 57, 60
**Wrigley Building** 10, 145
**Wrigley Field** 9, 13, 86–7, 179, 180

## X, Z

**Xerox building** 28
**zoos** 12, 170–71, 257

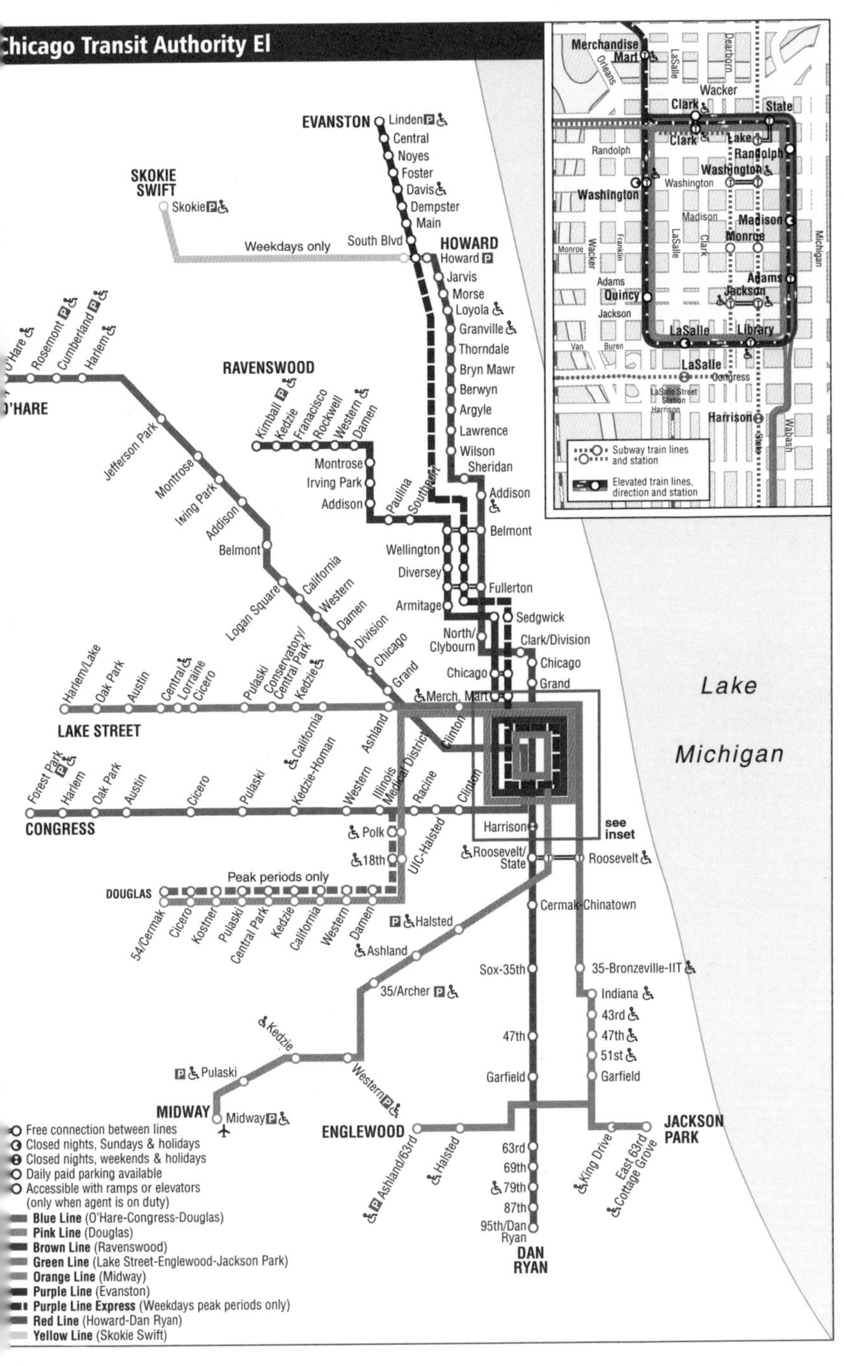
hicago Transit Authority El
EVANSTON
Linden
Central
Noyes
Foster
Davis
Dempster
Main
South Blvd
SKOKIE SWIFT
Skokie
Weekdays only
HOWARD
Howard
Jarvis
Morse
Loyola
Granville
Thorndale
Bryn Mawr
Berwyn
Argyle
Lawrence
Wilson
Sheridan
Addison
Belmont
Fullerton
Sedgwick
Clark/Division
Chicago
Grand
RAVENSWOOD
Kimball
Kedzie
Francisco
Rockwell
Western
Damen
Montrose
Irving Park
Addison
Paulina
Southport
Wellington
Diversey
Armitage
North/Clybourn
Chicago
Merch. Mart
O'Hare
Rosemont
Cumberland
Harlem
O'HARE
Jefferson Park
Montrose
Irving Park
Addison
Belmont
Logan Square
California
Western
Damen
Division
Chicago
Grand
Clinton
Harlem/Lake
Oak Park
Austin
Central
Laramie
Cicero
Pulaski
Conservatory/Central Park
Kedzie
California
Ashland
LAKE STREET
Forest Park
Harlem
Oak Park
Austin
Cicero
Pulaski
Kedzie-Homan
Western
Illinois Medical District
Racine
Clinton
UIC-Halsted
CONGRESS
Polk
18th
Peak periods only
DOUGLAS
54/Cermak
Cicero
Kostner
Pulaski
Central Park
Kedzie
California
Western
Damen
Harrison
see inset
Roosevelt/State
Roosevelt
Cermak-Chinatown
Halsted
Ashland
35/Archer
Kedzie
Pulaski
Western
MIDWAY
Midway
Sox-35th
47th
Garfield
35-Bronzeville-IIT
Indiana
43rd
47th
51st
Garfield
ENGLEWOOD
Ashland/63rd
Halsted
63rd
69th
79th
87th
95th/Dan Ryan
DAN RYAN
King Drive
East 63rd Cottage Grove
JACKSON PARK
Lake Michigan
Merchandise Mart
Orleans
LaSalle
Dearborn
Wacker
Clark
State
Lake
Randolph
Washington
Madison
Monroe
Franklin
Michigan
Adams
Quincy
Jackson
Van Buren
LaSalle
Library
Congress
LaSalle Street Station
Harrison
Wabash
Subway train lines and station
Elevated train lines, direction and station
Free connection between lines
Closed nights, Sundays & holidays
Closed nights, weekends & holidays
Daily paid parking available
Accessible with ramps or elevators (only when agent is on duty)
Blue Line (O'Hare-Congress-Douglas)
Pink Line (Douglas)
Brown Line (Ravenswood)
Green Line (Lake Street-Englewood-Jackson Park)
Orange Line (Midway)
Purple Line (Evanston)
Purple Line Express (Weekdays peak periods only)
Red Line (Howard-Dan Ryan)
Yellow Line (Skokie Swift)

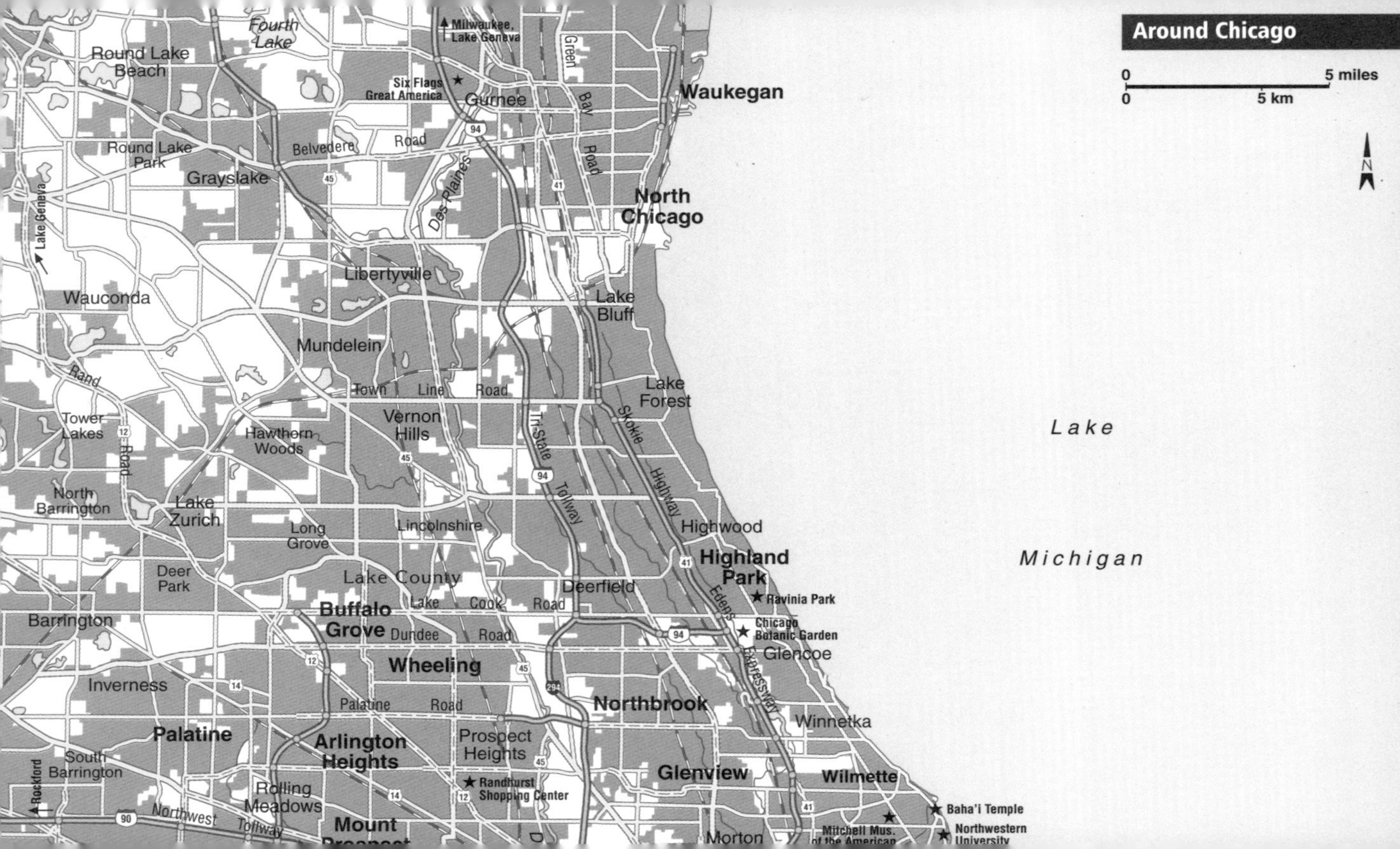
Around Chicago
0
5 miles
0
5 km
N
Lake
Michigan
Milwaukee,
Lake Geneva
Fourth
Lake
Round Lake
Beach
Six Flags
Great America
Gurnee
Green
Bay
Road
Waukegan
Round Lake
Park
Belvedere
Road
Grayslake
Des Plaines
North
Chicago
Lake Geneva
Libertyville
Wauconda
Lake
Bluff
Mundelein
Rand
Town
Line
Road
Lake
Forest
Tower
Lakes
Road
Hawthorn
Woods
Vernon
Hills
Skokie
Highway
Tri-State
Tollway
North
Barrington
Lake
Zurich
Long
Grove
Lincolnshire
Highwood
Highland
Park
Deer
Park
Lake County
Deerfield
Ravinia Park
Lake
Cook
Road
Edens
Barrington
Buffalo
Grove
Dundee
Road
Chicago
Botanic Garden
Glencoe
Expressway
Wheeling
Inverness
Palatine
Road
Northbrook
Winnetka
Palatine
Arlington
Heights
Prospect
Heights
South
Barrington
Glenview
Wilmette
Rolling
Meadows
Randhurst
Shopping Center
Rockford
Northwest
Tollway
Mount
Morton
Mitchell Mus.
Baha'i Temple
Northwestern
94
41
45
12
294
14
90